Perspectives in Motion

DANCE AND PERFORMANCE STUDIES

General Editors:
Helen Wulff, *Stockholm University,* and **Jonathan Skinner**, *University of Roehampton*

Advisory Board:
Alexandra Carter, Marion Kant, Tim Scholl

In all cultures, and across time, people have danced. Mesmerizing performers and spectators alike, dance creates spaces for meaningful expressions that are held back in daily life. Grounded in ethnography, this series explores dance and bodily movement in cultural contexts at the juncture of history, ritual and performance, including musical, in an interconnected world.

Recent volumes:

Volume 15
Perspectives in Motion: Engaging the Visual in Dance and Music
Edited by Kendra Stepputat and Brian Diettrich

Volume 14
24 Bars to Kill: Hip Hop, Aspiraton, and Japan's Social Margins
Andrew B. Armstrong

Volume 13
Lullabies and Battle Cries: Music, Identity and Emotion among Republican Parading Bands in Northern Ireland
Jaime Rollins

Volume 12
Singing Ideas: Performance, Politics and Oral Poetry
Tríona Ní Schíocháin

Volume 11
Staging Citizenship: Roma, Performance and Belonging in EU Romania
Ioana Szeman

Volume 10
Collaborative Intimacies in Music and Dance: Anthropologies of Sound and Movement
Edited by Evangelos Chrysagis and Panas Karampampas

Volume 9
Languid Bodies, Grounded Stances: The Curving Pathway of Neoclassical Odissi Dance
Nandini Sikand

Volume 8
Choreographies of Landscape: Signs of Performance in Yosemite National Park
Sally Ann Ness

Volume 7
In Search of Legitimacy: How Outsiders Become Part of an Afro-Brazilian Capoeira Tradition
Lauren Miller Griffith

Volume 6
Learning Senegalese Sabar: Dancers and Embodiment in New York and Dakar
Eleni Bizas

For a full volume listing, please see the series page on our website:
https://berghahnbooks.com/series/dance-and-performance-studies

Perspectives in Motion

Engaging the Visual in Dance and Music

Edited by
Kendra Stepputat and Brian Diettrich

First published in 2021 by
Berghahn Books
www.berghahnbooks.com

© 2021, 2024 Kendra Stepputat and Brian Diettrich
First paperback edition published in 2024

All rights reserved. Except for the quotation of short passages
for the purposes of criticism and review, no part of this book
may be reproduced in any form or by any means, electronic or
mechanical, including photocopying, recording, or any information
storage and retrieval system now known or to be invented,
without written permission of the publisher.

Library of Congress Cataloging-in-Publication Data

Names: Stepputat, Kendra, editor. | Diettrich, Brian, editor.
Title: Perspectives in motion : engaging the visual in dance and music / edited by Kendra Stepputat and Brian Diettrich.
Description: First Edition. | New York : Berghahn Books, 2021. | Series: Dance and Performance Studies; 15 | Includes bibliographical references and index.
Identifiers: LCCN 2020042174 (print) | LCCN 2020042175 (ebook) | ISBN 9781800730021 (Hardback) | ISBN 9781800730038 (eBook)
Subjects: LCSH: Dance. | Folk dancing. | Folk dance music. | Ethnology. | Kaeppler, Adrienne L., 1935–
Classification: LCC GV1588 .P43 2021 (print) | LCC GV1588 (ebook) | DDC 793.3/1—dc23
LC record available at https://lccn.loc.gov/2020042174
LC ebook record available at https://lccn.loc.gov/2020042175

British Library Cataloguing in Publication Data

A catalogue record for this book is available from the British Library

ISBN 978-1-80073-002-1 hardback
ISBN 978-1-80539-144-9 paperback
ISBN 978-1-80539-560-7 epub
ISBN 978-1-80073-003-8 web pdf

https://doi.org/10.3167/9781800730021

Research funding and support provided by

Contents

List of Illustrations	vii
Foreword	x
Nanasipauʻu Tukuʻaho	
Acknowledgements	xii
Introduction. Engaging the Visual in Dance and Music	1
Brian Diettrich and Kendra Stepputat	

PART I. GAINING INSIGHTS THROUGH DANCE VISUALIZATIONS

1. Kinetic Songscapes: Intersensorial Listening to *Hula Kuʻi* Songs *Kati Szego*	19
2. Using Motion Capture to Access Culturally Embedded and Embodied Movement Knowledge: A Case Study in Tango Argentino *Kendra Stepputat*	41
3. Transcription and Description: Tasks for Dance Research *Egil Bakka*	67
4. Moving into Someone Else's Research Project: Issues in Collaborative Research *Judy Van Zile*	90

PART II. RECONSIDERING MOVEMENT STRUCTURES

5. The Dancer's Voice: The Dancing Body as Sound Made Visible *Jane Freeman Moulin*	109
6. From Tonga to Malaysia: Utilizing Adrienne Kaeppler's Analysis of Dance Structure to Understand *Igal* of the Sama-Bajau in East Malaysia *Mohd Anis Md Nor*	138

7. Courting as Structured Movement in the Eastern Highlands of
   Papua New Guinea 158
   Don Niles

PART III. MUSIC AND DANCE AS AGENCY IN POWER STRUGGLES

8. Disturbing Bodies: Danced Resistance and Imperial Corporeality
   in Colonial Micronesia 179
   Brian Diettrich

9. Greek Politicians' Dancing: Theatrical Representations of
   Political Power 197
   Irene Loutzaki

10. Lalåi: Somatic Decolonization and Worldview-Making through
    Chant on the Pacific Island of Guåhan 214
    Ojeya Cruz Banks

PART IV. SIGNIFICANCE OF THE TANGIBLE

11. Intangible Dancing as Tangible Museum Exhibits 229
    Elsie Ivancich Dunin

12. Creativity and Ceremony in the Repatriation of King Ng:tja 244
    Kirsty Gillespie

13. The Weave Within: Being, Seeing and Sensing in *Barasili* –
    Solomon Islands 255
    Irene Karongo Hundleby

PART V. PERSPECTIVES FROM ADRIENNE L. KAEPPLER

**Interview with Adrienne L. Kaeppler. A Conversation with
the Kupuna** 279
   Ricardo D. Trimillos and Adrienne L. Kaeppler

Publications by Adrienne L. Kaeppler 293
   Jess Marinaccio (compiler)

Index 317

Illustrations

Figures

0.1. Tongan dancers perform at the Twelfth Festival of Pacific Arts on Guam. 2

0.2. Adrienne L. Kaeppler at the 27th Symposium and 50th anniversary celebration of the ICTM Study Group on Ethnochoreology, Irish World Academy of Music and Dance, University of Limerick, 2012. 8

1.1. Lia's drawing in response to 'Puamana'. 25

2.1. Real image and mocap representation of Homer Ladas and Cristina Ladas from five different perspectives. 44

2.2. *Ocho atrás* phases: a) starting position with closed feet, b) backstep, c) shifting weight to the back foot, d) closing front leg, e) turning, f) final position (same as image a) on other side). 50

2.3. Dissociation angle visualization. 54

2.4. *Ocho atrás* 3D data visualization. 55

2.5. *Ocho atrás* by six tango argentino dance experts. 58

3.1. Transcription excerpt of the *Ringlenner*. 81

3.2. Transcription of Mark Morris dancing 'Anger Dance'. 84

4.1. The same movement motif as performed in three different traditions (Kaeppler 1993: 244, 246, and 248). 96

4.2. Example of frame of reference choice for notating direction (Kaeppler 1993: 243). 97

4.3. Placement of four motifs together within the text for easy comparison (Kaeppler 1993: 74). 99

4.4. Excerpt from glossary, showing three motifs as performed in one tradition (Kaeppler 1993: 244). 100

5.1. Signal code used in the *tapriata* (also *tapiriata*) dance (Handy 1923: 308).	116
5.2. An earlier tripartite model of dance performance in Tahiti (Moulin 2011).	121
5.3. Tahitian tattoo with its *tiare tahiti* pattern in profile on the upper portion of the back and multiple flower shapes on the lower torso and thighs.	123
5.4. Close-up of the upper body flower motif.	124
5.5. Marquesan image of the womb in barkcloth folding (Omoa, Fatu Hiva).	124
5.6. The soundingness of Tahitian dance as represented by the *tiare tahiti* (Tahitian gardenia).	126
6.1. Music Transcription of *Titik Tarirai* (Santaella 2016: 79).	148
6.2. Examples of *Igal*'s morphokines and dance motifs.	152
7.1. Languages of Eastern Highlands Province, Papua New Guinea.	162
7.2. Courting styles in the Eastern Highlands.	163
8.1. Dancers in formation at the centennial Jubilee of the Catholic Church in Chuuk; Weno, Chuuk, 4 February 2011.	180
8.2. Men from Chuuk adorned for a community celebration, c. 1910 (Krämer 1932: Plate 8c).	185
9.1. Translation of Dialogue: 'The President [with his dancing] supports his friendship to Turkey.' / 'He danced the *zeibekiko* . . .'.	207
10.1. Mr. Leonard Iriarte (holding the staff) and I Fanlalai'an members at the grand opening of the 2016 Festival of Pacific Arts in Guåhan.	215
11.1. Photograph of barkcloth by Adrienne Kaeppler, 1975.	230
11.2. The Vardar dance zone.	234
11.3. Poster for the Romani exhibition in Zagreb's Ethnographic Museum.	240
12.1. Vera Ketchell making handprints on the box containing Ng:tja. Repatriation handover ceremony at the Australian Embassy in Berlin, Germany, March 2017, facilitated under the Australian Government's Indigenous Repatriation Program.	248
13.1. *Keke angi angi* (cricket cry) rhythm.	264

13.2. *Kisi kisi* (hand rattle) rhythm to signal the beginning of a dance. 265

13.3. Takwa Women's Barasili Group, September 2012. Kokosi and Adu wear *tafuli'ae* across their breasts and *fo'odara* across their brows. Upper arms are adorned with *'abagwaro* and *rii* plants. Wrists are decorated with *obi aba*. 267

13.4. *Ma'e'ae* made from plastic beads by Lawrence Fadaua, a respected designer and creator of traditional body ornaments. They rest upon a copy of Ben Burt's (2009) book, which family members use as a reference guide when ordering dance costume pieces. 269

Table

6.1. Upper and lower body morphokines and *igal* motifs. 149

Foreword

Nanasipau'u Tuku'aho

Perspectives in Motion: Engaging the Visual in Dance and Music, edited by Kendra Stepputat and Brian Diettrich, is a tribute to the work and career of Dr Adrienne Kaeppler, curator of Oceanic Ethnology at the National Museum of Natural History at the Smithsonian Institution in Washington, D.C.

Adrienne Kaeppler first visited the Kingdom of Tonga for the Pan Pacific and Southeast Asia Women's Association (PPSEAWA) Conference in 1964. At the time, she was studying Anthropology at the University of Hawai'i. Her Majesty Queen Sālote, who wrote many Tongan poems and dances, sent Adrienne to her choreographers to learn about Tongan dancing. That was the first of a continual stream of visits that Adrienne made to Tonga. In 1967, she completed her doctoral dissertation 'The Structure of Tongan Dance'.

Adrienne is widely recognized today for her expertise in Tongan dance and in particular the *lakalaka* – that is, composition, music, movements, the historical and cultural settings, the dancers and their positions. Adrienne has always been very thorough with her research, and she takes great care with the cultural details of her work. During times when Adrienne and I watched Tongan performances together, she would explain the instruments that were supposed to be used for that particular dance, and she would know whether it was being performed too fast or too slow. On 7 November 2003, The United Nations Educational, Scientific and Cultural Organization (UNESCO) proclaimed the *lakalaka* – Dances and Sung Speeches of Tonga – a Masterpiece of the Oral and Intangible Heritage of Humanity. Adrienne played a significant role in supporting this proclamation for Tonga.

Adrienne's love for Tonga also included learning about our traditional arts and crafts. She is deeply interested in art forms and their construction, but she is equally curious about the social constructs and the cultural systems behind the art forms produced. In 1998, she worked at the Tongan National Museum, setting up a special exhibition for the 80th birthday celebration of King Taufa'ahau Tupou IV. Adrienne has authored many influential books and articles about Tongan dance, music and art. I have had the special privilege of working with her, Elizabeth Wood-Ellem, and Melenaite Taumoefolau on the book *Songs and Po-*

ems of Queen Sālote (2004 and 2019) and with Adrienne and Mary Lynn Fonua on the book *Tonga's Royal Family: Photographs from Royal Collections* (2015).

Adrienne L. Kaeppler has dedicated her life to her scholarship. She has been faithful in sharing her deep understanding of Tongan dance and art as vital expressions of our history and our culture.

Nanasipau'u
Her Majesty Queen Nanasipau'u
The Kingdom of Tonga

Her Majesty Queen Nanasipau'u is the Queen Consort of His Majesty Tupou VI of the Kingdom of Tonga. Her lifelong passion has been to encourage women. At present she is President of the Tonga National Council of Women, President of Queen Sālote College Old Girls Association, Chairperson of the Women's Department, Free Wesleyan Church of Tonga, and Patron of the Women and Children's Centre. As the wife of the Head of State and as a Noble's wife, the Queen has special responsibilities for the people who live in their villages and estates. Due to Queen Nanasipau'u's extensive knowledge of genealogies and traditions, she has been a valuable contributor to Dr Adrienne Kaeppler's research and writings on Tonga.

Acknowledgements

This book developed from conversations among members of the International Council for Traditional Music (ICTM). After initial discussions and consultation, editors Kendra Stepputat and Brian Diettrich agreed to take on the project in 2017 and began inviting contributions. Some authors had been previously part of conversations, while others were newly approached. Because it was agreed early on that the project would be a surprise for Adrienne, work on the book remained clandestine. The authors assembled in the book include students and colleagues of Adrienne, senior scholars with long histories of work with her, as well as emerging researchers. Many authors have or have had roles in the International Council for Traditional Music, an organization for which Adrienne Kaeppler served as Executive Board Member (1999–2001), Vice President (2001–2005) and President (2005–2013). In acknowledgement of these connections, we thank the ICTM Executive Board Committee on Publications for agreeing to acknowledge the book with the ICTM name and logo.

We thank all contributors for their work and enthusiasm in completing this project, as well as everyone involved in seeing this project through despite the exceptional global circumstances from COVID-19 during the final stages of publication. We offer a special thanks to Queen Nanasipauʻu of Tonga for kindly agreeing to author the foreword to the book. Jessica Marinaccio compiled the bibliography of Kaeppler's works and Kurt Schatz provided valuable copy-editing assistance including indexing that helped improve the work, and the anonymous reviewers offered valuable feedback. We acknowledge and thank Barbara B. Smith for graciously offering financial support for the publication of the book, and the Land Steiermark Abteilung Wissenschaft for generously funding the project. We express gratitude to everyone at Berghahn books who encouraged and supported us in the process and worked towards the finalization of this book.

Finally, we wish to acknowledge Adrienne Kaeppler for inspiring this project through her dedicated and influential career, and her mentorship and friendship over many years. With this volume, we hope that future researchers may take inspiration from her scholarship on the place of dance and art in the world.

Introduction

Engaging the Visual in Dance and Music

Brian Diettrich and Kendra Stepputat

Young women standing in parallel rows gently turn their wrists inward. Smiling toward the audience, some follow their choreographed gestures with a spontaneous tilt of their heads to the side, the quick movement accentuated by the white feathers in their hair. Beside them, men take part with more vigorous actions as they turn and step in time with knees bent. The attire of the performers marks them of place and people, with skin anointed in fragrant coconut oil, and their voices reverberating with song in structured harmonies. The sung and danced lyrics – their 'poetry in motion' – make links between the ancestral past and present-day contexts of community. Spectators watch, some in novel admiration, and others with a watchful gaze of past knowledge and experience. This includes those who have learned the dance and those who can speak and write its history. Drawing meaning from dance offers many perspectives, the seen and unseen in an amalgamation of the senses, but with a broader acknowledgement of people, place, identity and global flow. These visions reflect back on our own experiences as embedded in the cultural movements around us.

'Seeing is believing', so the old saying goes. But seeing is never final; instead, it is a fluid domain of social meaning. We therefore reiterate the equally relevant saying, 'don't judge a book by its cover' (Walker and Chaplin 1997: 16). The physical act of vision is only one domain of seeing. Vision also encompasses a broader palate of knowing, questioning, perception and reflection. The chapters in this book explore a diverse range of visual understandings of dance and music in diverse contexts, just as they engage closely with the work of Adrienne Lois Kaeppler, one of the foremost scholars of Pacific dance and art. The specific context above that opens this chapter extends from imagery of Tongan dance performances, watched and discussed between Adrienne Kaeppler and Brian Diettrich at the Twelfth Festival of Pacific Arts, held on Guam in May 2016

(Figure 0.1.). The movements of the Tongan dancers in the performance above, as well as the imagery of the observing dance anthropologist, offer an appropriate point of departure to begin this volume, which focuses closely on the visual meanings of dance and music but also on the depth of scholarship crafted over five decades by Adrienne Kaeppler. *Perspectives in Motion* echoes the title of Kaeppler's 1993 book on Tongan dance, *Poetry in Motion*, just as it also references how authors of the present volume have expanded upon Kaeppler's scholarship in new directions over time. With this introduction we foreground our consideration of visual engagements with performance, just as we account for Kaeppler's impact on studies of dance and culture more broadly.

Engaging the Visual

The premise of engaging the visual prompts questions about the study of visual culture and its intersection with dance and music. How do we critically understand the visual in music and dance, and what visual cultural paradigms have scholars deployed for recognized and novel analyses? How might reconsidering visual analyses in music and/or dance offer new forms of insight into cultural practices but also prompt broader conversations about culture and politics, community and agency? Moreover, how might scholars employ new tools and methodologies for reflecting and communicating music and dance practices visually? In order to encompass such an expansive and open scrutiny into these questions,

Figure 0.1. *Tongan dancers perform at the Twelfth Festival of Pacific Arts on Guam. Photograph by Brian Diettrich, May 2016.*

this book brings together thirteen case studies on practices of dance and music. The chapters collected here offer a diversity of perspectives as they explore new insights into the meaning of visual culture in dance and music.

The examination of the visual in this book comes within a renewed shift toward the senses across diverse fields of study, within established frameworks and in new emerging pathways (Howles 2003; Le Breton 2017). At one level vision signifies basic perception concerned with the processing of complex phenomena undertaken alongside the other senses. As Walker and Chaplin (1997: 18–19) have noted, perception is complex and multilayered, as they describe with examples of synaesthesia, mental images and afterimages. Seeing as basic perception and observation is intricately tied to knowledge, as Jenks (1995: 1) commented about research in visual studies: 'looking, seeing and knowing have become perilously intertwined.' Understanding perception in dance and music has been most fully explored in emerging studies of phenomenology. Drawing on Maurice Merleau-Ponty and Edmund Husserl, Harris Berger (2009: 5), for example, has explored phenomenology for music and dance, to investigate 'the relationships between the person and the text, performance, practice, or items of expressive culture'. An early approach by Sheets-Johnstone (1979) focused on the perception of what is visible in dance, exploring the differentiation between objects in motion and movement itself. Such questions underscore the importance of experience in performance, and these in turn expand the meaning of how we understand consciousness.

In the study of imagery, a focus on the visual also implies a critical lens toward society and culture. In *Vision and Visuality*, Foster (1988: ix) offered an early differentiation between vision as a 'physical operation' and visuality as 'social fact' and a 'discursive determination'. With these important delineations, Foster (ibid.) articulated 'how we see, how we are able, allowed, or made to see, and how we see this seeing or the unseen therein'. As Walker and Chaplin (1997: 22) subsequently put it, 'visuality is vision socialized'. In the field of visual anthropology, scholars have maintained long-standing interests in art and objects, photography and film, but this work has increasingly considered 'the inescapable entanglement of the visual in all areas of life' (Banks and Ruby 2011: 16). Scholars have also interwoven new methods of critical analysis of visual culture together with new applied and activist research (Pink 2011). This current and expanded critical terrain offers new insights about visual culture across boundaries, transnationally and transculturally (Banks and Ruby 2011; Mirzoeff 2006), and across disciplinary lines. Writing with a node toward geography, for example, Schlottmann (2017: 7495) has examined 'visual practices of appropriating (spatial) reality and established ways of looking at the world – by society, cultural and social groups, or disciplines'. Sand (2012: 91), commenting from an Art History lens, 'asks us to look differently at familiar objects but also to turn our gaze on objects resistant to the traditional methods of our discipline'. Such studies offer new applications of visual modes of engagement that also open new critical terrain with which we expand upon in this volume.

Modernity has taken to heart that to see is to represent, and in turn, representing is a powerful means of seeing the world. From this then we understand that seeing is partial, 'a fracture, a bi-partition, a splitting of the being' as Lacan noted (2002 [1977]: 127) or perhaps a partial truth, to follow Clifford and Marcus (1986). Representation has been a rich area of exploration for visual culture and its theorization. The influential discourses unfolded in the work of Foucault and Lacan offered new understandings and cautions about modes of seeing, through the ocularcentrism of Western modernity (Jenks 1995), to comprehending the power of seeing through such scopic regimes as the panopticon (Foucault 1979). In this way, we are challenged to account for the role of the observer alongside that of the observed. For dance and music, a focus on the visual elements offers a staging ground to explore how performance might reinforce and/or resist such occurrences. Moreover, representation is closely allied to the power of seeing in a broader history of the visualization of music and dance. In early ethnographic projects, for example, the recording of images of Others was a powerful tool of representation alongside sound recording. For example, Pink (2006: 5) has described how the Torres Strait Island Expedition of 1898 – one of the earliest large expeditions to include technology of still and moving images as well as sound – documented and portrayed Indigenous practices with a focus on visualizing dance. From the earliest period of technological development, capturing and displaying the moving body has been central to not only the representation of movement but to critical methodologies of seeing as research. In a scoptic agenda intertwined with colonialism and racial ideas of both 'civilized' and 'primitive', scientists sought modes of visual documentary to record and portray 'primitive others' (ibid.). The rise of visual technology alongside the sonic expanded upon earlier efforts in print media and was closely aligned to what Mirzoeff (2002: 474) has called 'visual colonialism'. Deducing from this historical (mis)use of the visual, clearly an awareness and incorporation of different, culturally framed modes of seeing and understanding dancing bodies is needed in contemporary research (also see Schneider 2013).

In contemporary spaces, engaging the visual requires commitments to tracking imagery across performances, media, technology and in new contexts. Writing in 2011, Grau and Veigl (2011: 6) pointedly note that 'never before has the world of images changed so fast'. This changing ground has only accelerated in subsequent years. The analysis of visual culture has inherently moved toward multisensorial modes of description and comparison, long examined in areas such as photography (Edwards 2012, 2015; Lynteris and Stasch 2019) and film (Chion 1994; Jenssen 2005) but also with the cultural saturation of visual production through personal devices such as smartphones (Blaagaard 2013) and of course in social media (Shipley 2015). With the gradual move from formerly specialized equipment to everyday devices and practices, the continuity of visual production seems everywhere. In this new world of personal media, events of music, dance or theatre take on new lives through virtual imagery and visual experiences. Such new circumstances necessarily require additional perspectives for research. Moreover, as images move and transform across the globe at instantaneous speed and in numerous reconfigurations, they give rise to new questions of representation and ethics in access and consumption, in contexts such as museum exhibits and online events. Grau and Veigl (2011: 1), for example, have commented on 'the rise of the image as a virtual, spatial image – images that appear capable of changing interactively or even "autonomously" and formulating a lifelike, all-embracing audiovisual and sensory sphere where temporal and spatial parameters can be altered at will'. For Grau and Veigl (ibid.: 11), these new frontiers of visual culture prompt a focus on a reformulation of visualization, not merely image creation but now a 'translation of the invisible into the visible'. All of these formulations of visual culture offer new underlying questions about 'what images are and what they do, how they function and what effects they have' (ibid.: 6).

Visual Approaches to Dance and Music

Within ethnomusicology, research has historically focused on audible structure and has been closely linked to sound analysis (Titon 2008), and notwithstanding a small number of valuable studies that have explored visual elements of musical practice (Feld 1976; Kaeppler 1996; Killick 2014; Wade 1998). But work in music has also begun to challenge prior sound-centric domains. Predominantly in the field of music cognition, several important publications have focused on the visible aspects of sound-making, manifest in movement by musicians (e.g. Godøy and Leman 2010; Gritten and King 2011; Lesaffre, Maes and Leman 2017; Veroli and Vinay 2018). More recently subsumed under the term choreomusicology, studies in ethnomusicology have engaged with movement as a visual expression and important aspect of music making (e.g. Clayton 2007; Downey 2002; Mason 2017; Nor and Stepputat 2017; Van Zile 1988). Helena Simonett (2014: 119), referencing earlier periods of work, has stated that the 'antivisual' approach to previous studies in ethnomusicology deepened the 'fragmentation of the sensory experience' and has its foundations in 'the long intellectual history of dualistic thinking within Western philosophical and scientific discourses'. This dualism explains the separation of the visual and the auditive in prior ethnomusicological and ethnochoreological research. Working against this dualism, Simonett's work with Indigenous communities of Mexico asks for more holistic sensorial frameworks for understanding relationships to environment (Simonett 2014; also see Ingold 2011 and Helmreich 2010). In accordance with such ideas, the authors of this volume address the visual in music and dance as a complement to sonic and performative experiences across research methods and within diverse cultural contexts.

Comparable to the auditive focus in ethnomusicology, dance scholarship has placed much more focus on visual elements, often overlooking other sensorial domains. Exceptions include work by Grau (2011) and contributions to the ethnochoreology symposium dedicated to the topic of 'dance and the senses' (Stepputat 2017). Hannah (1979: 75), in exploring the communicatory aspect and arguing for dance as 'a whole complex of communication symbols', noted how 'even without being extraordinary, motion has the strongest visual appeal to attention'. Not surprisingly, dance being primarily a visual art, a great deal of the methods in dance research have focused on the gathering of visual data of human movement, whether through notation, recording or emerging technologies (Hutchinson Guest 1998; Sparti and Van Zile 2011). These efforts at capturing a performance have underscored the importance of temporality in dance research.

The visual communication of dance is dependent on time and thus of fleeting quality. Buckland (1999: 6) noted the resulting and inherent 'difficulties of textualization' stemming from the 'ephemerality of dancing'. Such features are also inherent in performance more broadly, which inspired Phelan (1993: 146) to state that 'performance cannot be saved, recorded, documented, or otherwise participate in the circulation of representations of representations: once it does so it becomes something other than performance'. And while Phelan saw disappearance, and thus invisibility, as a fundamental quality of performance, much dance research has invested instead in visualizations, in modes of capturing and preserving imagery, as a means of interpretation, but also in projects of preservation and heritage (e.g. Buckland 1999; Dunin 2015; Nor, Dunin and Von Bibra Wharton 2008). Although visual approaches play an important role in the capturing and analysis of dance, fewer publications address visual aspects connected to the culture and the elicitation of visual knowledge systems. An example of an edited volume on the topic are the 2004 proceedings of the ICTM Study Group on Ethnochoreology – in which several papers engage with the topic 'Visible and Invisible Dance', focusing on elements of cultural interpretation and symbolism in human movement (Dunin and Von Bibra Wharton 2008) – but also Farnell (2011), focusing on the dancing body in visual culture.

Another example is Adrienne Kaeppler's work on hula, in which, according to her, the dancer is mostly a storyteller, the dance being 'a visual extension and enhancement of sung poetry based on complex hand and arm movements' (Kaeppler 2011: 88). This storytelling element is visual, yet it is often a hidden element for some onlookers who may not be familiar with the stories and the culturally prescribed bodily movements. Kaeppler quoted travel writer Robert Louis Stevenson (cited in Kaeppler 2011: 88), who in 1900 wrote dismissively about hula and without cultural knowledge that 'The hula . . . is surely the most dull of man's inventions'. Kaeppler's writing, particularly about Hawaiian and Tongan dances, has offered foundational explorations of visual knowledge in Pacific performance contexts. In another example, Sally Ann Ness examined *sinulog*, a ritual practice from the Philippines, and with a focus on the change of emphasis on different senses depending on the context under which it is performed (Ness 1995: 2). She contrasted historical descriptions of *sinulog* as community ritual with those choreographed and performed annually in a competitive parade. In tracing how the visual aspects became the main medium in the individual ritual at the cost of the tactile and audible elements of the community practice, Ness addressed the change of visuality from the dancer's gaze and visual connection to the addressed deity to the focus on visual impressiveness for parade audiences (ibid.: 4–5). This work thereby captures a shift of focus in *sinulog* from the 'seeing' to the 'being seen'. In still another example, Hilary Vanessa Finchum-Sung (2012: 396) has written about the visuality of the Korean genre called *kugak* ('national music') – performances in which 'a sight-sound partnership has been and continues to be integral to performances'. In examining the contemporary experimental quality of *kugak* and its manifestation in performance events, video, photographs, staging and other imagery, Finchum-Sung (ibid.: 421) provides a case study of not only how visual aspects shape sound but the importance of visual cultural sensation in the contemporary musical practices of Korea. The case of Korean *kugak* suggests the importance of context and artistry in the sensorial landscape in diverse dance and musical practices. For her, and more generally applicable, a visual focus implies 'the socio-cultural, political, and historical implications of something that can be seen or witnessed at a particular point in time' (ibid.: 398). Yet another area of visual research is addressed by Nahachewsky (2017), who explores the use of the eyes in Ukrainian dance, differentiating between staged, choreographed performance and participatory social dancing. Among other elements, he explores the shift in the communicatory meaning of eye contact – for instance, from agreeing about the use of space between fellow performers in participatory dance – towards establishing a connection with an audience.

In a text propagating the need to not only notate, analyse and store dance but most importantly, to keep it actively practised in order to preserve it, Kaeppler (2017: 430) states that 'music and dance are multifaceted phenomena that include, in addition to what we see and hear, the "invisible" underlying systems of sound and movement recognised by specific cultures, the processes that produce both the system and the product, and the sociopolitical contexts in which they are embedded'. In her scholarship, Kaeppler has focused on both the 'visible' and 'invisible', offering insights and perspectives that have influenced research into dance, art and culture (Kaeppler 1996, 2010).

A Scholar of Dance and Art in the World

By way of offering visual perspectives on dance and music, the chapters in this volume are centred on the long-standing work of Adrienne Lois Kaeppler (born 1935), one of the foremost scholars of dance.[1] A scrutiny of the 318 research contributions that comprise Kaeppler's list of publications included in this book reveals a scholar with a rich legacy of significant contributions in depth and breadth to multiple fields of knowledge. Her corpus of research extends from her 1961 Master's thesis from the University of Hawai'i on Melanesian masks, to her 2019 contributions in the reprinted edition of *Songs and Poems of Queen Sālote* (2019) and additional essays in print during the completion of this book. Adrienne Kaeppler has offered pioneering contributions to anthropology, dance ethnology, ethnomusicology, museum and archival studies, art history, Pacific history, as well as speciality research in Polynesia, and with particular emphasis on Tonga, Hawai'i, and Rapa Nui, among other areas. Among her numerous books, encyclopaedia work, edited volumes, articles and chapters, Kaeppler has been a tireless reviewer of new research and willing to engage in critical debates on approaches, theories and interpretations. Her work has also included public engagement with research through popular publications such as museum catalogues but also in public exhibits internationally. Through her considerable research contributions, Adrienne Kaeppler is one of the most influential scholars of dance and performance across the second half of the twentieth century and early twenty-first century.

Figure 0.2. Adrienne L. Kaeppler at the 27th Symposium and 50th anniversary celebration of the ICTM Study Group on Ethnochoreology, Irish World Academy of Music and Dance, University of Limerick, 2012. Photograph by Mehmet Öcal Özbilgin.

A brief overview of her international affiliations, awards and publications offers further insights into her career. In addition to her long-standing position as Curator of Oceanic Ethnology at the Smithsonian Institute in Washington D.C., Adrienne Kaeppler has held positions at the Bernice P Bishop Museum (Honolulu), the University of Hawai'i, the University of Maryland (College Park) and Queen's University in Belfast, Northern Ireland. She has been affiliated with museums and cultural institutions across the Pacific region and internationally. Kaeppler has been influential in the development of the International Council for Traditional Music (ICTM) in her leadership roles as Vice President (2001–2005) and President (2005–2013). She has been an active member of both the ICTM Study Groups on Ethnochoreology and on Music and Dance of Oceania for several decades, contributing significantly to the development and recognition of both areas. In addition to her individual book awards, in 2003 Kaeppler received the prestigious Frigate Bird Award by the Pacific Arts Association for her lifetime contribution to and excellence in the study of Pacific Arts. For her contributions to the study of Tongan culture, in 1997 she was awarded the Silver Jubilee Anniversary Medal by King Tāufaʻāhau Tupou IV, and in 2015 she was invested with the Royal Order 'Commander of the Royal Tongan Household Order' during the royal honours ceremony for the coronation of King Tupou VI. She has given numerous distinguished lectures and keynote addresses, including the Charles Seeger Lecture for the Society for Ethnomusicology (2006), the Distinguished Lecture for the Association for Social Anthropology in Oceania (2010) and the Smithsonian Secretary's Distinguished Research Lecture Award (2010). In 2019, the Smithsonian Institute recognized Kaeppler as one of its leading women of science.

Kaeppler's influence has been considerable across multiple domains of scholarship, but here we emphasize selections of her work that we believe have been particularly meaningful. Perhaps one of her best-known theoretical contributions was her approach to structuralism through Pacific art, performance and culture, and appearing first in her doctoral thesis 'The Structure of Tongan Dance', from 1967. Kaeppler expanded and extended her ideas in several groundbreaking publications, including the articles, 'Tongan Dance: A Study in Cultural Change' (1970), 'Aesthetics of Tongan Dance' (1971) and especially 'Method and Theory in Analyzing Dance Structure with an Analysis of Tongan Dance' (1972). Ethnographically, she is best known for her in-depth scholarship on Tonga. In 1993, Vavaʻu Press in Nukuʻalofa, Tonga, published a compilation of her work on Tongan dance as *Poetry in Motion: Studies of Tongan Dance* (1993), which sets out as a major compendium of her scholarship with the Kingdom up to that time. This was followed in 2012 by the book *Lakalaka: A Tongan Masterpiece of Performing Arts*, published with rich illustrations by Vavaʻu Press, and which explores this important genre of Tongan dances and sung speeches.

In addition to her pioneering work in Tonga, Kaeppler's commitment to Hawaiian art and performance is evident in her scholarship on *hula*, demonstrated across many publications but perhaps most evident in *Haʻa and Hula Pahu, Sacred Movements* (Hula Pahu, Hawaiian Drum Dances, Volume I, 1991). Her influence as a preeminent scholar of Oceanic music and dance was demonstrated by her editing of – with Jacob Love – *Volume 9: Australia and the Pacific Islands* (1998), part of the *Garland Encyclopedia of World Music* and still the most comprehensive single resource on the region. The Garland volume thoroughly presented types of dance and music across Oceania, and Kaeppler and Love brought together a vast cohort of individual scholars and practitioners to contribute to the project. In addition to this work on dance and music, Kaeppler's output on the aesthetics and history of the visual arts of Polynesia and broader Oceania resulted in, among many publications, the major books: *The Pacific Arts of Polynesia and Micronesia* (2008), *Polynesia: The Mark and Carolyn Blackburn Collection of Polynesian Art* (2010), *Holophusicon – The Leverian Museum: An Eighteenth-Century English Institution of Science, Curiosity, and Art* (2011), and with Jo Anne Van Tilburg, *The Iconic Tattooed Man of Easter Island* (2019). Related to this is her important historical work on Pacific voyages, including her leadership role in the exhibition book *James Cook and the Exploration of the Pacific* (2009). Through her career at the Smithsonian Institution and earlier at the Bishop Museum in Honolulu, Kaeppler has collaborated with numerous international museums in organizing exhibitions and publishing exhibition catalogues, thereby advancing reflections of art and culture into the public consciousness. The breadth and depth of Kaeppler's scholarship have given rise to the studies that appear in this volume, in which authors reflect upon, extend, and challenge some of the themes and developments in her work, just as they offer new domains for future research.

Chapters in This Volume

In this volume, thirteen case studies build upon aspects of Kaeppler's work, in new explorations of music and dance. Several contributors – Judy Van Zile, Irene Loutzaki, Egil Bakka, Elsie Ivancich Dunin and Mohd Anis Md Nor – have shared a long scholarly history with Adrienne. They all have contributed chapters that not only present research in dance ethnology but also individually reflect on this long-time engagement with Adrienne's scholarly presence. Other authors in the volume build upon Kaeppler's writings and (critically) engage and expand her ideas and concepts, drawing on Kaeppler's ideas for new research approaches. Taken as a whole, the ensuing chapters represent a diverse range of analysis of visual culture, as applied to distinctive forms of expression, in past and present-day practice. In accordance with Kaeppler's research focus, a substantial portion of chapters in the book focuses closely on questions of dance and concentrate on case studies of Pacific Island cultures.

The first section of the book with the heading 'Gaining Insights through Dance Visualizations' explores new ways of representing dance visually across four chapters. The chapters in this part all focus on analytical aspects of dance as structured movement, building on Kaeppler's writings in dance anthropology. In a study that engages closely with phenomenology, Kati Szego explores Hawaiian hula through experiments in participant visualizations of dance. Afterward, Kendra Stepputat's chapter demonstrates the possibilities that motion capture technology offers for accessing embodied knowledge, in order to understand dance as both structure and culture. In the following chapter Egil Bakka explores the continuing importance of movement transcription as a time-honoured methodology for dance scholarship. In the final chapter of this section, Judy Van Zile writes elegantly about a past dance project she undertook with Kaeppler, and in doing so offers a reflective case study of collaborative research.

In the second section, called 'Reconsidering Movement Structures', each author takes a different tact to understand dance as structured movement, following the influential writings of Kaeppler. Jane Freeman Moulin writes about approaches to understand the intersections between dance, sound and experience in French Polynesian performances by offering a new model of conceptualizing dance and music for the Pacific. Following this, Mohd Anis Md Nor expands on Kaeppler's critical ideas about movement in society in order to explore *igal* performances of the Sama-Bajau in East Malaysia. A third chapter of this section, by Don Niles, examines historical descriptions of courting in Papua New Guinea as cultural forms of structured movement in the past.

The third section of the book, entitled 'Music and Dance as Agency in Power Struggles', addresses the active social meaning embedded in music and dance practices and in examples of visual art and media. Brian Diettrich explores dance performances in Chuuk in the Federated States of Micronesia as practices of active resistance during the German imperial administration of Micronesia, and as visualized in one of the earliest moving images of Pacific dance. Irene Loutzaki studies the close links between music and politics in a study of dances and their interpretation undertaken by Greek politicians in various forms of media. In the following chapter, Ojeya Cruz Banks explores what she calls 'somatic decolonization' in the chanted performances by the Indigenous Chamorro people on contemporary Guam.

The penultimate section of the book, called 'Significance of the Tangible', offers chapters that chart the connections of dance and music to museum contexts and material culture, topics of long interest to Kaeppler. In a reflective chapter, Elsie Ivancich Dunin describes how two past and contrasting museum exhibits on Yugoslavian dance and performance attire charted new ideas that blurred boundaries between tangible and intangible culture. Next, Kirsty Gillespie examines the role of creativity and performance in a recent repatriation project undertaken with Indigenous communities in Northern Australia, and a study that addresses the significance of the museum and museum practices for cultural healing. Finally, Irene Karongo Hundleby investigates how ideas of the senses and connectivity in Solomon Islands music, dance and instruments weave together Indigenous concepts and worldviews.

Given the close links throughout the book with Adrienne's ideas, we thought it only proper that she be given the final word. In 'A Conversation with the Kupuna', Ricardo Trimillos offers a delightful interview with Adrienne conducted in 2018, in which they speak about the trajectories of her career and research. This is followed by a comprehensive list of Kaeppler's work, compiled by Jessica Marinaccio.

Brian Diettrich (PhD, University of Hawai'i at Mānoa) is Senior Lecturer in Ethnomusicology at Victoria University of Wellington, New Zealand. His research has focused on Indigenous music and dance in Oceania and especially in the Federated States of Micronesia. Among his publications is the co-authored book *Music in Pacific Island Cultures: Experiencing Music, Expressing Culture*. Brian is an executive board member of the International Council for Traditional Music (ICTM), and he chairs the ICTM Study Group on Music and Dance of Oceania. Brian formerly taught music in the Federated States of Micronesia.

Kendra Stepputat is Assistant Professor in Ethnomusicology at the Institute of Ethnomusicology, University of Music and Performing Arts Graz, Austria. She is currently Chair of the ICTM Study Group on Sound, Movement, and the Sciences. Her research topics include Balinese performing arts, in particular *kecak*, and *tango argentino* in European perspective. Special focus in her research is on choreomusical aspects of performing arts. She has published articles in the Yearbook for Traditional Music, Asian Music, and is editor of *Performing Arts in Postmodern Bali* (2013) and co-editor of *Sounding the Dance, Moving the Music* (2017).

Note

1. To avoid duplication, full references to Kaeppler's publications in this section are found in 'Publications by Adrienne L. Kaeppler' at the end of this book.

References

Banks, M., and J. Ruby. 2011. 'History, Anthropology, and the History of Visual Anthropology', in M. Banks and J. Ruby (eds), *Made to Be Seen: Perspectives on the History of Visual Anthropology*. Chicago: University of Chicago Press, pp. 1–18.

Berger, H.M. 2009. *Stance: Ideas about Emotion, Style, and Meaning for the Study of Expressive Culture*. Middletown: Wesleyan University Press.

Blaagaard, B.B. 2013. 'Post-Human Viewing: A Discussion of the Ethics of Mobile Phone Imagery', *Visual Communication* 12(3): 359–74.

Buckland, T.J. 1999. 'Introduction: Reflecting on Dance Ethnography', in T.J. Buckland (ed.), *Dance in the Field: Theory, Methods and Issues in Dance Ethnography*. London: Macmillan, pp. 1–10.

Chion, M. 1994. *Audio-Vision: Sound on Screen*. Translated by C. Gorbman (ed.). New York: Columbia University Press.

Clayton, M. 2007. 'Time, Gesture and Attention in a "Khyāl" Performance', *Asian Music* 38(2): 71–96.

Clifford, J., and G.E. Marcus. 1986. 'Partial Truths', in J. Clifford and G.E. Marcus (eds), *Writing Culture: The Poetics and Politics of Ethnography*. Berkeley: University of California Press, pp. 1–26.

Collier, J., and M. Collier. 1986. *Visual Anthropology: Photography as a Research Method*. Albuquerque: University of New Mexico Press.

Downey, G. 2002. 'Listening to Capoeira: Phenomenology, Embodiment, and the Materiality of Music', *Ethnomusicology* 46(3): 487–509.

Dunin, E.I. 2015. *Dance, Narratives, Heritage: 28th Symposium of the ICTM Study Group on Ethnochoreology*. Zagreb: Institute of Ethnology and Folklore Research.

Dunin, E.I., and A. von Bibra Wharton (eds) 2008. *Invisible and Visible Dance, Crossing Identity Boundaries: Proceedings of the 23rd Symposium of the ICTM Study Group on Ethnochoreology*. Institute of Ethnology and Folklore Research Zagreb, Split: Redak.

Edwards, E. 2012. 'Objects of Affect: Photography Beyond the Image', *Annual Review of Anthropology* 41: 221–34.

———. 2015. 'Anthropology and Photography: A Long History of Knowledge and Affect', *Photographies* 8(3): 235–52.

Farnell, B. 2011. 'Theorizing "The Body" in Visual Culture', in M. Banks and J. Ruby (eds), *Visions of Culture: A History of Visual Anthropology*. Chicago: University of Chicago Press, pp. 136–58.

Feld, S. 1976. 'Ethnomusicology and Visual Communication', *Ethnomusicology* 20(2): 293–325.

Finchum-Sung, H. 2012. 'Visual Excess: The Visuality of Traditional Music Performance in South Korea', *Ethnomusicology* 56(3): 396–425.

Foster, H. 1988. *Vision and Visuality*. Seattle: Bay Press.

Foucault, M. 1979. *Discipline and Punish: The Birth of the Prison*. Translated by A. Sheridan. Harmondsworth: Penguin.

Godøy, R.I., and M. Leman (eds). 2010. *Musical Gestures: Sound, Movement, and Meaning*. New York and London: Routledge.

Grau, A. 2011. 'Dancing Bodies, Spaces/Places and the Senses: A Cross-Cultural Investigation', *Journal of Dance & Somatic Practices* 3(1,2): 5–24.

Grau, O., and T. Veigl. 2011. 'Introduction: Imagery in the 21st Century', in O. Grau and T. Veigl (eds), *Imagery in the 21st Century*. Cambridge: The MIT Press, pp. 1–17.

Gritten, A., and E. King (eds). 2011. *New Perspectives on Music and Gesture*. New York and London: Routledge.

Hahn, T. 2007. *Sensational Knowledge: Embodying Culture through Japanese Dance*. Middletown: Wesleyan University Press.

Hannah, J.L. 1979. *To Dance is Human: A Theory of Nonverbal Communication*. Austin: University of Texas Press.

Helmreich, S. 2010. 'Listening Against Soundscapes', *Anthropology News* 51(9): 10.

Howles, D. 2003. *Sensual Relations: Engaging the Senses in Culture and Social Theory*. Ann Arbor: University of Michigan Press.

Hutchinson Guest, A. 1998. *Choreo-Graphics: A Comparison of Dance Notation Systems from the Fifteenth Century to the Present*. Oxon and New York: Routledge.

Ingold, T. 2011. 'Against Soundscape', in A. Carlyle (ed.), *Autumn Leaves: Sound and the Environment in Artistic Practice*. Paris: Double Entendre, pp. 10–13.

Jenkins, H., S. Ford and J. Green. 2013. *Spreadable Media: Creating Value and Meaning in a Networked Culture*. New York: New York University Press.

Jenks, C. 1995. 'The Centrality of the Eye in Western Culture', in C. Jenks (ed.), *Visual Culture*. London: Routledge, pp. 1–25.

Jenssen, T.S. 2005. '"Cool and Crazy": Anthropological Film at the Point of Convergence between Humanities and Social Science', *Visual Anthropology* 18(4): 291–308.

Kaeppler, A.L. 1996. 'The Look of Music, the Sound of Dance: Music as a Visual Art', *Visual Anthropology* 8(2–4): 133–53.

———. 2010. 'The Beholder's Share: Viewing Music and Dance in a Globalized World', *Ethnomusicology* 54(2): 185–201.

———. 2011. 'The Hands and Arms Tell the Story: Movement through Time in Eighteenth-Century Dance Depictions from Polynesia', in B. Sparty and J. Van Zile (eds), *Imaging Dance: Visual Representations of Dancers and Dancing*. Hildesheim: Georg Olms Verlag, pp. 87–102.

———. 2017. 'Capturing Music and Dance in an Archive: A Meditation on Imprisonment', in K. Gillespie, S. Treloyn and D. Niles (eds), *A Distinctive Voice in the Antipodes: Essays in Honour of Stephen A. Wild*. Canberra: Australian National University Press, pp. 429–42.

Killick, A. 2014. 'Visual Evidence in Ethnomusicology', in T. Shepherd and A. Leonard (eds), *The Routledge Companion to Music and Visual Culture*. New York: Routledge, pp. 75–84.

Lacan, J. 2002 [1977]. 'What is a Picture', in N. Mirzoeff (ed.), *The Visual Culture Reader*. Translated by A. Sheridan. London: Routledge, pp. 126–28.

Le Breton, D. 2017. *Sensing the World: An Anthropology of the Senses*. London: Bloomsbury.

Lesaffre, M., P. Maes and M. Leman (eds). 2017. *The Routledge Companion to Embodied Music Interaction*. New York: Routledge.

Lynteris, C., and R. Stasch. 2019. 'Photography and the Unseen', *Visual Anthropology Review* 35(1): 5–9.

Mason, P. 2017. 'Combat-Dancing, Cultural Transmission, and Choreomusicology: The Globalization of Embodied Repertoires of Sound and Movement', in M. Lesaffre, P. Maes and M. Leman (eds), *The Routledge Companion to Embodied Music Interaction*. New York and London: Routledge, pp. 223–31.

Mirzoeff, N. 2002. 'Introduction to Part Three', in N. Mirzoeff (ed.), *The Visual Culture Reader*, 2nd edn. London: Routledge, pp. 473–80.

———. 2006. 'On Visuality', *Journal of Visual Culture* 5(1): 53–79.

———. 2009. *An Introduction to Visual Culture*. London: Routledge.

Nahachewsky, A. 2017. 'Using the Eyes in Ukranian Dance', in K. Stepputat (ed.), *Dance, Senses, Urban Contexts: Proceedings of the 28th Symposium of the ICTM Study Group on Ethnochoreology*. Aachen: Shaker Verlag, pp. 44–58.

Ness, S.A. 1992. *Body, Movement, and Culture: Kinesthetic and Visual Symbolism in a Philippine Community*. Philadelphia: University of Pennsylvania Press.

———. 1995. 'When Seeing is Believing: The Changing Role of Visuality in a Philippine Dance', *Anthropological Quarterly* 68(1): 1–13.

Nor, M.A.Md., E. Ivancich Dunin and A. von Bibra Wharton (eds). 2009. *Transmitting Dance as Cultural Heritage and Dance and Religion: Proceedings of the 25th Symposium of the ICTM Study Group on Ethnochoreology*. Kuala Lumpur: Cultural Centre University of Malaysia.

Nor, M.A.Md., and K. Stepputat (eds). 2017. *Sounding the Dance, Moving the Music: Choreomusicological Perspectives on Maritime Southeast Asian Performing Arts*. London and New York: Routledge.

Phelan, P. 1993. *Unmarked: The Politics of Performance*. New York: Routledge.

Pink, S. 2006. *The Future of Visual Anthropology: Engaging the Senses*. London: Routledge.

———. 2011. 'Images, Senses and Applications: Engaging Visual Anthropology', *Visual Anthropology* 24(5): 437–54.

Sand, A. 2012. 'Visuality', *Studies in Iconography* 33: 89–95.

Schlottmann, A. 2017. 'Visuality', in D. Richardson et al. (eds), *The International Encyclopedia of Geography*. Chichester and Hoboken: John Wiley & Sons, pp. 7495–97.

Schneider, K. 2013. 'Unexpected Horizons of Meaning', in G. Brandstetter and G. Klein (eds), *Dance [and] Theory*. Bielefeld: transcript Verlag, pp. 115–18.

Sheets-Johnstone, M. 1979. 'On Movement and Objects in Motion: The Phenomenology of the Visible in Dance', *Journal of Aesthetic Education* 13(2): 33–46.

Shipley, J.W. 2015. 'Selfie Love: Public Lives in an Era of Celebrity Pleasure, Violence, and Social Media', *American Anthropologist* 117(2): 403–13.

Simonett, H. 2014. 'Envisioned, Ensounded, Enacted: Sacred Ecology and Indigenous Musical Experience in Yoreme Ceremonies of Northwest Mexico', *Ethnomusicology* 58(1): 110–32.

Sparti, B., and J. Van Zile. 2011. 'Introduction', in B. Sparti and J. Van Zile (eds), *Imaging Dance: Visual Representations of Dancers and Dancing*. Hildesheim: Georg Olms Verlag, pp. 1–16.

Stepputat, K. (ed.). 2017. *Dance, Senses, Urban Contexts*. Proceedings of the 29th Symposium of the International Council for Traditional Music (ICTM) Study Group on Ethnochoreology. Aachen: Shaker Verlag.

Titon, J.T. 2008. 'Knowing Fieldwork', in G.F. Barz and T.J. Cooley (eds), *Shadows in the Field: New Perspectives for Fieldwork in Ethnomusicology*, 2nd edn. New York: Oxford University Press, pp. 25–41.

Veroli, P., and G. Vinay (eds). 2018. *Music-Dance: Sound and Motion in Contemporary Discourse*. London and New York: Routledge.

Wade, B. 1998. *Imaging Sound: An Ethnomusicological Study of Music, Art, and Culture in Mughal India*. Chicago: University of Chicago Press.

Walker, J.A., and S. Chaplin. 1997. *Visual Culture: An Introduction*. Manchester: Manchester University Press.

Van Zile, J. 1988. 'Examining Movement in the Context of the Music Event: A Working Model', *Yearbook for Traditional Music* 20: 125–33.

PART I

Gaining Insights through Dance Visualizations

Chapter 1

Kinetic Songscapes
Intersensorial Listening to *Hula Kuʻi* Songs

Kati Szego

The late twentieth and early twenty-first centuries generated a groundswell of scholarship on Indigenous Hawaiian[1] dance: its movement structures, poetic and musical repertoires; its histories of banishment and revival; its cosmological and social significances; its global circulation and consumption. Few have contributed as significantly to this literature as Adrienne Kaeppler. Kaeppler's most extended work on the subject is her 1993 tome on Hawaiian drum dances, which documents a particular genre of hula used to celebrate King Kalākaua's official coronation (1883) and fiftieth birthday jubilee (1886). As Hawaiʻi's first elected monarch, Kalākaua was keen to legitimate his status by traditional means, and to that end invited master practitioners of *mele oli* (chant) and *mele hula* (chant/song realized kinaesthetically) to perform in his honour. *Mele* (poetic) texts were strategically selected for those august occasions to link Kalākaua with the gods and thus consolidate his political/spiritual power (Kaeppler 1993: 24).

In terms of sound and accompanying movement, the various types of *mele hula* used to dignify Kalākaua were the products of different historical eras. *Hula pahu*, the near-exclusive focus of Kaeppler's book, is a pre-Christian movement style evolved from ritual worship of the Hawaiian pantheon. The court's chant and dance experts, like the monarch himself, were also masterful synthesizers active in the construction of two relatively new genres: *mele hula kuʻi* and its chanted counterpart, *mele hula ʻōlapa* (see Stillman 2005: 86). *Mele hula kuʻi* – songs accompanied by contemporized hula movement – were the hybrid designs of late-nineteenth century cosmopolitans. That genre, too, was powerful – not as much in its substantiation of divine presence as in its evocation of a trans-Pacific modernity.

This chapter has as its principle focus *mele hula kuʻi* as objects of aural apprehension. In asking the question, 'How do Hawaiians listen to *hula kuʻi* songs?', I uncover yet another kind of power – that is, the songs' capacity for calling forth meanings that are embodied through perception and imagination and, by virtue of their embodiment, across multiple modes of sense experience. In so doing, I extend the project of interrogating sounding *with* moving that Kaeppler initiated in the 1980s (Kaeppler 1981).

Accessing Meaning: How Do Hawaiians Listen?

In the early 1990s, I conducted research at the Performing Arts Department of Kamehameha Schools, a private school in Honolulu for Kānaka Maoli. Musically, Kamehameha still had many of the trappings of its nineteenth-century colonial beginnings: a marching band, an orchestra and a choir culture that held the state of Hawaiʻi in thrall during its annually televised choral song contest. Kamehameha was also riding high on a late-breaking wave of the second Hawaiian Renaissance,[2] offering courses in Indigenous chant and hula, as well as syncretic genres such as slack-key guitar. I was eager to know how young Hawaiians at the high school level navigated the differences and imbrications of Euro-American and Polynesian aesthetic systems and the meanings they made out of them. In an effort to wrestle free from master musicians' privileged narratives of meaning, I sought research participants who could represent a broader population of producers and consumers.[3] Kamehameha was ideal in this regard, as it was a crucible for young musicians and dancers developing their aesthetic competences with differing levels of commitment and mastery. I entered the Performing Arts Department's classrooms, rehearsal studios and hallways at an important historical juncture. Working to rehabilitate its colonial image and to imbue young Kānaka Maoli with a sense of cultural pride, Kamehameha's Hawaiian identity project was well underway by the time I arrived, and students spoke easily with me and their peers about the meanings they attached to Hawaiian musics and other expressive practices.

In querying how Kamehameha students traversed their musical terrain, I was interested not only in meanings they articulated intersubjectively, which could be gathered through dialogue and observation, but in their tacit readings and sensings – in apprehensions that are so evanescent, incomplete, automatic or commonplace as to be unremarkable, so powerful or socially contrary as to be unutterable, or so complex as to defy easy expression. As a method for getting at this silent/silenced realm, I asked students to listen to selected recordings of music, to reflexively observe their experiences during the period of listening, and to give those experiences expression. They did, by writing down the thoughts, images and sensations that manifested moment by moment. Quickly jotting keywords and phrases, they attempted to capture the flow of their experience; some even drew images. When the music ended, they elaborated and explained what they had captured on paper, either by writing more or in conversation with me.

A Phenomenological Perspective

I would like to consider the auto-representational listening–writing exercise as an approach that can help us fathom how people make meaning out of music. Here I am advocating expansion of the ethnographic toolkit to include another method informed by phenomenology, a philosophical tradition that offers insight into people's lived experience. Following a couple of streams in that tradition, this chapter takes as foundational three premises: 1) that experience is something individually constituted yet shaped by living together in the world (Hammond, Howarth and Keith 1991: 5–6); 2) that experience is constituted intersensorially – that is, with the totality of the body, rather than discrete senses – and through multiple modalities, such as perception and imagination; and 3) that the sensorial nature of experiential modalities such as perception and imagination is grounded in the embodied nature of all consciousness. One of the purposes of this chapter is to demonstrate how the meanings that emerge from young Hawaiians' apprehension of *hula kuʻi* songs engage the entire sensorium and are manifest in different modalities of lived experience.

Regarding the constitution of experience, Husserlian phenomenologists assert that subjects *perform* acts of perception and imagination. Rather than responding prescriptively to musical stimuli, for example, listeners actively, if unconsciously, bring lyrics, melodic structures, physical sensations and the like into their awareness. Humphreys (1991) has shown how acts of perception make it possible for a listener to apprehend an accelerating drum roll in subtly different ways as a function of attention. Through fore- and backgrounding, it can be heard as a 'gradual quickening of an otherwise constant pulse' or as a 'gradual contracting of the silences between sonic articulations' (Humphreys 1991: 288). The choice is the listener's, and that choice may be shaped, wittingly or not, by myriad sociocultural and musical factors. The point is that the listener actively constitutes the sound; she brings the drum roll into her lived experience in a particular way.

Human perception is always predicated on the presence of sense information and grounded in the sensorium. The same cannot be said for imagination. Many accounts of imagination describe it in terms that are independent of the apprehension of sense data or absent sense data altogether (see, for example, Lakoff 1987; Modell 2003). While this may be the case, Kamehameha listeners' imaginings were unambiguously tied to the sounds that hovered in their aural environment – that is, to the recordings I played for them. My analysis of listeners' imaginings benefits from phenomenologist Edward Casey's (1976) categorization and elucidation of imaginative phenomena, namely 'imaging' and 'imagining-how.' Imaging is an act of conjuring that calls upon a specific sense or senses, the most common of which, Casey surmises, is visualization (Casey 1976: 42). Fittingly, the sense that Kamehameha listeners registered most frequently was vision, and especially where *hula kuʻi* songs were concerned, the images they recorded were intimately tied to bodies – sometimes their own, but just as often others'.

It is the body – so conspicuous an object of visuality in the hula world, so foundational to consciousness – that takes centre stage in this chapter. My goal is not just to examine how listeners attended *to* the body but to interrogate how they attended *with* the body in constituting their musical experience. Listeners' jot notes and sketches revealed the body to be both a means of perception and an object of imagination. As the object of imagination, listeners visualized bodies (and other objects too), drawing liberally on 'conventional rich images' (Lakoff 1987: 446). The bodies that emerged in visual imagination were never isolated from the rest of experience but were inextricably tied to social identities such as gender, ethnicity and race. As the means of perception, listeners' gendered bodies were directly implicated in the act of listening via 'ghost gestures' (Behnke 1997), a concept I explore more fully later in the chapter.

While experience is located in individuals, the ways that they constitute their lived experience is both deeply personal and resonant with others. Human beings attend to music informed by living in the 'same world' (Ingold 2011: 136), by previous musical encounters, by communal ways of talking about music, by systems of musical pedagogy, by culturally shaped bodies that are the agents of perception, and so on. Ethnomusicologist Harris M. Berger suggests that 'each musical culture . . . possesses a unique social organization of attention . . . – a culturally specific style of *partially* sharing experiences' (Berger 1999: 43). It is those specificities I would like to approach now, by carefully scrutinizing Hawaiian youths' representations of their experience of listening to Hawaiian music. In the concluding portion of the chapter, I flesh out and critique the methodology I used that put research participants in the role of writers inscribing their perceptual and imaginative worlds.

Hula Kuʻi Songs

Most of my analysis will centre on the *hula kuʻi* song 'Puamana', which was composed in 1937 by Irmgard Farden ʻĀluli. *Hula kuʻi* is a song genre dating to the 1860s that combines (*kuʻi*) strophic Hawaiian poetry with Western diatonic melodies. Those melodies are frequently realized using Indigenous vocal techniques such as *haʻi* (breaking voice) and falsetto, and are accompanied by chordal instruments that provide the metric foundation for modern (*ʻauana*) hula movement (Stillman 2005: 86).

The lyrics of 'Puamana', written by Irmgard ʻĀluli's father, Charles Kekua Farden, celebrate the beloved Farden family home, called Puamana, located in Lahaina, Maui. Its beauties are extolled using a rather transparent poetic text (see below). An enduring 'hula hit' (Stillman 1998b), the recording of 'Puamana' that I used was one of the most familiar to people living in Hawaiʻi from the late 1980s to this day (Puamana 1986). It featured a group consisting of the composer herself (known affectionately as Aunty Irmgard),[4] her daughters Mihana Souza and A'ima McManus, and niece Luana McKenney. Singing in close harmony, the quartet accompanied itself on 'ukulele, guitar and bass, with added piano stylings by Mahi Beamer (see Salā 2011). In addition to instrumentation, *hula ku'i* songs like this one are instantly recognizable by their two-to-four-measure opening vamp in duple meter. Like most *hula ku'i* songs, the last verse is signalled by the phrase *ha'ina 'ia mai ka puana* (let the tale be told in the refrain) or some variant thereof.

Puamana	Puamana
Ku'u home i Lahaina	Is my home in Lahaina
Me nā pua 'ala onaona	With flowers so fragrant
Ku'u home i aloha 'ia	My home is so loved
Ku'u home	My home
I ka ulu o ka niu	Is surrounded by coconut trees
'O ka niu kū kilakila	That stand majestically
Napenape mālie	Gently swaying in the breezes
Home nani	A beautiful home
Home i ka 'ae kai	Nestled along the shore
Ke kōnane a ka mahina	With the bright moon light
I ke kai hāwanawana	Upon the whispering sea
Ha'ina	Told is the refrain
'Ia mai ka puana	For my beloved home
Ku'u home i Lahaina	Filled with much
I piha me ka hau'oli	Happiness and joy

(Translation: Hailama Farden. Text and translation courtesy of the Farden family.)

Imagining Bodies: Visualizing and Imagining-How

Listeners brought musical sound into their lived experience as visual images, either by recalling specific events they had participated in or witnessed, or by imagining new events with qualities of the old. A number of young men who listened to 'Puamana' envisioned a family *lū'au* or feast where 'Puamana' or a song like it had been played; as they listened, they visualized and carefully itemized the delicacies that festooned potluck tables:[5]

> luau's-birthdays-food, fish, poi, lomi salmon, kalua pig, rice, opihi, sweet potato, haupia, pineapple/my uncle who we dislike and only see at luau/ brother's graduation luau/cousin's first birthday luau/chicken long rice/ aunties singing at parties/family eating with me/talking to auntie

poi, fish, kalua pig, sweet potato, family, luau, happiness, haupia, kuloʻo, chicken long rice, squid, lomi salmon, pineapple/Hawaiian music/together happy, having a good time/crab[6]

These responses are examples of redintegration, a process by which a (sonic) morsel of the past can bring a fuller memory or new imagination to life.[7] As the first example intimates, the young men's mental images were also heavily populated with bodies – often a mother, grandmother, aunty or sister, singing or dancing hula at the festive occasion.

An alternative to family *lūʻau* scenes were images of performances for tourists, which similarly assigned hula dancing to women and were described in rich detail. Listener Kawehi[8] envisioned 'ukulele-strumming aunties at the airport, welcoming visitors, while others placed the musicians in the Royal Hawaiian Shopping Center or Kodak Hula Show, both located in Waikīkī, Honolulu's tourist mecca. The props and adornments used by the middle-aged aunties all portrayed a familiar sight of women attired in ankle-length dresses or *muʻumuʻu*, their long hair wrapped in a sleek, tight bun, set off with a large hibiscus.

Taken together, listeners' mental pictures had the properties of what George Lakoff (1987) calls 'conventional rich images' (CRIs). Drawing on 'typical cases, social stereotypes, paragons, and the like' (Lakoff 1987: 446), they are also finely elaborated.[9] 'Our conventional images', Lakoff says, 'may not all be exactly the same, but the degree of uniformity is remarkable' (ibid.: 447). Some female listeners who recalled their personal histories of dancing to 'Puamana' in tourist venues invoked CRIs of audience members: they were typically white, overweight, awkward, wore odd or inappropriate clothing (especially socks) and sported plastic flower leis.[10] Kawehi, for example, saw 'tourists getting off the plane/fat white bodies climbing down the stairs w/ straw hats & gaudy aloha wear'. Her visual evocation of the mid-Western American tourist CRI was laden with discerning humour; after all, locals rarely sport straw hats (or hats of any kind to shield them from the sun) and favour subtler colours and designs over eye-popping tourist kitsch. There is thus a sociopolitical sheen to Kawehi's visualization. Her CRI is a testament to encounters with tourists who cannot help but mark themselves as outsiders to Hawai'i even as they strive to blend in. Tourism is the single largest contributor to the state's gross domestic product, accounting for as much as 33 per cent of its economy and almost half its employment (Latzko n.d.). Many – perhaps even Kawehi – regard the almost inescapable imperative to serve tourists and the commercial tourist industry as extending the legacy of *haole* (white) American colonialism, which took hold in the early nineteenth century.

While remarkable in their consistency across persons, CRIs are not exactly the same, and listeners brought them into awareness in personally nuanced ways. 'Puamana' talks about sweet-smelling flowers, swaying palms and moonlight reflected on the sea. Another female listener, Lia, recorded her stream of thoughts and images as follows: 'hula dancer/sunset/beach/the mist/surfers/sitting and watching the ocean/the home in Lahaina/and everything like flowers, waves and people.' She was conversant with the lyrics of 'Puamana', so the sunset as well as the mist, surfers and hula dancer were of her own making. Lia represented her visual images with a drawing (see Figure 1.1.), which we later discussed.

Lia had a strong identification with this song because her grandmother, like the Farden family, had a seaside home on Maui. Not only was 'Puamana' one of the first hulas she ever learned, but she sometimes practised hula at her grandmother's beach house with her aunt. She described her image of the hula dancer as a self-portrait, made evident by the shortish hair. Young Hawaiian women, especially those invested in the competitive hula world, tend to grow their hair very long and display it either by splaying it voluminously or bundling it on top of their heads, sometimes in a tight knot.[11] Having short hair is thus a strong statement of gendered nonconformity. Lia was clear to point out, however, that

Figure 1.1. Lia's drawing in response to 'Puamana'. Photograph by Kati Szego.

she did not and would never have worn the apparel she depicted, which attired the dancer in a grass or cellophane skirt and a seashell brassiere. The choice of the commercial hula costume, she explained, was to represent her perception of 'Puamana' as 'kind of a tourist song', an observation she offered without apparent derision. While Lia drew on conventional rich images to depict dance dress[12] and oceanside scenery – umbrella and beach mat included – she did not merely reproduce them; she adjusted them carefully to portray herself and her memories of learning to dance at a beachside locale, as well as to comment on the song's emblematic status in the tourist sphere. By inhabiting the sartorially objectified body of the dancer who must cater to touristic desires, Lia blurred the boundary between self and other. Lia thus constituted an embodied memory that was at once a revision of her prior experience *and* imagined – a memory woven through with a visual stereotype and reflective of her understanding of the song's currency in the world of visitor entertainment. In appropriating a conventional visual trope and implicating herself in it, the drawing was shot through with a sympathetic irony. My sense is that Lia did not hold professional, commercially attired dancers in contempt because she did not see herself as being so very different from them: their dance training and dedication often equal, each would have been marked as a '[native] hula girl' (Desmond 1997: 86) by outsiders, though in very different ways. In the absence of more information, I can only speculate on other possible meanings of Lia's drawing. Did listening provide Lia and young Hawaiians like her with spaces for donning different masks? Did she invite the tourist gaze only to confront or frustrate it?[13]

I conclude this section on imagination with a brief example of 'imagining-how'. 'To imagine how', Casey writes, 'is to imagine what it would be like *to* do, think, or feel so-and-so, or *to* move, behave, and speak in such-and-such ways' (1976: 45; emphasis in original).[14] Imagining-how differs from the visualizing described heretofore in that it necessarily involves the imaginer's embodied participation in some sort of activity; as we have seen, visualizing is just as frequently focused on others' bodies.

The following example of imagining-how is 'Iolani's written response to another classic *hula ku'i* song, 'Hi'ilawe', performed by Gabby Pahinui (1978): 'what motions could go to this song[?] *I'm in hula [class] and trying to figure out my own motions, interpret [the text]*.' Unlike the 'Puamana' respondents quoted earlier, 'Iolani had not learned any choreographies to 'Hi'ilawe' but registered it as a familiar *hula ku'i* song. Recognizing the singer's voice, the melody, the extended opening vamp (featuring slack-key guitar) and Hawaiian language, she conjured the interpretive act of bringing the Hawaiian text to gestural life. Dreamily taking herself to hula class – the place where she routinely acquired and practised new hula gestures and learned to read songs for their representational potential – she visually imagined how she would choreograph and realize the text with her body. In 'Iolani's case, imagining-how stops just short of the impulse to move to the music or to act on that impulse – perceptual phenomena experienced by many other listeners and discussed in the next section of this chapter. Suffice it to say that it is easy to see how acts of imagination and perception may be tightly linked to each other.

Looking closely at the words that Kamehameha students wrote to capture the contents of their consciousness reveals their close attention to bodies – their own and others' – and their sharp eye for sartorial presentation. Lia's, Kawehi's, 'Iolani's and the young men's experiences speak to the visually imaginative constitution of musical experience. Each of them imported the sounds of 'Puamana' into their lived experience as finely grained mental images of bodies – images that spoke to their reiterative witness of dance-related occasions as disparate as airport welcomes and intimate family feasts. Both Lia's graphic inscription of the hula dancer's body – one that was simultaneously hers and not hers – and Kawehi's written depiction of the tourist body foreground racially savvy 'somatic modes of attention' (Csordas 1993). If Lia's drawing shed light on the symbolic economy of the 'Hawaiian hula girl', Kawehi's images of bodies burdened by whiteness and poor sartorial taste reversed the tourist gaze. Listeners' conventional rich images demonstrate how constituting sound in lived experience entails visualization and memory, both of which can open a window onto ethical stances and political dispositions.

Perceiving with Bodies: 'Ghost Gestures' and Kinetic Songscapes

Many written responses to 'Puamana' were registered in terms of the impulse to sing along and, even more commonly, to dance hula. The gendering of lived experience was again evident, as mostly women heard 'Puamana' with their dancers' bodies. Anthropologist Paul Connerton would have us think of these impulses as evidence of social memories 'sedimented' in the body (Connerton 1989: 72). They undoubtedly are, but unlike Connerton's culturally shaped embodied practices, which usually elude reflective scrutiny, hula was in the forefront of listeners' awareness. This is partly because of hula's reified aesthetic status as 'dance' rather than a set of practical movements tethered to the tasks of everyday living. More than that, hula was and still is a cornerstone of the Hawaiian cultural revival that emerged in the 1970s. Since that time, women have flocked to hula schools, to the extent that there is something of a duty to heritage for Hawaiian women, beginning in childhood, to study the dance. Under the tutelage of *kumu hula* (teachers), practitioners spend many years and countless hours rehearsing comportments and choreographies in preparation for public performance and competition.

During my time at Kamehameha, all of the women of the Concert Glee Club danced two modern hulas, one of which was 'Puamana'. The Concert Glee Club was Kamehameha's elite performing group and was frequently called upon by the school's upper administration to perform for dignitaries, for commemorative and other landmark occasions.[15] As 'ambassadors' of the school's increasingly Hawaiian-centric culture, dancing hula was an obligation that fell mostly to the young women; and it was a role that most embraced. It was no surprise, then, that when they heard 'Puamana', many (including women not in the Concert Glee) immediately recorded either the physical sensation of movement or their body's inclination to dance. From a phenomenological perspective, these are two separate categories of kinaesthetic experience. Corporeal sensations that are a by-product of the moving body are distinct from 'something volitional or quasi-volitional that remains when one abstracts from such sensations' (Cairns, cited in Behnke 1997: 183). Listeners' written comments, below, illustrate both kinds of lived experience. The first statement registers discrete physical sensations resulting from movements that were apparent only to the listener, while the second statement registers kinaesthetic volition in the absence of localized movement.

move foot and head *I felt the need to move along with the music* / [move] hands / sway slowly [during vamp] . . . / tap finger

it's hard to not get up and dance

The invisible or barely detectable movement of the listener's foot, head and hands resulting in corporeal sensation are part of a sedimented system of micromovements that, through rigorous somatic education, make a hula dancer's body. Phenomenologist Elizabeth Behnke describes this kind of bodily activity as a 'ghost of a gesture' – 'a kind of inner "quasi-gesture" . . . or tendency-toward movement that can persist in the body even when the large-scale gesture that the ghost gesture implies is not being performed' (Behnke 1997: 189). Ghost gestures exist in all bodies, returning to 'haunt' a person long after the occasions of their earliest enactments (ibid.: 191). What leaked through the young women's written responses to *hula kuʻi* songs was their corporeal habituation to the songs' signature sounds. The instant they heard the opening instrumental vamp to 'Puamana', rendered in a slow but danceable 4/4, they traced microscopic ghost gestures in the air with hands, feet and head, reproducing the back-and-forth *kāholo* step pattern and lateral arm movements that form the kinaesthetic infrastructure of modern hula.[16]

When lyric voices entered the sonic stream following the introductory vamp, ghost gestures took on another valence. As a legacy of colonial educational practices, Kamehameha students, like most young Hawaiians in the 1990s, had a limited Hawaiian vocabulary with which to decipher song lyrics (Szego 2003); hula practitioners, however, often knew many of the words to a song by virtue of the gestures they learned for dancing. In hula's representational movement system, gestures (especially those of the upper limbs and torso) are iconic of particular objects (e.g. *pali* [cliff]) and actions (e.g. *ua* [to rain]). Listening to *hula kuʻi* songs compelled many dancers to re-create sung words with their bodies, crossing experiential modalities, so that the denotative or connotative meaning of a Hawaiian poetic phrase could call forth a whisper of a gesture.

Such deeply sedimented processes signal the 'traffic and transformation of meaning' (Berger 2009: 43) between audition, vision and motility. If listening to hula songs gave rise to ghost gestures by foregrounding and focusing attention on certain elements in the mix of sound (e.g. the opening vamp's telltale melodic contour), then we may regard the embodied practice of micro-gesturing as part of listeners' constitution of sound. Many young women listened to 'Puamana' – that is, they brought the song into lived experience – with their hands and feet.[17]

By virtue of the writing task I set before students, they were attuned to – perhaps even hyperaware of – what their bodies were up to as they listened. In other words, they possessed and reported on consciousness of their somaesthetic and kinaesthetic sensations: they were reflexively aware of their tapping fingers and swaying torsos. Setting the writing task aside for a moment, I understand listeners' experience of ghost gesturing – that is, their embodied intentionality toward the music – as exercising a 'kinaesthetic consciousness' (Behnke 2011). Kinaesthetic consciousness is 'a consciousness or subjectivity that is itself characterized in terms of motility, that is, the very ability to move freely and responsively' (ibid.). In other words, hands and other parts of the body are the *means by which* sound is experienced. A Merleau-Pontian reading of this phenomenon – of women constituting sound with their hands and feet – would leave an exclusively intellectualist conception of human consciousness and intentionality behind, locating it firmly in the body. Arguably, the language I used to describe ghost gesturing where song lyrics are concerned suggests a relay quality to hula dancers' perceptual acts: she hears musical sounds, isolates distinct words and translates them, then represents them via her hands or other parts of her body. However, such a sequence makes movement 'a servant of [cognitive processes of] consciousness' (Merleau-Ponty 2012: 140), an approach from which Merleau-Ponty's phenomenology diverges. The body, he proclaims, directly mediates the world (ibid.: 147); it 'understands its world without having to go through "representations"' (ibid.: 141). The body's motor intentionality – here, its engagement with the world of sound – is pre-reflexive, and as a part of the female body's practical knowledge of hula, ghost gestures are irreducibly foundational rather than acts resulting from prior incorporeal cognition (see Hammond, Howarth and Keat 1991: 180; Merleau-Ponty 2012: 367).

In understanding how this plays out in hula dancers' listening practice, the sonic object equally warrants our consideration. I find Alain Corbin's deployment of the 'auditory landscape' metaphor, which speaks to the co-constitution of audition and vision, to be particularly apt here. Like a visual landscape that one learns to read (e.g. trees outlining the perimeter of a property), an auditory landscape helps to direct a listener's sensorial uptake (Corbin 1998: 306);

it 'comes with instructions for perceiving it' (Young 2018). We can think of 'Puamana' or 'Hi'ilawe' or any other *hula kuʻi* song bearing similar sonic features as 'kinetic songscapes' that speak to the co-constitution of audition and kinesis. Kinetic songscapes are equipped with a set of gestural and corporeal directions imparted almost exclusively to women. For female Hawaiian listeners immersively disciplined in the art of hula locomotion and lyric representation, *hula kuʻi* songs capacitate and guide dancers' bodies. There are certainly resonances here with having 'a song stuck in your body' (Miller 2017: 93), but I suggest that the corporeally possessive effects of kinetic songscapes are primarily generic. Hula dancers need not know a choreography to a particular song; rather, they need only to have incorporated and naturalized a gestural inventory that can be brought to hand through a set of normative genre-specific sonic cues: opening and between-verse vamps that lay down a II7-V7-I progression while tracing conventional melodic figures; Hawaiian lyrics parsed in two- or four-measure phrases; densely textured 'ukulele-guitar-bass accompaniment.[18]

Hula's ghost gestures had a generally positive valence for young Hawaiian women. After all, hula is a way for them to demonstrate extraordinary prowess and control over their bodies in a way that is valorised, and perhaps more than any other form of expressive culture or sport, hula visibly indexes Hawaiianness. Even so, some female members of the Concert Glee Club who had performed 'Puamana' failed to register ghost gestures or an urge to dance while listening to the song. One of them, Maile, wrote pejoratively, 'cows', later explaining to me that she had 'the grace of a cow' and that the Concert Glee women looked like cows in their matching floral dresses. Maile resisted participation in the hula world and had had a great deal of difficulty incarnating 'Puamana'; for that visible breach, she received gentle teasing from her male friends in the Concert Glee. The anxiety of not measuring up to the other dancers and not being able to fulfil gendered social expectations is reflected in her discomfited 'stance' (Berger 2009) toward the song. It was Maile's frustration at being unable to perform a compulsory choreography of visibly Hawaiian feminine beauty and cultural competence that drove her experience of 'Puamana'. I bring this example to the fore only to illustrate that bodies are not always obedient. The instructions for perceiving that accompany kinetic songscapes can be heeded but so too can they be ignored, shoved to the periphery, or supplanted by yet other instructions on condition of the listener's stance, of her particular relationship to hula. Where most young Hawaiian women clearly cherish hula and their bodies' mastery of it, some do not.

Only one young man registered a desire to dance to 'Puamana';[19] instead, the physical impulses male listeners noted took a different form as in, 'it makes you want to stand and pick up a uke and play along with them', suggesting a kinetic songscape with an alternative canon of embodied instructions. Here the listener's body again betrays a gender-specific mode of habituation. One of the continuing legacies of American colonialism in Hawai'i is the gendered division of aesthetic labour. Though there were important exceptions, in the early 1990s the role of hula dancer still fell mostly to women, while the role of singer/instrumentalist was dominated by men. Only 'Jawaiian' songs prompted ghost gestures or stirred an inclination to dance from both men and women. In the early 1990s, Jawaiian was still a relatively new genre of popular song enjoying heavy radio play. Glossed as 'Hawaiian reggae', it melded Hawaiian harmonic sensibilities with a reggae rhythm produced on acoustic or electronic percussion (see hoʻomanawanui 2006; Stillman 1998b; Weintraub 1993).[20] One of four Jawaiian songs I played for students was Manaʻo Company's 'Unity'.[21] Sounding its theme of universal brother- and sisterhood in English, the song spoke indirectly to the Indigenous Hawaiian ideal of *lōkahi* ('unity').[22] The song's up-tempo groove made it ideal for skanking, a ska-inspired dance form that is radically different from hula. Skanking (students usually wrote 'skankin') offered the possibility of moving in a more individuated style, often in male–female pairs, whereas hula's movements were lyrically guided and disciplined through gender-segregated group choreographies. Gender neutral, skanking bore none of hula's female associations or effeminizing stigma; it was a dance form that young Hawaiian men could engage without fear of others scrutinizing their sexuality (see Szego 2012, 2018).

Whereas hula's practitioners spanned many generations, Jawaiian was youth-centred. It was music for cruising – its boomy bass emanating from low-rider trucks overflowing with young 'bruddahs' heading for the beach to catch some waves. It follows, then, that 'Unity' evinced kinetic gestures that were not only concordant with reggae grooves but with other kinds of motility. Squirming in his seat, Kawika could barely contain his psychophysical energies as he listened to 'Unity' and scratched out this list:

> feeling nuts like going crazy
> feel like surfing
> feel like being with my chick
> surfing 20 ft.+ waves
> feel like cruising
> feel like dancing
> feel like smoking classes, drinking beer
> feel like ripping (waves)
> feeling high
> auxilirating [sic]
> feel like singing
> feel like surfing
> boogie boarding
> feel like acting stupid
> feel relaxed
> no worries
> clearing my mind

Registering volition more than sensate feeling, Kawika's writing reveals a restless body eager to take action: to cut classes and let loose, to cruise and drink beer with friends.

The larger point to be drawn from listeners' responses to 'Puamana', 'Hi'ilawe' and 'Unity' is that moving in habitual, gendered ways leaves tangible, visible and invisible records on the body that can later haunt its subjects. For young Hawaiian women in the early 1990s, the ability to assimilate sounds and song words through the gestural vocabulary of hula played a vital role in making meaning out of *hula ku'i* songs. This was true not only for women who knew a particular song and one of its choreographies but even for those who did not, who only imagined how they could or would render the song gesturally. Styles of movement tied to genres like *hula ku'i* can be so thoroughly sedimented in the body, so intimately folded into one's sense of self, that they are readily set in motion in the process of apprehending music. Embodied memories of hula dancing are, furthermore, so powerful a technology of female Hawaiian selves they may be hard to resist. In the world of *hula ku'i*, kinetic songscapes are the drivers of intersensorial listening experience, beckoning and leading but not determining dancers' motilities. It should be clear that 'Puamana' does not – cannot – mean any one thing. For all of the variability I tracked from person to person, however, there were also coherences, evidence of the partial sharing that enjoins people in that elusive and troublesome construct called 'culture'.

Conclusion: Experiential Writing as Phenomenological Method

Writing in Hawai'i

The listening–writing exercise briefly described in the introduction – wherein I asked students to listen and to represent contents of their consciousness to themselves (and ultimately to me) – stands out in the context of what was otherwise an aural project at Kamehameha, and it should be understood in historical, disciplinary perspective. Wary of a visual, especially literary hegemony permeating early musicological endeavours, not to mention literacy's imperialist misuses, ethnomusicologists came to privilege the aural mode in their ethnographic work. Even in Indigenous societies where ideography was cultivated and literacy was an important means of asserting identity or a form of empowerment (see, e.g. McLaughlin 1992), mystification of the living consultant as one who best spoke in an aural voice was a prevailing, tacit position in ethnomusicology; when I conducted research in the early 1990s, this was certainly the case. Since that time, sweeping technological changes, such as the development of the Internet, and efforts to Indigenize the academy have altered the interlocutory landscape considerably.[23]

Speaking to the Hawaiian scene, one of the most enduring outcomes of the American missionary presence in Hawai'i from 1820 is literacy. Members of the Hawaiian monarchy, while thoroughly grounded in oral traditions, embraced literacy for various purposes – not the least of which was writing poetry and music. In the nineteenth century, Hawai'i's *ali'i* (chiefly class) kept *mele* books, where they inscribed, in elegant cursive, their own and others' poetic texts (*mele*), which formed the backbone of a logocentric chant/song and dance culture. Documentary collections such as those housed in Honolulu's Bishop Museum Archives abound with *mele* books penned by Indigenous elites. Literacy, though, was hardly an exclusive pursuit. The broader population achieved widespread literacy by the middle of the nineteenth century, and by the 1860s, Hawaiians turned to Indigenous-language newspaper production in a way unprecedented in the Pacific. Of this independent press, Puakea Nogelmeier notes that, 'in five decades and in nearly 100 different newspapers, Hawaiian speakers filled more than 100,000 pages with their writings. During this time while literacy was at its highest, Hawaiians embraced the Hawaiian language newspapers as the main venue for news and national dialogue, and also as a public repository for history, cultural description, literature, and lore' (Nogelmeier 2003: xi).[24]

Though Indigenous Hawaiian literacy rates have suffered since the early twentieth century, it remains a core competence cultivated in Hawai'i's state-run and private school systems.[25] While asking Kamehameha students to write, then, was in keeping with school culture, I only did so after observing classes for a period of time. In one instance, teachers used essay writing with students who were learning chants and hulas about the Hawaiian islands. 'What', they were asked, 'are the mythological, Christian, and scientific explanations for the creation of the islands, and which explanation(s) do you most believe?' It was clear to students that there was no right answer, and the essay, once handed in, was deliberately never discussed. Writing was a way of debating potentially conflicting perspectives without bringing them into a public forum. This pedagogical exercise illustrated a general rule shaping a great deal of Hawaiian communication: that in face-to-face encounters, differences of opinion, and critique especially, will often be sublimated in order to maintain harmonious relations (Howard 1974). With this lesson in mind, and concerns about a potentially oppressive pedagogy at least partially relieved,[26] I asked students to listen to diverse musics of my choosing and put pen to paper.

Though there is much that can be said about the contexts in which Kamehameha research participants listened, I offer only a few comments here. In a very few cases, teachers gave their entire class over to me, in which case we used the classroom, usually furnished with chairs or desks. More often, students volunteered to listen together, sometimes with their friends, in a smaller studio space, where they sat comfortably on the carpeted floor, backs propped against the wall, writing on binders held in their laps. In either case, these environments were hardly as natural or rich as any of the musical scenarios that Hawaiian youth typically encounter, a shortcoming imposed, in part, by my institutionally sanctioned access to students.[27]

Writing as Intersensorial Representation

In terms of methodological efficacy, Charles Seeger's famous admonition not to confuse 'speech about music' (1977) with musical experience exposes one of the vulnerabilities of the self-monitoring/writing technique. The dilemma that Seeger recognized was that representation reconstitutes rather than reproduces experience, a hermeneutic condition that James Paul Gee (1992: 13) has called the 'paradox of interpretation' – that is, 'that an interpretation of a text is always just *another* text in "other words"'.

The effect of reconstituting experience is perhaps magnified by the self-monitoring/writing technique. At the most mundane level, there is the strain of constant metacognition and reflexivity for the listener; and while metacognition is hardly foreign to interpretive experience, some practice reflexivity with greater ease than others. Self-monitoring and writing also impose artificial attentional boundaries on experience; the physical act of writing can interrupt musical perception altogether or dislodge the act of perceiving or imagining from the foreground, moving it to the background or periphery. These attentional adjustments, in turn, surely cause listeners to register discrete instants of experience rather than their multilayered and seamless flow. Self-monitoring may also encourage listeners to settle on the least evanescent aspects of their experience.

Though reconstitution is a quality of all ethnographic inquiry, some, such as dance scholar Deidre Sklar, refuse to regard it as a diminishment of the 'real' thing. Exploring the ways that kinaesthesia can be translated into words for the sake of others' understanding, she maintains that 'writing is an aesthetic *embrace* that invites sensuous opening, almost as if words need to be irresistible, to partner bodily experience at all its levels of intensity, intimacy, and multiplicity' (Sklar 2000: 73; emphasis in original). While Sklar is speaking about ethnographic writing for academic audiences, I suggest that it was true too for some Kamehameha students who wrote about their musical experience. If it is at all possible, as Katharine Young has asked, to 'shape the contours of writing to those of experience' (cited in Sklar 2000: 73), I regard Kawika's response to 'Unity' as such an example. The repetitive fervour of his 'feel like' phrases, jotted in quick succession, animated the page. 'Permeable to their somatic reverberations' (Sklar 2000: 74), Kawika's words quiver with his embodied desire to rip waves, sing, dance, drink, go crazy. And at the conclusion of the song, his words settle into relaxed, worry-free tranquillity, leaving their intersensorial trace. In terms of conveyance, I do not think I could have elicited anything with the same rhythmic energy and vitality if I had engaged Kawika in casual conversation or an open-ended invitation to tell me what the song meant to him. His handwritten description demonstrates the 'mutually generative' possibilities offered by writing about embodied experience (Sklar 2000: 74).[28]

The effectiveness of any method – research-participant writing being just one – can rarely be determined in principle but by its express purposes and its application to particular research scenarios. In the midst of a social imperative to lubricate interpersonal relations dialogically, I surmised that inviting Kamehameha students to create written records of their experience could remove contentious face-to-face encounters and barriers to expressing culturally unacceptable thought. Clearly, the issues that attend the politics of representation cut in many different directions. Written texts can serve to broaden the set of techniques that ethnomusicologists use in the field, but they must also be weighed against their ability to censor or to suppress orality, or to reinforce colonially conceived cleavages between body and mind. Despite its epistemological shortcomings, the methodology provided glimpses into many of the subtleties of lived experience that are not always readily accessible through recall and rarely revealed in regular banter; the writing exercise and my direction of it, furthermore, was sufficiently school-like (i.e. it elicited school-like behaviours) in a study of school musical culture. Despite inherent and imposed limitations, the listening–writing exercise yielded, in the context of a larger, aurally centred ethnographic study, valuable insights into young Hawaiians' gendered, intersensorial percepts and imaginings of dance songs, and the kinetic songscapes that guided their bodies.

Kati Szego joined Memorial University of Newfoundland's School of Music in 1995, establishing its programme in ethnomusicology. Her ethnographic and archival projects on Hawaiian choral music, falsetto singing and yodelling are subsumed by larger interests in intercultural processes and discourses on vocal production. Kati is currently examining the roles of women in the North American 'ukulele revival and is in the process of reconstructing a libretto written by Queen Liliʻuokalani. From 2014 to 2017, Kati was General Editor of the *Yearbook for Traditional Music*, the flagship journal of the International Council for Traditional Music (ICTM).

Notes

I am grateful to the Farden family for generously granting permission to print the original Hawaiian text of 'Puamana' and Hailama Farden's translation. I also wish to thank Mandy Blake Bowers for clearing another path, Puakea Nogelmeier for his kind assistance, Keola Donaghy for his discographic sleuthing and close listening, and Bev Diamond and Harry Berger for their insightful feedback on a very early draft of this chapter.

1. By 'Hawaiian' I intend the Indigenous people of Hawaiʻi or Kānaka Maoli. Occasionally, as in this first instance, I use the redundant term 'Indigenous Hawaiian' to underscore aboriginality and to insist that 'Hawaiian' is not analogous to 'Californian'.
2. The second Hawaiian Renaissance came to fruition in the 1970s; it was prefigured by a revitalization of Indigenous arts (hula especially) during King Kalākaua's reign (1874–91), which is now thought of as the first Hawaiian Renaissance (cf. Carr 2014).
3. This excludes popular music studies, which have been largely youth-centred.

4. Aunty is a term of endearment commonly used in Hawai'i and applied to older women generally, not necessarily kin.
5. The backslash (/) indicates line breaks in the student's written response. Italics indicate the student's post-listening explanation of her/his jot notes.
6. The first written response was clearly identified by the student as a set of visual images. The second response was not so clearly identified. It is possible that the second list of foods was a conceptual description or an attempt to capture gustatory sensation rather than being visually imagined. Alternatively, the listener's experience may occupy a space between sensual and conceptual meaning.
7. In cognitive psychology, 'redintegration' has several meanings. In reference to phenomena in the field of memory, it can refer to 'the process of recovering or recollecting memories from partial cues or reminders, as in recalling a song when a few notes are played' (APA Dictionary of Psychology 2019).
8. Kamehameha student listeners have been provided with pseudonyms.
9. As an example, 'we have conventional images of people eating pizza – most likely a wedge-shaped slice of a round pizza, with the point going in the mouth first, and probably not with a clean bite but rather with the cheese pulling away in its usual stringy fashion' (Lakoff 1987: 447).
10. One reader of this chapter suggested that the presence of CRIs might indicate listeners' disengagement with what they were hearing, since CRIs constitute 'the most available description'. I do not read conventional responses as demonstrating lack of interest or engagement with the sonic material (or the listening exercise itself). Indeed, responses that invoke CRIs (or stereotypes and clichés of any type) should be expected for musics driven by convention and can, as I later suggest, imply critique.
11. The style of hula often determines how women's hair will be arranged. Performers of *hula kahiko* (ancient hula) tend to leave their wavy locks loose, while *hula 'auana* (modern hula, including *hula ku'i*) calls for a look that suggests more purposeful coiffing, especially in competition. To read a Hawaiian woman's perspective on long hair, read Takayama (2015).
12. I have seen coconut shell bras but never seashell bras in Hawai'i. I suspect that the popularity of the Disney film *The Little Mermaid* (1989), whose title figure wore a seashell bra (with shells placed sideways on the breasts), influenced Lia's rendering. Where attire (and hairstyle) is generally matched to repertoire in Hawaiian hula circles, a seashell or coconut bra is not appropriate to 'Puamana'. In fact, female Hawaiian hula dress has been, historically, very modest, even conservative. Tourists visiting Hawai'i are far more likely to encounter coconut shell bras in displays of more southerly Polynesian dance, for example from Tahiti (see also Desmond 1997: 84).
13. See Myers (1995) and Mitchell (2006) on the pitfalls of scholarly translation of visual images.
14. Casey (1976: 42–44) identifies yet a third mode of imagining – 'imagining that', which may or may not be sensuously realized. I did not recognize any cases of imagining-that in the listening data, so I do not deal with it here.
15. Kamehameha Schools is funded by the wealthy Bishop Estate; its high-profile trustees occasionally requested the presence of the Concert Glee Club (or some subgroup thereof) to perform at events of political or economic significance. As an example, a small contingent

of students sang and danced to mark its new partnership with Goldman Sachs in 1992 (see Norris 1992).
16. Similarly, Downey's (2002) phenomenological work on *capoeira* charts the intersensory dependence inherent in *capoeiristas'* audition and movement. Apprenticed as both martial artists and *berimbau* players, when *capoeiristas* hear the *berimbau*, they describe its sound not in terms of sonic parameters (e.g. rhythm, pitch) but as expressions of the musicians' physical movements (e.g. pressing stone against string) and the material qualities of the instrument's component parts (e.g. wood, steel belt). Even when listening to *capoeira* with their bodies at rest, *capoeiristas'* fingers are compelled to move, articulating counter-rhythms on a 'phantom berimbau' (Downey 2002: 498).
17. I am grateful to Harris M. Berger for helping me arrive at this conclusion.
18. There are many variations on and exceptions to these norms. Sometimes, for example, the vamp's chordal progression is as straightforward as V-I. Gabby Pahinui's rendition of 'Hi'ilawe' that I played for students was accompanied by slack-key guitar, not the customary trio, and in 'Puamana', piano is integral to the accompaniment. For an exposition of the role of the piano in *hula ku'i* accompaniment – in particular, detailed analyses of the vamp, 'lead-in' to the vamp, and use of melodic formulae – see Aaron J. Salā's thesis (2011).
19. There were twenty-eight male respondents to 'Puamana'.
20. The 'Ja' in Jawaiian is understood differently by various groups. Some claim that it combines the words 'Jamaican' and 'Hawaiian'. The Jawaiian group Simplicity claims that they coined the word from the expression 'Jamming Hawaiian'. Alternatively, 'Ja-' has been interpreted as 'Jah', the Rastafarian word for supreme being.
21. Danny Eli. 2018. *Mana'o Company Unity* [online video]. Retrieved 15 April 2019 from https://www.youtube.com/watch?v=7hhnQOwZqcc.
22. 'Unity' was considered key to sovereigntist aspirations (see Trask 2000).
23. Guilbault's (1993) account of *zouk*, inviting written contributions from other scholars, is groundbreaking in its use of alternative – that is, writing-based – methods of ethnographic research and representation. Of course, the emergence of Internet ethnography makes research participants' writings a commonplace in ethnomusicological texts today (e.g. Miller 2007), a move anticipated by the development of collaborative ethnography in the late 1990s. As an early example, Luke Lassiter's work with Kiowa co-writers and consultants Ralph Kotay and Clyde Ellis (1998) demonstrates the power of bringing non-academic Indigenous voices to the production of ethnographic texts (see also Lassiter 2005). Perhaps the richest example of this dialogical move is Caribbean bandleader Roy Cape's co-authored monograph (2014) with Jocelyne Guilbault, documenting his sprawling, storied career.
24. Amy Ku'uleialoha Stillman was the first to integrate the contents of *mele* books and newspapers into ethnomusicological and ethnochoreological analyses, laying new groundwork for Hawaiian genre theory (Stillman 1996, 1998a).
25. Literacy is cultivated alongside an increasingly treasured orality; there is great emphasis on orality and oral traditions in learning environments such as *hālau hula* (hula schools).
26. Kamehameha was still a colonial institution when I did research there; nonetheless, most of the teachers I worked closely with were painfully cognizant of Kamehameha's history and made assiduous efforts to both decolonize and Indigenize the school.

27. The stream-of-consciousness listening–writing exercise was only one piece of my early research. In retrospect, it is clear that my training as an ethnomusicologist and systematic musicologist in the late 1980s and early 1990s prepared me to look for large cultural shapes that the data might yield. That predilection was matched to the practical reality of Kamehameha students' structured class schedules; it meant that I did not have a great deal of time to spend with individuals to probe their listening experience. In revisiting listeners' writings and sketches, I am struck anew by their richness and occasionally embarrassed by the questions I regrettably could not or did not ask.
28. The phenomenon of the inscriptive body 'translating the encounter between word and sound' has most recently been theorized as 'sound writing' (Kapchan 2017: 12).

References

APA Dictionary of Psychology. 2019. 'Redintegration', *APA Dictionary of Psychology* [online]. Retrieved 15 April 2019 from https://dictionary.apa.org/redintegration.

Behnke, E. 1997. 'Ghost Gestures: Phenomenological Investigations of Bodily Micromovements and their Intercorporeal Implications', *Human Studies* 20: 181–201.

———. 2011. 'Edmund Husserl: Phenomenology of Embodiment', in J. Fieser and B. Dowden (eds), *Internet Encyclopedia of Philosophy*. Martin: University of Tennessee at Martin. Available at: https://www.iep.utm.edu/husspemb/.

Berger, H.M. 1999. *Metal, Rock, and Jazz: Perception and the Phenomenology of Musical Experience*. Middletown: Wesleyan University Press.

———. 2009. *Stance: Ideas about Emotion, Style, and Meaning for the Study of Expressive Culture*. Middletown: Wesleyan University Press.

Carr, J.R. 2014. *Hawaiian Music in Motion: Mariners, Missionaries, and Minstrels*. Urbana: University of Illinois Press.

Casey, E.S. 1976. *Imagining: A Phenomenological Study*. Bloomington: Indiana University Press.

Connerton, P. 1989. 'Bodily Practices', in *How Societies Remember*. Cambridge: Cambridge University Press, pp. 72–104.

Corbin, A. 1998. *Village Bells: Sound and Meaning in the 19th-Century French Countryside*. Translated by M. Thom. New York: Columbia University Press.

Csordas, T. 1993. 'Somatic Modes of Attention', *Cultural Anthropology* 8(2): 135–56.

Desmond, J.C. 1997. '"The Native": Body Politics in Contemporary Hawaiian Tourist Shows', *The Drama Review* 41(4): 83–109.

Downey, G. 2002. 'Listening to Capoeira: Phenomenology, Embodiment, and the Materiality of Music', *Ethnomusicology* 46(3): 487–509.

Gee, J.P. 1992. *The Social Mind: Language, Ideology, and Social Practice*. New York: Bergin & Garvey.

Guilbault, J., with G. Averill, É. Benoit and G. Rabess. 1993. *Zouk: World Music in the West Indies*. Chicago: University of Chicago Press.

Guilbault, J., and R. Cape. 2014. *Roy Cape: A Life on the Calypso and Soca Bandstand*. Durham: Duke University Press.

Hammond, M., J. Howarth and R. Keat. 1991. *Understanding Phenomenology*. Oxford: Blackwell.

hoʻomanawanui, k. 2006. 'From Ocean to O-Shen: Reggae, Rap, and Hip Hop in Hawaiʻi', in T. Miles and S.P. Holland (eds), *Crossing Waters, Crossing Worlds: The African Diaspora in Indian Country*. Durham: Duke University Press, pp. 273–308.

Howard, A. 1974. *Ain't No Big Thing: Coping Strategies in a Hawaiian-American Community*. Honolulu: University of Hawaii Press.
Humphreys, P. 1991. 'Time, Rhythm, and Silence: A Phenomenology of the Buddhist Accelerating Roll', in Y. Tokumaru (ed.), *Tradition and Its Future in Music: Report of SIMS Osaka*. Tokyo: Mita Press, pp. 287–93.
Ingold, T. 2011. 'Four Objections to the Concept of Soundscape', in *Being Alive: Essays on Movement, Knowledge and Description*. London: Routledge, pp. 136–39.
Kaeppler, A.L. 1981. 'From the Guest Editor', *Ethnomusicology* 25(3): v.
———. 1993. *Hula Pahu: Hawaiian Drum Dances. Vol. 1. Ha'a and Hula Pahu: Sacred Movements*. Honolulu: Bishop Museum Press.
Kapchan, D. (ed.). 2017. *Theorizing Sound Writing*. Middletown: Wesleyan University Press.
Lakoff, G. 1987. *Women, Fire and Dangerous Things: What Categories Reveal about the Mind*. Chicago: University of Chicago Press.
Lassiter, L.E. 2005. *The Chicago Guide to Collaborative Ethnography*. Chicago: University of Chicago Press.
Lassiter, L.E., R. Kotay and C. Ellis. 1998. *The Power of Kiowa Song: A Collaborative Ethnography*. Tucson: University of Arizona Press.
Latzko, D.A. n.d. *Tourism and Fluctuations in the Hawaiian Economy* [online]. Retrieved 15 April 2019 from http://www.personal.psu.edu/dxl31/research/articles/comove.pdf.
Mana'o Company. 1991. *True Inspiration* [cassette]. Kaniu Records MC1002. ['Unity']
McLaughlin, D. 1992. *When Literacy Empowers: Navajo Language in Print*. Albuquerque: University of New Mexico Press.
Merleau-Ponty, M. 2012. *Phenomenology of Perception*. Translated by D.A. Landes. London: Routledge.
Miller, K. 2007. 'Jacking the Dial: Radio, Race, and Place in Grand Theft Auto', *Ethnomusicology* 51(3): 402–38.
———. 2017. *Playable Bodies: Dance Games and Intimate Media*. New York: Oxford University Press.
Mitchell, L.M. 2006. 'Child-Centred? Thinking Critically about Children's Drawings as a Visual Research Method', *Visual Anthropology Review* 22(1): 60–73.
Modell, A.H. 2003. *Imagination and the Meaningful Brain*. Cambridge: MIT Press.
Myers, F. 1995. 'Representing Culture: The Production of Discourse(s) for Aboriginal Acrylic Paintings', in G. Marcus and F. Myers (eds), *The Traffic in Culture*. Berkeley: University of California Press, pp. 55–95.
Nogelmeier, M.P. 2003. 'Mai Pa'a i ka Leo: Historical Voice in Hawaiian Primary Materials, Looking Forward and Listening Back', Ph.D. dissertation. Honolulu: University of Hawai'i at Mānoa.
Norris, F. 1992. 'A Goldman Stake for Hawaiians', *The New York Times*, 28 April [online]. Retrieved 15 April 2019 from https://www.nytimes.com/1992/04/28/business/a-goldman-stake-for-hawaiians.html.
Pahinui, G. 1978. *Pure Gabby; I Just Play the Way I Feel* [cassette]. Hula Records HSC-567.
Puamana. 1986. *Have a Smile* [cassette]. Puamana Productions 002.
Salā, A.J. 2011. 'Claiming the Colonial and Domesticating the Foreign: A Native Hawaiian Aesthetic for the Piano in Hula Ku'i Music', MA thesis, Honolulu: University of Hawai'i at Mānoa.

Seeger, C. 1977. 'Speech, Music and Speech about Music', in *Studies in Musicology, 1935–1975*. Berkeley: University of California Press, pp. 16–30.

Sklar, D. 2000. 'Reprise: On Dance Ethnography', *Dance Research Journal* 32(1): 70–77.

Stillman, A.K. 1996. 'Beyond Bibliography: Interpreting Hawaiian-Language Hymn Imprints', *Ethnomusicology* 4(3): 469–88.

———. 1998a. *Sacred Hula: The Historical Hula ʻālaʻapapa*. Honolulu: Bishop Museum Press.

———. 1998b. 'Hula Hits, Local Music, and Local Charts: Some Dynamics of Popular Hawaiian Musics', in P. Hayward (ed.), *Sound Alliances: Indigenous Peoples, Cultural Politics and Popular Music in the Pacific*. London: Cassell, pp. 89–103.

———. 2005. 'Textualizing Hawaiian Music', *American Music* 23(1): 69–94.

Szego, K. [C.S.]. 1999. 'Musical Meaning-Making in an Intercultural Environment: The Case of Kamehameha Schools', Ph.D. dissertation, Seattle: University of Washington.

———. 2003. 'Singing Hawaiian and the Aesthetics of (In)comprehensibility', in H.M. Berger and M.T. Carroll (eds), *Global Pop, Local Language*. Jackson: University of Mississippi Press, pp. 291–328.

———. 2012. 'Review of Maiki Aiu Lake and Nā Kamalei: The Men of Hula', *Journal of the Society for American Music* 6(1): 139–41.

———. 2018. 'Singing Policemen, Dancing Firemen: Alliance-Building and Interethnic Remasculinization in Post-WWII Hawaiʻi', in F. Lau and C.R. Yano (eds), *Making Waves: Traveling Musics in Hawaiʻi, Asia and the Pacific*. Honolulu: University of Hawaiʻi Press, pp. 119–48.

Takayama, K.A. 2015. 'Thick as Blood', *Indian Country Today*, 10 March [online]. Retrieved 15 April 2019 from https://newsmaven.io/indiancountrytoday/archive/native-hawaiian-hair-is-thick-as-blood-says-essay-winner-HC_GD8sEKUKFOBCyoUD1sQ/.

Trask, H.K. 2000. 'Native Social Capital: The Case of Hawaiian Sovereignty and Ka Lahui Hawaii', *Policy Sciences* 33: 375–85.

Weintraub, A. 1993. 'Jawaiian and Local Cultural Identity in Hawaiʻi', *Perfect Beat: The Journal of Research into Contemporary Music and Popular Culture* 1(2): 78–89.

Young, K.G. 2018. 'Scrape, Brush, Flick: The Phenomenology of Sound', *Phenomenology in Ethnomusicology Conference, Research Centre for the Study of Music, Media and Place (MMaP), Memorial University of Newfoundland*. Retrieved 15 April 2019 from https://www.youtube.com/watch?v=isLv26LrpCo.

Chapter 2

Using Motion Capture to Access Culturally Embedded and Embodied Movement Knowledge
A Case Study in Tango Argentino

Kendra Stepputat

A continuous problem for working analytically with movement structures is the transfer of movement into any other medium. Today, the most commonly used medium that is closest to actual, living movement is film. When Adrienne Kaeppler wrote her text on 'Method and Theory in Analyzing Dance Structure' in 1972, film was still a rather expensive and impractical tool. Kaeppler's favourite way to work with 'informants' – the choice of words in those times – was to physically show them her version of a dance to get verbal feedback. She sometimes deliberately danced a wrong version to get feedback on what actually mattered or what was considered 'correct' within the boundaries of the culturally accepted (Kaeppler 1972: 175). Kaeppler (1972: 175) made the statement that 'Instant videotape, however, may be one solution to the dance ethnologists' dilemma.' Such a possibility, she hoped, would ease showing movements to bearers of a culture to get verbal feedback on it, surpassing the (deliberate or unintentionally) faulty reproduction by the researcher. Today, almost fifty years later, we have the tools to instantly film and watch; every simple smartphone has a video application that allows this without any additional costs or fuss. Yet the problem of having to understand the movement practice thoroughly – to be able to work academically with it – remains the same. Accordingly, if such instant filming were possible, Kaeppler pondered in 1972, it might still be better to physically show the movements than use film to reproduce it: 'Even with aids of this kind I submit that the ethnologist should be willing to do the "playback" for native identification and evaluation himself by performing' (Kaeppler

1972: 175). Since the 1970s, the importance of embodying a movement practice has not wavered; instead, it has become a valued research practice. Over the years, it has become understood that a researcher should be able to carry out the movement system they work with academically. The advantages of this 'fieldwork technique' are manifold.[1] They include: 1) the immersion into the dance and its culturally significant aspects, 2) the gaining of embodied insights, training the researcher's body in the movement system to be explored 3) having exchanges with fellow dancers, possibly teachers and prominent representatives of the dance culture, and all of this necessarily over a significant length of time.[2] Additionally, the researcher needs to be aware that not only the mind but also the body is 'cultured' (Csordas 2002: 58). The subjectivity not only of a researcher's intellectual interpretation but, equally important, the physical, embodied insights has become increasingly acknowledged. Sklar (2000: 71)[3] wrote that 'while it has been traditional practice to erase the researcher's body from the ethnographic text, "subjective" bodily engagement is tacit in the process of trying to make sense of another's somatic knowledge'. We can try to become fluent in many movement traditions to turn our body into a flexible 'research tool' but still need to be aware that we are continuously formed and shaped by everything we learn and do, and that the 'embodied point of departure' shapes our perception and subsequently the physical interpretation of a movement tradition significantly.[4]

Hence almost fifty years after Kaeppler's writing, both learning to perform or carry out a movement and capturing a movement for further analysis and communication about it with experts is still of great importance for dance researchers. Because even if we can embody a dance practice, we still need to transfer the movement system into another medium; words, symbols or graphics – digital or on paper – in order to communicate about it with others in academic and non-academic contexts. The manifold necessities, problems and advantages of capturing dance have been nicely summed up by Van Zile (1999).[5] Probably the most relevant issue concerning dance notation is that every transfer – or translation, as Van Zile (1999: 86) phrases it – from one medium (the movement system itself) to another (a representation of it) necessarily leads to a loss of information. What is added instead is the subjective perspective of the person making the transfer. This includes the decision of which medium to use, what to focus on, which information to capture and thereby which to neglect. Depending on the research question or particular interest, we make these decisions with the aim of having the most adequate form of transcription and representation of the movement system available for further analysis and/or communication. In addition to that, as soon as a transcription is put into form, and seen by another person, a second layer of interpretation is added. As a transcription does not speak for itself, we still need words – or movement – to explain and interpret the dance representation.

An option to reduce the loss of data in capturing and in translation could be to utilize the best capturing technology available. Having a precise record of movement as it is carried out would allow one to revisit the material at a later stage, to access recordings by others, and to look at valuable material with as little loss of information as currently possible. In general, this medium today is considered to be digital film. Increasing frame rates, data storage availability and affordable recording devices enable researchers to have high quality material at relatively low cost. A film of a dance event is a good representation and is quite close to the actual event, yet film always transfers a three-dimensional event into two dimensions. 3D cameras with two lenses capture a third dimension by adding depth to the picture but are still limited to one perspective. A way around this is the positioning of more than one camera, which enables us to see a movement from several directions. And yet, such an approach still lacks the depth of the third dimension. Fortunately, several devices have been developed that are able to capture in true 3D.

In this chapter, I present how motion capture can help to understand differences in style of a particular movement repertoire. I focus on the analysis of one basic tango argentino movement, the *ocho atrás*, to demonstrate how combining qualitative research with quantitative elements like data acquisition and statistical analysis can lead to a more thorough understanding of the movement itself.

Adding the Third Dimension

What is generally called motion capture (mocap) is actually a generic term that encompasses several technologies[6] for tracking and recording movement in 3D. These include, for instance, inertial systems that are based on measurements by accelerometers and gyroscopes, or optical systems that are based on visual capturing (Nymoen 2013: 18–19). All such motion capture systems today generally record movement data in 3D over time, by first sensing, then processing and finally storing data about the movement (Nymoen 2013: 13).[7] The system I focus on here is a marker-based optical motion capture system. The object of interest, in this case the dancers, are equipped with passive markers that reflect infrared light. The infrared light is emitted by a set of cameras that also record the reflections on the markers. For capturing dance movements, the cameras have to be fixed firmly on racks that are ideally detached from the floor, because vibrations on the floor translate to vibrations of the very sensitive cameras. The cameras – the more, the better – have to cover the same space but from different angles; most set-ups have the cameras overhead looking down on the recorded space. The cameras are connected to a central computer that records and processes all data. The downside of optical motion capture systems is that they are costly, time consuming to set up and hence depend on a neutral space, which can give the recording session the character of a 'laboratory test'. By current standards, data

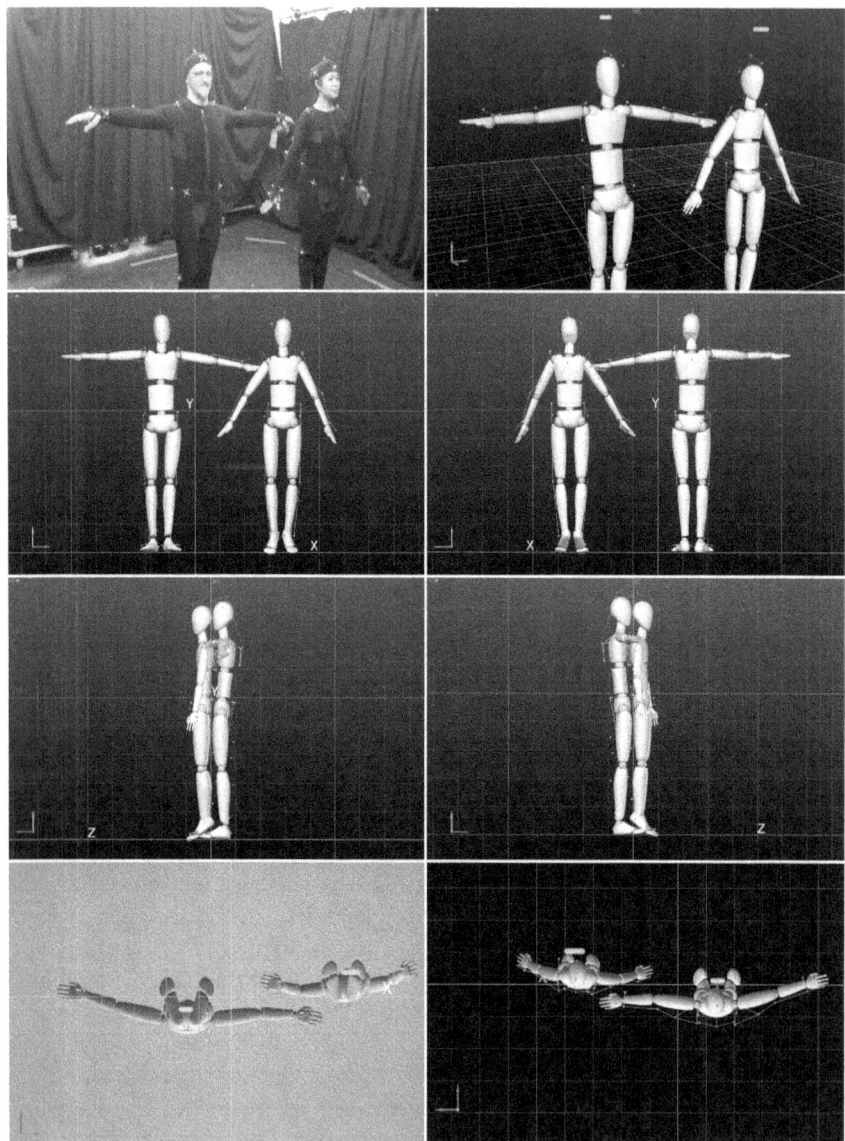

Figure 2.1. Real image and mocap representation of Homer Ladas and Cristina Ladas from five different perspectives. Photograph by Kendra Stepputat 2017, graphic by Christopher Dick 2019.

recorded with marker-based optical mocap is the most precise option to track movement in space and time.

Mocap technology adds the third dimension to a recording. It offers the possibility to change perspective at any time while watching the recording. In 1999, Van Zile (1999: 85) wrote that 'one of the most obvious values of movement notation is its ability to freeze an activity that occurs in time. ... Any analysis requires the ability to look at something repeatedly, often from different perspectives'. With mocap we can surpass the transfer of data into notation and still look at it at a later point, and – literally as well as figuratively – from different perspectives. We can access even more than can be seen by one researcher; it is possible to review the same recorded part again from any other angle and level of detail. It is even possible to watch from angles that are not accessible in reality; for instance, from below the surface or from within the body.

Mocap is a very useful medium for recording and later watching or showing a movement system. In addition, and most importantly so, mocap generates data about the movement. Information about every recorded marker can be analysed in relation to space, time and other markers. We are able to not only describe but measure speed, acceleration, amplitude, elevation and so forth. Currently, it takes a person skilled in relevant programming languages (e.g. Matlab, Python, R) and system-specific software by manufacturers like Optitrack or Vicon to work with the recorded data. Hopefully, over time, such tools will become more customer friendly, as has happened with other computational and technical possibilities. But even if a front-end software was developed, it would still be necessary to cooperate closely with a person – for instance, a data analyst or data scientist – trained in statistics, data visualization, manipulation and so forth to gain results that surpass basic correlations.

It could be argued, that 3D trajectory data is the most objective tool, compared to any other form of capturing a movement system. However, the large amount of data itself is meaningless on a semantic level; it conveys meaning only in the domain of abstract mathematical phenomena observable in the data set. The interpretation still relies on experts in the field of movement. We need to choose which elements and numbers to work with, which relations to analyse and how to visualize the results.[8] As in any other form of notation, the researcher chooses and selects which data to look at and analyse.

Case Study: Tango Argentino Styles

In order to show how mocap can be incorporated into an ethnochoreological research process, I present a case study from a recent research project in which I explored the 'Tango-danceability of music in European perspective'.[9] The movement system studied in this project is translocal tango argentino, a cosmopolitan dance and music form that originated in Buenos Aires (Argentina) and Montevideo (Uruguay) at the turn of the nineteenth to twentieth century. Since the

1910s, tango argentino as coupled social dance has spread to other countries and continents, and through a constant back and forth of people and trends between Argentina and – mainly – Europe, it has developed into the translocal, socially practised dance form known today.[10] In tango argentino, a couple improvises jointly, interpreting or inspired by the music. The two general roles in the couple are the 'lead' and the 'follow', though advanced dancers see their joint dance more as a dialogue than a unidirectional lead–follow relation.

One of the research questions of the 'tango-danceability' project is concerned with the development of different tango argentino styles and their dissemination in the current European tango argentino community. The term 'style' here refers to a particular way to carry out the genre. Kaeppler (2001) examines in more detail what style stands for, how it can be determined and how individuality in carrying out a movement (an allokine) turns into a more general way of practising a genre – that is, a style. Kaeppler's examinations have proven to be very helpful for my approach and overlap to a large extent with my experiences in the tango argentino community. Kaeppler calls the dance genre the 'structure', built from distinct structural elements that are 'the building blocks – the essential elements that determine how a specific dance is constructed and how dances differ according to genre'. She continues that 'style is the *way* of performing – that is, realising or embodying the structure' (Kaeppler 2001: 52). Kaeppler puts emphasis on the fact that beholders of the embodied knowledge are foremost those who determine style and what is considered to be 'stylistic': 'Which elements are stylistic must be recognised by the performers themselves' and 'Depending on the knowledge of the beholders, they may (or may not) recognise the style – the way of performing – in which the structure of the dance is embodied' (Kaeppler 2001: 57). This is an important fact that I became aware of when I started to look into tango styles from the perspective of an experienced tango dancer. Where I – after fifteen years of dancing and watching a countless number of expert and lay dancers – see significant differences in tango dance style, people who are not trained and embedded in tango argentino will be able to differentiate the genre (or 'structure' in Kaeppler's terms) as tango argentino but maybe not recognize stylistic details within the genre. This is of course a generalization: on what level a person is able to differentiate movement always also depends on the person's abilities to recognize and analyse movement visually. But the fact remains that 'beholders' of a movement structure (in theory and/or practice) will more likely be able to determine different styles and with less effort.

The question is why determining style is of such importance to practitioners of a dance genre, as it definitely is in tango argentino. Kaeppler (2001: 57) brings forth the issue of 'distancing' and 'differentiating': 'I suggest that canon and style can both be distancing concepts, used to contrast, separate, or differentiate performances from one another and the performers of one group from the "other"'. Such a distancing can also be seen in the translocal tango argentino scene. A group brought together by aesthetic, athletic, organizational, philosophical or any other preference in dance style seems to need a label to put on their own practice, to be able to communicate about it and, on a simple organizational level, find each other. At the same time, such a label, in this case a term for a tango dance style, gives the option to exclude those who do not want to practice this tango style and everything that comes along with it, like rules on and off the dance floor. But above the inclusion, exclusion and communicative elements, putting a style label on a way to dance tango can also be for economic reasons, especially if professional dance teachers are a driving force. Apprill writes about the codification of dance in terms of movement repertoire since the early nineteenth century and relates this to tango argentino practice in the 1990s. Although Apprill focuses on the movement repertoire itself, the practice is of course closely related to the style label this codified dance vocabulary is given: 'The codification has thus always been regulated by this desire to maintain the economic profitability of the profession of dance teacher. . . . Today, the same principle of economic rentability influences the codification of the tango through the accreditation of the salon style as a way of dancing exclusively in the ball' (Apprill 1999: 85).[11] Liska focuses on the competitive issue between rivalling teachers and venues creating the need to define clearly separate styles. She writes that in the 1990s, during the revitalization phase of tango in Buenos Aires, at least three stylistic tango variants were labelled, which were *milonguero*, *salón* and new tango (*tango nuevo*). She states that due to the competition between the practitioners and milonga venues 'disputes arose regarding the antiquity, authenticity, popularity and validity of the styles' (Liska 2017: 7).

The need to label tango styles obviously exists, with differing and changing agendas, and is an important force in the organization and development of the translocal tango argentino. Looking more closely into existing tango styles is therefore a highly relevant research topic for understanding the phenomenon of tango argentino as a whole. Above that, answers from such research can be of potentially high relevance for practitioners themselves.

Apart from reasons for defining separate styles, it is interesting to look into what the definition of tango styles is based on. Several authors, all experts from within the tango argentino domain, have suggested different approaches. Benzecry Sabá, for instance, states that styles can be differentiated by the way a dancer embraces, by belonging to a certain neighbourhood, in accordance with a historical tango period, or 'in imitation of a teacher's way of dancing, either in his honour or because it coincides with our own dance aesthetics' (Benzecry Sabá 2010: 69). Apprill adds yet another possibility of distinguishing styles. He states that the dance style can differ in accordance with the music the tango is danced to, yet he adds that 'this differentiation in interpretation can truly be exercised only by experienced dancers',[12] and is therefore not very practical (Apprill 1999: 85–86). Carozzi[13] focuses on different approaches to determine style – in particular by tango dancers in Buenos Aires up to the 1980s – and thereby showing not only how ambiguous the approach was but also how ambiguous the attempts at a definition were, and still are:

> Thus, through a common verbal practice among *milongueros*, he [El Chino Perico, a renowned tango dancer] creates a complete map of tango in the city from a trajectory that traveled a few neighborhoods. Other *milongueros* resorted to a taxonomy that distinguished between the tango *salón*, the *orillero*, the *canyengue*, the *fantasía* and *for export*. Even though many adhered to the same denominations, there was little agreement among them about what were the distinctive characteristics of each of these ways of dancing. Certain versions even included two terms as alternative denominations of the same style. (Carozzi 2015: 135–36)[14]

We see that there were and are many attempts to categorize tango styles based on a variety of aspects. Of course, all of those styles have at the core a difference in aesthetics, some variants in movement repertoire or body dynamics. But even if an attempt at categorization is solely based on movement repertoire, there is no general agreement in the tango community about its particular features. One reason for this is that tango styles continue to change constantly, as Bolasell states. He claims that there are actually no distinct and different styles but rather 'tendencies'. Because tango evolves constantly, styles that have just separated can be combined again for (and by) the next generations of dancers (Bolasell 2011: 163). Nevertheless, I will briefly sum up the more common terms that have shown persistence over the last decades. Apprill designates three main styles, which are *milonguero*, *salón* and *fantasía* (Apprill 1999: 84–85). There is a clear distinction between *fantasía* (also called *escenario* and *for export*) and the other two. *Fantasía* is a choreographed genre designed for staged performances, whereas *milonguero* and *salón* belong to tango styles that are danced socially at events called *milongas*. Other frequent terms for socially danced tango styles, as for instance described by Benzecry Sabá, are *canyengue*, *liso* and *orillero* (Benzecry Sabá 2010: 71–77). These all have historical connotations dating back to the early twentieth century when tango was still in its early developmental stage.[15] A further important term is *tango nuevo* or *neotango*. This way of dancing developed in the 1990s and revolutionized body dynamics in terms of lead/follow concepts and use of space (Carozzi 2013: 155–56).

I do not want to embark on a detailed discussion of all possible terms for tango argentino styles, their historic developments, manifold definitions and connection to economic and group dynamic factors. Such an endeavour must be left to future publications. What is important for this text is the fact that there are no agreed upon definitions of styles, yet certain terms for styles are regularly and commonly used. For the project, we[16] focused on three common dance styles that can be differentiated following the concept mentioned by Benzecry Sabá (2010: 69) and elaborated on by Krüger, which is the embrace. Krüger differentiates between tango in close embrace (*cerrado*, which she sees as representative of *milonguero* style), *abierto* (open embrace, which she relates to *neotango*), and *cerrado, pero flexible* (closed but flexible), a contemporary combination of the two that allows for more flexibility in movement and expression (Krüger 2012: 188–95). Accordingly, the experts we worked with are known for their dancing in mostly open embrace, a flexible semi-open embrace, and close embrace. Yet of course it should be assumed that not only the embrace differs but that there are also differences in the movements, in particular in the legs. On the level of description, several authors have narrowed down such characteristics. For the time being, I can state from my own experience and insights that close embrace dancing includes smaller and more intimate movements – the feet stay close to the floor, and the dancers have physical contact from the chest down to the hips. The current often-used term for this is tango *milonguero*.[17] In open embrace, dancers have much more freedom in their individual movements, and the only contact between them is with their arms. Leg movements are much more space consuming with a lot of turns, leg entanglements and high kicks. This tango style can be called *tango nuevo* or *neotango*. The flexible embrace, shifting between close, open and semi-open, generally incorporates elements from open and close embrace, keeping complex leg figures yet staying closer to the partner. This style is increasingly often called *tango (de) salón*.

Because it is next to impossible to look at all features of a dance style and stay within the framework of a book chapter, we chose to narrow the movement repertoire we looked at for this chapter down to one particular element[18] in tango argentino, which is the *ocho atrás*.

The *Ocho Atrás* as Style Determinant: Three Different Perspectives

Kaeppler examined individual dancers' movements as representative of different schools in a stylistic analysis of the Hawaiian dance *hula pahu* 'Kaulilula' (2001: 55). The approach in my research project was similar to this. We worked with three representative expert dance couples. The three couples were chosen because of their influential positions in the European tango argentino dance community. All of them are accomplished teachers in tango argentino social dancing with very distinct styles, although naming those styles is not equivocal. The first couple was Yanina Quiñones and Neri Píliu, who term their tango 'tango salón'. The second couple was Homer Ladas and Cristina Ladas, who came up with the term 'organic tango' for their way of dancing, though they are hesitant to call it their 'style'.[19] Maja Petrović and Marko Miljević, the third couple, call their dancing cautiously 'tango milonguero'.[20] All of them were asked to perform a number of dance and tapping tasks to several musical stimuli (Stepputat, Kienreich and Dick 2019).[21] One of the tasks was a common tango dance movement called *ocho atrás* (backward eight). The term *ocho* refers to the floor pattern drawn by the dancer's feet, which resembles the figure eight. A rough description of the dance movement is as follows: the dancer starts with a dissociation in the spine. The upper body (hip upward) faces the dance partner; the lower body (hip downward) is rotated to the outside of the dance couple, up to ninety degrees. From this position the dancer does a step backwards with the outside leg, which because of the dissociation is in parallel to the dance partner. Following is a complete shift of weight onto the extended back foot, and the closing of the front leg, which stays free of any weight after closing. By releasing the dissociation until the body is straight, facing the partner, and without pause instantly going into a counter-dissociation, the dancer turns the lower body about 180 degrees on the standing leg, rotating backwards towards the free leg while keeping the upper body as stable as possible and facing the dance partner (see Figure 2.2).

The basic aim of using mocap technology to capture *ocho atrás* was to determine what constitutes *ocho atrás* technique in general. Moreover, the recordings were used to find out details about individual movement executions. In other words, we wanted to find out what exactly defines individual style, and if detected features can be used to determine the styles *milonguero*, *salón* or organic tango. Instead of forming hypotheses, the more useful method seemed to be an open, exploratory approach in which the recorded data sets were examined for significant and distinct features and then analysed and interpreted.

The use of mocap in ethnochoreological research is still quite unusual. There is no established methodology for using mocap, hence any research done at this stage is at the same time – and maybe even foremost – an exploration of methods. In order to test the possibilities and features mocap offers, develop useful methods, and find ways to usefully include them into 'traditional' movement structure analysis, I compared already established approaches in movement analysis with mocap. Probably the most complex and most established system for notating movement is Labanotation.[22] A person educated in Laban's system of movement notation has advanced skills in looking at movement in close detail and the abil-

Figure 2.2. Ocho atrás phases: a) starting position with closed feet, b) backstep, c) shifting weight to the back foot, d) closing front leg, e) turning, f) final position (same as image a) on other side). Dancer Federica Rubattu, photographs by Amalia Asaro 2020, graphic by Kendra Stepputat 2020.

ity to dissect small movements and their relevance, depending on the research question or analytical interest. A dance notator being educated in Labanotation is of course influenced by the way the body in space and time is conceptualized in this notation system, which shapes their perception of the movement (see Hutchinson Guest 1998: 180). This shaped perception is different from that of a data analyst, who looks at a body and its movement mostly with a biomechanical understanding, focusing on measurable properties based on body mechanics (e.g. Knudson 2007; Koutedakis, Owolabi and Apostolos 2008; Wilson and Kwon 2008). Then again, both of these approaches and shaped perspectives on movement will probably differ from that of a movement system practitioner ('beholder'), which in this case would be a tango dancer.[23] The beholder describing dance movements verbally makes use of the existing vocabulary shared in the dance community, focusing on those elements in the dance that are considered to be of importance or relevance; for example, in teaching and learning.

In the following, I will present the three perspectives of 'tango dancer', 'data analysis' and 'Labanotation' separately, based on insights by three dance researchers working together in this project.[24] The separation here is of course artificial. By talking about the data and sharing our insights, we of course already influenced each other's thinking, and by trying out movements together we also modified our different embodied experiences. A joint learning process was initiated that only for the sake of argument is put into different sections here.

The Tango Dancer Perspective

The material I used for the following embodied perspective description is the cleansed 3D motion capture data.[25] The data was visualized with the tool 'mokka', which allows you to look at all captured markers separately and simultaneously, from all possible perspectives, and at different speeds. I mostly looked at all markers in combination, in half speed of the original tempo, and from back, front and top perspective.

As a tango dancer for fifteen years, if I look at the visualization of the recorded movements, I do see obvious differences in the six dancers' execution of the movement. First, I notice that all six are highly skilled dancers, although the three dancers being used to the follower role are more skilled in this particular movement. This comes as no surprise, because *ocho atrás* is carried out mostly while dancing as follower. Trying to verbalize why the followers' *ochos* look better than the leaders' brings me to vocabulary like: the movements are smoother, more regular, more elegant. Being trained in executing *ochos atrás* myself, I see that they all use the same technique in generating the initial dissociation. They actively rotate their hips first, both by giving an initial impulse in the aspired turning direction of the upper body (chest) and rotating on their standing leg. Right after the initial impulse initiated by the chest, the shoulder line is readjusted to be stable to the front, while the hips and standing foot continue to turn until the maximum dissociation is reached. In tango terminology, this preparatory movement could be called 'generating turning energy', or 'going into a dissociation', or, as Homer (2019, pers. comm., 4 August) states, 'creating the contralateral movement from the floor through the torso'. Until this phase of the *ocho*, there are no clearly distinguishable style differences between the six dancers. All six dancers turn with slightly bent knees and keep at a more or less stable absolute height throughout the whole movement. This horizontal stability is something that all tango teachers put emphasis on as being 'good *ocho* technique'. A significant difference between the couples, though, is the absolute height. In the turn, Yanina and Neri bend their knees more than the other two couples. In order to straighten their free legs (Yanina in particular, not so much Neri), their steps must be bigger than those of the other two couples because taking a step with a bent knee elongates the step and widens the covered floor space. Interestingly, in terms of body height, the other two couples are taller than Yanina and Neri. Bending their standing legs to reach further and carry out bigger steps is an obvious feature of Yanina and Neri's way to dance tango. This is even more visible in their regular steps but leaves its marks on their *ocho* technique.

Hip movement is something that is rarely addressed in tango lessons. This in itself is interesting because of course hips are a major part of the moving system but obviously not considered of importance for the *ocho*. Something students often hear in their first tango lessons is 'keep the hips in line' or 'keep the hips stable', even 'hip movement is for salsa, not so much for tango'. The ideal seems to be no lateral pelvic tilting – that is, to keep the left and right hip horizontally stable on one line. However, we do see that Maja, differing from all other dancers, does a lateral pelvic tilt, which is an important part of her personal walking style. She comments on her technique: 'the hip in tango does exactly the same thing as in "normal" life or everyday walking: it absorbs the weight of the body when we step on the foot. Like this, the weight transition is smooth and effortless (less muscle work) and we keep the knees straight' (Maja Petrović 2019, pers. comm., 31 July). It is particularly visible after she shifts weight; the hip of the free, still extended front leg goes down while she stretches it. The hip moves up again to the same level as the other hip after closing for the rotation and the backstep. Homer, Marko, Neri and Cristina all have yet another way of tilting: the anterior pelvic tilt, or as colloquially stated, 'sticking out their buttocks'. All do this anterior tilting when they initiate the backstep, getting back into straight position when shifting weight to the back foot. Yanina's hips are the most horizontally (lateral and anterior) stable of all dancers, which might explain the particular smoothness we see in her *ochos*. One more thing that catches the eye when looking in detail at the hip movement: all leaders do a lateral hip movement while turning; they lift the hip of the free leg. Laterally tilting the hip while turning disturbs the central vertical axis; counter- movements in another part of the body are needed, for instance, by slightly leaning out sideways on the standing leg. This movement might be a reason why their *ochos* do not look quite as stable and smooth as those of the followers.

In summary, having the 3D data available helps immensely in actually seeing differences in the movement styles. 3D data offers the possibility to focus on the abstract bone structure, visualized as dots, as an exact representation of the dancers' bodies. In addition, being able to change perspective, even into a 'naturally impossible' one, enriches possible insights. From my tango dancer perspective, and from conversations with the dancers, I was able to see some significant factors that determine individual style, and in one instance – differences between leader and follower – also the level of training of a particular movement.

The Data Analysis Perspective

The basis for this analysis is the same data set as that used for the visual analysis described before.[26] The difference is that for this part the data itself instead of the visualization was used – that is, the exact information of every marker at any given point in space and time. Possibilities for the analysis of the captured data are almost unlimited. To narrow down options, and be able to ask useful questions, we incorporated the tango dancer's perspective and knowledge. Nevertheless, the biomechanical approach is still contained in the choice of analysed elements. We chose to focus on two elements of the *ocho atrás* that are very hard to see even in the motion capture visuals. The first one is the angle between shoulders and hips, what I call the dissociation angle. In order to determine the angle between shoulder and hip line, vectors had to be calculated. Left and right side were looked at separately. We used calculated joints as reference points, which are computed as the centroid between several markers as defined by Toiviainen and Burger in the *MoCap Toolbox Manual* (2015). For the shoulder joint, we used the 'shoulder top' and 'shoulder back' marker. The centre of the body between the shoulders is called 'neck', calculated based on 'left shoulder top' and 'right shoulder top'. The alignment of the right and left shoulder respectively is indicated by the vector from the neck out towards the shoulder joint (see Figure 2.3, right side). On the level of the hips, the same approach is based on the calculated joint 'root' (centre of the body, based on left and right 'waist front' and 'waist back') as well as 'hip', based on 'waist front' and 'waist back'. By calculating the angle between the two vectors on each side, the relative dissociation within the body between shoulder line and hip line can be determined.[27]

In Figure 2.4., the progress over time (shown in frames) of the change in angle on the left side of the body (lower grey line) and right side of the body (upper grey line) are shown. The lines go in parallel with an approximate forty degree angle difference. This difference derives from the fact that on hip level all three calculated markers are on one horizontal line, whereas the shoulders are further back than the 'neck' point, which adds about twenty degrees (that is, minus twenty degrees on the left side) to the measured angle (see Figure 2.3., left side).

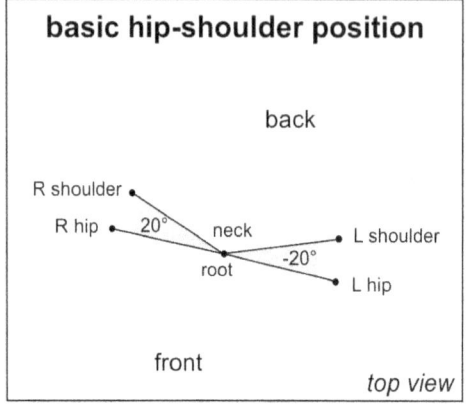
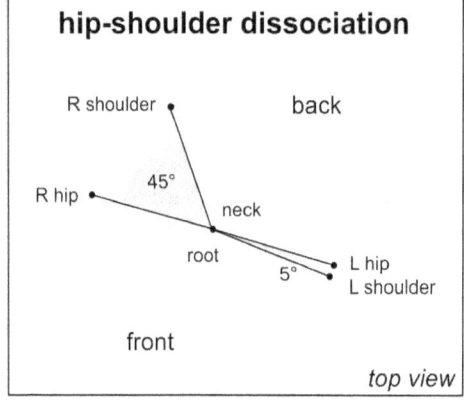
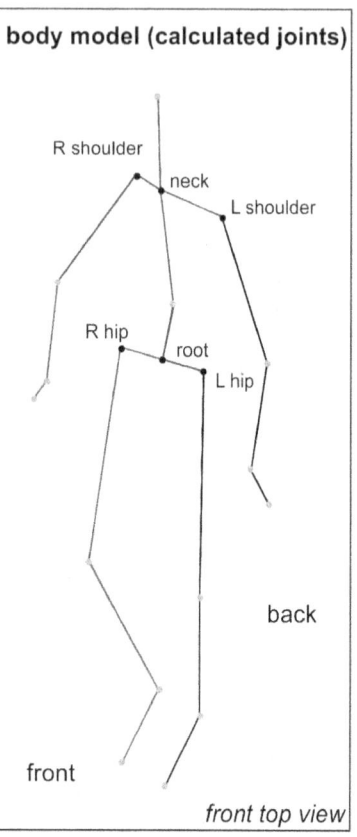

Figure 2.3. Dissociation angle visualization. Graphic by Kendra Stepputat, 2019.

The second set of marker information we analysed is the opening and closing of the feet. We determined this through the absolute distance of the ankle joint (calculated on the markers 'ankle out' and 'ankle in') between the left and right foot. In Figure 2.4., you see the ankle distance shown in the black line in exact reference over time with the dissociation angles. For comparison, the ankle distance and dissociation angle data of all six dancers are shown here. The starting point in the graphic – defined as the beginning of an *ocho atrás* – is the moment when the dancer starts to stretch the free leg to the back and is already in a significantly dissociated position. We see that all six dancers have a very stable length in their steps and regularly close and open over time.

Looking at the relation between ankle distance and dissociation angle, we see, for instance, that all dancers have the maximum ankle distance before they reach the maximum dissociation angle, or before they release the dissociation phase. This means that all of them continue to actively dissociate after they have

Using Motion Capture ■ 55

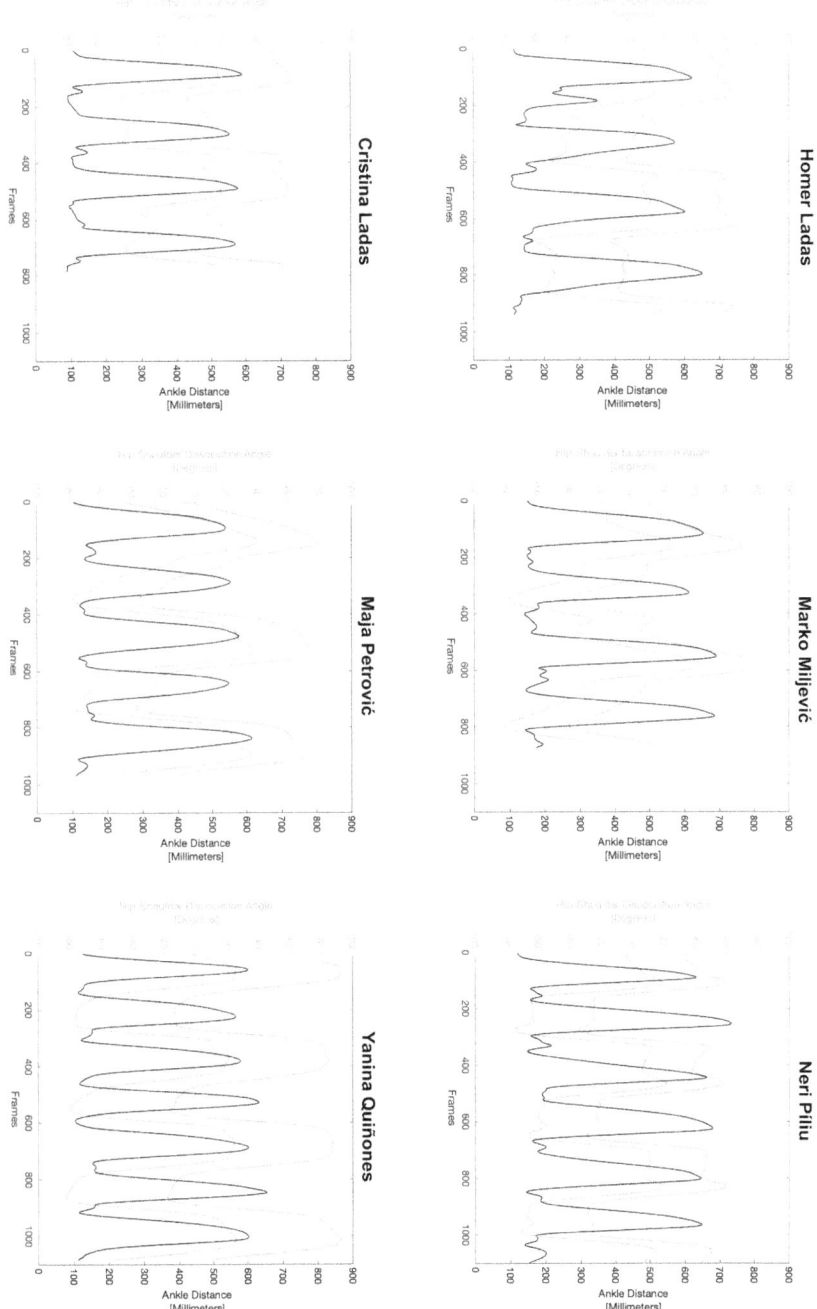

Figure 2.4. Ocho atrás *3D data visualization. Graphic by Kendra Stepputat and Kurt Schatz.*

finished the backstep. This moment when dissociation into one direction is released to start the counter-dissociation is used by all as the initial movement to start the turning. Additionally, if the beginning of the turn is defined as the moment at which the maximum dissociation is released to go into counter-dissociation, it is interesting to look at the state of the ankle distance at exactly this point: all six dancers have not yet reached the minimum ankle distance when they start the counter-dissociation, which means that they all initiate the turning while still closing the feet. Based on this data, it is safe to say that the timing of rotating and counter-rotating in relation to the closing is essential for proper *ocho atrás* technique as presented by all of the recorded tango dancers; it is an essential technique element of the *ocho atrás* motif. Looking closer at the chosen data, however, we do see some individual or 'style' differences. For instance, five of the dancers have several peaks in their dissociation graphs, a phenomenon I would like to call 'dissociation variations'. For instance, Homer (frame -450), Cristina (frame -380) and Marko (frame -420) shortly release their dissociation into a counter-movement and dissociate further in the middle of the turning movement (when the ankles are closest). Neri also releases the dissociation temporarily (frame -320) still in the turn and dissociates further when shifting weight. Homer has a second dissociation variation when shifting weight (Homer frame -540). Maja has a very slight dissociation variation at the time of shifting weight but is not going into a counter-movement, only keeping the dissociation stable before further dissociating (frame -450). Yanina, however, has next to no dissociation variations; her dissociation angle graph has a very regular shape. We clearly see individual variations in the execution of the *ocho atrás* based on the *regularity* of the dissociation. Generally, the followers, who in regular tango dancing are much more used to carrying out *ocho atrás*, are much better trained in controlling the dissociation and keep it stable into the counter-dissociation. Here we have one possible answer to the question of why *ocho atrás* by well-trained tango dancers looks 'smoother' than those by less skilled or trained dancers. With all caution, it could be said that the more regular the dissociation angle graphic, the smoother the visual impact of the *ocho* movement.[28]

To sum up, with the mocap data chosen for analysis here, we can clearly show important features of what is considered by tango dancers to be 'good *ocho* technique': stability in the length of steps, regularity in carrying out the steps over time, a stable and regular dissociation and counter-dissociation on both sides, and the turning with closed feet. We also see significant differences in individual execution, which can be related to training, or a focus on the visual impression of smoothness in the movement, which is obviously related to the regular transition from dissociation to counter-dissociation. What we do not see in this sample and this set of data is a difference in tango style. For this, we would have needed significant similarities between the two dancers in a couple, or even stronger differences between the three followers.

The Labanotation Perspective

As in the tango dancer approach, the basis for Laban's system of movement notation perspective was the mocap recorded material, made visible in mokka. The notation process was as follows: first, all possible variants by one dancer were notated separately to understand the general movement. Looking at the notated variants, it then became possible to see which movements were carried out regularly and which could be considered exceptions from an ideal as seemingly conceptualized by the dancer. As a next step, those separate variants, with a focus on those movements that seem to be the norm across all variants, were combined into one 'standard' *ocho atrás*, representative of every dancer recorded. It is clear that depending on the research question, an exact notation of all variants over time might be more enlightening. However, for this publication, we decided to focus on the 'ideal' version of each individual's *ocho atrás*.[29] In addition, the aim here was an approach best described as 'as detailed as necessary, as simple as possible'. In the six notations below, one bar of 4/4 is notated for each dancer, with a preparatory part that each dancer carries out before starting the first *ocho*. In each bar, the dancers carry out two *ochos atrás*, first to one side, then to the other. The following descriptions are based on the notation in Figure 2.5.

The notations show that although all of them are doing the same movement, every individual has a slightly different way of carrying it out. The differences start with the length of the backsteps; where Homer, Maja and Marko carry out a 'normal' step, Cristina and Neri do a 'long' step, and Yanina a 'very long' step. The steps by Neri and Yanina are prolonged by a sliding movement on the floor with the pad or tip of the toe.[30] Time progression in the notation is marked by the 4 quarters of the bar. We see that the dancers show different time relations between turn and step. Homer does a long step and a quick turn, which is possibly connected to his putting down the free foot right after the turn, to stop the turning movement. Cristina, his dance partner, shows the same pattern. Maja and Marko start with a quick step and leave much more time for the turn. Yanina and Neri use about equally much time for the turn and the step. It must of course be added that the step and turn are not clearly separated but often overlap. The 'turning time' has here been captured as the time from the moment the standing leg starts to rotate on the floor until it stops. With these timing differences, we do see obvious differences between the couples. Whether these differences are individual or can be considered a 'style' must be decided by a tango dancer with more knowledge of the couples and their dancing.

A closer look at the overlapping of the turn and the twisting of the body, what is called 'dissociation' in tango, reveals differences again. The release of the dissociation is marked here with the sign for 'cancellation of rotation' after the notating of a twist in the augmented chest, which states the moment when the front of the chest and the pelvic coincide. Marko is the only dancer who has a moment of stability between the twist and untwist. He starts to twist at about the

58 ■ Kendra Stepputat

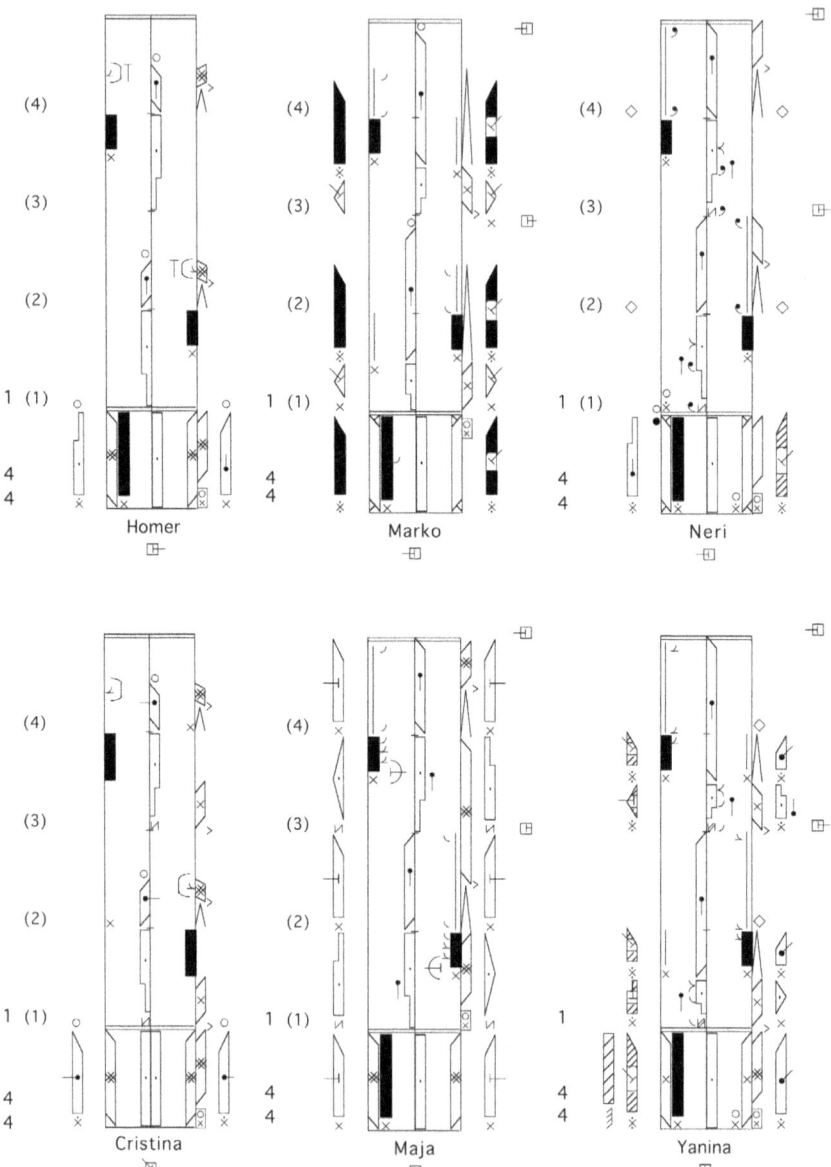

Figure 2.5. Ocho atrás by six tango argentino dance experts. Notation in Kinetography Laban by Raymundo Ruiz González, 2019.

same time as he starts to step and release in the turn, which is the same pattern as that of Maja. A difference is that Maja already starts to twist in the opposite direction while still in the turn and therefore never stays untwisted. Neri goes into the twist before stepping, stays in this twisted position while stepping and starts to 'release' in the turn. This is the same pattern as that of Homer, with the aforementioned difference that Homer turns much faster, which causes a shorter release time. Yanina similarly starts the step in an already twisted position, continues to twist until she starts turning, and releases when the turn begins. A significant difference between Yanina and all other dancers is that her hips are much more active in the untwisting, while the augmented chest[31] stays more stable in space. Finally, Cristina twists before stepping, continues to twist while stepping and holds the twisted position in the second half of her step. As all the others, she starts to untwist at the beginning of the turn.

A further obvious difference is the continuity in the movement. Homer and Cristina have relatively long pauses between the first *ocho* and the second, Marko does only a very small but recognizable pause, while there is no visible pause in Maja's, Neri's or Yanina's movements. A final observation is that Neri and Yanina's levels are slightly more down – that is, they dance with knees slightly more bent than the other four dancers (a second degree of contraction in Laban terms). All dancers are relatively stable in their horizontal axis.

In summary, there are visible differences between individuals, sometimes between couples. The continuity of movement, timing of twisting and stepping and overlapping of turning and stepping are differences on an individual level. Both partners in a couple show the same pattern in comparison to other couples in the length of their steps, the bending of their knees, and in relation to the time between turn and step. Whether these last elements actually define a style, and not only for one representative couple, cannot be answered without more insights into tango dancing.

New Methods, New Insights

In the course of working on the analysis presented in this chapter, in an iterative, evolving process, we established a method that is promising and applicable for future projects and other movement forms. As expected, it involves a combination of all approaches mentioned here, bringing together advantages and knowledge of the three perspectives as well as the possibility to mutually review and reduce potential mistakes or avoid ignoring important data. Our working procedure to achieve this started with the dance perspective, which alone can decide which research questions are of importance to both the researcher and the dance community. Which elements to look at and how is also within the realm of the dance perspective. The data has then to be captured properly with the help of motion capture, cleansed and then analysed based on mathematical procedures in regard to the research question. When the data is ready to be worked with, a movement expert can examine the mocap recordings, working on a notation and analysis based foremost on the visualization of the captured data. The ideal situation would of course be that this movement expert was already involved in the recording and working with the dancers, to give them a better and more thorough impression of the people and the context. At the same time as the movement experts examine the recordings, data analyses of movement features can be carried out. At this step, a constant back and forth between data analysis, notation and dance knowledge is initiated. The data can be used to double check notation, while insights from the movement notation can be used to understand data output. In the course of this process, new ideas might develop, advancing the initial approach. This back and forth between movement notation and data analysis must of course be in close cooperation with the dance perspective, to keep the aspired insights in focus. Finally, results should be cross-checked with the dancers themselves, who, after all, should always be in focus with the embodied and implicit or explicit knowledge of the movement system.

We first developed and then followed this pattern in the course of trying to find out what determines style in the comparison of the three representative tango dance couples. I will give only one example of how the combination of insights enabled a clear definition of one couple's style element. In comparing the backstep in the *ocho*, the data visualization of the ankle distance (Figure 2.4.) shows clearly that Yanina and Neri, the couple dancing in *tang salón* style, make the widest steps, in particular if considering that they are the smallest couple in terms of body height. In the Labanotation, we see that they transfer the weight after a short sliding of the tip or pad of the toe, which prolongs the reach of their steps. This movement can only be accomplished by bending the knee further. From both the dancer and notation perspectives, it is obvious that they do bend their knees much more, in their turns and in their steps, than the other two couples. This is obviously closely connected to the reach of the steps, but it also produces a certain aesthetic. Having become aware of this particular feature, I double checked random filmed examples of a broad range of *tango salón* dancers, both prominent and regular community dancers. With all caution – considering that styles change, overlap and develop over time – we can say that a backstep with a short sliding phase before transferring weight by bending the standing leg further, both in walking and in the *ocho atrás*, is an important aesthetic technical feature of current *tango salón*. In the course of working with the *ocho atrás* recordings, we found many small elements that if combined into a bigger picture and cross-checked with the other perspectives can be regarded as elements of a particular style. The backstep as presented here is so far the most prominent example of a style element.

Summary and Conclusion

In this chapter, I compared motion capture to already established approaches of movement analysis in ethnochoreology, which were Labanotation and a dancer's embodied and explicit knowledge. The objective was to explore possibilities mocap offers and develop an ethnochoreological method to work with mocap data. As an example, we examined the tango argentino motif *ocho atrás*, in particular with differences in individual execution of the movement by six representative expert tango dancers. The aim was to detect style differences between *milonguero*, *salón* and *nuevo* (organic) tango dancing. First, we clearly identified movement elements – for instance, the overlapping of step and turn, or the continuity of dissociation and counter-dissociation – that are an essential part of the motif yet variable in execution. Connected to that, we detected significant individual ways of executing the movement, or 'individual style'. By this, it is possible on a movement analysis level to explain and pinpoint the similarities in movement by students and their teachers, or admirers and their idols. That a dancer's individual execution of tango movements 'looks like' somebody else's is indeed a common issue in the tango community. On the style level of the three couples, fewer but also obvious differences do exist. This includes, for instance, the length of steps and duration of turns. If the couples' detected style elements are typical representations of *milonguero*, *salón* or *nuevo*, needs to be investigated on a much broader level. For one example – the execution of the *ocho atrás* backstep in *tango salón* – such a generalization could be made by cross-checking insights from the analysis with a larger sample of *tango salón* dance film recordings.

The impact this research could have for the tango dance community is first of all more detailed information about particular styles and the knowledge that tango styles definitely do have more concrete differences in terms of movement execution than the way of embracing and can at least partly be determined by them. Since the translocal tango community has a very active communication culture – mainly based on social media – such information will probably be a welcome basis for discussions with an economic, aesthetic or a stylistic background etc., all mentioned above when discussing why communities feel the need to define style. Furthermore, on a more practical level, the teachers recorded here can use the recordings for their own benefit,[32] to improve or reconsider their teaching or even their dance technique. This relates to the fact that the data visualization gives concrete insights into level of training, as seen here by the generally smoother movements by the followers compared to the leaders.

On a methodological level, we found that mocap can actively further the ethnochoreological analysis of structured movement systems by opening up new technical possibilities as well as broadening research questions and approaches. Motion capture, if applied in ethnochoreology, should not be considered as a replacement for other forms of capturing and analysis but instead as a valuable supplement and tool to access embodied and culturally embedded knowledge. In developing a method that combines insights and approaches to understanding a movement system, we were able to advance the knowledge about the dance form significantly, which had not been possible without any of the involved experts and their diverse expertise. I would like to turn back to Kaeppler's aforementioned analysis approach from the 1970s: she put emphasis on learning the dance to understand it better and be able to communicate about it, get feedback from the practitioners and work closely with a second person to notate and analyse the movements.[33] In a way, the method shown here is a forward evolution of that setup, with significantly more technical advancements and arguably more emphasis on a regulated, less hierarchical cooperation between all people involved. I hope that the results from this project encourage more researchers to include mocap into their research design and thereby advance our possibilities in understanding human movement.

Kendra Stepputat is Assistant Professor in Ethnomusicology at the Institute of Ethnomusicology, University of Music and Performing Arts Graz, Austria. She is currently Chair of the ICTM Study Group on Sound, Movement, and the Sciences. Her research topics include Balinese performing arts, in particular *kecak*, and *tango argentino* in European perspective. Special focus in her research is on choreomusical aspects of performing arts. She has published articles in the Yearbook for Traditional Music, Asian Music, and is editor of *Performing Arts in Postmodern Bali* (2013) and co-editor of *Sounding the Dance, Moving the Music* (2017).

Notes

1. For an in-depth discussion of fieldwork concepts, including the necessary reinterpretation of 'the field' from a movement perspective, see Gore (1999). For aspects in ethnomusicology, see, for instance, Nettl (2015: 199–210).
2. Similarly, in ethnomusicology, practically learning to play a music tradition is considered to be an important part of learning to understand, as originally promoted by Mantle Hood (1960). See also Trimillos (2004) for a good overview of the concept and the incorporation of 'learning to perform' into ethnomusicology curricula.
3. See also the discussion of impossible objectivity in understanding dance cross-culturally by Ness (2004).
4. Due to limited space, I am not able to include kinaesthetic, somatic or phenomenological aspects of movement knowledge here. For general information on related concepts and discourses in dance studies, see, for instance, Sklar (2001, 2008), Parviainen (1998), Horton Fraleigh (1987). See also Hahn (2007) or Daniel (2005) as examples of ethnochoreological studies of embodied knowledge production.
5. In addition, see Hutchinson Guest (1998) and Jeschke (2017) for an overview and comparison of dance notation approaches in historical perspective.

6. For a brief historical introduction into the development of different motion capture technologies since the 1970s, see Dick (2015: 68–73).
7. A thorough overview of motion capture technologies is given by Nymoen (2013: 13–22).
8. For an introduction to data visualization, see Tufte (1983).
9. The four-year project (V 423) was financed by the FWF (Austrian Science Fund) within the Elise Richter grant programme.
10. See, for instance, Cara (2009), Goertzen and Azzi (1999) or Fares (2015).
11. 'La codification a ainsi toujours été réglée par ce souci de maintenir la rentabilité économique du métier de professeur de danse. . . . Aujourd'hui, le même principe de la rentabilité économique influence la codification du tango à travers l'accréditation du style salon comme façon de danser exclusive dans le bal.'
12. 'Cette différenciation dans l'interprétation n'est véritablement réalisée que par les danseurs expérimentés.'
13. For a detailed historical and sociological overview of the development of different tango styles in connection to learning to dance tango in Argentina from the 1950s to the early twenty-first century, see Carozzi (2015: 133–64).
14. '[El Chino Perico] crea así, mediante una práctica verbal común entre los milongueros, un mapa completo del tango en la ciudad a partir de una trayectoria que recorría unos pocos barrios. Otros milongueros recurrían a una taxonomía que distinguía entre el tango salón, el orillero, el canyengue, el fantasía y el for export. Aun cuando muchos adherían a las mismas denominaciones, existía escaso acuerdo entre ellos sobre cuáles eran las características distintivas de cada uno de estos modos de bailar. Ciertas versiones incluso sostenían que algunos pares de términos eran denominaciones alternativas del mismo estilo.'
15. See Torp (2007) and Azzi (1996) for the early development of tango argentino in the Rio de la Plata delta.
16. The research presented here is a team effort, based on the knowledge and expertise of many. To acknowledge this, I use first person plural ('we') phrasing whenever I refer to results or insights that are based on contributions by several people. In the course of the project, experts from a variety of fields were involved and contributed significantly to the general outcome.
17. See Carozzi (2015: 160–64) on the introduction of *milonguero* as a new label mainly by Susana Miller, in the 1990s. *Tango milonguero* as a present concept or philosophy behind dancing tango has also been termed *tanguedad* – a feeling for and in tango – by Cara (2009).
18. The *ocho atrás* could be called a 'motif' as defined by both Kaeppler and Giurchescu and Kröschlova (2007: 33).
19. Homer Ladas (2019, pers. comm., 5 August) stated: 'I use organic tango to explain my philosophy but not style. Although you could argue that they are bound together.'
20. Maja (2019, pers. comm., 3 August) specifies: 'I think our style would be the closest to "milonguero" style, although it is not completely the same thing. For the purposes of distinguishing and naming different styles, I guess this would be the most accurate description.'
21. We had access to an Optitrack system with twelve cameras, with MatLab software version R2019a Update 3 (9.6.0.1135713). We used a body model with forty markers per captured person (see Figure 2.1.).
22. For a thorough introduction to the history, theory and practice of notation systems based on Rudolf Laban's concepts, see Hutchinson Guest (2005), and Fügedi (2016) as an

example of the use of Kinetography Laban in ethnochoreological research. Labanotation, Laban Kinetography and Kinetography Laban are different but related approaches to Laban's system of movement notation. The term 'Labanotation' is commonly used as an umbrella term, therefore I will continue to use this term together with the more neutral 'Laban's system of movement notation' in this chapter.

23. See also Dils and Crosby (2001) for an exemplary dialogic approach combining movement knowledge and Labanotation.
24. I am very grateful for the fruitful cooperation with Raymundo Ruiz González and Christopher Dick, on which the following contents is based. Christopher Dick was the computer technician and analyst for all mocap recordings we did during the project. Raymundo Ruiz González added his advanced knowledge in Laban's system of movement notation. Both Christopher and Raymundo are trained in many dance traditions but not the tango argentino. In September 2018, we spent time watching the recorded data of *ocho atrás* together and discussed possible ways to analyse, interpret or simply understand the relevant movement structures. We realized quite quickly that what we 'saw' differed immensely and depended on our individual skill and training, both theoretically and physically.
25. Often during a recording information of single markers is temporarily lost and needs to be manually added at a later stage. I thank Christopher Dick and Siavash Moazzami Vahid for weeks of data cleansing for the tango danceability project.
26. Christopher Dick worked on the project from 2016 to 2019. Kurt Schatz took over all computer-based technical and analytical tasks from July 2019, including the data presented here. The approach to this data analysis part is based on Christopher's biomechanical insights as well as my own experiences and interpretations after three years of working with mocap.
27. We computed the dissociation using the vector dot product between corresponding shoulder (v1 l/r) and hip vectors (v2 l/r). The positive and negative degrees result from the way the angle was calculated in MatLab, where the angle is 'measured in a counterclockwise direction from v1 to v2. If that angle would exceed 180 degrees, then the angle is measured in the clockwise direction but given a negative value' (R. Stafford, 24 February 2014, see https://de.mathworks.com/matlabcentral/answers/180131-how-can-i-find-the-angle-between-two-vectors-including-directional-information).
28. I would like to add that Cristina's *ocho* movement shown here is not particularly representative of her ability to carry out 'smooth' *ochos*. For the mocap recording, she chose to break the *ocho atrás* down into clearly distinguishable parts, which caused interruptions in the movement that were visible in the overall slowness and the small changes in angle.
29. For a discussion of the advantages and disadvantages of exact versus idealized dance notation, see Ruiz González (2019), also Bakka in this book.
30. Raymundo (2019, pers. comm., 16 August) stated that a major disadvantage with watching the mocap recordings in comparison with watching a film is that it is hard to determine which part of the sole has contact with the floor. The body model we used for the recording covers each foot with only four markers, which gives no information about individual toe movement. Other more detailed foot models are in use, for instance, in gait analysis (see Leardini and Caravaggi 2016).
31. The augmented chest in Labanotation is defined as 'chest plus waist' (Hutchinson Guest 2005: 220).
32. All 3D recordings have been shared with the dance couples for their own perusal.
33. See Van Zile's chapter in this book on the cooperation between notator and researcher.

References

Apprill, C. 1999. 'De la Musique à la danse, l'autre cople du tango', *Musurgia* 6(2): 73–88.
Azzi, M.S. 1996. 'Multicultural Tango: The Impact and the Contribution of the Italian Immigration to the Tango in Argentina', *International Journal of Musicology* 5: 437–53.
Benzecry Sabá, G. 2010. *New Glossary of Tango Dance: Key Tango Argentino Dance Terms*. Stuttgart: Abrazos.
Bolasell, M. 2011. *La revolución del tango: la nueva edad de oro*. Buenos Aires: Corregidor.
Cara, A.C. 2009. 'Entangled Tangos: Passionate Displays, Intimate Dialogues', *The Journal of American Folklore* 122(486): 438–65.
Carozzi, M.J. 2015. *Aquí se baila el tango: Una etnografía de las milongas porteñas*. Buenos Aires: Siglo Veintiuno Editores.
Csordas, T. 2002. *Body/Meaning/Healing*. New York: Palgrave Macmillan.
Daniel, Y. 2005. *Dancing Wisdom: Embodied Knowledge in Haitian Vodou, Cuban Yoruba, and Bahian Candomble*. Urbana: University of Illinois Press.
Dick, C. 2015. 'Movement and Music: It is not a Dance, but Capoeira: A Motion Capture Analysis of Capoeira's Ginga', Master's thesis. Vienna: University of Vienna.
Dils, A., and J.F. Crosby. 2001. 'Dialogue in Dance Studies Research', *Dance Research Journal* 33(1): 62–81.
Fares, G. 2015. 'Tango's Elsewhere: Japan', *The Journal of the Midwest Modern Language Association* 48(1): 171–92.
Fügedi, J. 2016. *Basics of Laban Kinetography for Traditional Dancers*. Budapest: Institute for Musicology, Research Centre for the Humanities, Hungarian Academy of Sciences.
Giurchescu, A., and E. Kröschlova. 2007. 'Theory and Method of Dance Form Analysis. Revised Version of the ICTM Study Group on Ethnochoreology Collective Work: "Foundation for Folk Dance Structure and Form Analysis" (1962–1976)', in A.L. Kaeppler and E. Ivancich Dunin (eds), *Dance Structures*. Szeged: Department of Ethnology and Cultural Anthropology, University of Szeged, Akadémiai Kiadó Budapest, pp. 21–52.
Goertzen, C., and M.S. Azzi. 1999. 'Globalization and the Tango', *Yearbook for Traditional Music* 31: 67–76.
Gore, G. 1999. 'Textual Fields: Representation in Dance Ethnography', in T.J. Buckland (ed.), *Dance in the Field: Theory, Methods and Issues in Dance Ethnography*. London: Macmillan Press, pp. 208–20.
Hahn, T. 2007. *Sensational Knowledge: Embodying Culture through Japanese Dance*. Middletown, CT: Wesleyan University Press.
Hood, M. 1960. 'The Challenge of "Bi-Musicality"', *Ethnomusicology* 4(2): 55–59.
Horton Fraleigh, S. 1987. *Dance and the Lived Body: A Descriptive Aesthetics*. Pittsburgh, PA: University of Pittsburgh Press.
Hutchinson Guest, A. 1998. *Choreo-Graphics: A Comparison of Dance Notation Systems from the Fifteenth Century to the Present*. Amsterdam: Gordon and Breach.
———. 2005. *Labanotation: The System of Analyzing and Recording Movement*, 4th edn. New York: Routledge.
Jeschke, C. 2017. 'Reflecting on Time while Moving: Dance Notations from the Nineteenth to the Twenty-first Century', in P. Veroli and G. Vinay (eds), *Music-Dance: Sound and Motion in Contemporary Discourse*. London and New York: Routledge, pp. 93–106.
Kaeppler, A.L. 2001. 'Dance and the Concept of Style', *Yearbook for Traditional Music*, pp. 49–63.

———. 1972. 'Method and Theory in Analyzing Dance Structure with an Analysis of Tongan Dance', *Ethnomusicology* 16(2): 173–217.
Knudson, D. 2007. *Fundamentals of Biomechanics*, 2nd edn. New York: Springer.
Koutedakis, Y., E.O. Owolabi and M. Apostolos. 2008. 'Dance Biomechanics: A Tool for Controlling Health, Fitness, and Training', *Journal of Dance Medicine and Science* 12(3): 83–90.
Krüger, J. 2012. *Cuál es tu tango? Musikalische Lesarten der argentinischen Tangotradition*. Münster: Wexmann.
Leardini A., and P. Caravaggi. 2016. 'Kinematic Foot Models for Instrumented Gait Analysis', in B. Müller et al. (eds), *Handbook of Human Motion* [s.l.]: Springer, Cham, [n.p.].
Liska, M. 2017. *Argentine Queer Tango: Dance and Sexuality Politics in Buenos Aires*. Lanham, MD: Lexington Books.
Ness, S.A. 2004. 'Observing the Evidence Fail: Difference Arising from Objectification in Cross-Cultural Studies of Dance', in G. Morris (ed.), *Moving Words: Re-writing Dance*. London and New York: Routledge, pp. 245–69.
Nettl, B. 2015. *Ethnomusicology: 33 Discussions*. Urbana, IL: University of Illinois Press.
Nymoen, K. 2013. 'Methods and Technologies for Analysing Links between Musical Sound and Body Motion', Ph.D. dissertation. Oslo: University of Oslo.
Parviainen, J. 1998. *Bodies Moving and Moved: A Phenomenological Analysis of the Dancing Subject and the Cognitive and Ethical Values of Dance Art*. Tampere: Tampere University Press.
Ruiz González, R. 2019. 'The Cultural Construction of Laban's System of Movement Notation: The Situated Perspectives of Three Approaches: Laban Kinetography in Hungary, Labanotation in Ohio, and Language of Dance in New York', Master's thesis. Trondheim: Norwegian University of Science and Technology Trondheim.
Sklar, D. 2000. 'Reprise: On Dance Ethnography', *Dance Research Journal* 32(1): 70–77.
———. 2001. 'Toward Cross-Cultural Conversation on Bodily Knowledge', *Dance Research Journal* 33(1): 91–92.
———. 2008. 'Remembering Kinesthesia: An Inquiry into Embodied Cultural Knowledge', in Noland C. and Ness S. (eds), *Migrations of Gesture*. University of Minnesota Press, pp. 85–112.
Stepputat, K., W. Kienreich and C. Dick. 2019. 'Digital Methods in Intangible Cultural Heritage Research: A Case Study in Tango Argentino', *ACM Journal on Computing and Cultural Heritage* 12(2): [n.p.].
Toiviainen, P., and B. Burger. 2015. *MoCap Toolbox Manual*. University of Jyväskylä.
Torp, J. 2007. *Alte atlantische Tangos: Rhythmische Figurationen im Wandel der Zeiten und Kulturen*. Hamburg: Lit Verlag.
Trimillos, R. 2004. 'Subject, Object, and the Ethnomusicology Ensemble: The Ethnomusicological "We" and "Them"', in T. Solis (ed.), *Performing Ethnomusicology: Teaching and Representation in World Music Ensembles*. Berkeley and Los Angeles: University of California Press.
Tufte, E. 1983. *The Visual Display of Quantitative Information*. Cheshire, CT: Graphics Press.
Van Zile, J. 1999. 'Capturing the Dancing: Why and How?', in T.J. Buckland (ed.), *Dance in the Field: Theory, Methods and Issues in Dance Ethnography*. London: Macmillan Press.
Wilson, M., and Kwon, Y.H. 2008. 'The Role of Biomechanics in Understanding Dance Movement: A Review', *Journal of Dance Medicine and Science* 12(3): 109–16.

Chapter 3

Transcription and Description
Tasks for Dance Research

Egil Bakka

At the ICTM world conference in Edinburgh in 1969, I listened to Adrienne Kaeppler present her work on dance in Tonga. As a first-timer with a rather weak command of English but still having experience in fieldwork and dance analysis, I was very impressed by her presentation. She was one of the young stars there, and I may have stuttered a few words to her at some point. As far as I can remember, the two of us did not meet again until around 1990, when the ICTM Study Group on Ethnochoreology made a new start, attracting anthropologists of dance from the USA and Western Europe. Before that, through the 1970s and 1980s, I worked intensively with documenting traditional dances of my country for research purposes, but even more for the purpose of supporting their transmission, as a cultural value for the communities from which they came, and I mostly published in Norwegian for a Nordic readership. In the same period, Adrienne worked intensively at the Bishop museum in Honolulu and from 1980 at the Smithsonian Institute in Washington DC, also with fieldwork, research projects and publications in English.

Norwegian Discussion

My perspective on work with dance first came from my strong involvement in the organized Norwegian folk dance movement but also from the attitudes of the mostly old traditional dancers and musicians, as well as from some young people in their communities. They saw traditional dance first of all as valuable heritage, which also became part of the vision for my professional work at the Norwegian Centre for Traditional Music and Dance. I felt pressure from many sides of the research environment against the validity of treating dances or immaterial folk culture as objects of value. My teachers of folkloristics in the 1960s – Svale Solheim, Olav Bø, Brynjulf Alver and Reimund Kvideland – all grew up in rural environments close to folk culture and did teach us with an attitude to folklore as value for the community, but all were quite distant from dance as a topic. At the same time, Alver argued for new methods and approaches in tune with international trends of the discipline (Heggli 2013). Ballads, fairy tales and other folklore genres had been collected as isolated texts almost without context since the middle of the nineteenth century, and large text archives had been established. Alver argued that current collecting should be based on research projects defining what and how to collect. I found that understandable from the field of folklore but problematic for dance, which had hardly any collections in our country.

The only academic in Norway who had engaged with dance as part of his discipline at that time was Jan-Petter Blom, who already worked as a social anthropologist at the University of Bergen. He was never my teacher but inspired me and advised me on my magister dissertation. In our many discussions, he teased me as a student of folklore, criticising folklorists for lack of theory, a point that was stressed even more when I moved to Oslo to study Regional Nordic Ethnology. The curriculum at the end of the 1960s was about to change. It had a specialization in material folk culture, including traditional house building, agricultural implements, traditional costumes, social customs etc. taught by people working in museums. This was suitable for people aiming for careers in traditional museums with large collections of objects from the past. Under the leadership of Knut Kolsrud, the programme kept some of that orientation for a while but slowly developed towards a more theory-based discipline based particularly on American anthropology. I remember reading Alfred Kroeber and Robert Redfield. The study of old rural objects, their forms, history and distribution, slowly gave way to contemporary culture, with less emphasis on objects. It was my interest in traditional culture that attracted me to folklore and ethnology, and I felt that much concrete and practical knowledge about life in the past that was still needed was being left behind. On the other hand, I felt the engagement with the present to be necessary. It may have been one reason why I started documenting twentieth-century dances, such as tango and rock 'n' roll already in the mid 1970s, even if my priority was on older material. Building a national archive for traditional dance, I saw the need to not turn a blind eye to other dance genres.

Meeting with European Folk Dance Research

Abroad, I met researchers who had similar experiences in folk dance collecting but who had different opinions. Roderyk Lange[1] had worked with traditional dance in his home country Poland and stresses in several articles how dances change when they move from the rural context to the urban, as for example when they were taken up as 'national dances' by the upper classes in the early nineteenth century (Lange 1976: 38). He was also sceptical about what could be achieved by a folk dance revival:

> Many attempts have been made to keep the peasant version of *kujawiak* alive. But this has never really been possible. Even the 'regional' dance groups which try to retain the dance heritage consist in many cases of young people who are already at a distance from the old ways of life. For them, the musicians have to play a set version of dance melodies instead of improvising. The spell arising out of improvisation and the interaction between the musicians and the dancer has been broken. (Lange 1974: 50)

During long discussions, it turned out that Lange and I had different views on the possibility of continuing traditional dancing. He felt that the dances would change too much to be of value and interest in a new setting and had ended up with the conclusion that the traditional dances could not be transferred from their old rural settings to the urbanized population of today. I felt that changes could be minimized, particularly where the dances were used in the communities they came from, even if it was in new functions, and that they were of value in spite of the changes.

Jean Michel Guilcher, who together with his wife collected and analysed French traditional dance as a lifelong endeavour, was also critical of the amateur folk dance revival movement and its way of dealing with the material. He felt the values in past movement systems and movement skills were hardly transferable to new generations but did, however, look at good revival work with some understanding:

> The members of our current folklore groups, in applying themselves to seize from outside the forms of movement out of use, have little chance of living through them the same psychic state as the members of the peasant communities of the past. Men of another time and another society invested something else in the dances, and consequently make another dance. This means that the traditional dancers' dancing can only be understood by the milieu, the culture, the mentality, where it flourished and was transmitted. The link that we perceive between a movement structure and psyche is of its environment and of its time. (Guilcher 1971: 31)[2]

My comments to Guilcher would be that dances and movements of the upper classes in Europe of the eighteenth and nineteenth centuries, at least the ballet and the classical music have been transferred, despite all changes that have occurred and the big differences in living conditions for even the practitioners. Why then, would the dance and music culture of the lower classes be so much less valuable to transfer? One understanding that is not usually explicated might be that the arts of the upper classes were made with other intentions and had other qualities, something I would question.[3] So I retained my point of departure and got surprising support for it through the UNESCO Convention for the Safeguarding of Intangible Cultural Heritage when it was established in 2003, which I was engaged with from the beginning (Bakka 2015).

Impressions from American Discussions

In the 1970s, while Adrienne worked at the Bernice Pauahi Bishop Museum in Hawai'i, she carried out a regional research programme on music and dance in Oceania for UNESCO with Barbara Smith at the University of Hawai'i (*The Journal of American Folklore* 1974: 369). She did extensive fieldwork, produced publications and participated in the North American debates and conferences. Then around 1980, she was employed at the Smithsonian Institute in Washington DC., which presents itself as 'the world's largest museum, education, and research complex' (Smithsonian Institution [n.d.]).

In that time, Adrienne engaged in basic discussions on dance research; for instance, in a review of Judith Lynne Hanna's book *To Dance Is Human* from 1979. The core of her criticism was that Hanna does not support her theories with sufficient empirical data, and she evaluates the present state of dance research as follows: 'There are too few detailed studies of human movement and those who feel the need to theorize will continue to be hampered by lack of empirical data until more relevant studies have been carried out and published' (Kaeppler 1981: 218–19). Her publications on Tongan dance were already well known and are ideal examples of careful study combined with analysis of movement structures and theory. Hanna (1981: 808–10) wrote an answer to defend her book, which I think gives an interesting impression of different views on dance research at that time:

> Researchers operate on the basis of theory, whether they make it explicit or not. It is appropriate to develop theory on the basis of what is known, to make the theory explicit, and then to modify it as relevant data are collected and analyzed. On the basis of current theory and knowledge, including my own fieldwork in several settings, the book presents a dynamic communication model which combines textual (movement) and contextual (culture, society, history, ecology) approaches with human evolution and symbolic interaction. The communication theory systematizes and makes explicit much of what is usually segmented and implicit. It attempts to encompass both surface phenomena and the underlying reality of which the observer or participant may be unaware.

In a much later article, Adrienne again stresses the importance of dealing with movement but in balance with how it functions in society:

> What anthro/ethno/indigenous fieldworkers do with their data and how it is presented in publication varies widely. But all of these researchers

focus our attention on movement content as well as social, cultural and political concerns such as gender, the body, ethnic, cultural and national identity, the negotiation of tradition, and turning the ethnographic eye on any society. In order to find the larger view as advocated here, fieldwork is not only recommended but is necessary in order to bring movement into focus as part of a total cultural system. (Kaeppler 2000: 116–25)

Why, then, is technical engagement with movement still unusual? Many researchers may still think that producing well researched descriptions of dance forms that can be of direct use for practitioners is not academic work. Having described some two hundred different dances, based on an average of three to four transcriptions each, I know very well that this is very time consuming, cumbersome and demanding work. It may seem that dance description is not necessary for the study of dancing as a social phenomenon and that transcription and description in most cases does not take us anywhere far for such purposes. It is much easier to write up our descriptions and discussions about how dance interacts with gender, the body or identity based upon our general impressions or participant observation of dancing in the community we study. It may seem that we can glean the necessary information about dancing from what the dancers tell us. However, it seems that Kaeppler and others have somewhat different views: 'Kaeppler cautions us to put the same value on movement events as members of the group one is studying; and Keali'inohomoku reminds us that: "Dance should be studied because it is important to the people involved"' (Frosch 1999: 261). This quote may sound alarm bells about lingering colonial attitudes where researchers study 'the other' to glean knowledge about 'man'[4] for the needs of the colonial powers and Western research communities. Keali'inohomoku's point that research should also be done for the needs of the communities studied could be achieved by outsiders as well as by community members themselves. Adrienne stressed this in more careful wording on several occasions, and this viewpoint probably contributed to two of her awards.[5]

Revisiting Work in the ICTM Study Group on Ethnochoreology

The Study Group took as its first task at its start in 1962 the development of a common terminology, which then became a work on how to analyse dance structure. In 1974, a syllabus to this end was published (The I.F.M.C. Study Group for Folk Dance Terminology 1974). Adrienne Kaeppler had submitted her Ph.D. dissertation on Tongan dance (1967), and I had submitted my magister dissertation on Norwegian couple dances (Bakka 1973); both had structural analysis as the core theme. But there had not been any contact between any of us before the mythical meeting and chat in a bathroom at the ICTM Conference in Bayonne in 1973, between Anca Giurchescu from Romania and Adrienne Kaeppler, USA. They both individually and together told us colleagues of the Study Group how amazed they were when they realised to be working with so similar questions and ideas about structural analysis. The bathroom meeting came to represent a 'first contact' event between East European and North American dance research for our group. However, we did not, as far as I remember, discuss these contrasting perspectives much in the ICTM Study Group on Ethnochoreology, where Adrienne and I had many discussions during the decades around the turn of the century. The members of the group may have assumed that we had more similar opinions than we actually had, which slowly dawned on me at least.

Looking back at the work with structural analysis, I now realize that in spite of the seemingly similar point of departure there were basic differences in the way we in the Study Group created and used our material. The Hungarian work with transcribing dance from films to Labanotation was based on the principle of notating each dancer's dancing exactly as it happened on one particular film from beginning to end (Fügedi 2018).[6] The method of structural analysis claims to be based on such transcriptions.[7] In practical terms, however, the examples used do not refer to filmed realizations. They rather seem to be written down by Labanotators from their own experience and memory or from the standard taught forms in the folk dance movement.[8] These forms, therefore, do not represent single instances but a system level and muddles up what the structure of a dance as presented in the East European system for structural analysis represents (Giurchescu and Kröschlova 2007).

If we have a dance with many variations, the structure of a single realization does not represent the total vocabulary and grammar of the dance. Transcriptions of many realizations of the dance, however, could show more of the totality that we in Norwegian dance research have called the dance concept: 'We suggest that dance has two dimensions: the realization and the concept. The realization is the actual dancing of a dance. The concept for the same dance is the potential of skills, understanding, and knowledge that enables an individual or a dance community to dance that particular dance and to recognize and relate to each particular realization of it' (Bakka and Karoblis 2010: 172–73). A transcription of a standardized form where variations have been taken out can only show the structure of that form and not what might have been there in any non-standardized version. So, the formula showing the structure of a dance is well suited to show one realization of a dance but not the ensemble of variations between the different realizations of one dance.

Adrienne Kaeppler avoided this point by analysing the elements that could be used to build dance motives and how the elements could have a series of allokines, versions that carry the same meaning and can replace each other in the dance composition (Kaeppler 1972). She did not go into the total pattern of one realization or one dance, and since the Tongan dances are choreographies using these elements to create a dance, the question of differences between realizations did not come up in the same way.

Adrienne Kaeppler and the Safeguarding of Intangible Cultural Heritage

Adrienne always stressed that for an anthropologist of dance the aim was to understand a community through the dance rather than the dance itself. It was, therefore, a surprise for us, her colleagues, that she engaged with the UNESCO Convention for the Safeguarding of Intangible Cultural Heritage and was instrumental in getting dance onto the UNESCO lists and that she praised the safeguarding measures put in place in the Tongan Kingdom. Her main argument was that she realized the value dance had for Tongans:[9]

> Lakalaka is a unique legacy to Tonga and is considered by the Tongans as the living cultural history of the community. Through performance, lakalaka have become chronicles of the history of the Tongan people. Lakalaka is in danger of disappearing, due primarily to the lack of means for safeguarding and protecting this oral and intangible form. (Kaeppler 2004: 2–3)

The consequence was a recognition of researching the dance also for its own sake, as Intangible Cultural Heritage, and it is interesting to see how Adrienne also engages with this idea, stressing the importance of oral transmission:

> Tongan musicians believe that the music of the lakalaka cannot be written down. Notation could be made (with difficulty) by listening to a tape recording and writing down what occurred on a specific occasion. But this does not cover the possibilities of how a lakalaka could or should be sung. Each time a lakalaka sung speech is performed, it is performed differently and each rendition is 'correct'. Indeed, the music can only be perpetuated through the oral tradition – both for known historic lakalaka, and the structure and strictures of lakalaka composition. Likewise, Tongans believe that the dance movements of lakalaka cannot be written down, but must be passed in the oral tradition by learning the dance and reconstructing it each time the lakalaka will be performed. (Kaeppler 2004: 3)

In these two quotations, Adrienne points to the core problem of notating traditional dance. Transcription of one performance (or realization in our Norwegian terminology) is not sufficient, but she does not go on towards the question of transcribing, analysing and comparing many realizations in order to find out as much as possible about the dance concept, the source of knowledge and skills in the practitioner's bodies from which the realizations spring. Her solution is to support the oral tradition, and I agree that needs to be the ultimate aim. My experience, however, is that an oral tradition under pressure tends to shrink and become more and more simple. If it is supported by conventional systematic teaching, the danger for standardization and simplification is even larger.

In my mind, the best tool for safeguarding is a systematic survey of all that is collected and known about a dance, including films, interviews, notations and transcriptions. Such a survey can also be built on as time passes and should not be regarded as a fixed standard at any given time. Instead, it should be a pool of knowledge about the dance concept that can support the re-creation of different realizations just as in the traditional context.

In her classic and renowned work, Adrienne has to a certain degree described such a dance concept by identifying the elements and the morphology for combining them as learnt directly from the performers. But the step from understanding the principles of building motives to the building of a full choreography that could be performed is, as far as I can understand, missing. In her defence, it should be said that the idea of making a description that could directly support learning the dance was probably very far from the aims of a dance anthropologist in those days. Her article from 2004 about the safeguarding of Tongan dance ends with Tonga's National Action plan, which includes 'Field research to identify and record lakalaka practitioners, research in Tongan and overseas archives to find texts and other information about lakalaka, workshops given by recognized practitioners and composers and a national lakalaka festival' (Kaeppler 2004: 4). It is my impression that many anthropologists are sceptical or even very critical of the 2003 UNESCO Convention (Brown 2012: 93–97; Keitumetse 2006). To me and other supporters, it was encouraging that Adrienne took a strong lead in support of it from the very beginning. In one of her latest articles, she also stresses how historic film footage of music and dance in archives needs to be made available to the communities it came from and how it can help the continuation of practices (Kaeppler 2017).

The Tools of Transcription and Description

This introduction above was meant to serve as a backdrop for the presentation of two concrete, simple and flexible tools that I think can be helpful in dance research, and particularly with regard to the dilemma that Adrienne found among practitioners at Tonga – that they believed their dance could not be notated because of its changeability. My proposed tools are not meant to be stand-alone methods but combined into larger methodological approaches. The following is also an argument for the study of dance movements in a way that only film documentation allows. It should in my opinion cancel some of the reservations that dance researchers have expressed against the use of film recordings as research material. As researchers, I think we should base our work on documentation that can be re-examined, on stringent observation and advanced analysis of material if we want to support safeguarding.

The tools I present here are 'transcription' and 'description'. In order to show how I understand and use the terms differently from other fields, I want to sum up shortly how the terms are used here.

Generally, the term transcription is often used for the converting of the content of one specific process of human expression into some kind of writing or notation. For instance, transcription of speech is understood as taking down the words or the sounds spoken. It is also possible to transcribe the content of documented events or other kinds of human interaction, again listing how the process is running from beginning to end. A transcription is most often based on a sound or film recording of the process and lists the content of the specific recording in the order elements occur, from the beginning to the end. For dance transcription, it can be a Labanotation score recording precisely what is shown on a piece of film. If, for instance, somebody gives you a recording of a dance that is danced three and a half times before the recording ends and asks you to make a notation of it to be published in a dance manual, you will write it down as it can be danced once. It is not relevant that it was performed more times in that one specific case. Your task is to describe the dance or how it should be danced in general, not how it was danced on that specific occasion. The problem of how such a notation represents the possible spectre of variations is usually not raised. If a piece of music is transcribed, one option is to take down exactly what is recorded within certain parameters, or the way a specific composition should or could be carried out, an idealized or standardized version. Such kinds of transcription are called 'descriptive transcriptions' in ethnomusicology (see Nettl 2015: 78; Seeger 1958). However, this definition of transcription in my view is not suitable for the approach I present here.

My proposal is to define the tools 'transcription' and 'description' based on some specific principles: transcription, as used here, is the transfer of a filmed dance realization into writing in the order the movements occur, referenced through time codes or other means to keep track of the timing. The transcription takes down one specific process or action as it happened at one specific point in time and as it was documented while it happened. If it turns out that there are variations in the dance, meaning that it is not danced in quite the same way each of the three and half times, a transcription will show you that. Notations may show or refer to variations, but most often they do not, or at least not in a systematic way. If you make several precise transcriptions first, it enables you to make a notation of the dance for the collection, where the variations can be included in a systematic way if you wish. You can put the variations as alternative options, for instance in footnotes.

The term 'description' refers to a document that is built by comparing a set of transcriptions of different realizations. It lists the elements from all compared transcriptions and explains how the combination of elements is done. It is, in other words, the description of the vocabulary and the grammar of a practice. This perhaps complex description can help people who give workshops or teach the practice to understand the complexities and help them adapt their teaching to that understanding. Teaching can still be simple but build up little by little to a basis for developing complexity and deeper understanding and variation (Bakka 2017: 223–40).

Dance Movement Transcription

This chapter presents dance movement transcription as the converting of one person's specific movement sequence into a kind of writing or notation. It requires that the movement sequence is filmed so that the transcriber can study the recording and take down the movement elements in the order they occur.[10] The transcriber can define the level of detail or the aspects of movement recorded in the transcription but should keep to the level and the aspects he or she takes down as consistently as possible throughout the transcription. This means that a transcription records as much as possible of a totality, but that it also records only selected aspects of a dance such as arm movements or step patterns. The level of detail or the aspects chosen depends on the focus of the study and the questions asked (Hutchinson Guest 2014: 177–78). Transcription is, in other words, to systematically take down in writing or notation the movement content of a dance realization. Bakka and Karoblis have explained a dance realization in the following way:

> We suggest that dance has two dimensions: the realization and the concept. The realization is the actual dancing of a dance. The concept for the same dance is the potential of skills, understanding, and knowledge that enables an individual or a dance community to dance that particular dance and to recognize and relate to each particular realization of it (Bakka, Aksdal and Flem 1995: 21; Gore and Bakka 2007: 93). We argue that the approach to dance through its realization is underestimated in anthropological research and ethnographic work in general (Bakka 2005: 72). A realization is the only full and proper way in which a dance becomes available for us. We consider demonstrations, rehearsals, and illustrated explanations as secondary and only as hints to a full expression of the dance. Consequently, we see the full, normal realization as the primary source to, and the only fully valid form of, dance. The realization makes dance available perceptually. (Bakka and Karoblis 2010: 172–73)

One main argument for recommending this kind of movement transcription is that it allows us to establish a firm empirical basis for studying movement patterns. Each element or aspect of the dance that is transcribed refers to a specific point in the documented realization and can be revisited and re-evaluated. The description or classification the transcriber is giving for each element he or she transcribes can be verified, questioned or falsified. A process of transcription is of course influenced by the background, knowledge and opinions of the transcriber. Still, working from documentation with a stringent transcription system will more easily enable a critical distance to the movement material.

The usual approach to making notations for practical purposes was[11] to look at a dance being shown several times and then take down what the collector considered the best version or the most typical version based on impressions and observation and perhaps notes. If the collector looks at the dance and then makes statements that generalize about the totality, based on impressions and opinions, it may be sufficient for practical purposes but for research it is a shortcut to a notation that is not properly supported.

Theatrical dance is usually seen as works, and researchers in this field tend to comment on the work as a totality of the choreographer's and the dancers' intentions and maybe the audience's interpretations or understanding. One realization is then seen as an imperfect version of the abstract totality, and the latter cannot be reached or observed directly. Only the descriptions, opinions and understandings of the artists and the audience will be available for characterizing the abstract totality, which can be seen as a dance concept. With such material, it can be difficult to break out of the conventional and internal discourses of the artistic field and find a critical distance. The analysis of realizations may enable the researcher to bracket his or her preconceptions and see a Western theatrical dance work as if it is unknown to her or him (Buckland 1999; Keali'inohomoku 1983). With transcriptions of realizations – that is, individual performances – one will be able to compare them to see to what degree they are different and, if so, how they are different.

To sum up: transcriptions as described above could be used as a firm empirical basis for discussing techniques, intentions or aesthetical ideals with the choreographer and the readings or interpretations with critics or members of the audience.

The problem with transcribing as it is proposed here is that the system has to be learned at the beginning by every new reader, and it is dependent on written language for explications. It does not have the benefit of Western staff notation, which is generally known, or Labanotation, which has at least some readers internationally. My transcription, however, has the benefit of giving beginners in analysis a simple start, and it can register just a few simple aspects of dance patterns. It also enables a person with knowledge of the terminology of the piece he or she wants to analyse the possibility to use that in the transcription, which can also be helpful and facilitate the work. A full Labanotation score will often give redundant information if the questions asked are simple. Shorthand techniques in Labanotation can probably have similar benefits as transcription in terms of avoiding redundancy. It is also possible to take terms such as motive, phrase or cell, or other basic ideas from various models of structural analysis, as presented in Kaeppler and Dunin (2007).

As a conclusion to the argumentation for using the principle of transcription, I refer to a piece of basic information from Penn State University Libraries (2019): 'Empirical research is based on observed and measured phenomena and derives knowledge from actual experience rather than from theory or belief.' This links with the following statement: 'A bottom-line in our argument is that, despite all the cumbersome work it takes, generalizations need to be based upon the explorations of singular events, such as realizations of dance. We argue that there is a need for dance research to work systematically with empirical material and to strive for transparency about how singular events bring us to generalizations' (Bakka and Karoblis 2010: 187). We think that Ethnochoreology and Dance Anthropology would benefit from strengthening the empirical basis for its research and hope that use of transcription as a simple and easy tool will make that easier, since it is open to a broad range of adaptations.

An Example of a Round Dance Transcription: Ringlenner from Røros

The transcribed dance in this example belongs to what I have proposed to call the dance paradigm of round dances – that is, a kind of couple dance that dominated in Europe in the nineteenth century (Bakka 2005). In the Nordic countries, we investigated round dances in a large shared project where we documented them in twelve locations, two each in Denmark, the Faroe Isles,[12] Finland, Iceland, Norway and Sweden (Urup, Sjöberg and Bakka 1988). The project developed terminology for the round dance paradigm, and I will use part of that terminology with some adaptation for the transcriptions and description.

The Nordic project classified the motives found in a selection of 299 dance realizations that were analysed and used for a video publication. There were many couples dancing in most realizations, and the total number of individual dances documented was considerably higher. The project identified five main types of motives (Urup, Sjöberg and Bakka 1988: 257):

> *Promenade motives*: The two dancers in a couple hold each other and move forward, backwards, sideways or diagonally along but on their side of the circular line of direction. In the transcription, these motives are listed as P-Motive 1 and P-Motive 2.
>
> *Turning motives*: The two dancers in a couple face each other. They hold each other and turn clockwise or counterclockwise around their own axis while moving counterclockwise along a circular path forming a circle together with the other dancing couples. There are two subtypes: one-measure turning (T-Motive 1 m), where the couple makes one full turn on one measure of the music, and two-measure turning (T-Motive 2 m), where the turn takes two measures.
>
> *Rest figure motives*: the couple faces each other and uses the steps from the two-measure-turning while moving from side to side and/or along the line of direction. It is a variant of two-measure-turning where the couple rests from the turning. These motives are listed as (T-Motive 2 m) and not specified, to reduce the detail level.

In place motives: The two dancers in a couple travel no more than a few paces in one direction, but dance, forth and back, across an imagined spot.

Miscellaneous motives: Motive that does not fit into the other motive types.

Promenade and turning motives were the most usual motive types in the 299 dance realizations project material, and only these types are listed in the transcriptions and description of the dance analysed here. The dance, however, also has some rest figure motives, which function as variations to two-measure-turning motives; I have, however, just counted those as two-measure-turning motives to keep it simple. I have also left out details of the dance fastening,[13] all gestures of free leg and small variations in the directions the dancers use etc. If the aim of a project is to produce a description for teaching the dance, such details would need to be added in transcriptions and the resulting description. The film documentation would be used to illustrate the work of the teacher and give students a deeper visual impression. The aim here is not so much to make a full description for transmission but rather to show how transcriptions are necessary as a point of departure for a description of dances with many variations.

The dance name *Ringlenner* is a local version of the German Rheinländer, a dance name that is mostly found in German, Norwegian and Danish sources. In Swedish and English, the same dance is mostly called *Schottis/Schottische*. The *Reinlender/Schottis/Schottische* as described by dancing masters was a very simple form following the structure of the music with two measures of P-Motive 2 and two measures of T-Motive 1. An example of this can be observed in a film that shows the German dance teacher couple by the name of Fern teaching a standardized Rheinländer form for German television in 1967. The basic dance structure shown here was commonly danced by late nineteenth-century lower classes, and during my fieldwork in all parts of Norway between the late 1960s to the late 1980s, this version was common almost everywhere except for eastern Norway, where forms were more complex. The simple form was taken up by the dancing masters towards the very end of the nineteenth century. We find close parallels to the simple form taught by the Ferns in the books of the dancing masters from the late nineteenth and early twentieth centuries (Dodworth 1888: 60; Isachsen 1886: 46; Zorn and Sheafe 1905: 247).

Step 1: Transcription

The transcription form shows seven couples dancing the *Ringlenner* at a recording in Röros, Norway, written into a spreadsheet.[14] The first column gives the time code from the recording at the beginning of each repetition and, below, how many seconds the repetition took. Then, there are three columns for each of the seven couples dancing. The first column gives the steps of the male dancer, the second the steps of the female dancer, and the third the couple motives. There are some cells filled with colour, stressing the lengths of musical repetitions and couple motives. Coloured letters in red and green are used to show how the step patterns crossing measures (barlines) are placed. The first pattern is given in red; the following in green. The codes used for transcribing steps are:

L = Left
R = Right
S = *Svikt* (a movement down and up on one foot)[15]
Ss = Double *Svikt* (a movement down and up and down and up again on one foot)
T = Transfer of weight (a movement that takes over the up-movement from the previous S)

In the couple motives columns:

P-motive stands for Promenade motives, and there are two versions of them
T-motive stands for (couple) Turning motives, and there are two versions
1 m stands for 1 measure turning
2 m stands for 2 measure turning
/v stands for variation

Step 2: Description

Having shown the process of transcription, the next step is to make a description based on an analysis of the transcriptions, and this can take many forms. One of them can be a summary of the findings from the analysis, to function as an answer to the questions the researcher may have asked. The aim may be to build it into a broader discussion of the dancers' attitudes and understandings of choreo-musical relationships. Then aspects or details considered irrelevant for the questions posed may not be transcribed or not described. Another form of description can be made for transmission purposes and be formulated as a systematic explanation of how the dance was done in the available transcriptions. This should then be quite detailed and will have a similarity to dance descriptions in manuals but include the variations of a motive as alternatives, and explain how the dance structure can be built. In the following, I present two exemplary analyses focusing on music–dance relationships and elements of the dance respectively.

Music-Dance Relationship

The film used for this transcription gives us a common version of a *Ringlenner*; the musicians play a melody with two parts (A and B) with eight bars each. They play each part twice (AA, BB) and then repeat all again, so that the total is AA BB AA BB, adding up to a total of sixty-four bars. The seven dance couples start dancing at slightly different times, and they stop when the music ends.

	Measures	Step Man 1	Step Woman 1	P-Motives C1	Man 2	Woman 2	P-Motives C2
00:01	1	Black shirt	White blouse		White shirt	White top	
	2	Denim jeans	Black skirt		Black slacks	Black Shirt	
	3	VS HS VSs	[HS VS HSs]		VSs HSs	HSs VSs	
	4	HSs VS HS	[VSs HS VS]		VS HS HS	HSs VS VS	
	5	VSs HSs	HSs VSs		HSs VSs	HSs VSs	
	6	VS HS VSs	VS HS HS VS	P-Motive 1	HSs **WAIT**	VSs **HS VS**	P-Motive 1
	7			Two			Three
	8			Times			and
00:13	9	HS VS HSs	HS VS HS VS	P-Motive 2	VS HS VSs	HS VS HSs	to
00:12	10	VSs HSs	**HSs VSs**	P-Motive 2/v	HSs VS HS	VSs VS HS	third
	11	VSs HSs	HSs VSs	T-Motive 1-m	VSs HSs	HSs VSs	Times
	12	VSs HSs	HSs VSs	T-Motive 1-m	VSs HSs	HSs VSs	T-Motive 1-m
	13	VS HS VSs	HS VS HSs	T-Motive 2-m	VSs HSs	HSs VSs	T-Motive 1-m
	14	VS HS HSs	VS HS VSs	T-Motive 2-m	VSs HSs	HSs VSs	T-Motive 1-m
	15	VS HS VSs	HS VS HSs	T-Motive 2-m	VSs HSs	HSs VSs	T-Motive 1-m
	16	HS VS VSs	VS HS VSs		VSs HSs	HSs VSs	T-Motive 1-m
00:26	17	VS HS VSs	HS VS HSs	P-Motive 1	VS HS VSs	HS VS HSs	T-Motive 2-m
00:13	18	HSs VS HS	VSs HS VS		HS VS HSs	VS HS VSs	T-Motive 2-m
	19	VS HSs	HSs VSs	Two	VS HS VSs	HS VS HSs	T-Motive 2-m
	20	VS HS VSs	VS HS VS HS	Times	VS HS VSs	VS HS HSs	T-Motive 2-m
	21	HS VS VSs	HS VS HSs	P-Motive 2	HS VS VSs	HS VS HSs	T-Motive 2-m
	22	VSs HSs	HSs VSs	T-Motive 1-m	VS HS HSs	HS VS HSs	T-Motive 2-m
	23	VSs HSs	HSs VSs	T-Motive 1-m	HS VS VSs	HS VS HSs	T-Motive 2-m
	24	HS VS VSs	HSs VSs	T-Motive 1-m	HS VS HSs	HS VS HSs	T-Motive 2-m
00:39	25	VS HS VSs	HS VS HSs	T-Motive 2-m	VS HS VSs	VS HS HSs	P-Motive 1
00:13	26	HS VS HSs	VS HS VSs	T-Motive 2-m	HSs VS HS	HSs HS VS	Three
	27	HS VS VSs	HS VS HSs	T-Motive 2-m	VS HSs	HSs VSs	
	28	HS VS VSs	VS HS VSs	T-Motive 2-m	VSs HSs	HSs VSs	Times
	29	VS HS VSs	VS HS HSs	T-Motive 2-m	HSs **VSs**	VSs **HSs**	
	30	HS VS HSs	HS VS VSs	T-Motive 2-m	VSs HSs	HSs VSs	T-Motive 1-m
	31	VS HS VSs	VS HS VS HS	P-Motive 2	VSs HSs	HSs VSs	T-Motive 1-m
	32	HS VS HSs	HS VS HS VS	P-Motive 2	VSs HSs	HSs VSs	T-Motive 1-m

Figure 3.1. Transcription excerpt of the Ringlenner. Transcription by Egil Bakka, 2019. The full transcription is available at https://berghahnbooks.com/downloads/chapters/StepputatPerspectives_03_Appendix_Bakka.pdf.

In most versions of *Reinlender/Schottis/Schottische*, all step patterns are corresponding to one 4/4 bar of the music, but the version from Røros breaks this clear and square dance–music relationship, making it ambivalent. The P-Motive 1 takes one and a half bars of music (six beats), which by itself disturbs the clarity. It also influences the dance–music relationship in the rest of the dance, enabling even the step patterns that cover just one bar of music not only to start on the first beat of the bar, as usual, but also to start on the third beat of the bar. Through this, the dance pattern spans two half bars (beat 3 and 4 of one bar plus 1 and 2 of the next). A dancer accustomed to the clear and square dance–music relationship when dancing the *Reinlender* will have an uneasy feeling if another couple 'divides' (particularly the T-Motive 2 m) between two bars. One may get the feeling that the other couple is out of beat. The difference between the couples is easily observable when a couple that carries out a pattern within one bar, and a couple that shifts the pattern to span two half-bars (T-Motive 2 m) are dancing next to each other. In the transcriptions, we see male dancer 7 hesitate and stop a couple of times to switch from dividing a one-bar pattern over two half-bars to the standard version. Male dancer 2 makes a similar change, waiting for two beats but without hesitation.

We can take this phenomenon of ambivalence on to a more general level. Having discovered this seeming ambivalence in the transcriptions, we can interview the practitioners about their understanding and experience. Can they confirm that there is some ambivalence, and how do they feel about it? Siri Mæland has interviewed dancers inspired by the explicitation interview technique, which is very promising (Mæland 2019). The question can even be taken out into broader spheres, such as the tension between the regulated, unison and transparent opposed to the irregular, individual and ambivalent. The *Reinlender* is a typical example: some forms are simple and square; other forms are complex and advanced. It could, for example, be investigated by putting the findings from the transcription and interviews in relation to aesthetic feelings of communities, intrinsic qualities of social dancing and the related musical culture.

The Elements of the Dance

The dance recording of the seven dancers has four kinds of motives mostly occurring in the following order:

> Promenade motives
> P-Motive 1 is used by all except one couple and is danced 2 or 3 at a time.
> P-Motive 2 also used by all except one couple and is mostly danced 1 to 2 at a time.
>
> Turning motives
> T-Motive 1-m is used by all couples and is danced between 2 to 6 at a time but most often 3.

T-Motive 2-m is used by all couples and is danced between 4 to 8 at a time, most often 6 or 8.

It is interesting to take the motives apart into cell elements, according to the East-European structural analysis method (Giurchescu and Kröschlova 2007). It shows that the whole dance is built on three different motive cells taking two beats each. These elements relate to the musical structure so that they will always start on beat 1 or beat 3 of the measure:

1. Foot-1S Foot-2S
2. Foot-1Ss
3. Foot-1S Foot-2T Foot-1S (Used by couple two, most visible in the last part of their dance)

Finally, the motive cells are built on three different types of paces, an S-pace, an Ss-pace and a T-pace. A pace is the period from the moment a foot takes support till the support has been taken by the other foot. The traditional way of registering or notating the relationship between footwork and music is to give the time value for each pace – that is, from the moment a foot takes on weight till the foot loses the weight. If the weight is taken off the foot through elevation and ends back to the same foot, however, the time value of the stepping part and the landing part are each registered by themselves.

An Example of a Theatrical Dance Transcription

The following example is a transcription of a small Mark Morris piece (see sawing14s 2019 for the video link). Mark Morris is an American dancer, choreographer and opera director (Jordan 2015). In this piece, Morris is performing a danced interaction with three puppets to the 'Anger Dance' by Henry Cowell.[16] The point is to demonstrate concretely how the choreography is constructed in terms of movement and 'narrative'. We can ask how the interaction is constructed in terms of regularity and irregularity and look at the dance–music relationship, and by adding more aspects to new columns more questions can be asked. The aim here is not to explicate on the similarity or difference between Norway and the USA in terms of methodology but to demonstrate that the method can be used on very different kinds of dance material and help to answer very different questions.

Step 1: Transcription

In the transcription, I register the interaction between Mark Morris and three puppets. I have established four categories: *Move* means a movement that is not directed to the other agents, *Command* is a move giving someone else a command, *Imitation* is that the agent imitates someone else. The use of light grey

Time Code	Measure 1-2-3-	Mark Morris	Animal 1	Animal 2	Animal 3	Phrase	
00:01	1	Move					1
	2	Command					
00:03	3		Immitation				
	4			Immitation			
	5				Immitation	5 bars	
	6	Command					2
	7		Immitation				
	8			Immitation			
	9	Move			Immitation	4 bars	
	10	Move					3
	11		Immitation				
	12			Immitation			
	13				Immitation	4 bars	
	14	Command					4
	15		Immitation				
	16			Immitation			
	17				Immitation	4 bars	
	18				Move		5
	19			Immitation			
	20		Immitation			3 bars	
	21	Move					6
	22	Move				2 bars	
	23	Move	Immitation	Immitation			7
	24	Move	Immitation	Immitation			
	25	Move	Immitation	Immitation	Immitation		
	26	Move	Immitation	Immitation	Immitation		
	27	Move	Immitation	Immitation	Immitation		
	28	Move	Immitation	Immitation	Immitation	6 bars	
	29	Reaction	Reaction	Reaction	Reaction		8
	30	Reaction	Command	Command	Command		
	31	Reaction	Command	Command	Command	3 bars	
	32	Reaction					9
	33	Reaction					
	34	Reaction	Command				
	35	Move				4 bars	
	36	Command	Immitation	Immitation	Immitation		10
	37	Move					
	38	Move					
	39	Command					
	40		Immitation	Immitation	Immitation		
00:40	41	Move	Immitation	Immitation	Immitation	6 bars	

Figure 3.2. Transcription of Mark Morris dancing 'Anger Dance'. Transcription by Egil Bakka, 2019.

(yellow in the colour version) indicates that the puppets imitate movement that comes from Morris; the use of dark grey (green in the colour version) indicates imitations of movements initiated by the puppets. A reaction is that one agent *reacts* towards another agent.

Step 2: Instead of a Description

In this case, as we have only one realization of the dance, and since the dance may be intended as a fixed choreography, a description process may not make sense, but a summary of findings is still possible.

The categories of interaction as transcribed above could certainly be developed and more precisely defined; they are just simple examples. The music is simple and circling around a motif of two bars that is repeated most of the time. If we look at the movement phrases, most of them start on even number bars, somehow breaking with the two-bar pattern in the music. The phrases are of different length, and both these features create tension with musical regularity.

As for the interaction categories, the *move* category belongs to Morris, whereas the *imitation* category belongs to the puppets; the other categories are done by Morris as well as the puppets. There are some problems with using the video for movement analysis: it has many cuts and some pieces where we cannot see all the agents. It does give the impression, though, that it is a continuous dance and that the pieces are shot simultaneously with different cameras, but most likely it is pieces recorded at different times pasted together. The continuity of sound and movement patterns still enables us to analyse it as one piece of dance. We could have made a column for the camera clips to see how a change of camera influences our reading of the dance. We could have also made columns for the movements performed and a number of other aspects.

Epilogue

In this chapter, I have revisited a past shared with a dear colleague, reflecting on some common and some different threads in the histories of our lives. We have in common that we have dealt with the movement content of dance, by analysing it in detail but for different purposes; Adrienne in order to learn about the society, and me for the sake of transmitting it to new generations. The 2003 Convention, however, made us both work for the same purpose, although still in different ways and with different understandings. Adrienne has shown through her work that the values of the communities she researched mattered to her, and she promoted them, maybe without explicating that as much as I have done. She has not continued to develop the impressive system for analysis of movement that she started with her Ph.D., instead moving on to other issues, whereas I have found movement analysis in all its aspects ever more interesting and important. This is why I have taken the liberty to combine the revisiting of the past with a piece aiming to inspire my students and colleagues towards more movement analysis by proposing some strategies that are not so demanding and that take advantage of online publishing, which allows much more efficient video illustrations than before. Works about dance have been difficult to write and even worse to read because it is such a challenge to imagine and understand dance from descriptions and notation. The possibility to combine seamlessly the watching of a dance film with the reading of its analysis is in my mind a revolutionary progress. The potential of this technology can be taken much further than here, but I hope the attempt can be an inspiration.

Egil Bakka is professor emeritus at Program for Dance Studies, Department of Music, Faculty of Humanities, Norwegian University of Science and Technology and former director of the Norwegian Centre for Traditional Music and Dance. His fields of expertise include Ethnochoreology, Dance history and Dance analysis. His latest publication is Erlien, T., and E. Bakka. 2017. 'Museums, Dance, and the Safeguarding of Intangible Cultural Heritage: "Events of Practice"– A New Strategy for Museums?', *Santander Art and Culture Law Review* 2(4): 135–56.

Notes

1. In the summer of 1983, I stayed several months in Lange's centre at Jersey to learn Labanotation from him.
2. 'Les membres de nos actuels groupes folkloriques, en s'appliquant à saisir du dehors des formes de mouvement sorties de l'usage, n'ont guère de chances de vivre par elles le même état psychique que les membres des communautés paysannes d'autrefois. Hommes d'un autre temps et d'une autre société, ils y investissent autre chose, et par suite en font une autre danse. C'est dire que la danse des danseurs traditionnels ne se comprend que replacée dans le milieu, la culture, la mentalité, où elle s'est épanouie et transmise. Le lien que nous percevons entre une structure de mouvement et un psychisme est de son milieu et de son temps.' (Translated from French by Bakka)
3. It may not have been seen as necessary to argue for the value of classical music and ballet, but a parallel argument for the superiority of modern or expressive dance permeates a book such as McFee (1994).
4. For an example of the historical use of the term 'man' in social anthropology, see Linton (1964 [1936]).
5. Kaeppler was awarded a prize by the YWCA (World Young Women's Christian Association) in 1977 for increasing the 'understanding of world cultures', and the International Tribal Art Book Prize in 2009 (Wikipedia [n.d.]).
6. Janos Fügedi (2019, pers. comm., 17 February) confirmed my understanding explicitly.
7. Form analysis as carried out by the Study Group for Folk Dance terminology takes into consideration a dance instance and not a dance system as a whole (Giurchescu and Kröschlova 2007: 22).
8. Fügedi (2019, pers. comm., 17 February) explains: 'Most probably: the notator learned the dances, either from text or after demonstration. . . . the issue of generalization in case of both dances [used as examples] may have a certain validity. . . . the notation implies a

definite, strict structure that meets the musical structure, which indicates a sort of steady performance, . . . [which] present the main, let us say, the "socially expected" or "socially accepted" features of that particular dance.'
9. In retrospect, my impression is that many anthropologists did not study dance forms with an aim to support safeguarding as a legitimate task for their research, and I think many still keep that opinion. Even if most researchers see the dances they study as valuable, they may not see it as legitimate to engage with questions of value. I think Adrienne's change of mind was about the willingness to engage with such issues and was not a question of value in itself.
10. It could be argued that it is possible to transcribe a movement sequence while observing it live. It would depend upon the density of the material and level of detail aimed for if it is practically realistic. Additionally, if a transcription should be available for revisiting and re-evaluation, documentation would be needed, which is why transcribing without documentation is not included in the definition here.
11. The method was typical for folk dance collectors, many of whom did not have film recorders at least in the first half of the twentieth century.
12. Although the Faroe Isles are officially part of the Kingdom of Denmark, we brought them into the project as a separate unit.
13. A general term for the kinds of ways people hold each other when dancing, proposed by William C. Reynolds (Bakka, Aksdal and Flem 1995: 107).
14. The recording is available online at https://www.youtube.com/watch?v=IGj6k7jVd5U.
15. The video with the Ferns has a simplicity that may help to observe the svikt patterns. They both do: S – S – S(s) S – S – Ss (here with a hop between S and s) STS STS STS S(s).
16. Morris appeared on Sesame Street (Episode 3682) in a segment with the three rod muppets 'Baby Tooth and the Fuzzy Funk' (Muppet Wiki [n.d.]a, [n.d.]b).

References

Bakka, E. 1973. 'Springar, gangar, rull og pols: Hovudliner i eldre norsk folkedanstradisjon', Mag.avhandl. thesis. Oslo: University of Oslo.

———. 2005. 'Dance Paradigms: Movement Analysis and Dance Studies', in E.I. Dunin, A.v.B. Wharton and L. Felföldi (eds), *Dance and Society: Dancer as a Cultural Performer*. Budapest: Akadémiai Kiadó, pp. 72–80.

———. 2015. 'Safeguarding of Intangible Cultural Heritage: The Spirit and the Letter of the Law', *Musikk og Tradisjon* 29: 135–69.

———. 2017. *Theorising and 'De-theorising' Dance*. Poznań: Polskie Forum Choreologiczne.

Bakka, E., B. Aksdal and E. Flem. 1995. *Springar and Pols: Variation, Dialect and Age: Pilot Project on the Methodology for Determining Traditions Structures and Historical Layering of Old Norwegian Couple Dances*. Trondheim: Rådet for folkemusikk og folkedans, The Rff-Centre.

Bakka, E., and G. Karoblis. 2010. 'Writing a Dance: Epistemology for Dance Research', *Yearbook for Traditional Music* 42: 167–93.

Brown, M.F. 2012. 'Safeguarding the Intangible', *Museum Anthropology Review* 6(2): 93–97.

Buckland, T. 1999. 'All Dances are Ethnic, but Some are More Ethnic than Others: Some Observations on Dance Studies and Anthropology', *Dance Research* 17(1): 3–21.

Cowell, H. 1925. *Anger Dance*. New York: Breitkopf Publications.

Dodworth, A. 1888. *Dancing and its Relations to Education and Social Life: With a New Method of Instruction: Including a Complete Guide to the Cotillion (German)*. New York: Harper & Brothers.

Frosch, J.D. 1999. 'Tracing the Weave of Dance in the Fabric of Culture', in S.H. Farleigh and P. Hanstein (eds), *Researching Dance: Evolving Modes of Inquiry*. London: Dance Books, pp. 249–80.

Fügedi, J. 2018. 'Notating Dances from Films: A Method in Hungarian Ethnochoreology', *Journal of Movement Arts Literacy* 4(1): 5.

Giurchescu, A., and E. Kröschlova. 2007. 'Theory and Method of Dance Form Analysis', in A.L. Kaeppler and E.I. Dunin (eds), *Dance Structures: Perspectives on the Analysis of Human Movement*. Budapest: Akadémiai Kiadó, pp. 21–52.

Gore, G., and E. Bakka. 2007. 'Constructing Dance Knowledge in the Field: Bridging the Gap Between Realisation and Concept', in A.C. Albright, D. Davida and S.D. Cordova (eds), *Re-thinking Practice and Theory: Proceedings Thirtieth Annual Conference. Cosponsored with CORD. Centre National de la danse, Paris 21–24 June 2007*. Riverside: Society for Dance History Scholars, pp. 93–97.

Guilcher, J.M. 1971. 'Aspects et problèmes de la danse populaire traditionnelle', *Ethnologie française* 1(2): 7–48.

Hanna, J.L. 1981. 'The Anthropology of Dance: Or, Who Collects Butterflies?', *American Ethnologist* 8(4): 808–10.

Heggli, G. 2013. 'Brynjulf Alver (1924–2009)', in B. Rogan and A. Eriksen (eds), *Etnologi og folkloristikk: En fagkritisk biografi om norsk kulturhistorie*. Oslo: Novus forlag, pp. 267–82.

Hutchinson Guest, A. 2014. 'Choreo-graphics: A Comparison of Dance Notation Systems from the Fifteenth Century to the Present'. First published 1989 by Gordon and Breach. Oxon and New York: Routledge.

Isachsen, J. 1886. *Lommebog for Dansende: til Støtte for Erindringen ved Menuet, Françaize, Lanciers, Fandango med flere af de mest brugelige Nutidsdandse: samt Anvisning til nogle Cotillontoure*. Kristiania: Cammermeyer.

Jordan, S. 2015. *Mark Morris: Musician, Choreographer*. Binstead: Dance Books.

Kaeppler, A.L. 1967. 'The Structure of Tongan Dance', Ph.D. dissertation. Honolulu: University of Hawai'i.

———. 1972. 'Method and Theory in Analyzing Dance Structure with an Analysis of Tongan Dance', *Ethnomusicology* 16(2): 173–217.

———. 1981. 'Reviewed Work: To Dance is Human: A Theory of Nonverbal Communication by Judith Lynne Hanna', *American Ethnologist* 8(1): 218–19.

———. 2000. 'Dance Ethnology and the Anthropology of Dance', *Dance Research Journal* 32(1): 116–25.

———. 2004. 'Safeguarding Intangible Cultural Heritage. The Tongan Lakalaka: Sung Speeches with Choreographed Movements', in *The Regional Meeting on the Promotion of the Convention for the Safeguarding of the Intangible Cultural Heritage for countries of Europe and Northern America Kazan (Russia), 15–17 December 2004* [online]. Retrieved 17 August 2019 from https://eclass.uoa.gr/modules/document/file.php/MUSIC165/Intagible%20Heritage/Online%20Article_Kaeppler%20Safeguarding%20Intagible%20Cultural%20Heritage_Lakalaka.pdf.

———. 2009. *James Cook and the Exploration of the Pacific*. Exhibition Catalogue. London: Thames and Hudson.

———. 2017. 'Capturing Music and Dance in an Archive: A Meditation on Imprisonment', in K. Gillespie, S. Treloyn and D. Niles (eds), *A Distinctive Voice in the Antipodes*. Canberra ANU Press, pp. 429–42.

Kaeppler, A.L., and E.I. Dunin. 2007. *Dance Structures: Perspectives on the Analysis of Human Movement*. Budapest: Akadémiai Kiadó.

Keali'inohomoku, J. 1983. 'An Anthropologist Looks at Ballet as a Form of Ethnic Dance', in R. Copeland and M. Cohen (eds), *What is Dance?*. Oxford: Oxford University Press, pp. 533–49.

Keitumetse, S. 2006. 'UNESCO 2003 Convention on Intangible Heritage: Practical Implications for Heritage Management Approaches in Africa', *The South African Archaeological Bulletin* 61(184): 166–71.

Lange, R. 1974. 'On Differences between the Rural and the Urban: Traditional Polish Peasant Dancing', *Yearbook of the International Folk Music Council* 6: 44–51.

———. 1976. 'Some Notes on the Anthropology of Dance', *Dance Studies* 1: 38–46.

Linton, R. 1964 [1936]. *The Study of Man*. Appleton: Appleton Press.

Mæland, S. 2019. 'Dansebygda Haltdalen – Knowledge-in-Dancing in a Rural Community in Norway: Triangular Interaction Between Dance Music and Partnering', Ph.D. dissertation. Trondheim: Norwegian University of Science and Technology.

McFee, G. 1994. *The Concept of Dance Education*. London and New York: Routledge.

Muppet Wiki. [n.d.]a. 'Baby Tooth and the Fuzzy Funk', in *Muppet Wiki* [online]. Retrieved 17 August 2019 from https://muppet.fandom.com/wiki/Baby_Tooth_and_the_Fuzzy _Funk.

Muppet Wiki. [n.d.]b. 'Mark Morris', in *Muppet Wiki* [online]. Retrieved 17 August 2019 from https://muppet.fandom.com/wiki/Mark_Morris.

Nettl, B. 2015. *The Study of Ethnomusicology: 33 Discussions*. Urbana, Chicago and Springfield: University of Illinois Press.

Penn State University Libraries. 2019. 'Empirical Research in the Social Sciences and Education', *Penn State University Libraries* [online]. Retrieved 17 August 2019 from http:// guides.libraries.psu.edu/emp.

Reynolds, W.C. 1974. 'Foundations for the Analysis of the Structure and Form of Folk Dance: A Syllabus', *Yearbook of the International Folk Music Council* 6: 115–35.

sawing14s. 2009. '(Mark) Morris Dancing', in *Youtube* [online video]. Retrieved 17 August 2019 from https://www.youtube.com/watch?v=MX3B31ZNXw0.

Seeger, C. 1958. 'Prescriptive and Descriptive Music-Writing', *The Musical Quarterly* 44(2): 184–95.

Smithsonian Institution. [n.d.]. 'Welcome', *Smithsonian Homepage* [online]. Retrieved 2 January 2019 from https://www.si.edu/.

The Journal of American Folklore. 1974. 'Notes and Queries. Music and Dance: Oceania', *The Journal of American Folklore* 87(346): 369.

Urup, H., H. Sjöberg and E. Bakka (eds). 1988. *Gammaldans i Norden: Komparativ analyse av ein folkeleg dansegenre i utvalde nordiske lokalsamfunn – Rapport fra forskningsprosjektet*. Dragvoll: Nordisk forening for folkedansforskning.

Wikipedia. [n.d.]. 'Adrienne L. Kaeppler', *Wikipedia: The Free Encyclopaedia* [online]. Retrieved 2 January 2019 from: https://en.wikipedia.org/wiki/Adrienne_L._Kaeppler.

Zorn, F.A., and A.J. Sheafe. 1905. *Grammar of the Art of Dancing, Theoretical and Practical: Lessons in the Arts of Dancing and Dance Writing (Choreography), with Drawings, Musical Examples, Choreographic Symbols and Special Music Scores: Translated from the German*. Boston: [Heintzemann Press].

Chapter 4

Moving into Someone Else's Research Project
Issues in Collaborative Research

Judy Van Zile

Sometime in the 1980s, Adrienne Kaeppler spoke with me about a research project she was working on, a project subsequently published by Hawai'i's Bishop Museum Press in 1993 titled *Hula Pahu: Hawaiian Drum Dances*. She was doing an extensive analytical study and given her background in Labanotation and movement analysis wanted to include Labanotation scores to illustrate, augment and support the movement components of the project. Although trained in Labanotation herself, she asked if I would create the notation material.[1]

The goal, she informed me, was to notate the lower body movement motifs of what she described as three different hula traditions. Although I anticipated the potential challenge in notating the very important hip movements of hula, I thought I remembered seeing only a few lower body motifs. In addition, I suspected each of the traditions likely used several different motifs, the majority of which had a consistent movement core, with variations or embellishments between styles. The project seemed feasible. Little did I anticipate that before the project ended I would learn a great deal about hula, experience first-hand some of the ways in which collaborative research can occur, and create Labanotation scores for thirty-seven motifs and sixteen complete dances.

My purpose here is to draw on personal memory of how my work with the project unfolded in order to describe and interpret my changing relationship to it as I created the Labanotation scores. I note issues I confronted wittingly or unwittingly and how collaborative research can take on many different forms, some that reiterate definitions reported in existing literature and others that may be unique to particular projects.

A Disclaimer

My research training and background taught me what has become increasingly foregrounded in doing and reporting on historical and fieldwork-based research: memory is slippery, and the views of one individual do not constitute grounds for generalizing across a group or entire community. Events of the past are not only interpreted differently but are frequently remembered differently. This became vivid as I reflected on how I made the decision to work on Adrienne's project in order to write about it here.

I recall my initial reaction to Adrienne's request as surprise, since I was a rather naïve newcomer to dance research and had learned of her scholarly reputation. But I was also eager. I wanted very much to contribute to the slowly growing body of Labanotation scores dealing with dance forms other than ballet and modern or contemporary dance. As I considered the request, however, I became increasingly concerned. I studied *hapa haole hula* (literally half foreign hula; a relatively modern style of hula) as a youngster growing up in Chicago, but when I relocated in 1971 to begin a teaching position at the University of Hawai'i, I decided not to actively engage in research on hula.[2] Additionally, the focus of Adrienne's project was *hula kahiko* (ancient style hula), with which I was minimally familiar. How could I meaningfully notate hula with such little knowledge about it?

Adrienne sought to entice me by reiterating that I would only notate lower body motifs of three important traditions as exemplified by three contemporary *kumu hula* (hula masters) and that there were not many motifs. My belief in Labanotation's value as an important analytical and documentation tool, and its ability to record and further the understanding of many different kinds of movements, together with Adrienne's affirmation of the limited scope of the task, transformed my reluctance to anticipation of an interesting experience – one with potential for deepening my understanding of Adrienne's research process, expanding my knowledge of hula, and providing a record for use by future researchers and interested individuals.

While the project in which I participated exemplifies several kinds of collaborative research processes, my report here does not. When inviting contributions to this book, editors asked that since it was intended to be a surprise for Adrienne contributors not inform her about their work. Without the opportunity to discuss my recollections with her, I could not validate them nor collaborate with her on interpretations of them, two cornerstones of what constitutes collaborative research for many scholars today.[3] Adrienne might recall what occurred during the course of my involvement with her project differently, interpret things differently and write a very different report than this one. It is important, therefore, to acknowledge that the reflections leading to the content presented here and the chapter itself do not constitute collaborative undertakings. I draw solely on personal memory and anecdotal experience in the manner of autoethnography, and try to avoid simply engaging in confessional research.[4] I am simultaneously the subject of the material presented here, the observer of events that transpired and the interpreter of those events. I seek to explore the nature of collaborative processes beyond the immediate instance and am solely responsible for the way I remember and interpret things.[5]

Collaboration in Determining the Scope of My Involvement

Collaborative, or team, research today often means including the 'subjects' of research, now sometimes referred to as 'consultants', in the entire research process – from project design to execution and final reporting. While this may have described Adrienne's relationship to the *kumu hula* with whom she worked, it was not the nature of my original involvement with the project. I was not the subject of Adrienne's research, and when I became involved with it, many decisions had already been made and a great deal of work accomplished. Adrienne had determined the people she would work with and established relationships with them, learned a tremendous amount of information about her topic, and delimited what she wanted me to do. There was a specific task to accomplish, and I was called on to accomplish it. In effect, I was one of the tools for her research and might have been considered a kind of research assistant. Because of my lack of familiarity with her topic, in order to do my work properly I had to tackle, at the outset, a number of tasks beyond simply providing Labanotation scores for movement I observed. I needed to fully understand Adrienne's goals, align what I observed with her movement understandings and the ways the *kumu* described and taught particular movements, and be true to the latest developments in the Labanotation system. As I confronted these tasks I felt myself moving away from that of research assistant and toward that of a partner in one, albeit important, facet of Adrienne's work.

This was evident as we proceeded with the notation and decided, together, to expand the scope of my work. We talked about the fact that lower body motifs were consistently repeated within complete dances, and Adrienne suggested notating several complete dances might be an additional, but therefore easy, task. Our discussions then focused on considering the pros and cons of expanding my undertaking. Doing so, Adrienne noted, would allow her to exemplify easily the importance of gestures and compare how several of the same dances were performed by different *kumu* and in the traditions she examined, and could provide more extensive documentation for use by future researchers.[6] But, I pointed out, considerably expanding the scope of my task would translate into time. The time required to notate only lower body motifs would be a good deal shorter than that required to notate not one but sixteen complete dances. Not only would there be more material to notate, the range and complexity of upper body movements would take more time to understand and record. The decision to expand the scope of the project, therefore, had to be made jointly. As discussions ensued, my role seemed to move closer to that of a partnership. Instead of accepting an assigned task as an assistant, I became involved in determining the extent of both my work and of part of the larger project.

As the scope and the time to execute it expanded, so too did the time needed to check the scores and prepare copy for publication. Because of the complexity of some dances and hence their notation scores, there is a formal process in place for having a second Labanotation specialist check scores and obtain official certification of accuracy from the Dance Notation Bureau. Although scores can be published without having them checked, and the checking process contributes to adding time to do the checking, make any corrections and complete publishable copy, I considered these steps important for Adrienne's project and for providing the most meaningful documentation of an important corpus of hula material. This meant an increased time lag between completing the scores and hence publication of Adrienne's book. I needed to make an argument for having the scores checked and hence maintaining what I considered the integrity of one component of the project.

The time lag also required a statement in the publication regarding when the scores were completed and adding pages to describe some of the specific Labanotation practices used. This was important because Labanotation is continually evolving. Things considered standard practice at one time change, and new symbols and uses of existing symbols that adhere to the basic principles of the system emerge as new dances and new kinds of dance are notated. As developments within the system evolve, they are published, but there can be a time lag between when they are decided upon and publication of them. Hence some processes I used might not be known to all Labanotation practitioners. Additionally, at the time of the project, the preparation of manuscript versions of Labanotation scores was done in pencil copy by the notator. This was then transcribed into inked, camera-ready copy for publication by a professional Labanotation autographer, contributing again to the need for additional time.[7] Collaborative decisions had to be made, this time relating to both the scope of my task and the ultimate publication of the project.

What began as a clearly defined small undertaking expanded, and the nature of my role in the larger project continued to evolve.

Collaboration in the Fieldwork Setting and Beyond

During the course of Adrienne's research, she studied with many hula practitioners. In *Hula Pahu*, one of the things she does is trace hula lineages – who people studied with, who they passed their knowledge on to and who they considered perpetuators of their line of hula knowledge. When I became involved with the project, I observed and worked with three then-contemporary *kumu*, whose repertoire Adrienne analysed: Edith McKinzie, Pat Bacon and Noenoelani Zuttermeister. The lineage of these *kumu* is described in *Hula Pahu*, and details about Bacon and Zuttermeister are more fully elaborated on in Kaeppler's 2015 essay 'Two Hawaiian Dancers and Their Daughters'.

Adrienne had established strong rapport and working relationships with these *kumu* before I entered the project. It was critical, therefore, that further rapport had to be established between myself and each of these individuals in order for us to carry on with the project. It was the willingness of McKinzie, Bacon and Zuttermeister to allow me into the fieldwork setting, for which I am most grateful, that established a kind of consortium of individuals all engaged in various kinds of collaborations and enabled me to pursue my task. While I worked with each of the *kumu* at different times and in different ways, their contributions to the notated material were sometimes tied to a particular motif or dance. In the end, however, it was the insights, descriptions and demonstrations of each that crossed over and ultimately contributed to impacting not only my understanding of a single motif or phrase within a dance but to hula movements in general. Thus, while I do not identify them individually in each situation described here, I fully acknowledge their direct or indirect collaboration in my ability to complete all of the notated material.

At the beginning of my involvement with the *hula pahu* project, prior to moving into a fieldwork setting and working directly with the *kumu*, Adrienne provided me a great deal of preparatory information in the form of discussions, demonstrations of movements she had learned and differences she perceived in these movements between the three traditions, and filmed materials of some of the repertoire I was to notate. This enabled me to sketch out parts of some of the scores and formulate questions to address in order to clarify some things. It also allowed me to begin to engage with issues of etic and emic distinctions, which I knew were very important to Adrienne's movement analysis methods. But I needed clarifications in order to successfully complete the notation scores in a manner that accounted for both the integrity of the Labanotation system and Adrienne's goals for her project. I became concerned about the planned visits with the *kumu* and how best to obtain the answers. I did not know the *kumu*, had not established any link or rapport with them and had not participated in the fieldwork setting with Adrienne. How could I most easily move into one component of someone else's research?

I also became concerned with what might be expected of me by the *kumu*. Adrienne had a great deal of first-hand knowledge about the movements of each of the traditions she was studying; my knowledge was minimal and largely secondhand. I wondered if assumptions would be made as to what I should know – because of what Adrienne already knew – and of what she had described to me. I was concerned about the possible need to revisit things previously covered by Adrienne, and with efficiently using the time spent with each *kumu*. There were no easy resolutions for these matters as we set out to meet with the *kumu*. I needed to be mindful of them as we moved forward.

When we entered the fieldwork setting, Adrienne obviously took the lead. She introduced me, explained a little about Labanotation and my specific task and then moved on to finding answers to questions we had discussed by using one way she attempts to tease out emic movement perspectives. She asked the *kumu* to demonstrate a particular dance or movement; we both observed and I notated and took notes in whatever form was most relevant for me at that moment. I remained somewhat of an outsider, quietly observing and refraining from intruding with questions. As the need to untangle some of the complex movements and notation decisions increasingly emerged, I decided to continue as a quiet outsider and first discuss things separately with Adrienne. These discussions did answer some questions but left others for validation or further answering by the *kumu*.

As we visited each of the *kumu* again, Adrienne again took the lead, but I now began to feel a bit more comfortable. With Adrienne's encouragement, I was able to establish my own rapport with the *kumu*, ask my own questions and demonstrate movements myself to obtain information I needed. My role in the fieldwork setting was morphing into that of a co-researcher, and as we proceeded I also embarked on a kind of sub-project – one in which Adrienne herself became the subject and I became the researcher. This occurred as I observed one of her research methods and tried to use it myself.

Adrienne uses a procedure essentially like that of an optometrist when trying to determine the intensity of corrective lens a patient needs: as the lens placed before the patient's eye changes, the optometrist asks, 'Which is clearer, A or B?' At times, Adrienne demonstrated one way to perform a movement and asked if her performance was acceptable. She then demonstrated 'the same' movement performed in a slightly different way and asked if that was acceptable or which version she had performed was better. With this process, it was sometimes easier for a *kumu* to identify or to perform herself the version she considered correct than if she had been verbally asked how to best perform a motif.[8] As I observed and began to participate in this process, rather than remaining a silent observer, it became a kind of five-way collaboration between Adrienne, the three *kumu* and me, a collaboration that facilitated my understanding of how each *kumu* thought about particular movements and what components of them were especially important within the individual traditions, as well as my understanding of hula movements at a much broader level.

This then impacted my notation choices. In some instances, Labanotation offers alternate ways to document 'the same' physical movement. Elsewhere, I describe Labanotation as a kind of translation, an endeavour in which something that exists in one medium is put into another medium.[9] Even if the media involved are of the same basic nature, as when translating a verbal text from one written language to another, choices are made that can lead to differing subtle, but often quite important, meanings. In Labanotation, the choice to notate a movement one way as opposed to another can make the difference between providing an emic as opposed to an etic score.[10] One example of this in Adrienne's project is evident in the choice of direction used to describe the motifs shown in Figure 4.1 here.

Labanotation allows for describing directions in several different ways, each one based on the 'frame of reference' used. As I watched each *kumu* perform this motif, I perceived small inconsistencies in its execution. Rather than muddy the fieldwork session with details, I decided to at least initially discuss this with Adrienne. As I pointed out the different notation choices I had, she suggested we return to the *kumu* to find the most appropriate decision. In doing so, we asked each *kumu* to teach Adrienne and me the movement and proceeded to get their advice on performing it correctly. As I saw Adrienne do in other contexts, she performed the movement one way and asked if she was doing it correctly, and then in another way and asked the same question. The movement involved a small turn of the torso, the amount varying among the *kumu* and sometimes between performances by the same *kumu*. This occurred simultaneously with

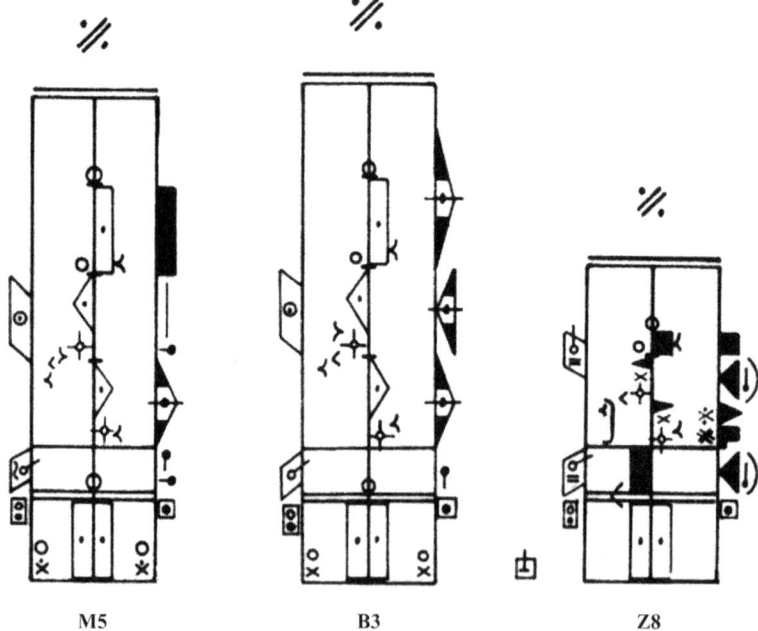

Figure 4.1. The same movement motif as performed in three different traditions. Note: Adrienne used letters adjacent to motif scores to identify the kumu *who represented the tradition shown in the score. She assigned consecutive numbers to each motif within a single tradition. For example, M5 refers to the fifth motif of* kumu *Edith McKinzie (Kaeppler 1993: 244, 246, and 248). Image courtesy of Bishop Museum Archives.*

a weight transfer I initially perceived as a step directed toward a back diagonal in the performing space or to a back diagonal in relation to the dancer's overall facing – depending in part on just how far the torso turned. But the amount of torso turn varied from one performance to another by one of the *kumu* and was different among the three *kumu*.

As I puzzled over how to deal with this and listened to the verbal instructions each of the *kumu* gave, I realized that despite the differences in amount of turn executed, all three verbally provided a common description for the direction of the step: 'Step to the side'. This directional description emphasized the lateral plane within the body rather than the diagonal directional description I had considered. In this case, the shared verbal description of the *kumu* rather than a kinaesthetic embodiment indicated a notation choice based on the body cross of axes, a frame of reference within the body. It emphasized a flat bodily sidedness as the important feature, regardless of how much torso turn was performed, and was a commonality among the *kumu* and traditions. This provided the rationale for the Labanotation choices I made and allowed the scores to reflect an emic perspective as well as structural differences between the performances by each *kumu*. In addition, a note, shown in Figure 4.2. here, was provided in the glossary for the notation in order to draw attention to the rationale for the notation used. This again constituted a five-way collaboration, even if not intended, between me, the three *kumu* and Adrienne as we clarified the emic movement description and I determined the most appropriate Labanotation translation of it.

The need for collaborating beyond the fieldwork context occurred as we tried to align Adrienne's verbal descriptions of movements and my notation scores. This was necessary so Adrienne could communicate to readers not familiar with Labanotation her comparison of the movement dimension of the three traditions analysed, and to avoid contradictions between the words and scores. Differences between the Labanotation system's ability to handle movement details as opposed to possibilities available with words emerged quite clearly. As is shown in the ex-

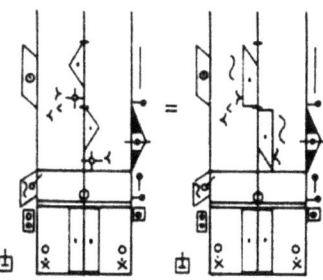

The body cross of axes has been used to allow for the supports to be described as "sideward" — the manner in which they are conceptualized within the tradition.

Figure 4.2. Example of frame of reference choice for notating direction (Kaeppler 1993: 243). Image courtesy of Bishop Museum Archives.

amples described here, Labanotation can record small, but important, movement details very easily, often using a minimal number of symbols. A verbal description of the same details can take long paragraphs and become almost unintelligible. Adrienne acknowledged this when she wrote: 'The descriptions presented here [in the *Hula Pahu* book] can capture only the broad outlines of the movement. More detail is found in the notations' (Kaeppler 1993: 253, note 19). She also emphasized the ability of the scores to record an emic perspective when she said: 'The notations can be said to be "emic," as they record what the performers say and think they are doing. Thus, the notation is at least partially prescriptive' (ibid.).

As Adrienne wrote the verbal movement descriptions, we engaged in extensive discussions to determine the easiest way to convey the level of detail important to her analysis, without doing a 'word-for-word' translation of the notation symbols but to assure that the symbols directly related to her words. Readers of the final publication can determine for themselves the success of this collaborative process, but a testament was suggested while I worked in my office one day after the book was published. I received a telephone call from a woman who said she had studied hula for some time and wanted to know where she could learn Labanotation so she could study and perform the details of the movements suggested in words but that were contained only in the scores.

Collaboration in Publication Layout

Beyond the collaboration needed for some of the publishing decisions already described here, there was a larger one Adrienne and I discussed. This related to placement in the book of the scores for the motifs and complete dances. Adrienne divided the material in her book into separate chapters for each of the three traditions. She then followed a consistent format within each chapter to present the tradition's background, repertoire and a conclusion. The question arose as to whether the notation scores should be placed within each of the three chapters or in a single section at the back of the book. We arrived at different solutions for the motifs and dances. We decided repetition of some of the motifs would be wise. Individual motifs within a tradition were placed in the body of the text in the relevant chapter as they were described. Motifs from different traditions were placed side by side in chapters in which they were compared, as shown here in Figure 4.3. All motifs were then repeated in the glossary at the end of the text, where all the motifs from a single tradition were shown together, as in the excerpt in Figure 4.4. here.

Rather than place all of the full dances at the end of the volume, we decided it would be best to place the dances for each tradition at the end of each of the tradition's chapters, again closer to the related text discussion. This made it easier for the reader who knew Labanotation to link the detailed scores with Adrienne's verbal narrative in the respective chapters.

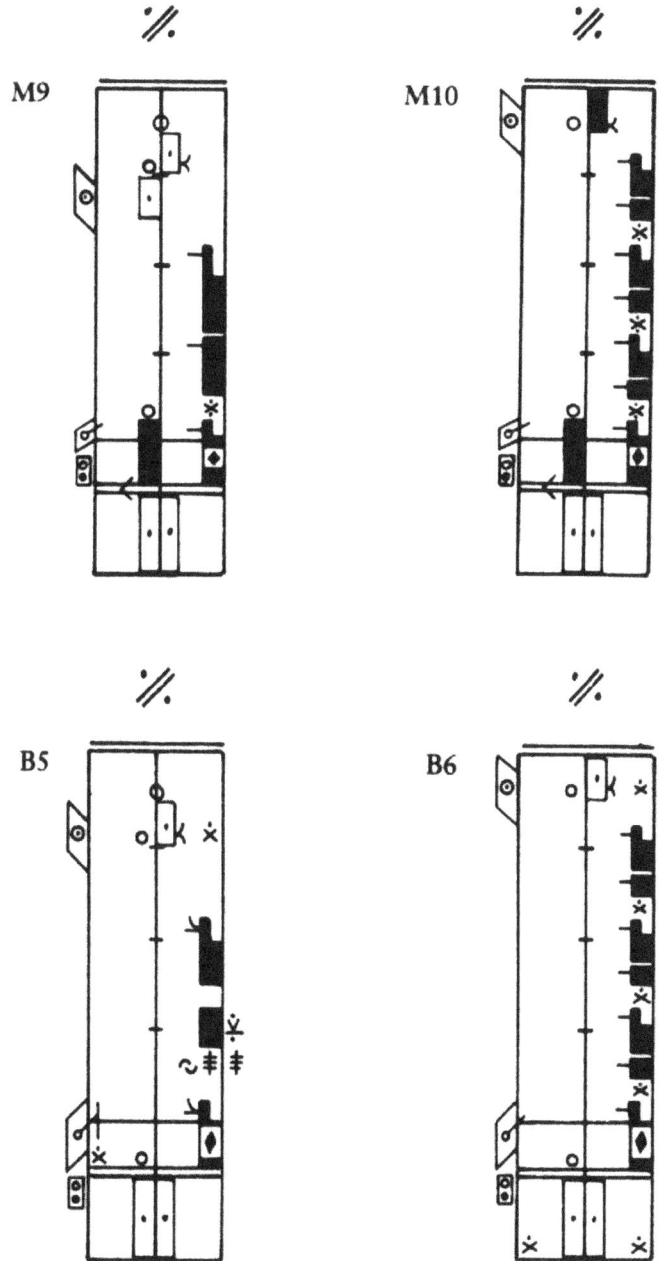

Figure 4.3. Placement of four motifs together within the text for easy comparison (Kaeppler 1993: 74). Image courtesy of Bishop Museum Archives.

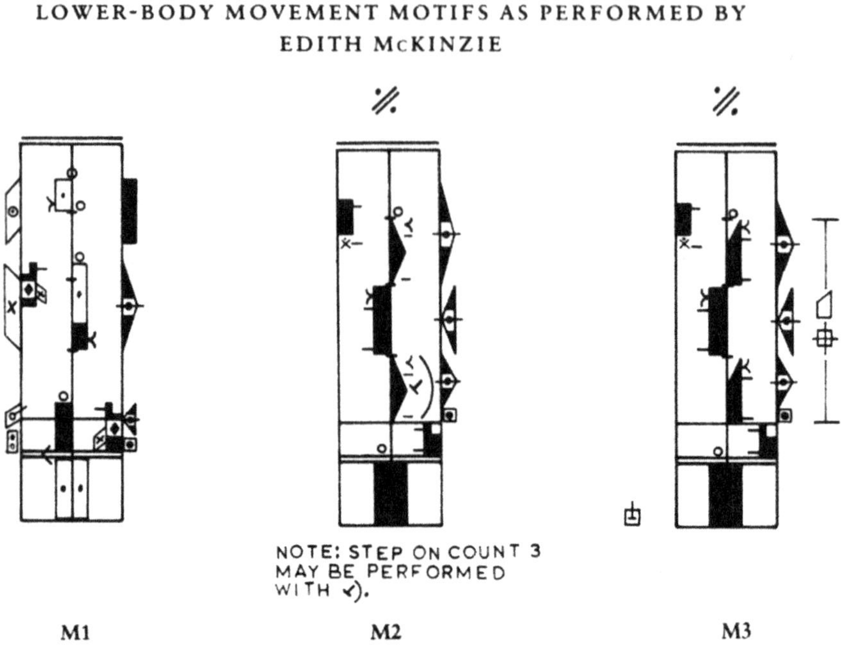

LOWER-BODY MOVEMENT MOTIFS AS PERFORMED BY EDITH McKINZIE

```
                    NOTE: STEP ON COUNT 3
                    MAY BE PERFORMED
                    WITH ✓).
    M1                    M2                    M3
```

Figure 4.4. Excerpt from glossary, showing three motifs as performed in one tradition (Kaeppler 1993: 244). Image courtesy of Bishop Museum Archives.

Considering and Reconsidering Collaborative Research

There is an abundance of literature that explores types of research methods and methods specifically identified as collaborative. As early as 2005, Lassiter pointed out that while various models for collaborative research had existed for a long time, 'collaboration with research subjects is today [in 2005] becoming one of the most important ethical, theoretical, and methodological issues in anthropology' (Lassiter 2005: x).[11] Besides books and journal articles by individual scholars, three years later, in 2008, an entire journal, *Collaborative Research*, was founded to establish a platform for discussions about the topic. The research processes described in the chapter here both exemplify and differ from descriptions and issues raised in such publications.

One topic frequently discussed is the relationship between the researcher and the subjects of the research. In the case of Adrienne's project, this relates to Adrienne and the *kumu*, whose repertoires she studied. Using such descriptors as 'collaborative', 'team' and 'partnership', studies point to the involvement of the researcher and the 'subjects' or 'informants' or 'collaborators' in defining the project, determining some of the methods used, involvement with presenting results of the study and, where relevant, the uses to which results might be put. I do not know the extent to which these kinds of things applied to Adrienne's project. But there was an additional component in her research contributing to what might best be described as a co-researcher. Initially, I was neither the subject nor the primary researcher. I was another researcher who brought with her a particular tool to facilitate the work of the project and the tasks the primary researcher wanted to accomplish. As the work proceeded, this brought the potential, and in some instances the need, for other kinds of involvement. In what way(s) could the tool (Labanotation) and the individual tasked with using the tool (myself) be most effectively used and serve the needs of the project?

At the outset, my role was to complete a task using the tool, and as described earlier here, I considered myself, in fact, to be a kind of tool. I sat apart from decision-making processes and tasks beyond that originally assigned to me. But as my own work progressed, the nature of my role changed. I needed to become involved in more collaborative ways, and Adrienne seemed to consider this appropriate. I was always mindful that this was Adrienne's project and was based on her goals. In that regard, I was not, as some literature describes, a truly equal partner, nor did I participate in all aspects of the project.[12] But it became increasingly clear to me that the task I was doing impacted the ways in which some parts of the project proceeded and that I could not complete parts of my task without posing some of my own questions to both Adrienne and the *kumu* and contributing to some decisions that impacted the project as a whole. The nature of my role needed to be fluid, moving between research assistant, partner, co-researcher and collaborator.

Referring largely to research involving topics related to Indigenous peoples and identity, Lassiter (2005: 5) talks about ethnographic research that has 'seemingly displaced the politically charged, asymmetrical metaphor of "reading over the shoulders of natives" with that of "reading alongside natives"'. During my involvement with the project, I came to consider myself sometimes an unequal partner and at other times an equal partner, but the latter only in some specific circumstances, not in the entire project. At times I read over Adrienne's shoulder as well as the shoulders of the *kumu* to determine my own movement observations and how to translate these into Labanotation. Inequality was inherent because I did not have the knowledge Adrienne did of the subject she was studying or the knowledge possessed by the *kumu*. At other times, I had to read alongside both Adrienne and the *kumu*, especially to arrive at emic perspectives. This was critical because my knowledge specifically related to the tool I brought to the project, and I needed to serve Adrienne's project and also take advantage of the opportunities Labanotation provided.

In Adrienne's essay that discusses Bacon, Zuttermeister and other *kumu* who serve as the basis for much of her work, she makes a point of acknowledging their involvement in the *Hula Pahu* book: 'We all worked together on my *Hula Pahu* book, because they wanted this material to be preserved as they taught it, along with their insights. This article [the 2015 essay] is an offshoot of our work together and was approved by Pat Bacon and Noenoelani Zuttermeister' (Kaeppler 2015: 206).

During the entire process of the notation component of Adrienne's project, I was cognizant of the fact that the *kumu*, unlike 'subjects' in research that is reported largely in words, could not read my version of what they did. While they contributed to what I notated by virtue of the equal, collaborative research relationship we had established, they could not validate or question what I ultimately did. Unlike Adrienne's ability to obtain their approval of her verbal work, they had to trust that my work adequately represented their repertoire and the tradition they each represented, and our relationship was distinctly unequal.[13] The latter is what contributed, in part, to my concern with having the scores checked and certified as well as with spending considerable time with Adrienne assuring that her verbal descriptions and my scores, apart from level of detail, said the same things.[14]

In the case of Adrienne's *hula pahu* project, I consider myself overall to have been what Lassiter (2005: 13, 24) describes as a 'consultant' or 'co-intellectual'. But unlike Lassiter, I consider these attributes both positive and appropriate in this case. The issue was not equality in the total project but rather our flexibility to allow equal participation when it was relevant, given the nature of what I could contribute. This, I believe, is what Lassiter (2005: 77) refers to as 'cointerpretation' and what I have described here as a co-researcher. For Adrienne's project, it applies specifically to understanding movement and translating it into both words and Labanotation.

The *hula pahu* project is Adrienne's project. In this chapter, I am subject, topic and researcher. The success of *this* collaboration is based on whether or not I was able to move back and forth between these three roles and allow them to interact – indeed, collaborate – with each other. Perhaps the content presented here and the way the chapter is presented constitute yet another kind of collaborative research.

Judy Van Zile is Professor Emerita of Dance at the University of Hawai'i at Mānoa. A Fellow of the International Council for Kinetography Laban, she holds Advanced Level and Teacher certification in Labanotation. Her research centres on Asia, particularly South Korea (for which she received a special award in 2017 from the Korea Dance Critics Society), and embraces movement analysis and documentation while focusing on issues of identity and change. She has published widely in journals and book chapters, including translation into French, Korean, Japanese and Chinese. Author of *The Japanese Bon Dance in Hawai'i*, her book *Perspectives on Korean Dance* earned an Outstanding Publication Award from the Congress on Research in Dance. She has served as consultant on dance projects in Asia, Australia and the US, for five years was editor of *Dance Research Journal*, and has done guest presentations and teaching in the US, Europe and Asia.

Notes

1. Adrienne's initial work on Tongan dance was based heavily on movement analysis and Labanotation. This was part of her doctoral degree, completed at the University of Hawai'i in 1967. Portions of her dissertation were subsequently published in a journal article in 1972. Because her study of Labanotation and her Tongan research occurred considerably earlier than her *hula pahu* project, it is possible she considered currency of knowledge of practices in the Labanotation system when asking me to do the Labanotation for *Hula Pahu*. The system is constantly evolving, and since my studies and usage of it were considerably more recent than hers, I was more familiar with developments that might prove useful to the project.
2. I felt that while knowledge of hula was certainly important to my position as a dance professor at the University of Hawai'i, it would be best for me to remain outside some of the political ramifications of engaging deeply with participating in and researching about hula until I had a better understanding of the local dancescape. Hence, my familiarity with hula was based on an almost osmosis process that comes from living in Hawai'i for an extended period of time and on seeing hula in the many contexts in which it exists there, as well as reading and attending as many lectures, discussions and presentations about hula as I could.
3. Definitions of collaborative research have evolved over time, with emphases shifting. See, for example, Lassiter (2005), which includes a substantial discussion and bibliography of related work.
4. For discussions of autoethnography, see, for example, Adams, Holman Jones and Ellis (2015), Chang (2008), Ellis and Bochner (2000), Ellingson and Ellis (2008), Lassiter (2005) and Maréchal (2010). For a discussion of confessional research, see, for example, Lassiter (2005: xx, 107). I use the concept of autoethnography here to describe my reflection, considerably after the fact, on my own experiences during a research process in order to see what light such reflection might shed on that process, and hence on future undertakings. I seek to contribute to knowledge about different kinds of collaborative research. My focus during the hula project was on tackling the work at hand. While I took copious notes on details relating to the production of the final notation scores, I did not take notes during the course of fieldwork to record my own process of what I was doing and experiencing. I never envisioned writing a reflective piece such as this one.
5. For comments on confessional research and the idea of the self as a spectator of the self, see Behar, quoted in Lassiter (2005: 110, 115). Behar also comments on going beyond 'navel-gazing' to explore larger issues and the challenges in diverting attention toward the self and away from the larger issues (ibid.).
6. I use 'the same dance' here to refer to four different choreographies of dances identified as 'entrance dances', three different choreographies identified and performed to the chant identified as Kaululua, two different choreographies identified and performed to the chant identified as 'Au'a 'ia, and two different choreographies identified and performed to the

chant A Koʻolau Au. In doing so, I recognize that I base the notion of 'the same' on the title of the dances. Others may consider each of these instances 'different dances' based on the differing choreographies. The occurrence of differing choreographies for the same chanted or sung text is common in hula and is seen in the choreography of different *kumu* as well as when performing movement to the same text when both are performed in *kahiko*, or ancient style, as opposed to ʻ*auana*, or modern style. See the discussions in Adrienne's book for details relating to the same dances as performed in different hula traditions.
7. Nowadays the time needed to prepare final copy is reduced by virtue of computer software that enables the notator herself to produce camera-ready copy as she works. Statements regarding autography, score certification, time frame for practices used in the scores and a number of other explanations are provided in the Labanotation glossary on pages 238–42 of Kaeppler's book. I am grateful to Irene Politis, who created the camera-ready score copy for the book, all of which was drawn manually by her.
8. For a discussion regarding providing movement information and corrections kinaesthetically versus verbally, see Van Zile (2014).
9. See Van Zile (1985/1986, 1999, 2014, 2018).
10. Besides Adrienne's early work on Tongan dance, Farnell (1995) provides important examples of this from her work with Plains Indian Sign Language.
11. Although referring specifically to anthropology, his comments focus on ethnographic research – a type of research directly relevant to the disciplines known as ethnomusicology and dance ethnology, ethnochoreology or dance anthropology.
12. In his 2005 publication, Lassiter discusses issues of equal partnership throughout the volume, referring to his own work as well as to the writings of many other scholars whose works represent many different areas of research.
13. Dance notation scores are generally created by individuals other than the creators, and frequently performers, of the dances they record. Although not discussed specifically in terms of equality and ethics, these matters are addressed in my 1985/1986 article 'What is the Dance', as well as in Farnell's work on Plains Indian Sign Language.
14. Lucy Venable (1926–2019), former Professor and then Professor Emerita, Ohio State University, checked the scores. It is important to note, however, that in this case the checking was to validate accuracy of Labanotation practices and an assumed understanding, on her part, of the movement intention. A different level of checking can be obtained if the score checker looks at the material notated either as performed live or filmed, to see that the notation precisely represents the movement performed. Although Venable did not do this more specific level of checking, we did communicate verbally on a number of occasions when she asked if what she understood the symbols to be saying was, indeed, what I had intended. Venable was an extremely accomplished notation specialist but only very broadly familiar with hula. Her task, therefore, was tremendous, and I am extremely grateful for the time she took to assure a high level score accuracy.

References

Adams, T. E., S.L. Holman Jones and C. Ellis. 2015. *Autoethnography: Understanding Qualitative Research*. New York: Oxford University Press.

Chang, H. 2008. *Autoethnography as Method*. Walnut Creek, CA: Left Coast Press.

Ellingson, L., and C. Ellis. 2008. 'Autoethnography as Constructionist Project', in J. Holstein and J. Gubrium (eds), *Handbook of Constructionist Research*. New York: Guilford Press, pp. 445–66.

Ellis, C., and A. Bochner. 2000. 'Autoethnography, Personal Narrative, Reflexivity: Researcher as Subject', in N. Denzin and Y. Lincoln (eds), *The Handbook of Qualitative Research*. Thousand Oaks, CA: Sage, pp. 733–68.

Farnell, B. 1995. 'It Goes Without Saying – But Not Always', in T. Buckland (ed.), *Dance in the Field: Theory, Methods and Issues in Dance Ethnography*. London and New York: Macmillan Press and St. Martin's Press, pp. 145–60.

Kaeppler, A. 1967. 'The Structure of Tongan Dance', Ph.D. dissertation. Honolulu: University of Hawaiʻi.

———. 1972. 'Method and Theory in Analyzing Dance Structure with an Analysis of Tongan Dance', *Ethnomusicology* 16(2): 173–217.

———. 1993. *Hula Pahu: Hawaiian Drum Dances. Volume I. Haʻa and Hula Pahu: Sacred Movements*. Honolulu: Bishop Museum Press.

———. 2015. 'Two Hawaiian Dancers and Their Daughters', *Journal of the Polynesian Society* 124(2): 189–207.

Lassiter, L.E. 2005. *The Chicago Guide to Collaborative Ethnography*. Chicago and London: University of Chicago Press.

Maréchal, G. 2010. 'Autoethnography', in A. Mills, G. Durepos and E. Wiebe (eds), *Encyclopedia of Case Study Research*. Thousand Oaks, CA: Sage, pp. 43–45.

Van Zile, J. 1985/1986. 'What is the Dance? Implications for Dance Notation', *Dance Research Journal* 17(2) and 18(1): 41–47.

———. 1999. 'Capturing the Dancing: Why and How?', in T. Buckland (eds), *Dance in the Field: Theory, Methods and Issues in Dance Ethnography*. London and New York: Macmillan Press and St. Martin's Press, pp. 85–99.

———. 2014. '(Re)Searching the Field: "Just Do It Naturally!"', in A.M. Fiskvik and M. Stranden (eds), *(Re)Searching the Field: Festschrift in Honour of Egil Bakka*. Bergen: Fagbokforlaget Vigmostad & Bjørke AS, pp. 201–10.

———. 2018. 'Aesthetics of Korean Dance: Concepts and Techniques', *Gensha* [Journal of Hitotsubashi University Graduate School of Language and Society, Japan] 12: 88–118 [online]. Retrieved 22 March 2019 from: http://ezproxy.lib.hit-u.ac.jp/rs/bitstream/10086/29158/1/gensha0001203190.pdf.

PART II

Reconsidering Movement Structures

Chapter 5

The Dancer's Voice
The Dancing Body as Sound Made Visible

Jane Freeman Moulin

Most of those involved in the wonderful world of Pacific music and dance scholarship have been influenced and inspired in various ways by Dr Adrienne Kaeppler's long-standing and ongoing research – work that has touched everything from dance analysis, to oral poetry, musical structure as related to larger social systems, museum re/presentation, the visual arts and so much more. Her scholarship spans journals with wide-ranging foci, to the point where it is a challenge to keep up with her active and extensive bibliography and her obvious interest in *everything* Pacific. For decades, she has provided – and continues to provide – stimulating thought to those who engage with the domains of ethnomusicology, anthropology, ethnochoreology and museum studies as well as those who perpetuate Pacific arts.

For me, Kaeppler's research and comments have had a marvellous way of circling around to revisit me often on my own research path. For example, many years ago, Kaeppler called for Pacific scholars to address the theme of multipart relationships in the music of Oceania (Kaeppler 1981: v). The notion of many interrelated parts resonated with my experiences in French Polynesia, and the inseparable linkage of poetry with music and dance in Polynesia formed a crucial framework for my doctoral dissertation on Marquesan performing arts (Moulin 1991). Intrigued by the idea that multidimensional expressive culture could entail so much more, I kept returning to these multiparts and, over time, explored instrumental music as text (2002), costuming as an integral feature of Tahitian dance (2010), initial thoughts on the aurality of Tahitian dance (2011) and even olfactory sensation and the importance of scent in Polynesian dance culture (2013). In what follows, and with a nod to Feld's terminology (2000: 184), I examine the 'soundingness' of Tahitian dance by expanding the elements of performance inquiry and then view the whole within a framework of experiential practice and knowledge – moving from product/object to action (performing) and to the meanings embedded in that shared experience. It is in the spirit of *still* reflecting on these multipart relationships and what they signify for performers and viewers that my humble contribution here continues to take to heart her call of so many years ago.

Kaeppler's research on song texts as oral poetry and the interconnectedness of poetry with music and dance is legendary. She foregrounds the crucial role of dance as a medium to present and elaborate the meaning of a song text or story and takes readers to an appreciation of the sophisticated use of metaphor, simile and other established poetic conventions employed by Polynesians (Kaeppler 1967, 1976, 1993a, 2004, 2013). Indeed, the underlying goal of most dance presentations in Polynesia is to assist in conveying a text to the audience, with comprehension aided by focusing audience attention, through gesture, on selected words in the sung poetry. Hawaiian hula master Hokulani Holt instructs her dancers to 'dance the poetry, not the choreography' (Goldman 2013), and Kaeppler nicely captures it all in the title of her compilation of essays, *Poetry in Motion* (Kaeppler 1993b). In a system that celebrates the combination of the word with movement and sound, the multiparts of performance come together, creating meaning from a Polynesian perspective and shedding light on the priorities and the dynamics of artistic presentation.

Even with this expanded view of the performing arts, however, scholars of Pacific expressive culture have remained unsatisfied by the terminological and conceptual boundaries imposed by Western divisions of the arts, with Kaeppler pushing back against such limiting categories in her article that explores 'music as a visual art' (Kaeppler 1996).[1] The present chapter also endeavours to tug at imposed restraints by weaving together different threads of thought with a broad perspective of what the temporal arts encompass. Flipping Kaeppler's phrase on end – dance as a sounded art – discussion here takes a step beyond the honoured realm of poetry and the tripartite model of poetry–dance–music to explore a vital and additional aspect of presentation, the dancer's 'voice'. I utilize voice as a metaphor for expression through sound – but, importantly, not only structured vocal production. I first examine the dancer as a medium for producing sound and then turn to the dancer as the physical embodiment and visualization of musical sound, exploring phenomenology as a tool for understanding the sounded world of dance. Taking into consideration Indigenous epistemologies that link dance with nature, procreation and related arts such as tattoo and *tapa* (bark cloth) beating, I then present the Tahitian gardenia (*tiare tahiti*) as a visual model for both embracing the totality of multidimensional dance presentation and exploring dance as the manifestation of and vehicle for expressing deep-rooted cultural values that link eye and ear in particularly Pacific ways. Finally, I look to the world of experience as the active setting where the arts, the cultural stream and the different participants all interact to create social meaning, reinforce the belongingness of community and celebrate the shared relations of the performative moment. In an effort to highlight features that reach across the broader region, there are occasional references to other Polynesian cultures, but my focus is specifically on the presentation of traditional dance on Tahiti, one of 118 islands that make up French Polynesia. I am interested in the sonic dimension of dance and the dancing body as an agent for sound made visible.

Dance as an Aural Experience

In a collection of essays that explore the multiple threads of connection inherent in music and dance – including sonic, tactile, visual, relational, gendered and contextual – the volume *Sounding the Dance, Moving the Music: Choreomusicology in Maritime Southeast Asia* (Nor and Stepputat 2017) argues for an inseparability that has long been the mantra of Pacific scholars. A recurrent theme in the work is the importance of learning from emic ways of engaging with and 'knowing' performance as well as the implicit call to consider a much-expanded view of what the study of performative culture includes. The notion of dance as an aural phenomenon embraces this spirit of interconnectedness as an 'overlapping, multifaceted intermingling of sounds and movements' (Stepputat 2017: 31), interpreted and appreciated through experiential knowledge. As I will explain shortly, the concept of experience and the notion of dance as a 'socially significant space of relationships' (Hughes 2020) are crucial elements underpinning the whole.

The turn to the aural dimension of movement requires an explanation of what the world of sound encompasses in Tahitian dance. Elements of performance include, among other things: the verbalization of poetic text; music (including singing, its elaboration through improvised harmonies and the use of musical instruments); dance (including dance implements and the sounding elements of movement, such as stamps, hand claps, body percussion); costume (both in sounding props and as occasional costume sound); the shouts of the group (including musicians who signal the musical form, shouted instructions of the troupe leader and the spontaneous vocalizations of dancers and troupe leader); sounded response from the audience (shouts and applause); and oration that may be integrated as part of the dance performance.[2] In exploring dancer voice and the aurality of dance, my comments draw on my years as a professional dancer in Tahiti, multiple extended field trips and in-depth interviews with Tahitian performers, choreographers and cultural specialists – all experiences that have shown me how Tahitian essence and meaning touch on an expanded field that is multidimensional and, specifically, neither music nor dance per se. Rather, there is a place where the layers of sonic activity converge in a soundingness of performance that helps to create the potent and vital moments that Polynesians experience and express through their performing arts. The expectation of and desire for an animated sound space is a vital part of dance in Tahiti. Without this action of multilayered aurality, the presentation may still be 'correct' in terms of technical execution but seems sterile, incomplete and unsatisfactory as a lived experience.

This layered, multidimensional aesthetic includes both structured and unstructured sounds – an aural space that involves both expected, scripted action and unplanned, spontaneous, emotive reaction. Tahitians do not have a specific term that embraces the totality of the sounded experience arising from music and dance performances. Rather, the sounds that come to life in the act of performing become enmeshed as an integral part of the performing event itself – *'ua heiva te heiva*.[3] *Heiva* signifies a dance presentation, an assembly for dancing or entertainment. One does not dance a *heiva* or sing a *heiva*. By saying 'the *heiva heiva-ed*', the totality is comprised within, and articulated as, the act of coming together through dance – a realm that includes the layered sound that Tahitians view as a positive, interactive, enlivened and shared aural environment. The phrase is typical of Polynesian languages and reveals the close integration of the arts in emic thought by encompassing *all* of the different aspects of performance – the poetry, the music, the gestures, the voices, the costumes, the perfumed garlands worn by the performers, *le tout*. It is in their combination that Islanders conceptualize dance. Similarly, without a specific word to isolate the soundingness of performance, dance embodies that concept of the whole as understood by Tahitians without having to resort to separate, and separating, terminology.

In initially thinking about this topic of voicing the dance, I was struck by the comments of Bojana Kunst in her 2009 article 'The Voice of the Dancing Body' and particularly her vivid depiction of the ballet body as

> dancing voicelessly, gliding along and challenging the limitations of gravity without any sound. The breathing of the body must be silent, its physical efforts inaudible . . . gliding along the dance floor, flying in the air and touching its dance partner in silence. . . . Paradoxically, when dancing as language, the body actually goes silent. (Kunst 2009)

How curious, I thought. What an amazing contrast to dance in the Pacific and, specifically, the role of the Tahitian dancer in performance. If the absence of dancer sound is an expectation of performers and viewers of ballet, I was intrigued by the internal standards, expectations and potentials for Polynesian audiences and how sound contributes – for all participants, whether audience or performer – to connecting emotionally with dance as expressive culture and to the overall experience of the dance. If the beauty of the ballet body centres on silence and effortless expression, how does sound and effort-*full* expression contribute to Pacific expectations and aesthetics of presentation?

The dancing body in Tahiti takes on multiple roles. It is simultaneously a sound producer and a re-enforcer and extension of sounded elements, a bringing together of gesture and sound production that is explored in an important and very broad body of literature (e.g. Fatone et al. 2011; Hatten 2004; Kealiinohomoku 1965; King and Gritten 2016; Le Guin 2006; Mashino 2017; Mason 2014; Nor and Stepputat 2017; and many others). In the Pacific, body slapping/hand claps/foot stamps are all elements of dance; however, they are not accidental by-products of visual priorities, as in a gesture that just happens to produce sound.[4] Rather, their deliberate audibility also renders them actual instigators of movement and confirms sound as a specifically desired aesthetic element of the choreography. Taken to its fullest development in Sāmoa, this idea blooms as the energetic body percussion that accompanies the *fa'ataupati* dance performed by men and the related sound-producing slapping movements (also called *fa'ataupati*) performed by the *aiuli*[5] during the *taualuga* dance. The importance of movement as sound becomes evident in looking at Islander terminology. In the Marquesas Islands, for example, the vocabulary for body percussion includes at least ten terms for the different dancer hand claps and audible body striking gestures that Marquesans consider vital to the sounds of artistic presentation through music and dance (Moulin 1997: 266). In addition to the use of movements as choreographed sound, in many Polynesian cultures dancers also generate sound by means of various dance implements.[6] Far from being an incidental feature of performative culture, the concept of the dancer as a sound producer is fully integrated into Polynesian aesthetics and practices.

The Body as Sound; Sound as the Body

Polynesian concepts of the dancing body extend to the use of the body – and the dancer – as 'musical instrument', but it is also worth noting other connections between the body and sound production. First, aside from using the dancer as sound producer or to engage with external sound producers, Polynesian beliefs draw further connections between the human body and musical instruments. Second, the aesthetics of performance in most Polynesian archipelagos view the dancer as not only a producer of rhythmic sound but also as the primary source for the delivery of text and vocal music. Each of these points demands some further elaboration.

The strong association of the body with musical instruments is apparent on both the visual and conceptual levels. It is an idea that permeates many Pacific cultures. Eastern Polynesians, for example, often view drums as anthropomorphic, as in the Cook Islands where the parts of slit and skin drums include the sides, back, eyes, ears, mouth, lips, tongue and voice (Jonassen 1991: 36; Lawrence 1993: 105, 107, 113, 129). The Hawaiian *ipu heke* (double gourd drum), similarly, has a body, head, neck and voice. According to *kumu hula* (hula master) Kapono'ai Molitau, 'The first *kani* [sound] of a drum is like a baby's first cry . . . It has a life now' (Wianecki 2014), whereas hula master Holt offers a sense of cultural depth and attachment by affirming, 'The sounds that emanate out of the *pahu* or *ipu heke* are the voices of the ancestors and gods' (ibid.). Bestowed with a personal name, decorated with the same garlands worn by performers and viewed as a form of human sound, the *ipu heke* also personifies a special emotional attachment between player and sound-producing instrument. When flying from Hawai'i to perform at the Smithsonian Folklife Festival in Washington D.C. (1989), *kumu hula* Noenoelani Zuttermeister was asked to remove the *pahu* (drum) cradled on her lap in order to place it in the baggage hold. She responded: 'I wouldn't put my child with the luggage; why would I put my *pahu* there?' (Zuttermeister 2005, pers. comm.). In the hands and the mind of the Hawaiian performer, the drum is infinitely more than artefact or mere sound producer. Incarnated as a cherished being, it is the ancestral voice conveyed, manifest and revered in a consciously humanized form. Similar connections appear elsewhere in Eastern Polynesia. Drums in the Marquesas Islands, for example, incorporate decorations of human hair and bone that replicate human ornaments but, more strikingly, utilize those parts of the actual human body that are highly charged with *mana* and socio-religious significance.[7] The link between human form and drum is seamless; the body functions as instrument and the instrument as embodied sound.

Notwithstanding the interjection of percussive sound as movement and the connecting link between the human body and musical instruments, in many Polynesian dance cultures, the body's primary use in producing sound is through vocalization and the established use of the dancer as singer. Conveying the all-important song text is both a prime component of the dance system and a confirmation of the dancers' contribution to the potency and dynamism of the performative moment. With no dividing line between musician and dancer, the dancer is both the singing and the moving body.

The role of sound as power comes into play as well. Just as a big group presents a commanding visual presence and projects an image of community strength and vitality, the sound produced by large groups of singing dancers establishes a sonic power that causes listeners to sit up and take notice. For this reason, there is a preference for large performing groups in Tahiti and many parts of Polynesia. Part of this sonic power derives from not only the sheer numbers of dancer–singers but also an aesthetic that ensures all are singing at the highest possible volume. This is not the realm of subtle dynamic nuance.

Aural elaboration of the musical parts further amplifies and enhances the sonic power of dance. A standard feature of dance songs in French Polynesia is that the dancer provides more than only the words to a known melody. He or she is also expected to have the musical sensitivity, familiarity with the song tradition and creativity to harmonize freely in providing a rich multipart musical experience that changes with each delivery to heighten the overall aural experience while also responding to the communal occasion and ambiance of the event. This ability to harmonize is a socialized, learned skill and one encouraged by a society that believes 1) anyone can sing and dance and 2) song and dance performance is a way to contribute to a collective socio-musical effort expressed through and aided by the moving body. Thus, the expectation is that the dancer is a skilled singer and a singer who expertly uses gesture to share the stories and meanings of the song text.

The Visualization of Sound

From a Polynesian viewpoint, dance is not only visual; it is also visualized sound. Sung poetry and gesture combine perfectly in the body of the Polynesian dancer, helping to establish the direct link between the words of the song text and its delivery as 'poetry in motion'. The gestures that accompany dance songs are not abstract movements; they represent sounded words or the ideas underlying them. For knowledgeable viewers, the gestures of the moving body function in an intertextuality that unlocks the layers of poetic meaning. Given the complex poetic metaphors that Polynesians admire, the intertextuality of gesture allows the informed viewer to move beyond the obvious and to delight in added levels of song comprehension. Those with in-depth knowledge of the text and the system of gestures derive additional layers of meaning.[8]

While the gestures accompanying song provide the link between dance movement and musical sound, one genre of Tahitian dance – the *'ōte'a* – underscores a perspective that amplifies how sound can be visualized through the dancer's body as a representation of text. Acknowledging that the movements of dance in sung genres illuminate the meaning of the song text subsequently raises questions concerning the purpose of textless dance, specifically the *'ōte'a*, a choreographed, large group dance accompanied by a drumming ensemble. Three features of the dance hint at connections to the world of words. First, Lawrence (1992: 133) points out that on Manahiki (in the Cook Islands), the related *fōtea* and *hupahupa* dances are based on rhythms associated with chanted texts, with the rhythms of the drums following closely the speech rhythms of the text. This information potentially explains Tahitians' use of the term *pehe* (a song; to sing) to designate the drumming rhythms that accompany the *'ōte'a* dance and hints that perhaps these dances – whether at point of origin or at subsequent destinations where they travelled – were not always devoid of performed words.[9] Preliminary research by Wehrman (1996) establishes a link between drum rhythms and the normative speech patterns of the Tahitian language, meaning that although text is not present as articulated words in *'ōte'a* dances, it may still be present as an underlying system of linguistically organized rhythmic sound. This supposition supports the comments of Tahiti's best-known choreographer, the late Coco Hotahota, who insisted that the slit-drums accompanying the *'ōte'a* dance 'speak' (Terau Piritua 2020, pers. comm., 20 February). Second, there is evidence from the Marquesas Islands that the gestures and arm positions of the *tapriata*[10] (also *tapiriata*) – a dance related to the *'ōte'a* and imported from Tahiti in the late 1800s – may have been influenced by the alphabetical code of the word-based semaphore practised on the European ships that visited the islands (Handy 1923: 308). Some dance movements still known in the Marquesas actually spell out words, something resembling movements for the song 'YMCA'. The signal code illustrated by Handy (Figure 5.1.), and purportedly based on semaphore, certainly aligns with known dance positions of twentieth- and twenty-first-century *ōteʻa*. Third, although the *ōteʻa* has developed in modern Tahiti as a textless dance, it nevertheless intends to convey a larger overall story through movement and music. In both contemporary interpretation and what we might assume to have been historical practice (as seen through terminology and associated dance styles), the dancer still relates a word-based text visualized in the realm of dance – even when audible words are not present. In addition, an introduction to the overall story or theme of the *ōteʻa* or overall performance may be communicated verbally through the art of *ōrero* (oratory) that precedes the dance but is tied to it as part of the overall presentation.

While the movements of the *ōteʻa* performer allow the dancer's voice to exist as visual rather than sung expression, this visual plane is certainly not devoid of sound. Rather, dancer voice is informed and shaped by a thorough understanding

Figure 5.1. Signal code used in the tapriata *(also* tapiriata) *dance (Handy 1923: 308).*

of how sound prompts certain physical actions. Underscoring the multimodal nature of perception, Jordan (2011) addresses a phenomenon known in psychology as 'visual capture', in which 'coincident sound and movement is perhaps experienced as a perceptual unity' and 'capitalizes on a model of optimal combination . . . [that] combines the information from each medium into a composite interpretation that makes the most sense' (Fogelsanger and Afanador 2006: 6).

> In other words, visual stimuli . . . are strong enough to influence people to interpret simultaneously presented auditory stimuli as somehow related. The phenomenon can also work in the opposite direction, as "auditory capture", sound stimuli affecting our perception of visual information. (Jordan 2011: 50)

Movement in the *'ōte'a* is tied inseparably to the percussive sounds of the drums and to a set of shared expectations surrounding the interpretation of the drum rhythms. Through movement, the dancer *becomes* the physical embodiment and visualization of the musical sound, the medium that allows the audience to perceive the rhythm as interpreted and portrayed by a particular dancer. There is flexibility and room for creativity, but major departures from the norm require the dancer or choreographer to offer a convincing and stimulating way to *see* the sound in a new light. The movements of the dance provide coherency to the structure of the drumming patterns as well as the specific occurrence and aural characteristics of the sound, the whole functioning as an amplification of the *pehe* through the body's conveyance of the audible.[11] In a good Tahitian dancer, movement and sound are one and must match up perfectly. In the words of Berger (2015), 'Here, the body is not an output device for some underlying musical cognition; rather, it is the social and musical means by which music structure itself is created.' The body becomes the medium through which music is understood, communicated, visualized and made meaningful by the audience.

Audible shouts of performers and audience add further layers of sound and expand the aural space to create bonds within and between the interacting groups. Part of this aural environment includes the various shouts of the musicians as they cue each other and the dancers. Shouts may indicate upcoming drum patterns as well as sectional divisions of the music, such as the closing formula that will either terminate the dance or provide a structural 'comma' before introducing a new rhythmic pattern. Dancers must know how to respond to these cues because, apart from highly formalized occasions, musicians have some freedom to modify the music in response to the physical or artistic needs of the moment. Given this flexibility, the shouts become an indispensable element that makes musical structure apparent and renders cues an integral part of the overall soundingness of the dance. Encouraging calls or instructions from the *ra'atira* (director), who is an onstage performer in the troupe at grand events, further enliven presentation and invigorate the performers. In addition, the spontaneous vocalizations of the dancers and the *ra'atira* allow them to express individual emotive reactions to the feelings produced through the act of dancing; such shouts also stimulate other dancers and establish a meshwork (Ingold 2007: 81, 84) of multiple, direct, personal, emotional and verbalized connections to the audience, within and between different sets of performers, and between individual performers. In short, many layers of sound that stretch beyond instrumental music or sung text are essential to the event. An enthusiastic director and rousing musicians animate the dance and energize the dancers, who – through actions and vocalizations – generate emotive reactions in the audience and in fellow performers. The audience responds vocally when moved or to give encouragement, creating a shared interactive space that is an accepted and expected part of the sociality of performance.

By considering dancer 'voice' and 'soundingness' as vehicles for expressing the deep-rooted cultural values surrounding artistic presentation, the soundscape of Tahitian dance broadens extensively. The spontaneous and exuberant shouts of the dancers or audience, the musicians' cues, and inspiring calls of the *ra'atira* (director) are all part of the interactive social space that is performance. The soundings reinforce dance as a relational experience and underscore the value of those created relationships.

Understanding Soundingness and the Phenomenal Body

Scholars of music deal primarily with structured sound – whether precomposed or improvised – and it is easy to overlook or place less analytical importance on things like dance gestures as sound, the cues, shouts and grunts of performers, or the yells from the audience. In earlier work, I initially drew on a multidimensional approach to Polynesian performing arts in an effort to extend the analytical focus to include such additional elements as colour, fragrance and costume materials. Kunst's article (2009) on silence, however, forced me to realize that I did not include soundingness as a point of investigation, despite its ubiquitousness in Tahitian dance and accepted place in audience reactions to artistic presentation. Recognizing the central place that sound – in its many forms – assumes in Polynesian views of dance in turn prompts an adjustment in scholarly approach. In exploring this realm, I admit to having less concern with definitions and theories of sound than with an interest with its actual use and with the process of sounding. My intent is to recognize and guide understanding of the *action* over concepts of sound as an object. This emphasis harkens back to the Polynesian valorization of process as a highlight of performance and as integral to *'ite* (knowledge, understanding) as well as Kaeppler's (1996: 140) statement 'this art lies in the process of performing'.

Berger's work, *Stance* (2009), encompasses this notion of process and the need to recognize fully its importance, not as the study of the products of texts (used in its wide sense) but as 'the product of texts *in experience*' (ibid.: IX). Acknowledging the role of phenomenology in understanding the lived meanings created through expressive culture, he further elaborates: 'By the phrase *structures of experience* I mean something very specific: the relationships between parts in experience and the ways in which awareness is shaped and organized' by 'socially situated people [who] engage with texts and bring them into lived experiences' (ibid.: xi–xii). He argues for the importance of considering these structures of experience and contends, 'if we fail to account for such structures, many of the most powerful elements of artistic behavior become inaccessible or mysterious' (ibid.: xii).

Embracing these ideas posits that experiencing the soundings of dance is part of multidimensional performance in the Pacific. This approach, however, moves beyond the individual multiparts to that experiential place where these parts find value and significance through actions that resonate with Islander performers and audiences. For example, the shouted elements are an important part of the performer/audience encounter for Tahitians, both for those who express themselves vocally as well as for those who appreciate these additions as part of the overall experience. Not only does the director animate the moment with calls of encouragement or directive but the musicians' cues, the dancers' spontaneous vocalizations and yelled responses of the audience all contribute to both the sounding of artistic presentation and to the creation of feelings and meanings derived from it. The dancer's voice, thus, gives rise to audience voice in the interactive, shared space of performance. In French Polynesia, the synergistic aurality of singing dancers, sonic power with multipart elaboration, instrumental accompaniment, sounded gestures, musician cues, *ra'atira* (director) calls and spontaneous shouts of dancer excitement and audience reaction become part of a vibrant experience in which the dancer's voice and multiple types of sound are crucial to the social relationships and interactivity of the performative moment. A soundless delivery of dance does not exist in the framework of traditional Tahitian dance. In fact, even a presentation that includes singing with accompanying gestures and music would, for Tahitian audiences, feel somehow flat and sorely lacking if the other elements were absent. Without the range of expected aurality, the audience does not recognize and sense the socially created meanings that are both crucial to enjoyment and anticipated as part of the shared experience.[12]

This focus on connections and experience returns discussion firmly to the realm of phenomenology and what it holds as promise for understanding Pacific temporal arts. Turning to Merleau-Ponty's view of perception as an act that engages the *entire* body, the idea of intertwined senses emerges:

> each sensation gives us a particular manner of being in space and, in a certain sense, of creating space. It is neither contradictory nor impossible that each sense constitutes a small world within the larger one, and it is even because of its particularity that it is necessary to the whole

and that each sensation opens onto the whole. (Merleau-Ponty 2012 [1945]: 230)

Those interested in multimodal approaches argue for a view that recognizes an interlinked world of sensory perception. Simonett (2014: 120) reminds us: 'Studies in neuropsychology have shown that in perceptual practice our senses cooperate so closely, and with such overlap of function, that their perceptive contributions are impossible to tease apart. Seeing, then, is a kind of hearing and hearing a kind of seeing.' It is a conclusion that supports Carman's summarization of Merleau-Ponty's core philosophy of perception as being 'both intentional and bodily, both sensory and motor, and so neither merely subjective nor objective, inner nor out, spiritual nor mechanical' (Carman 2012: XIII). In an increasingly entangled meeting of related fields, cross-modal investigations into music and gesture, embodiment, intercorporeality, cognitive musicology, choreomusicology and multisensory integration and imagery search for more comprehensive ways to understand and speak about music, bodies and performativity.[13] Works by Sheets-Johnstone (1966, 1984) and Fraleigh (1987, 1998) underscore the need to engage with phenomenology as it applies to perception, experience and corporeality, while a new generation of scholars has come forward to question certain precepts, including: its universalist values, first-person perspective, notion of aesthetic reception being located in the body (now proven by cognition studies to be a function of the brain) and even assumptions about the primacy of the body (summarized in Franko 2011). In response to such challenges and the needs of new avenues of inquiry over the years (such as embodied cognition or kinaesthetic empathy), new scholarship continues to reinterpret, reshape and reuse phenomenology as a dynamic methodology for writing and thinking about dance (Kozel 2007; Legrand and Ravn 2009; Pakes 2011; Rothfield 2010; Warburton 2011).

Merleau-Ponty views language as a central feature of culture and, in doing so, opens paths of inquiry to the integrated art form that is Polynesian dance. It is a perspective that allows for the performance and the performer – as the 'singer–dancer–conveyor of poetry and feelings' – to be experienced and understood as a totality, not as individual parts that detach the performer from the body and from other types of artistic expression and sensual appreciation. The crucial question becomes, how do these ideas align with Indigenous epistemologies of dance and the embodied understanding of how these parts relate?

Imaging Performance

When I first presented my thoughts on soundings in dance at the Society for Ethnomusicology conference in 2011, Kaeppler approached me afterwards to comment that rather than the overlapping circles of my tripartite design (Figure 5.2.), she viewed the multiparts of dance as the petals of a flower. Expanding my model

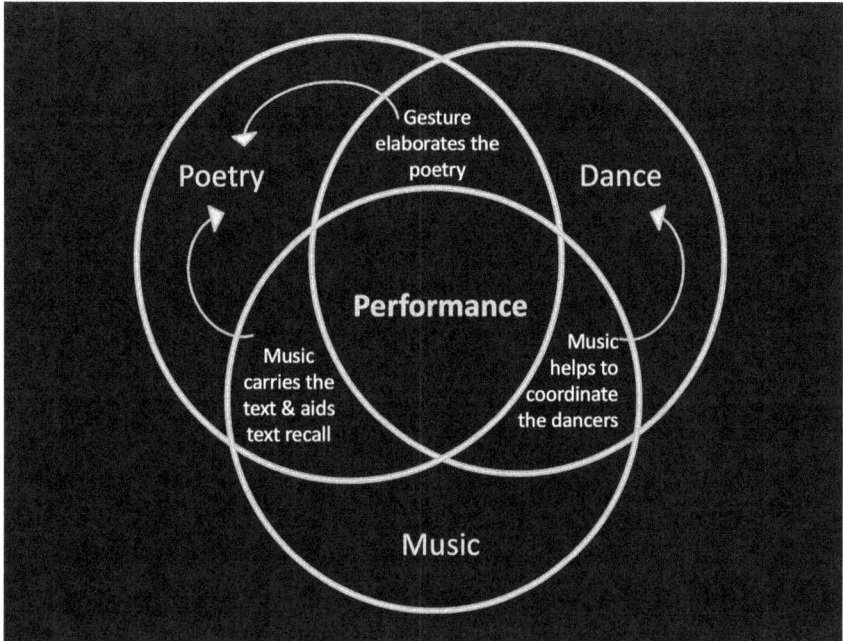

Figure 5.2. An earlier tripartite model of dance performance in Tahiti (Moulin 2011).

to embrace more than the original three areas of performative activity but still 'thinking in nouns' (e.g. dance, music, text, performance) and circles, I struggled to see how Kaeppler's petals might overlap to allow for the level of interactivity I sought between all the parts.

By reimagining the sounding elements not as individual petals but as units growing from a single base, I came to recognize that the place where the many elements of performance come together is in the *action* of experiencing, not in the fixed and bounded artefact/noun of performance or in the juxtaposition of its objectified parts. Through embracing the Polynesian emphasis on process, it became clear that it is the interactive space of the performative moment that allows those who engage in the arts to construct and value the meanings that secure these petals as lived experience.

In assembling the multiple petals of dance presentation, I found that the resultant flower echoed traditional visual motifs found in the Tahitian arts of tattoo and *tapa* (barkcloth) as recorded during the early nineteenth century. I divert momentarily to unpack some of the layers inherent in my usage of this motif, and I do so specifically to demonstrate how this shift moves to a level of cultural understanding that would be completely overlooked by staying with two-dimensional overlapping circles, linear presentations and a focus on static objects/nouns.

As a visual aid for understanding the soundings of dance presentation, I selected the *tiare tahiti* (lit. Tahitian flower; Tahitian gardenia, *Gardenia tahitensis* [*taitensis*]), the flower depicted in profile in its budding form on the upper part of an early nineteenth-century body tattoo (Figure 5.3. and Figure 5.4.). The flower is, of course, a lovely, poetic symbol that invokes long-held representations of the islands, but I am convinced it also embraces and functions on a much deeper level of cultural knowledge, experience and prioritization. The multiple uses of different flower motifs on both upper and lower body in this one drawing underscore an importance that lies far beyond a mere visual ornamentation.

The literature affirms a lack of information about the signification of the patterns embodied in seventeenth- and early eighteenth-century Tahitian tattoos; however, potential clues to the meanings of the imagery appear when stepping back to assemble the various pieces of the puzzle that exist in other domains, such as legends, etymology, cultural practice and acknowledged symbolism. For example, the elderly woman who recounted the legend of the *tiare tahiti* (Montillier Tetuanui 2016: 89, 91) specified emphatically that the flower represents the female *hua* 'vagina' (Montillier Tetuanui 2019, pers. comm., 6 April).

> The sex of the woman then changed into a tiare tahiti (flower, Gardenia tahitensis) [sic] that is where the name of the island Huahine originated. The interior of the flower looks like the *hua* (vagina) of the *hine* (woman). The flower grew, replacing this woman. Her beauty bloomed into a flower but it is a vagina and not of [sic] a face which figures this beauty. (Montillier Tetuanui 2016: 91)

In relating this story, the narrator of the legend, Ma'iari'i 'Arutahi, specifically explained that 'the beauty of the sexual organ, represented by the interior of the *tiare* (*Gardenia tahitensis* [*taitensis*]) where the pistils are, was by no mean[s] inferior to the beauty of the face' (ibid.: 93). Given this, the wearing of the flower takes on new meaning by representing both external and internal – specifically procreative – female beauty.

Looking past Tahitian shores, the word for flower, *pua,* is a well-known cognate throughout Polynesia (Greenhill and Clark 2011). In Hawai'i and the Marquesas Islands, *pua* is also a metaphorical reference to progeny (Dordillon 1904: 234; Pukui and Elbert 1986: 344), whereas contemporary Tahitians use *pua* mainly to refer to a beautiful girl – revealing what may be vestigial linkage to the notion of descendants and to the sexual organs and sexuality of women, especially in light of the legend above. It is worth noting that the reduplication of the word, *puapua,* refers to petals, the pistil (part of the reproductive organ) of a flower, and female genitalia in New Zealand Māori (Moorfield 2011) and on Pukapuka in the Cook Islands (Greenhill and Clark 2011). The symbolic representation of female physical characteristics also appears in other art forms. In the

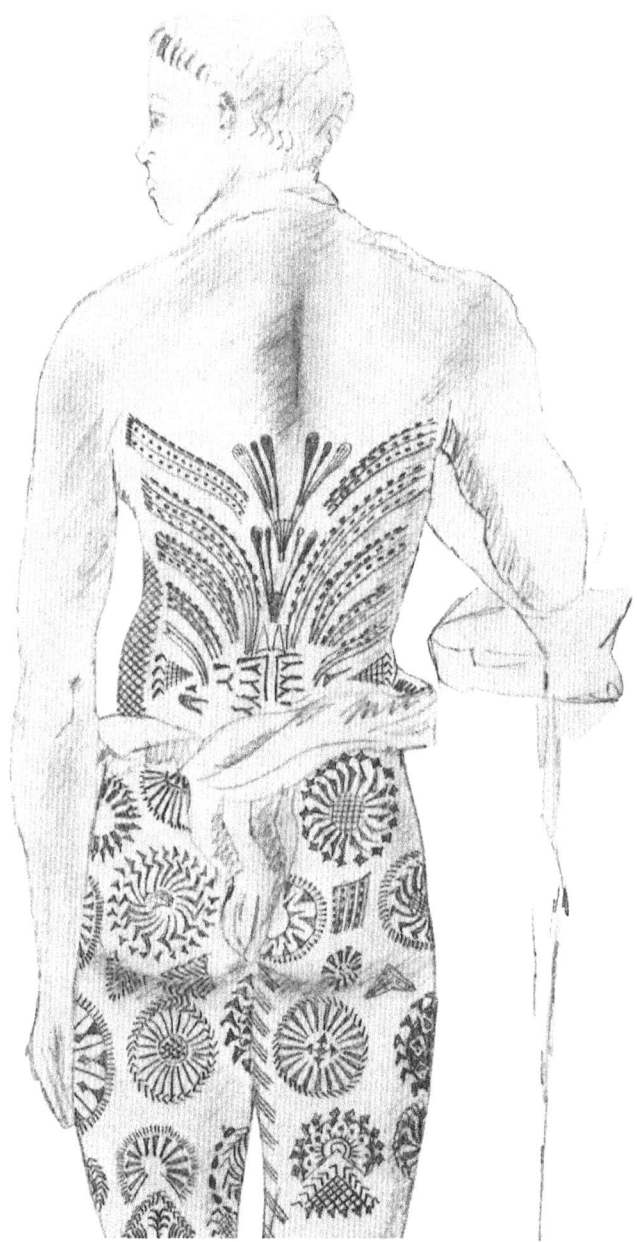

Figure 5.3. Tahitian tattoo with its tiare tahiti *pattern in profile on the upper portion of the back and multiple flower shapes on the lower torso and thighs.*
Image from Smyth 1825–26, FL3270079, Mitchell Library, State Library of New South Wales.

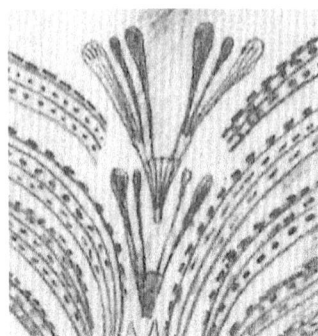

Figure 5.4. Close-up of the upper body flower motif. Image from Smyth 1825–26, FL3270079, Mitchell Library, State Library of New South Wales.

Marquesas Islands, for example, the production of *tapa* involves a folding process that results in an image of the womb (Figure 5.5.), which is also present in a prevalent design pattern, *ipu*, found in Marquesan tattoos (*Patutiki* 2018). Far from being an isolated case, this association with and visualization of the female body travelled widely across the Polynesian world, where the term for barkcloth (*tapa*) means 'thigh or groin' in Tahiti but refers specifically to the vulva in the neighbouring cultures of Hawai'i, New Zealand and Rarotonga (Greenhill and Clark 2011). As women performed their act of tapa creation, they purposely visualized female beauty when beating their mark into the tree bark to produce a culturally significant cloth, whether for everyday use or as attire for grand occasions and for ceremonial gifting and presentation.

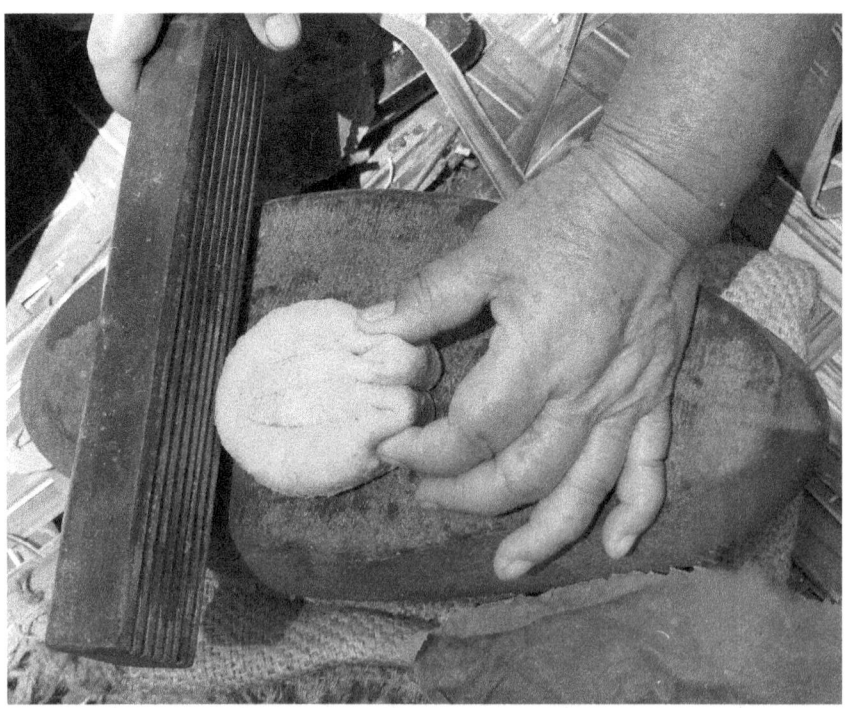

Figure 5.5. Marquesan image of the womb in barkcloth folding (Omoa, Fatu Hiva). Photograph courtesy of Heidy Baumgartner Lesage.

Given these widespread associations, it is possible that the flower pattern in Figure 5.4. references both generation and generations, and genealogical connections documented in other Polynesian tattoos lend support for this notion. In discussions about the use of flower imagery, Marquesan tattoo specialist and researcher Teiki Huukena (2019, pers. comm., April 7) confirmed: 'I am convinced that there is a relationship with fertility.' The direct connection of the *tiare tahiti* flower to the *hua vahine* certainly suggests, on the ancestral level, a possibility of similar thought that broadens our understanding of Polynesian imagery and opens the door to a range of possibilities that demand further exploration and contemplation.

The flower remains a powerful expressive symbol for contemporary Tahitians as well, whether manifested in the flower worn on the ear or in the multitude of songs dedicated to different types of flowers, their glorification in festivals and dance presentations or the delight Tahitians take in sporting flowered crowns for all sorts of occasions. Within this set of signification, the beloved *tiare tahiti* carries special connotations, with elicited responses foregrounding heightened sentiments and experiential reactions rather than disengaged facts. The descriptors provided – simple elegance, perfection, beauty, perfume (as in heady or intoxicating), allure, welcome, celebration, emotion, memories and island life – all touch on emotive experiences. It is in this sense of lived feeling that I draw on the multipetaled *tiare tahiti* (Figure 5.6.) to depict the performing moment as a powerful site for creating experience and shared emotion.

I have often wondered over the years why the *tiare tahiti*, as physical object and imagined symbol, resonates *so* very strongly with Tahitians. Without knowledge of the possible rich meaning behind this physical manifestation, however, I saw only the surface level and attributed this to merely the physical and olfactory characteristics of the flower and its power in Tahiti to beautify a person and attract the opposite sex. The notion of the flower as attached to female sexuality and procreation, however, frames the *tiare* drawing in a much deeper metaphoric sense that links present to past. Even if many people today are not aware of that potential relationship, the concept as vestigial cultural memory brings the flower, its use and its importance into perspective. I am reminded of Diettrich's look at the role of 'forged' memory and ancestrality in performative practice on Chuuk (2018a: 12–13). The performative ritual of placing a flower on the ear reaches into the ancestral world, attaching the wearer to the repeated practice of generations and to both nature and fertility, even if this is reduced today to merely sexual attraction rather than specifically procreation and generation. With a base that serves as the site of creation and connection, the *tiare tahiti* image comes alive – not as a simple drawing but as a setting for experience, shared emotion and attachment/belonging.

True to Tahitian practice, Montillier Tetuanui looked at the tattoo pattern I shared with her (Figure 5.3.) and dutifully counted out the petals of each *tiare* –

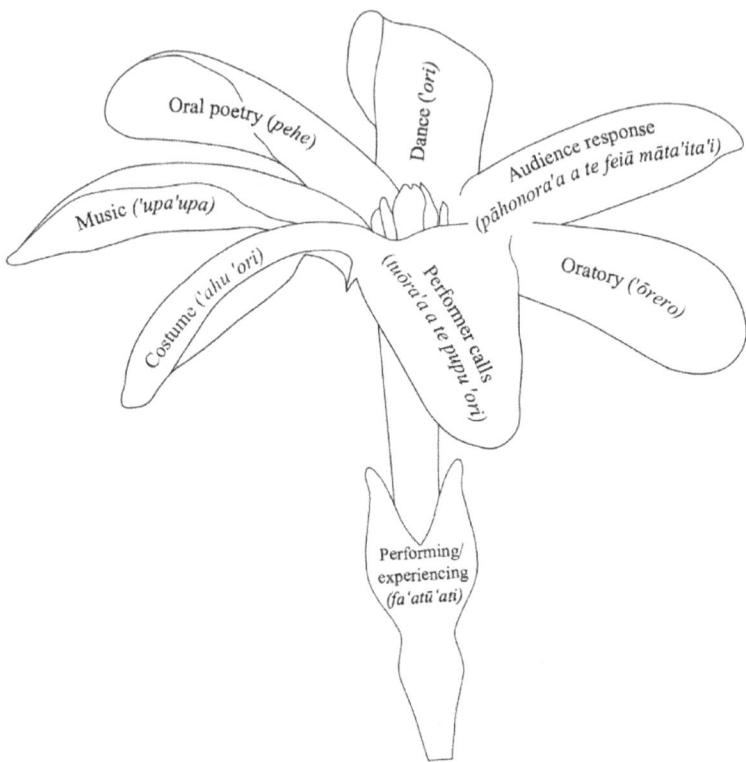

Figure 5.6. The soundingness of Tahitian dance as represented by the tiare tahiti *(Tahitian gardenia). Drawing by Andreas Dettloff.*

musing that there are only six petals in the historic illustration, rather than the eight she would have expected as a number associated with women. In the spirit of expressing hope and growth over the generations, she noted what might be the representation of a second generation (the uppermost flower) in this tattoo; her interpretation was that this flower appeared more resplendent than the one on the bottom.

All of this expands the meaning of the flower in infinitesimal ways and renders the use of this motif to describe music and dance even more appropriate than previously imagined. The flower is composed of the many petals of performance, all fused together through artistic action/performing/experiencing to become the locus of both ancestral connection and contemporary 'birth', a linking of past and present that results in an ongoing and resplendent continuation of the arts. The various petals (*raupua*) of performance unite in the corolla (*'apu raurau*), that portion of the flower that encompasses and protects the reproductive organs as the place of creation and generation. The protective envelope of the calyx (*vehipua*) at the bottom houses the performing moment and the process of experiencing. It also safeguards the ovary of the flower (*puna huero*), allowing the seed of creation to grow and to nurture the processes of *'ite* (seeing, understanding, knowing, and perceiving), thereby giving life to individual and social meaning. The flower in its totality thus connects the petals of ancestral performativity – all the cultural knowledge that is passed on through performance – to the experiences of today in a linking I refer to as *fa'atū'ati* (the deliberate action of connecting things or people in the desire for integration). The word *fa'atū'ati* demands that something intervene to make the connection happen, and that something is the act of performing.

The connection with ancestral knowledge represented in the *tiare* is an important facet of Tahitian dance, regardless of how 'modernized' the dance may appear to some outside observers. As Downey notes in his study of the sound and movement of capoeira (2002):

> When one moves in relation to the berimbau, one's body becomes inhabited, not only by sound, but by conventional movements and gestures peculiar to that sound space, borrowed from one's teacher. A player subsequently becomes a descendent from kinesthetic ancestors, a link in the chain of bodily transmission and transformation. (Downey 2002: 502)

Many contemporary Tahitians seek this kinaesthetic connection to the past and express their desire for involvement in music and dance as both an intense passion for the arts and as a way to maintain culture. Music, dance and the performing moment provide the desired link that Tahitians seek, for both performers and audience.

The flower as a model offers possibilities for expansion. More than one Tahitian friend involved in the arts, for example, viewed this flower as blossoming on a tree of culture, a tree firmly grounded in the Tahitian soil and with roots extending deep into the land. Given the strong Polynesian sense of attachment to land, these roots become metaphorically anchored in place and people. The attachment to land is performed in Tahitian rituals, such as the traditional practice of placing the placenta (*pūfenua*) in the earth after a birth. The *pūfenua* (literally center, core or pit of the land) 'reinforces the continuity of mutual belonging and assimilation between the person and the earth' (Saura 2000a: 133), creating a link between the child, ancestral property and the island of birth (Saura 2000b: 14). Families also plant a fruit tree (such as coconut, mango or breadfruit) on the site of the *pūfenua* that serves as a visual memory of the birth, the number of children in the family and the approximate age of each (ibid.: 12), but the meaning is much deeper:

The essential does not reside in the process of attaching an individual to a young tree that will grow with him and symbolize his individual identity, but rather in the harmony and even the continuity of the elements in which man and plants participate and that the burying of the placenta demonstrates. (Ibid.: 6) (Translation J. Moulin)

The ties between humans and the land, performance and the natural world, and creation and plants all open interesting doors for exploration. Certainly, a discussion of how performance relates to culture and the sense of being 'rooted' becomes an obvious focus for future research. Additionally, with its links to creation and the generations, the flower becomes infinitely more than merely a pretty blossom, prompting the question of whether the event of the performance ultimately nurtures, supports and reaches ever deeper to represent the notion of life itself.

By highlighting Tahitian approaches to performance, the imagery of the flower provides a tool for understanding not only the wide range of senses invoked but also the profound feelings enlivened and shared in the presentation of Pacific dance. It also underscores Berger's contention that '[H]ighlighting the dynamics of experience that would otherwise be grasped in a peripheral fashion . . . can get us close to the people and things we care about' (Berger 2009: 26).

With focus on the *experiences* of all those who engage in and with the performative arts of the Pacific, we move closer to knowing about their lives and priorities, values and expectations. Such a focus demands that scholars look at how Islanders engage with all of the processes of expressive culture and the ways in which they grapple to make sense of the phenomena and to appreciate them, whether resonating as openly articulated thoughts or deeply felt connections. Islanders' lives and their arts become infinitely deeper and more potent when considering the meanings and multifacets of experience rather than merely analysing the individual parts.

Therefore, with my *tiare tahiti* in hand, simple in design but rich in meaning, I extend my sincere thanks to Kaeppler for her suggestion that allowed me to consider, explore and appreciate the flower motif as a locus for artistic generation, shared experience and attachment to the ancestors. To Adrienne, *eie atu te 'ūa'a tiare hau'a no'ano'a ma tō na raupua rau 'e mahora nehenehe nā 'oe* (here is a fragrant flower, in full bloom with its varied and splendid petals open for you).

Conclusions

Viewing both the visual *and* aural forms of perception as key to understanding music allows for the types of elaboration so important to Polynesian artistic expression. Polynesian dance combines colours, surfaces, shapes – much like painting, sculpture, architecture or other visual arts – but does not confine them to a fixed or physically motionless space. Instead, the dancer interlaces these with text, movement, music and even the flower-laden scent of the dance troupe to present the whole while moving, singing and sounding in time and space. Dance not only complements and expands the inner world of music; it *completes* the experience as an enriched temporal art. Sound is intimately tied to the movement; the gestures of the song cannot be separated from the poetic text that is their *raison d'être*; soundingness is secured in performance structure, perception and emotional connection; scent links to colour, to the content of the poetic text or the overall theme of the performance. These are not separate provinces, because it is through simultaneity of their occurrence and their connection in the mind and body of the beholder and performer that they take on meaning. What we find is an absolute linkage of language, movement, scent, colour/texture and sound – with all of its spontaneous richness – in a connecting moment where the elements are so intertwined that they cannot be fully understood as unrelated phenomena. Through expression as an interconnected and inseparable art, performance in Polynesia moves to an expanded and heightened sensual plane that enriches the shared experience on multiple levels to establish a sense of community, shared values and the feeling of making (and enjoying) music together.

The consideration of sound in Tahitian expressive culture takes analysis firmly into the realm of lived experience. While the songs and their texts, accompanying instruments, body percussion, improvised part-singing and shouted verbalizations constitute the expressive aural elements so appreciated by Tahitians, an analysis of dance culture also must look to the ways in which these soundings create value for those engaged as performers, listener/viewers and observers of culture. It is in the relationship of the parts and the players that the performative arts provide a space to interact and where the dancer's voice swells to become infinitely more than nouns like poetry, music and dance. Ingold's imagery of 'meshwork' to describe the relational trails that are interwoven through experience is a helpful one in considering the resultant, myriad linkings of people and performative elements prompted by the 'journey' performers and audiences share in that moment of performance (Ingold 2007: 81–84). This is echoed as well by philosopher Alva Noë, who describes the transformation that takes place: 'It's understanding; it's seeing connections, it's knowing your way around' (Noë 2008 at 14:14.). Performers and audience enter a space of 'trying to make worlds, enact experience' (ibid. at 17:55), meaning that 'the perceiving, the seeing is not something to catch from that coupling; it *is* the coupling' (ibid. at 5:29). It is this meshwork of knowledge and relationships that Diettrich also addresses in his article on the importance of understanding Islander connections to the sea, stating: 'At the centre of this Indigenous knowing and experiencing the sea are relationships and, by extension, belonging' (Diettrich 2018b: 64).

Two key points are apparent in the analysis of a multidimensional approach to movement presented here. First is the recognition that Polynesian dance involves bringing together and expertly combining several related phenomena into a total experience that heightens sensory awareness on multiple levels. Sound is not external to dance; rather, it is a phenomenon manifest through the bodies of the performers and is an integral part of the process of dancing. As an expanded realm of being, it requires an expanded perception on the part of both participants and observers. Second, rather than viewing the multiparts as coming together in a construct known as performance, we should view the performative event as the moment where the *action* of experiencing gives these parts both individualized and collective importance. In many ways, this focus on action aligns squarely with Polynesian values that recognize the *doing* of performance as something infinitely richer than only the resultant artefact of it. It is in that act of doing and being – in singing, using poetic gestures, linking gesture with sound, visualizing rhythm, appreciating the various soundings, smelling the perfumes of carefully selected flowers and fragrant leaves and the sharing of feelings – that the dancer's voice emerges as central and integral to the creation of meaning and the confirmation of a sense of community.

In French Polynesia, aurality is a fundamental element of the meaningful context created through dance presentation; it is also a socially approved expression of inner feelings within the framework of lived experience and the social relationships established through the multiparts of artistic expression. As scholars continue to explore the multidimensions of music and dance called for by Kaeppler so long ago, we must remain open to new paths that lead us to an enhanced understanding of Polynesian arts and the people who produce and support them. It is through a broad appreciation of dancer voice, the many soundings of performance and the action of shared experience that the multiple values of Tahitian performative arts are revealed to scholars and admired by Islander audiences.

Acknowledgements

I acknowledge with deepest gratitude my Tahitian teachers in music and dance and the continued conversations and exchange of ideas over the years with many Tahitian colleagues, who have contributed to my understanding of Tahiti's performative arts. The *tiare* model presented here represents the thoughts and efforts of all of those who so kindly shared their resources, ideas and knowledge, including Véronique Clément, Teiki Huukena, Michael Koch, Denise and Robert Koenig, Lars Krutak, Heremoana Maamaatuaiahutapu, Vavitu Mooria, Vāhi Tuheiava Richaud, Heretu Tetahiotupa and Natea Montillier Tetuanui. A very special thanks goes to Vāhi and Natea for their careful consideration of language questions and for the wonderful discussions that were crucial to opening my eyes and to helping me refine the model and its concepts as well as to Andreas Dettloff for so graciously supplying the *tiare* drawing presented here. I also wish to thank Aya Kimura and Christine Yano for their in-depth comments and feedback on the earlier conference paper from which this chapter grew. In its expanded form, I am indebted to Brian Diettrich and Kendra Stepputat for their valued critique and kind assistance in accessing resources while I was in Tahiti and for their unfailing dedication in guiding this volume through the publication process. *Māuruuru 'e māuruuru roa.*

Jane Freeman Moulin (PhD in Music, UCSB; MA in Ethnomusicology, UCLA; BA Music *cum laude*, University of Hawai'i) is Professor of Ethnomusicology and Chair of Undergraduate Studies in Music at the University of Hawai'i. A singer with the *pupu hīmene* of Papara district and former dancer with Tahiti's top professional dance troupes (Te Maeva, Tahiti Nui and the touring company The Royal Tahitian Dancers), she has participated in five years of prize-winning performances at the Heiva i Tahiti. Publications include journal and encyclopaedia articles on the music and dance of French Polynesia and the books *The Dance of Tahiti, Music of the Southern Marquesas Islands* and co-authored *Music in Pacific Island Cultures: Experiencing Music, Expressing Culture*. Her current research concerns *'ori Tahiti* away from the homeland and the history of music in the Marquesan church.

Notes

1. The dilemma continues over two decades later, with scholars bemoaning that 'much of current scholarly discourse continues to frame itself in terms of dyadic and bounded categories' (Trimillos 2017: 1).
2. The specific goal here is to explore the aural dimension of expressive culture in Tahiti; this does not negate the presence or importance of other sensory realms discussed elsewhere (e.g. scent or costume colour and texture).
3. My thanks to Natea Montillier Tetuanui for suggesting this phrase.
4. See Jensenius et al. (2010: 23) for discussion of the functional aspects of sound-producing gestures.
5. *Aiuli* dancers represent the *tulafale* (talking chief) and provide vigorous, humorous or uncontrolled movements intended specifically to contrast with and draw attention to the elegant and graceful movements of the *taupou*, the featured dancer representing the high chief. While usually a male *aiuli* performs the *fa'ataupati* during the *taualuga* dance, a woman with the traditional female *malu* tattoo may also act as *aiuli*, performing the *fa'ataupati* and showing off her tattoos (Kuki Tuiasosopo 2018, pers. comm., 28 November).
6. The idiophones played by hula dancers are prime examples; in French Polynesia, choreographers may include sound producers that relate to the overall dance theme. At Tahiti's annual Heiva celebrations, for example, this has included drums played by male dancers (Les Grands Ballets, 1998), half coconut shells worn on dancers' feet (Rapa, 2012), or wooden platters and pounders sounded to depict making the mashed taro paste *pōpoi* (Tahiti Nui, 1975).
7. Given the high *mana* contained in such objects, a Marquesan cultural group placed protective *noni* leaves in their clothing and hair before entering Bishop Museum in 2003, saying 'we don't know whose bones and hair we are going to encounter.'

8. Indian Bharatanatyam offers an interesting point of comparison as a gestural art that encompasses four communicative modes: the body, the face and movements; words, literature or drama and their delivery; decoration such as proper costume, ornaments and make up; and acting out different states of mind, feelings or internal emotions (Sharma 2013: 15). While overlaps with Polynesian dance exist, one notable difference is that the French Polynesian dancer is also the singer. Another critical distinction surrounds the notion of 'acting out'. Kaeppler has long held that the Polynesian dancer is a storyteller, not an actor: 'the performer did not become an actor or character in a drama, but told a story audibly and visually about a person, place, or event. The performance was not *dramatic*: there was no conflict, nor were emotions portrayed' (Kaeppler 2010: 188). Although modern changes start to challenge traditional practice in French Polynesia and elsewhere, this performative difference remains an important feature of Polynesian dance.
9. My purpose here is neither to confirm nor deny Lawrence's contention that Tahitian dance originally came from Manahiki. I simply wish to signal that information about Manahiki dispels earlier unanswered questions about the Tahitian use of the term *pehe* to designate the rhythmic sequences played on drums.
10. In my 1989 fieldwork, Hiva Oa residents confirmed *tapriata*, the term given by Handy in 1923, insisting on the lack of a vowel between p and r. I also noted, however, the alternative spelling (*tapiriata*) on written announcements concerning rehearsals or performances.
11. Nannyonga-Tamusuza's work (2015) on the interdependent, dialogic nature of Bagandan music and dance resonates strongly with many elements prominent in Polynesian approaches to rhythm and performance. She observes 'because the Baganda conceptualize drumming as movement action, they do not "play" drums; rather, they "beat/strike" drums to articulate the movement involved' (ibid.: 84). She also presents an intriguing methodology for visualizing how the use of individual body parts corresponds with drum rhythms.
12. I reference here what Tahitian audiences experience in a typical community performance in French Polynesia. As the event shifts place (e.g. to tourist venues or festival performances and tours abroad) expectations of both performers and audience may not connect in the same way. As Kaeppler (2010: 186) states, 'the beholder, and what he or she brings to a performance, determine how the performance is decoded'.
13. Wide-ranging works provide introductions to the fields of gesture and embodiment, intercorporeality, music and cognition, choreomusicology, perception and phenomenological dance studies (Albright 2011; Downey 2002; Felföldi 2001; Fisher and Lochhead 2002; Fogelsanger and Afanador 2006; Godøy and Leman 2010; Haumann 2015; Hodgins 1992; Jensenius et al. 2010; Jordan 2011; Mason 2012; Meyer, Streeck and Jordan 2017; Noë 2008, 2015; Nor and Stepputat 2017; Schneider 2010; Warburton 2011; Young 2011). Research also embraces related cross-modal investigations in motor theory, multisensory integration and imagery, kinaesthetic perception, and motion sonification (Godøy and Leman 2010; Hahn 2007; Lacey and Lawson 2013; Schneider 2010; Sklar 2001; Vines et al. 2006).

References

Albright, A.C. 2011. 'Situated Dancing: Notes from Three Decades in Contact with Phenomenology', *Dance Research Journal* 43(2): 7–18.

Berger, H.M. 2009. *Stance: Ideas about Emotion, Style, and Meaning for the Study of Expressive Culture*. Middletown, CN: Wesleyan University Press.

———. 2015. 'Phenomenological Approaches in the History of Ethnomusicology', *Oxford Handbooks Online*. Retrieved 27 December 2018 from http://www.oxfordhandbooks.com/view/10.1093/oxfordhb/9780199935321.001.0001/oxfordhb-9780199935321-e-30?

Carman, T. 2012. 'Foreword', in M. Merleau-Ponty [1945], *The Phenomenology of Perception*. Translated by D. Landes. New York: Routledge, pp. VII–XVI.

Diettrich, B. 2018a. '"Summoning Breadfruit" and "Opening Seas": Toward a Performative Ecology in Oceania', *Ethnomusicology* 62(1): 1–27.

———. 2018b. 'A Sea of Voices: Performance, Relations, and Belonging in Saltwater Places', *Yearbook for Traditional Music* 50: 41–69.

Dordillon, R.I. 1904. *Grammaire et dictionnaire de la langue des Îles Marquises*. Paris: Belin Frere.

———. 1931. *Grammaire et dictionnaire de la langue des Îles Marquises*. Paris: Institut d'Ethnologie.

Downey, G. 2002. 'Listening to Capoeira: Phenomenology, Embodiment, and the Materiality of Music', *Ethnomusicology* 46(3): 487–509.

Fatone, G. et al. 2011. 'Imagery, Melody and Gesture in Cross-cultural Perspective', in A. Gritten and E. King (eds), *New Perspectives on Music and Gesture*. Burlington, VT: Ashgate, pp. 203–20.

Feld, S. 2000. 'Sound Worlds', in P. Kruth and H. Stobart (eds), *Sound*. Cambridge: Cambridge University Press, pp. 173–200.

Felföldi, L. 2001. 'Connections between Dance and Dance Music: Summary of Hungarian Research', *Yearbook for Traditional Music* 33: 159–65.

Fisher, G., and J. Lochhead. 2002. 'Analyzing from the Body', *Theory and Practice* 27: 37–67.

Fogelsanger, A., and K. Afanador. 2006. 'Parameters of Perception: Vision, Audition, and Twentieth-Century Music and Dance', *Congress on Research in Dance 38th Annual Conference, 2–5 November*. Tempe, Arizona: CORD.

Fraleigh, S.H. 1987. *Dance and the Lived Body: A Descriptive Aesthetics*. Pittsburgh: University of Pittsburgh Press.

———. 1998. 'A Vulnerable Glance: Seeing Dance through Phenomenology', in A. Carter (ed.), *The Routledge Dance Studies Reader*. London: Routledge, pp. 135–43.

Franko, M. 2011. 'What is Dead and What is Alive in Dance Phenomenology?', *Dance Research Journal* 43(2): 1–4. Retrieved 29 December 2018 https://doi-org.eres.library.manoa.hawaii.edu/10.1017/S0149767711000015.

Godøy, R.I., and M. Leman (eds). 2010. *Musical Gestures: Sound, Movement and Meaning*. New York: Routledge.

Goldman, R. 2013. 'Kino Lau: Finding the Spirit of the Divine in the Ordinary World', *Maui Nō Ka 'Oi Magazine* (September/October) [online]. Retrieved 21 December 2018 from https://www.mauimagazine.net/kino-lau/.

Greenhill, S.J., and R. Clark. 2011. 'POLLEX-Online: The Polynesian Lexicon Project Online', *Oceanic Linguistics* 50(2): 551–59. Retrieved 25 April 2019 from https://pollex.shh.mpg.de/search/?field=entry&query=pua.

Hahn, T. 2007. *Sensational Knowledge: Embodying Culture through Japanese Dance*. Middletown: Wesleyan University Press.

Handy, E.S.C. 1923. *The Native Culture in the Marquesas*. Honolulu: Bishop Museum.

Handy, E.S.C, and J.L. Winne. 1925. *Music in the Marquesas Islands*. Bulletin 17. Honolulu: Bernice P. Bishop Museum.

Hatten, R.S. 2004. *Interpreting Musical Gestures, Topics, and Tropes: Mozart, Beethoven, Schubert*. Bloomington: Indiana University Press.

Haumann, N. 2015. 'An Introduction to Cognitive Musicology: Historical-Scientific Presuppositions in the Psychology of Music', *Danish Musicology Online*. Retrieved 22 June 2019 from http://danishmusicologyonline.dk/arkiv/arkiv_dmo/dmo_saernummer_2015/dmo_saernummer_2015_musik_hjerneforskning_01.pdf.

Hodgins, P. 1992. *Relationships between Score and Choreography in Twentieth-Century Dance: Music, Movement, and Metaphor*. Lewiston, NY: Edward Mellon Press.

Hughes, Teuila. 2020. 'Vā and the Dancing Body: Articulations of Current Samoan Dance Practices'. Public lecture given at the University of Hawai'i on March 5.

Ingold, T. 2007. *Lines: A Brief History*. London: Routledge.

Jensenius, A. et al. 2010. 'Musical Gestures: Concepts and Methods in Research', in R. Godøy and M. Leman (eds), *Musical Gestures: Sound, Movement, and Meaning*. New York: Routledge, pp. 12–35.

Jonassen, J. 1991. *Cook Islands Drums*. Rarotonga, Cook Islands: Ministry of Cultural Development, Government of the Cook Islands.

Jordan, S. 2011. 'Choreomusical Conversations: Facing a Double Challenge', *Dance Research Journal* 43(1): 43–64.

Kaeppler, A.L. 1967. 'Folklore as Expressed in the Dance in Tonga', *Journal of American Folklore* 80(316): 160–68.

———. 1976. 'Dance and the Interpretation of Pacific Traditional Literature', in A.L. Kaeppler and H.A. Nimmo (eds), *Directions in Pacific Traditional Literature: Essays in Honor of Katharine Luomala*. Bishop Museum Special Publication 62. Honolulu: Bishop Museum Press, pp. 195–216.

———. 1981. 'From the Guest Editor', *Ethnomusicology* 25(3): V.

———. 1993a. 'Poetics and Politics of Tongan Laments and Eulogies', *American Ethnologist* 20(3): 474–501.

———. 1993b. *Poetry in Motion: Studies of Tongan Dance*. Nukualofa, Tonga: Vavau Press.

———. 1996. 'The Look of Music, the Sound of Dance: Music as a Visual Art', *Visual Anthropology* 8(2–4): 133.

———. 2004. 'Queen Sālote's Poetry as Works of Art, History, Politics, and Culture', in E. Wood-Ellem (ed.), *Songs & Poems of Queen Sālote*. Nuku'alofa, Tonga: Vava'u Press, pp. 26–65.

———. 2010. 'The Beholder's Share: Viewing Music and Dance in a Globalized World', *Ethnomusicology* 54(2): 185–201. [Charles Seeger Lecture Presented at the 51st Annual Meeting of the Society for Ethnomusicology, 2006, Honolulu].

———. 2013. 'Chanting Grief, Dancing Memories: Objectifying Hawaiian laments', in A. Corn, R.L. Martin, D. Roy and S. Wild (eds), *One Common Thread: The Musical World of Lament. Humanities Research Journal* XIX(3): 71–81. Retrieved 30 December 2018 from http://press-files.anu.edu.au/downloads/press/p245301/pdf/ch06.pdf.

Kealiinohomoku, J.W. 1965. 'Dance and Self-Accompaniment', *Ethnomusicology* 9(3): 292–95.

King, E., and A. Gritten (eds). 2016. *New Perspectives on Music and Gesture*. Surrey: Routledge, ProQuest Ebook Central. Retrieved 10 April 2019 https://ebookcentral.proquest.com/lib/uhm/detail.action?docID=679214.

Kozel, S. 2007. *Closer: Performance, Technologies, Phenomenology*. Cambridge, MA: MIT Press.

Kunst, B. 2009. 'The Voice of the Dancing Body' [originally published in *Frakcija* (51–52)], *Wordpress* [online]. Retrieved 19 December 2019 from https://kunstbody.wordpress.com/2009/03/20/the-voice-of-the-dancing-body/.
Lacey, S., and R. Lawson (eds). 2013. *Multisensory Imagery*. New York: Springer.
Lawrence, H.R. 1992. 'Is the "Tahitian" Drum Dance Really Tahitian? Re-Evaluating the Evidence for the Origins of Contemporary Polynesian Drum Dance', *Yearbook for Traditional Music* 24: 126–37.
———. 1993. 'The Material Culture of Contemporary Music Performance in Manihiki, Northern Cook Islands', Ph.D. dissertation. North Queensland: James Cook University.
Legrand, D., and S. Ravn. 2009. 'Perceiving Subjectivity in Bodily Movement: The Case of Dancers', *Phenomenology and the Cognitive Sciences* 8(3): 389–408.
Le Guin, E. 2006. *Boccherini's Body: An Essay in Carnal Musicology*. Berkeley: University of
Mashino, A. 2017. 'The Body as Intersection: Interaction and Collaboration of Voice, Body and Music in Balinese Arja', in M.A.Md. Nor and K. Stepputat (eds), *Sounding the Dance, Moving the Music*. London and New York: Routledge, pp. 96–107.
Mason, P.H. 2012. 'Music, Dance and the Total Art Work: Choreomusicology in Theory and Practice', *Research in Dance Education* 13(1): 5–24.
———. 2014. 'Tapping the Plate or Hitting the Bottle: Sound and Movement in Self-Accompanied and Musician-Accompanied Dance', *Ethnomusicology Forum* 23(2): 208–28.
Merleau-Ponty, M. 2012 [1945]. *The Phenomenology of Perception*. Translated by Donald Landes. New York: Routledge.
Meyer, C., J. Streeck and J.S. Jordan (eds). 2017. *Intercorporeality: Emerging Socialities in Interaction*. New York: Oxford University Press.
Montillier Tetuanui, N. 2016. *Nau 'ā'ai nō te mau ta'amotu: Légendes des archipels*. Ethnologie de Tahiti et des îles, no. 1. Punaauia, Tahiti: Service de la culture et du patrimoine de Polynésie française.
Moorfield, J.C. *Māori Dictionary*. Auckland: Pearson. Retrieved 8 April 2019 from https://maoridictionary.co.nz/maori-dictionary [Based on: Moorfield, J.C. 2011. *Te Aka Māori-English, English-Māori Dictionary and Index*. 3rd edn.].
Moulin, J.F. 1991. 'He Koʻina: Music, Dance and Poetry in the Marquesas Islands', Ph.D. dissertation. Santa Barbara: University of California.
———. 1997. 'Gods and Mortals: Understanding Traditional Function and Usage in Marquesan Musical Instruments', *Journal of the Polynesian Society* 106(3): 250–83.
———. 2002. 'Kaputuhe: Exploring Word-Based Performance on Marquesan Musical Instruments', *The Galpin Society Journal* 55(April): 130–60.
———. 2010. 'Dance Costumes in French Polynesia', in J.B. Eicher (ed.), *Australia, New Zealand and the Pacific Islands*, Encyclopedia of World Dress and Fashion vol. 7. Oxford: Berg/Oxford, pp. 419–24.
———. 2011. 'The Dancer's Voice', *National Conference of the Society for Ethnomusicology, 16–20 November*. Philadelphia: University of Pennsylvania.
———. 2013. 'The Marks of a Sensual Person: Music and Dance Performance in the Marquesas Islands', in F. Kouwenhoven and J. Kippen (eds), *Music and the Art of Seduction*. Amsterdam: Eburon Publishers Delft, pp. 15–35.
Nannyonga-Tamusuza, S. 2015. 'Music as Dance and Dance as Music: Interdependence and Dialogue in Baganda Baakisimba Performance', *Yearbook for Traditional Music* 47: 82–96.

Noë, A. 2008. 'Dance as a Way of Knowing: Interview With Alva Noë', *YouTube* [online video]. Retrieved 17 April 2019 from https://www.youtube.com/watch?v=FbWVERm5bsM.
———. 2015. *Strange Tools: Art and Human Nature*. New York: Hill and Wang.
Nor, M.A.Md., and K. Stepputat (eds). 2017. *Sounding the Dance, Moving the Music: Choreomusicology in Maritime Southeast Asia*. London and New York: Routledge.
Pakes, A. 2011. 'Phenomenology and Dance: Husserlian Meditations', *Dance Research Journal* 43(2): 33–49.
Patutiki, l'art du tatouage des îles Marquises, directed by Heretu Tetahiotupa and Christophe Cordier. 2018. Produced by: Les Studio Hashtag, Eka Eka Productions, Association Patutiki, and Sydélia Guirao. 55 min.
Pukui, M.K., and S.H. Elbert. 1986. *Hawaiian Dictionary: Hawaiian-English, English-Hawaiian*. Honolulu: University of Hawai'i Press.
Rollin, L. 1974 [1929]. *Moeurs et coutumes des anciens Maoris des îles Marquises*. Papeete: Stepolde.
Rothfield, P. 2010. 'Differentiating Phenomenology and Dance', in A. Carter and J. O'Shea (eds), *The Routledge Dance Studies Reader*. Second edition. London: Routledge, pp. 303–18.
Saura, B. 2000a. 'Continuity of Bodies: The Infant's Placenta and the Island's Navel in Eastern Polynesia', *Journal of the Polynesian Society* 111(2): 127–45.
———. 2000b. 'Le placenta en Polynésie française: un choix de santé publique confronté à des questions identitaires', *Sciences Sociales et Santé* 18(3): 5-28.
Schneider, A. 2010. 'Music and Gestures: A Historical Introduction and Survey of Earlier Research', in R.I. Godøy and M. Leman (eds), *Musical Gestures: Sound, Movement, and Meaning*. New York: Routledge, pp. 69–100.
Sharma, P. 2013. 'Bharatanatyam: The Crescendo of Non Verbal Communication', *Impact* 1: 13–22.
Sheets-Johnstone, M. 1966. *The Phenomenology of Dance*. Madison, WI: University of Wisconsin Press.
———. 1984. 'Phenomenology as a Way of Illuminating Dance', in M. Sheets-Johnstone (ed.), *Illuminating Dance: Philosophical Explorations*. Cranbury, NJ: Associated University Presses, pp. 124–45.
Simonett, H. 2014. 'Envisioned, Ensounded, Enacted: Sacred Ecology and Indigenous Experience in Yoreme Ceremonies of Northwest Mexico', *Ethnomusicology* 58(1): 110–32.
Sklar, D. 2001. 'Five Premises for a Culturally Sensitive Approach to Dance', in A.C. Albright and A. Dils (eds), *Moving History/Dancing Cultures*. Middletown: Wesleyan University Press, pp. 30–32.
Smyth, W. 1825–1826. 'Sketchbook of Places Visited during the Voyage of H.M.S. Blossom, 1825–1826'. Ms in Mitchell Library, State Library of New South Wales. Items 25–26 and FL3270075.
Steinen, K.v.d. 2007 [1925–1928]. *L'art du tatouage aux îles Marquises*. D. Koenig, R. Koenig, and J. Nottarp-Giroire (eds). Papeete: Haere Po.
Stepputat, K. 2017. 'The Balinese Kecak: An Exemplification of Sonic and Visual (Inter)relations', in M.A.Md. Nor and K. Stepputat (eds), *Sounding the Dance, Moving the Music*. London and New York: Routledge, pp. 31–41.
Trimillos, R. 2017. 'Understanding Performance in Maritime Southeast Asia: Rethinking Paradigm and Discourses, an Introduction', in M.A.Md. Nor and K. Stepputat (eds), *Sounding the Dance, Moving the Music*. London and New York: Routledge, pp. 1–12.

Vines, B. et al. 2006. 'Cross-modal Interactions in the Perception of Musical Performance', *Cognition* 101(1): 80–113.

Warburton, E.C. 2011. 'Of Meanings and Movements: Re-Languaging Embodiment in Dance Phenomenology and Cognition', *Dance Research Journal* 43(2): 65–83.

Wehrman, R. 1996. 'Tahitian Drumming: Rhythmic Structure and Its Origin'. Manuscript in the Ethnomusicology Archive, University of Hawai'i at Mānoa.

Wianecki, S. 2014. 'The Heartbeat of Hula: Like Choreography, Gesture and Chant, Rhythm Conveys the Story', *Maui Nō Ka 'Oi Magazine* (July/August) [online]. Available 21 December from https://www.mauimagazine.net/the-heartbeat-of-hula/.

Young, K. 2011. 'Gestures, Intercorporeity, and the Fate of Phenomenology in Folklore', *Journal of American Folklore* 124(492): 55–87.

Chapter 6

From Tonga to Malaysia

Utilizing Adrienne Kaeppler's Analysis of Dance Structure to Understand *Igal* of the Sama-Bajau in East Malaysia

Mohd Anis Md Nor

From the 1980s onwards, Adrienne Kaeppler's pioneering method and theory in dance research contributed greatly to Southeast Asian ethnochoreology, particularly in Malaysia. As a leading scholar on Polynesian and specifically Tongan dance, Kaeppler's lifelong interest to understand the implicit as well as the explicit aspects of dance and related performance, with connections to aesthetics and socio-political-religious implications, offered new approaches for Southeast Asian scholars to analyse dance from the beholders' perspective. Analysis of structured movement systems pioneered by Kaeppler's ethnotheories and ethnoscientific concepts of structuralism (Kaeppler 1978, 1986), with etic/emic distinctions through 'contrastive analysis' (1967), inadvertently introduced Bronislaw Malinowski, Franz Boas, Kenneth Pike, Ferdinand de Saussure and Noam Chomsky into Southeast Asia dance discourse. Examples of these ideas include Boas' view that 'if we choose to apply our [Western] classification to alien cultures we may combine forms that do not belong together ... If it is our serious purpose to understand the thoughts of a people, the whole analysis of experience must be based on their concepts, not ours' (Boas 1943: 314); Malinowski's concept that 'to grasp the native's point of view, his relation to life, to realize his vision of his world' (Malinowski 1961 [1922]: 25); and Kenneth Pike's dictum that we should 'attempt to discover and to describe the pattern of that particular language or culture in reference to the way in which the various elements are related to each other in the functioning of the particular pattern' (Pike 1954: 8). These now largely accepted ideas were effective in Kaeppler's examinations of movements and choreographies globally, and they became new perimeters toward understanding the underlying systems of dance analysis in Southeast Asia.

Southeast Asian scholars took note of Kaeppler's rationalizations that underlying systems cannot be merely observed but must be derived from the social and cultural construction of specific movement worlds in order to discover cultural theories about local movement systems (Kaeppler 1991: 15). Proficiency in understanding these systems is paramount for recalling movement motifs and imagery, which come together in compositions that produce social and cultural meaning in performance. Kaeppler's ethnoscientific concept calls for proficiency in learning the rules for constructing compositions in order to deconstruct movements into culturally recognized pieces.[1] The resulting description is comparable to a grammar, which enables the description of dance to be subjected to 'emic' analyses of movement systems from the point of view of the holders of the tradition themselves. This embedded knowledge of the tradition holders relates to the cognitive learning of shared rules of specific dance traditions acquired in much the same way as competence in a language. Kaeppler's analysis of movement structure borrows from structural linguistics as an emic discourse and places the holders of the tradition as the significant emic elements, as does a linguist. Kaeppler's approach using linguistic analogy to weave movement poetry into prosaic analysis in the dances of Polynesia have influenced the studies of structured movement systems of Southeast Asia, laying the foundation for those who are interested in socially constructed movement systems to understand the structure of dance in its cultural context.

Ethnochoreology in Malaysia

Writings on dance or dance-related activities of maritime Malay societies in the early twentieth century were limited to colonial narratives in the form of subtexts of 'cultural events' for the administrative head offices in Asia and Europe. At best, these writings gave superficial glimpses of dance and music from a colonial gaze, whilst writings on dance and music in the Indigenous languages were in the form of appendices attached to reports on customs and practices of the royal courts and commoners (Cuisinier 1936; Holt 1967; Saleeby 1905; Sheppard 1969; Sim 1946; Swettenham 1895). In this work, there was an absence of epistemological discourse on Indigenous dance cultures from the native mind and on what dance meant to Indigenous beholders. This situation lasted until the third quarter of the twentieth century. Provoked by the awareness of the obvious lacunae in epistemological discourse on Indigenous dance, Southeast Asian dance scholarship began to seek new approaches and theories to find answers to their own ethnographical questions (Amilbangsa 1983; Bandem and De Boer 1981; Ness 1992; Nor 1986, 1993; Rutnin 1993; Sheppard 1983; Soedarsono 1984; Stepputat 2013; Villaruz 2007). Dance ethnology that was developed in the 1960s in North America was unknown in Southeast Asia until the early 1980s. Emerging Southeast Asian scholars from North American dance ethnology or dance anthropology programmes in the 1980s introduced dance ethnology as a discourse to respond to the prevailing gaps in Indigenous dance studies. By the end of the 1980s to the early 1990s, reference materials from North American scholars were widely used by researchers in Southeast Asia, particularly in Malaysia.

Scholarship by Gertrude Kurath, Judith Lynne Hanna, Anya Peterson Royce, Joann Kealiinohomoku, Adrienne Kaeppler, Suzanne Youngerman and Drid Williams became standard reference materials for ethnochoreological studies. Adrienne Kaeppler's writings, in particular, generated interest about the meta-discourse of dance from emic perspectives as Indigenous dance scholars searched for alternative frames to interrogate the meanings of dance from the beholder's point of view. Diachronic studies on dance, framed by the synchronicity of specific time and place, emerged from this new literature in dance ethnology and ultimately enabled new perspectives and novel research trajectories.

In the 2000s, references from European sources began to emerge through scholarly engagements of Asian dance and music scholars in the Study Group on Ethnochoreology, part of the International Council for Traditional Music (David 2008, 2010; Paetzold and Mason 2016; Stepputat 2013; Van Zile 2001; Wharton 2009). However, Southeast Asian scholars were interested in researching their own Indigenous dance traditions rather than pursuing the conventional Western-centric ethnological interest of studying dance genres abroad or across migrant groups. Southeast Asian ethnochoreologists were keen to study their own dance traditions from the perspectives of national and cultural representations and from local interdisciplinary standpoints. Scholarly engagements with ethnochoreologists in the International Council for Traditional Music (ICTM) had enabled Southeast Asian ethnochoreologists to reinvent their work beyond the conventional discourses of history, ethnography, notation and aesthetics.

As an emerging ethnochoreologist in the l980s, the above-mentioned changes were influential in the way I looked at ethnochoreology as an important discourse of knowledge alongside ethnomusicology. For example, I used my training as an ethnochoreologist to evaluate and appraise theories and methods in comprehending the dancing body as a cultural construct in Malaysia and insular Southeast Asia, while the training I had in ethnomusicology enabled me to explore the interdependency of dance movements and music as part of an integral performative entity. It was pertinent that I examine methodologies for contextualizing cultural and first-person experiences of dance to elucidate broader meanings and intentions of structured movement systems within the Malay psyche. I was also greatly influenced by Kaeppler's definition of dance as a structured movement system – a product of action and interactions as well as the processes through which these actions and interactions take place (Kaeppler 1985: 92–118). A structured movement system may be viewed quite distinctively from performances that are primarily participatory or when performed as presentation pieces for an audience. Kaeppler's description of the structured movement systems that are visual manifestations of social relations impacted my understanding of similar structured movements within social activities and social duties that may be categorized quite distinctly by culture holders.

It is within these new trajectories that I began to explore issues of the dancing body while examining methodologies for contextualizing cultural and first-person experiences of dancing. Influenced by Kaeppler, I couched my own appraisal of dance as structured movement systems within an Indigenous system of knowledge, and a product of action and interaction as well as processes through which action and interaction takes place. Being intangible and transient in form, dance as structured movement system is a visual manifestation of social relations, which deals with matters of consciousness and structured content that are both performative and phenomenological. Methodological analysis and cultural evaluation of culturally structured movement systems within the Malay or Austronesian psyche have brought me to question my understanding of dominant theoretical positions and to resituate the theoretical framework that shaped my research and writings.[2] It also brought me to evaluate theories about the dancing body as a cultural construct and as experience. Alan P. Merriam's ideas that 'dance is culture and culture is dance' and that the 'entity of dance is not separable from the anthropological concept of culture' (Merriam 1974: 17) further inspired my work to embrace the notion of dance as being a cohesive and integrative part of culture. My inquiry was equally stimulated by Kealiinohomoku's definition of dance culture as 'an entire configuration, rather than just a performance . . . the implicit as well as explicit aspects of the dance and its reasons for being; the entire conception of the dance within the larger culture, both on a diachronic basis through time and on a synchronic basis of the several parts occurring at the same time' (Kealiinohomoku 1974: 99). Merriam and Kealiinohomoku augmented my interest in Kaeppler's ethnoscientific concept of dance analysis with the aim of understanding the implicit as well as the explicit aspects of dance, which led me to look at the structure of consciousness and hermeneutics of a structured movement system's phenomena. The structure of consciousness is inherent in the mind of the dancer, whose body narrates the phenomena of any movement system. The hermeneutics of the phenomena, meanwhile, are subscribed within the emic tenets of genre, repertoire and performance. Guided by these questions, my ethnochoreographic research veered towards methods of dance analysis to unveil dance context as culture, although such analysis is not an end in itself. I was motivated to furnish data and tools for further analysis, drawing on epistemological and hermeneutical discourse. Adrienne Kaeppler's pioneering work on the structural analysis of Tongan dance (Kaeppler 1972: 173–217) brought me to understand dance in its cultural context through understanding the society of the beholders. It brought me to understand what dance means and how it is understood within the social-cultural and spatial context of the beholders. In due course, my research on Malay dance and dances of other Indigenous communities in Malaysia focused on topics such as recreation as dance, the dancing body, semiotics and dance iconography and oscillated from intangible cultural heritage to invented traditions and hybrids. My work has been explicitly ethnographic and implicitly cultural through systems of knowledge and signifiers of meaning under investigation.

Dance as Play-Performance

Adrienne Kaeppler's emic analysis borrowed from Kenneth Pike's directive to 'discover and to describe the pattern of that particular language or culture in reference to the way in which the various elements of that culture are related to each other in the functioning of the particular pattern' (Pike 1954: 8). This stimulated my quest for an emic definition of structured movement in my dance research amongst the maritime societies in Malaysia, Indonesia and the Philippines. I had to achieve some level of communicative competence in order to understand movement, performers and the observers of a specific dance tradition being investigated. Kaeppler's description of Polynesian dance helped to leverage the differences that I was looking for in analysing dance from the observer's point of view, from the various types of dance existing in a society and how to isolate traits such as movement patterns, motifs, lines of direction and repetitions as an ethnochoreological discourse. Kaeppler (1983: 8) described dance in Polynesia 'as traditionally a stylized visual accompaniment to oral literature hence texts were the basic and most important feature in Polynesia music rendered melodically and rhythmically to incorporate hidden meanings through metaphor and illusion and could be interpreted on more than one level'. Essentially a storyteller, the Polynesian dancer conveyed poetic text primarily through movements of the hands and arms. Rhythmic body and leg movements add to the aesthetic qualities of the dance but were generally not essential to the storytelling function. Movements of the hands and arms kinaesthetically connect the selected words of the poetic text melodically and rhythmically to enhance the story. Dancers perform the poetry, and the audience listens to understand the deeper meaning embodied in the allusive poetry and dance movements.

Given that dance uses the body as its primary means for expression, and which evolves through space and time, I was convinced that Adrianne Kaeppler's method and theory of analysing dance structure would help to articulate the embodiment of specific subjectivities in the Malay case. To this end, I had to understand the abstract concepts of structured movement in Malay culture to avoid assuming that such concepts are equivalent to a Western concept of 'dance'. On the contrary, such concepts are the surface manifestation of a deep structure that awaits philosophical and ethnochoreological enquiries to understand how the dancing body conceptualizes and experiences its practices. There was a need to discover how dancing bodies combined grammatical movement knowledge in performance and how performance can be understood as 'movement in specific cultural contexts'. Such analysis necessitates deconstructing the movements into culturally recognized pieces and learning the rules for constructing compositions according to the system (Nor 2007: 358). This is mainly because the shape of dance within the scope of ethnocentric terminology must engage with the issues of form and structure. Unless structure is defined through the 'emic' concepts, the form and style of a particular structured movement system may not be Indigenous and autochthonous.

The implicit and explicit meaning of the term 'dance' in Malay has to be investigated from a larger view of structured movement. The terms that are most commonly used to describe dance in the Malay language are *tari, tandak, igal, sayau, totor, gencok, joget* and *main*. These terms are local and reflect specific forms or styles of structured movement systems peculiar to a region, dialect group or community. Dance in this context interfaces the notion of 'playing' (*main*) with an improvised set of movements and within a specific format performed according to a peculiar style. Performing an improvised set of movements verbalizes the playing-dancing of a structured movement system, overstretching the boundaries of dance as understood in the Western concept. It is within these contexts that the concept of dance as a structured movement system in Indigenous Malaysian societies could be understood for the purpose of sourcing and identifying the artistic idioms that have shaped and challenged their dance repertoires. Indigenous Malaysian dance is shaped by a specific structured movement system in a playing-dancing discourse. The act of playing-dancing through the processes of casual imitation and formal structuring embodies the physique, spectatorship and aesthetic appreciation of Indigenous dance (Nor 2007: 357–58). Thus, the realms of Indigenous dancing involve the sharing of space that is brought to life by the 'playful' interaction of community members, who are both performers and spectators (Nor 2001: 238).

Application to and Analysis of Malaysian Dance

The need to understand the theory and methodology of interpreting dance as playing-dancing in Malaysian sociocultural and spatial contexts led me to revisit and re-evaluate Kaeppler's pioneering method and theory of analysing dance structure through linguistic analogies and emic approaches. Building on Kaeppler's ethnoscientific analysis, I realized that analysing movement systems is not just about understanding the structure of a dance but rather the significance of its cultural context. It is necessary to comprehend the 'communicative competence' or knowledge embedded by traditional beholders. Competence relates to the cognitive learning and understanding of a dance tradition in the way *langue*, as espoused by Saussure (1972 [1916]), is acquired. Such competence will allow the understanding of a grammatical movement sequence found in a performance. Competence in understanding the actual rendering of a movement sequence is analogous to competence in communication: 'and if one does not know the movement conventions, he or she will not have communicative competence and will be unable to understand what is being conveyed' (Kaeppler 2007: 56). Communicative competence in understanding the beholder's knowledge of dance involves deconstructing movements into culturally recognized elements and learning the rules for constructing compositions (Kaeppler 1999: 19).

Units of Indigenous dance movements are put together in a way that forms a grammar of rules and syntax by distinguishing movement as analogous to the two basic units of linguistic analysis: phonemes and morphemes. Kaeppler's structural analysis of dance recognizes these movement analogues of phonemes and morphemes as kinemes and morphokines. Kinemes are actions or positions that are the basic units from which a given dance tradition is built, but they themselves have no specific meaning. The second level of construction is the morphokines, defined as the smallest unit that has meaning. Following this, the third level of movement construction is known as the motif and is a combination of frequently occurring morphokines. When motifs are constructed, a culturally grammatical sequence of movements associated with meaningful imagery emerges. A combination of several motifs becomes a choreme, a culturally grammatical choreographic unit made up of a constellation of motifs that occur simultaneously and sequentially. Motifs and choremes are the building blocks of dances and are implicated not only in structure but also in style (Kaeppler 2007: 56–89).

As an example of these principles of analysis from Malaysia, I focus on the *igal* dance of the Sama-Bajau people from the Southeast coast of Sabah in North Borneo. Sama-Bajau or Sinama speaking people inhibit the many islands of the Sulu-Archipelago in the Philippines, northern and eastern Borneo and throughout eastern Indonesia, including the Celebes sea. The Sama-Bajau have often been referred to as the 'sea gypsies' or 'sea nomads' in the past but within the last seventy years have become strand dwellers in Semporna, Sabah, many of whom live in sprawling stilt villages over the water whilst maintaining their traditional maritime lifestyles. Today, the strand dwelling Sama-Bajau are differentiated from their nomadic cousins, the Pala'u Bajau, who still maintain their old nomadic life on boats (Hussin and Santamaria 2008; Saat 2003; Sather 1997; Sulehan and Nurdin 2017; Warren 2007).

Igal connotes a structured movement system of playing-dancing Indigenous to the Sama-Bajau. Particular forms and styles of performances are synonymous with the place of practice, named after strand villages in Semporna, such as Bangau-Bangau and Labuan Haji on Bum-Bum Island, and villages on Danawan Island, Maiga Island, Omadal Island, Mabul Island, Tetagan Island, Larapan Island and Kulapuan Island (Hamza 2013: 47). The verb *magigal/angigal* refers to the act of playing-dancing (henceforth to be referred as dance), and the prefixes *mag-* or *ang-* imply the act of dancing (*mag-igal/ang-igal*). *Magigal* or *angigal*, as cognate of *igal*, to the Sama-Bajau or Sinama-speaking people in Semporna means playing-dancing within specific kinaesthetic and variations of movement motifs. The terms can have a slightly more converged meaning that involves *musiking* – performing musical instruments, playing-dancing or partaking in the *magigal/angigal* event as engaged participants (Nor 2017b: 85). The term musicking, as coined by Christopher Small (1998), suggests that musical performance is an encounter between human beings that takes place through the medium of sound organized in specific ways, which involves activities by all present and who bear responsibility to social identity via music and music-making. Musicking as human activity 'covers all participation in a musical performance . . . to take part, in any capacity, in a musical performance, whether by performing, by listening, by rehearsing or practicing, by providing material for performance . . . or by dancing' (Small 1998: 9). The meaning of *igal* crosses the boundary between music and dance as understood in common parlance (Nor 2017b: 85).

Igal includes play-dancing and music-making by members of the community within the performative space and by the interaction of performers and spectators. The act of making music and play-dancing *igal* privileges the Indigenous beholders of their perceptions, cognitions and/or memory of their deep-rooted tradition that serves secular and ritual purposes. Sustained by the need to celebrate specific occasions, *igal* are performed for wedding celebrations (*pagkawin*), ritual healings with spirit mediums (*magpaigal-jin*) or social dancing (*maglami-lami*) (Nor 2017a, 2017b; Nor and Hussin 2011, 2012; Quintero and Nor 2016).

Music from the *tagunggu'* ensemble consists of *kulintangan* (a set of small kettle gongs on a rack), with one to three *agung* (large hanging gongs) and one *tambul/tambol/tambur* (a double-headed brass snare drum) (Chan, Hamza and Santaella 2015). The music carries specific melodic and rhythmic motifs coloured with interlocking rhythms within an ostinato layer and over a rapid or leisurely tempo. The playing of *tagunggu'* requires rhythmic dexterity and skill just as in dancing *igal* (*magigal/angigal*). Playing *tagunggu'* (*magtagunggu'*) is dominated by senior female members of the community playing the melodic and ostinato parts of the kettle gongs. Similarly, women outnumber male dancers in most *igal* performances. The gender-separated groups demarcate stylistic differences in dance movements. Female dancers are extremely fluid with their hands, extending, curling and flexing their fingers with or without finger extensions (*sulingkengkeng*) to accentuate and amplify hand and finger movements. This is done while undulating their arms, by extending or folding the upper and lower arms whilst sustaining a relatively upright torso. The male dancers, on the other hand, are agile and display masculine movements associated with *langka* or *kuntaw* dance movements. They may not command the fluidity of flexing fingers like the female dancers, but they generally display great flexibility in arm movements, good footwork and sustenance of energy. Their dances are performed for the pleasure of spectators to exhibit a combination of movement styles and skills. Accurate playing of rhythmic patterns and melodic lines of the *tagunggu'* is an absolute necessity for the dancers. This is to ensure that the dancers feel the melodic-rhythmic motif as it rises and descends along melodic contours to satisfactorily interlock with the overall rhythms of the music.

Igal is collectively associated with the aesthetics of abstract stylization. Arabesques and curvilinear designs woven on fabrics, painted on adornments and in the visual art of the maritime Sama-Bajau echo virtues of infinite form in *igal* that seemingly continue and multiply in space and time from a single point, while the lines and curvilineal movements of the arms and hands demarcate vertical and horizontal spaces. Avoidance of body contact in dance, the absence of overly sensuous gestures and the highly repetitive and symmetrical nature of dance sequences conform to the abstract quality of stylized gestures. The symmetrical repetition of dance motifs within a prescribed floor plan invokes the visual artistic elaboration of a never-ending dance and music pattern (Nor 2003: 179). In the same way, the dance is aesthetically pleasing when the flexed but stiff fingers, quavering outwards with thumbs apart (*tangan palantik*), are accentuated with the rise and fall of shoulders (*kijjut bahu*) and undulating arms, footsteps brushing sideways (*a ngakkai*) into larger step-brushes (*a ngagis*), abrupt stamping of the foot or tapping of the foot and lifting it (*tendek-tendek* or *sintak tape'*) while sustaining a curvaceous silhouette of the body by thrusting the hip to the opposite direction of the head or arms. This is done with almost minimal movement of the hip or torso; thus, the torso is akin to trellises that are the superstructure for climbing foliage that dangles and slithers in and out of the main trunk of a plant, just as the body is to the dancer. Here lies the essence of the Sama-Bajau aesthetics, where curvilinear designs in dance motifs with foliage-like movements in twisting trunks quantify the curvilinear spaces in a never-ending succession representing a continuum of abstract motifs, infinite and endless (Nor 2017b: 87–88).

As embellishments, the ornamentations of dance motifs are encouraged through improvisations that are based upon prearranged concepts of designs in the form of floor plans, kinaesthetic use of space and minute body accentuations (shimmering of shoulders, flexing and folding of fingers, intricate footwork, bending and turning of torso). These are individually executed by the dancers as personal signatures that are culturally accepted within the Indigenous terminologies by the community of dancers. The ornamentations are analogous to creeping foliage that branches out from a single stem of a dance motif. Each of the dance motifs are modular structures that provide enough room for improvisation as the dance progresses into an abstraction of curvilinear conjunction.

Similar aesthetics are fused and imbued in *igal* and in the music of the *tagunggu'* ensemble (Nor 2017b: 86–87). The melodic-rhythmic patterns and interlocking ostinati of the *tagunggu'* kettle gongs, beating of drums and wooden or bamboo beaters display the dynamics of accentuated beats, timbres and ascending and descending melodic-rhythmic motifs. An analysis of *igal tarirai* by Mayco Santaella reveals that sound and movement are of a single emic musicking structure (2016: 70–90). Santaella's analysis is based on the observation made of Hajjah Intan Sulga K.K. Tiring, a *pangigal* (*igal* dancer) and daughter of a respected *panglima* (headman) among the Bajau Laut community of Bangau-Bangau village in Semporna. The dancer uses *bola'-bola'* (wooden or bamboo castanets) to perform *igal tarirai* to the accompaniment of *titik tarirai* (a *tarirai* tune). This piece is rather distinctive, as it consists of a recurring cycle of a syncopated melody with four melodic motifs, which provides the structure for the execution of movement choremes (the largest units of movements) by the *pangigal* (dancer). The movements of *igal tarirai* are focused on the legwork, shoulders and arms alternating with right- and left-hand strokes of the castanets. Movements such as a sudden lifting of the legs (*sintak tape'*), walking with slow steps (*ni lengngan-lennganan*) and shifting the feet left and right (*a ngangginsil*) are executed spontaneously in each melodic motif. These movements are complemented by the rise and fall of the shoulders (*kijjut bahu*), arms swaying forward and backward (*a ngalimbai*), gentle turning of the wrists (*a ngolles*) and gentle movement of the upper torso (*lemma'baran*). The hands accentuate the melodic motif by carrying out the rhythmic ostinato with the castanets within the rhythmic density of the *tambul/tambur* (double-headed brass snare drum).

The *titik tarirai* tune begins with the *kulintangan* player introducing the melody and tempo. Thus, the *titik* (tune/piece) sets the foundation for *igal tarirai*. The *tambul* begins the rhythmic accompaniment after the first eight-beat melodic motif, played with the greatest rhythmic density and maintaining a steady subdivision of the beat throughout the piece. After the *kulintangan* and *tambul* players have synchronized rhythmically, the lower and higher pitched *agung* players gradually begin their patterns with the third melodic motif. By the end of this melodic cycle, the *igal* dancer gradually adds another rhythmic layer with the *bola'-bola'* accompaniment at the rhythmic density of the *tambul* in order to begin the movements of *igal tarirai*. The *pangigal* in this case generates both sound and movement through the *bola'-bola'* accompaniment, a correspondence between the rhythmic structure of the castanets and the movement motifs. The tempo of the *bola'-bola'* may differ slightly at times with the rhythm of the *tagunggu'* ensemble as it accompanies each movement motif (Santaella 2016: 79–80).

Morphokines, Motifs and Choremes: Improvising *Igal*

The structural configuration of *Igal* from the smallest units of movement (kinemes) to the largest (choremes) through a constellation of morphokines and

Tarirai

Figure 6.1. Music transcription of Titik Tarirai *(Santaella 2016: 79).*

motifs are symbiotically linked to deliberate or subtle movements of the head, shoulders, neck, arms, elbows, wrists, fingers, knees, ankles and toes. *Igal*'s aesthetics necessitate continuous fluidity of movements creating curvilinear arms and hand movements without body or space held for specific poses and with minimal upward and downward movements of the torso. The combination of morphokines into a constellation of dance motifs is based on the tunes (*titik*) of the *tagunggu'* corresponding to the specific musical repertoires as shown below:

Types of *Igal*	*Titik* (tunes/piece)
• *Igal Limbayan*	: *Titik Limbayan*
• *Igal Lellang*	: *Titik Lellang*
• *Igal Tabawan/Lubak-Lubak*	: *Titik Tabawan/Lubak-Lubak*
• *Igal Tarirai* (with *bola'-bola'* [castanets])	: *Titik Tarirai*
• *Sayau*	: *Titik Lubak-Lubak*
• *Kuntau*	: *Tititk Tabawan/Lubak-Lubak*

Igal morphokines enhance the infinite designs of abstract forms into self-contained dance motifs, which are harmoniously serialized into a constellation of motifs. The design resembles an infinite journey that only pauses when *igal* is completed. Each *igal* dance motif becomes a part of a visual decoration carrying more motifs as it flows apparently unending, until it reaches a point of rest. There is neither a single climax nor a focal point, but the movement continuously evolves. *Igal* dance movements are arranged according to individual or group preferences with freedom for improvisation. This enables *igal* dancers to rearrange and embellish the sequences of *igal* dance motifs at random.

Table 6.1. *Upper and lower body morphokines and* igal *motifs.*

Head Movements and Facial Expressions (Morphokines)	
1. *Pahangad-hangad*	tilting the head backwards
2. *Pahanduk-handuk* (male dancers in *Igal Sayau*)	tilting the head backwards and forwards
3. *A ngiddat*	lifting of the eyebrows
4. *Takium*	smiling
Improvised morphokines 1–4 for head motifs	

(*continued*)

Table 6.1. Continued

Torso (morphokines)	
1. A nekang	in a state of readiness
2. Pareo'- reo'	the body is lowered slightly
3. Paengket	the body is raised up
4. Pagiling	turning the body without lifting the foot
5. Pabulivud	a turning movement
6. Pattaddung	to turn one's back
7. Lemma' Baran	move the body gently
8. Kijjut Baha	shoulders shrugged
Improvised morphokines 1–8 for torso motifs	

Arm Movements (morphokines)	
1. A ngalimbai	swaying the arms forwards and backwards
2. Sinayangan	arm tossed gently upward
3. Pabettad	arms flexed
4. Pahettad	arms stretch outward with palm facing upward (place high)
5. A ngolles	turning the wrists
6. Sinulavai	both arms swaying in opposite directions
7. Siku Palantik	hyper extending the elbow
8. Tangan Palantik	flexing the hands
9. Tinaut Taut	gently moving and swaying the arms
Improvised morphokines of 1–9 for arm motifs	

Arm Movements for Men (morphokines)	
1. Sinayangngan	swinging a hand-held weapon – i.e. *gayang* or *tombak* (spears) for *igal sayau*
2. A ngalagpak	hand-clapping as in *kuntaw*
3. A ngalasti	clapping the backs of the hands as in *kuntaw*
4. A ngansom	teasing and feinting in *igal sayau*
Improvised morphokines of 1–4 for men's arm motifs	

Table 6.1. Continued

Footwork (morphokines)	
1. *A meka'*	step with toe touching the floor softly
2. *Pahenggel*	lifting both heels
3. *A ngangginsil*	shifting the feet left and right
4. *A ngengket Tape'*	lifting one leg
5. *A ngengsod*	shifting one foot sideway alongside the leading foot; shifting forward middle
6. *Ni Lengngan–lengnganan*	walking in slow steps
7. *A ngagis*	tiptoe shifting
8. *Sintak Tape'*	sudden lifting of legs
Improvised morphokines of 1–8 for footwork motifs	

Additional Footwork for Men (morphokines)	
1. *Maglaksu – laksu*	to jump
2. *Tendek*	foot stamping
3. *Erek- Erek*	shaking legs and thigh
4. *A ngakkai*	one foot shifting on the floor
Improvised morphokines of 1–4 for men's footwork motifs	

The aforementioned examples of *igal* morphokines are improvised with abstract stylizations serialized into a constellation of motifs to form the genre's choremes. Dancers embellish their motives with posture and gesture to create choremes that represent their strand-dwelling villages or communities. The nuances of *igal*'s choremes signify place of origin supported by specific *titik* (tunes) played by the *tagunggu'* ensembles.

Summary and Epilogue

The shared aesthetics of *igal* and *tagunggu'* are essential to the extant performance traditions of the Sama-Bajau. *Igal* performances are fundamental for Sama-Bajau wedding celebrations (*pagkawin*), ritual healings with spirit mediums (*magpaigal-jin*) and social dancing (*maglami-lami*) in Semporna. In these contexts, performers play-dance constellations of morphokines and motifs to become grammatical choreographic units (choremes) to the accompaniment of the *tagunggu'* ensemble. Competence in improvising an *igal* structural configuration rests in the shared knowledge embedded in the memory of *igal* dancers and *tagunggu'* musicians, the

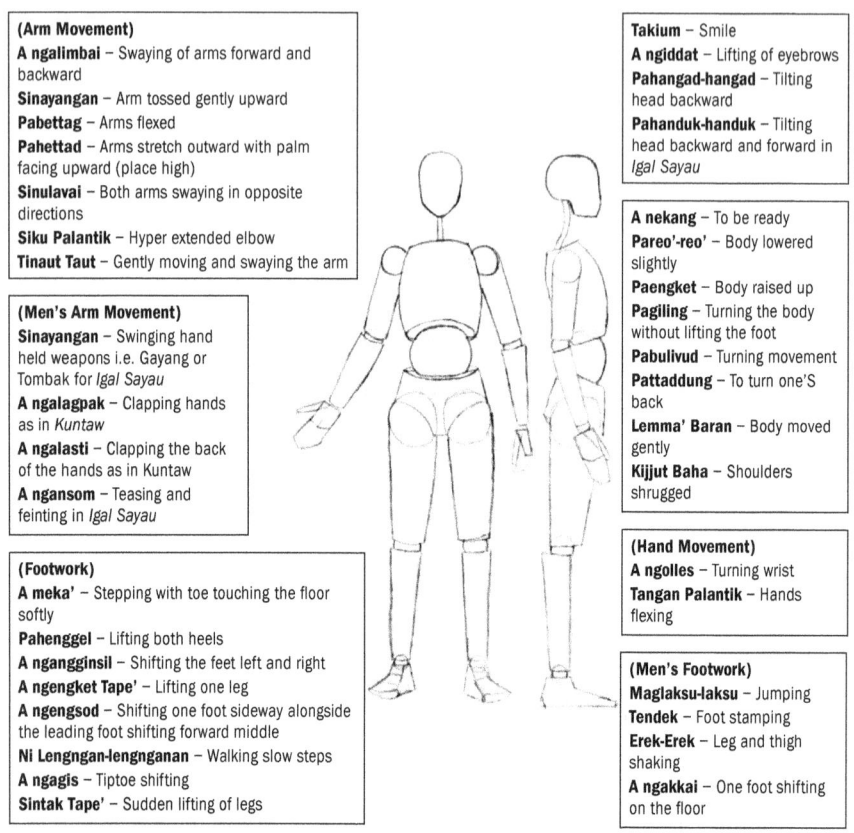

Figure 6.2. Examples of Igal's *morphokines and dance motifs.* © *Mohd Anis Md Nor.*
Note: There are several variants to the terms used by the Sama-Bajau in Semporna. These terms presented here were categorized by the Sama-Bajau in Semporna for the igal *competitions, first held at the International* Igal *Festival in 2017.*

beholders who not only gave *igal* its own identity and form in Semporna but who also make the dance and music an integral part of Sama-Bajau traditions.

In this chapter, I have examined *igal*'s structural analysis as an ethnochoreological discourse to contextualize cultural and first-person experiences of dancing, as well as analysing and interpreting *igal* as a cultural representation of the dancing body. Through the above discussions, I have posited that the evaluation and appraisal of theories on the dancing body as a cultural construct from Kaeppler's structural analysis can become an instrument of dance research, which may further appraise dance as heritage. Since the terms for dance reflect forms and styles of structured movement systems peculiar to a region (Peninsular Malaysia or Sabah and Sarawak in East Malaysia) or a dialect group (Malay or Sama-Bajau), or in a community, then understanding meanings from emic perspectives necessitates the need to deconstruct dance into meaningful units of movement for an in-depth understanding of local aesthetics.

Ethnoscientific analysis provided a framework to analyse Indigenous Malaysian and maritime Southeast Asian dance in order to understand the structured movement systems in their cultural context. Kaeppler's descriptions of Polynesian dance helped me to leverage the differences and similarities in understanding culturally coherent choremes through the communicative competence of *igal* practitioners. According to Kaeppler (1993), Polynesian dance is 'poetry in motion', rendered melodically and rhythmically to incorporate meanings through movements that are connected to the poetic text and that enliven through metaphor and illusion. In contrast, *igal* does not tell stories but instead focuses on the aesthetic qualities of the dance. *Igal* is prosaic, expressing aesthetics through improvised motifs that seemingly continue in space and time from a single point. The lines and curvilineal movements of the arms and hands in the dance are the means to quantify spatial horizons. The infinite designs in their abstract form offer significant cultural links to natural sources, in the flora and fauna of the surrounding environment. This abstraction through movement has enabled *igal* dancers to rearrange and embellish sequences of dance motifs at random and arrange them according to individual or group preferences. As in broader Sama-Bajau visual arts, the improvised play-performance of movements flow unendingly into choreographic phrases that are recalled and re-embodied as *igal* by the Sama-Bajau.

Mohd Anis Md Nor is a former Professor of Ethnochoreology and Ethnomusicology at the Cultural Centre (School of Performing Arts) University of Malaya and is currently an Adjunct Professor at Sunway University in Kuala Lumpur. He is the Managing Director of Nusantara Performing Arts Research Centre (www.nusparc.com), a non-profit organization that focuses on research, documentation and publication of traditional and contemporary performing arts of Southeast Asia. He has pioneered the study of Zapin dance and music in Southeast Asia and has published widely on the same topic. He is the Past Secretary General of World Dance Alliance (WDA Americas, WDA Asia Pacific and WDA Europe), Chair of the ICTM Study Group on Performing Arts of Southeast Asia (International Council for Traditional Music – PASEA) and was the Program Committee Co-Chair for the 70th ICTM Anniversary and 44th ICTM World Conference (2017) at the University of Limerick, Ireland.

Glossary

gencok commonly refers to social dance in Northwest Peninsular Malaysia
igal refers to dance amongst Sama-Bajau groups in Sabah
joget generic term for dance in Malaysia
kuntaw derived from the Hokkian word *kûn-thâu*, a term for movements in martial arts
langka footsteps that mock combat
main literally means 'playing' or 'gambolling' in a structured movement system
sayau term for dance by the Dusunic people of Sabah
tandak Malay social dances
tari generic term for dance in Malay/Indonesian
totor a term referring to dance amongst the then Indigenous people in North Sumatra – i.e. Tapanuli Utara, Humbang Hasundutan, Toba Samosir and Samosir

Notes

1. The concept of ethnoscientific perspective came into anthropological theory in the 1960s. It is often referred to as 'Indigenous knowledge', based on a completely emic perspective, which excludes all observations, interpretations and or any personal notions belonging to the ethnographer. The taxonomy and classification of Indigenous systems is adapted from a linguistic analysis, hence understanding the language and the native people's linguistic system is one method of understanding a native people's system of knowledge of organization and the complex relationship between environment and culture. Kaeppler's ethnoscientific orientation required analysing the structure of dance and movement systems that should reflect dance movements as known and performed by the carriers of the tradition themselves based on ethno-semantic categories.
2. The term Austronesian refers to the dispersed peoples who descend from the Austronesian linguistic family, distributed in parts of Asia, including maritime Southeast Asia, Madagascar and the Pacific Islands.

References

Amilbangsa, L.F. 1983. *Pangalay: Traditional Dances and Related Folk Artistic Expressions*. Manila: Filipinas Foundation, Inc.

Bandem, I.M., and F.E. De Boer. 1981. *Kaja and Kelod: Balinese Dance in Transition*. Kuala Lumpur: Oxford University Press.

Boas, F. 1943. 'Recent Anthropology', *Science* 98(2545): 311–37.

Chan, H., H.Z. Hamza and M.A. Santaella. 2015. *A Bajau Heritage: Warisan Bajau*. Tanjung Malim: Sultan Idris Education University.

Cuisinier, J. 1936. *Danses Magiques de Kelantan*. Paris: Institut D'Etnologie.

David, A.R. 2008. 'Local Diasporas/Global Trajectories: New Aspects of Religious "Performance" in British Tamil Hindu Practices', *Performance Research* 13(3): 89–99.

———. 2010. 'Gendering the Divine: New Forms of Feminine Hindu Worship', *International Journal of Hindu Studies* 13(3): 337–55.

Hamza, H.Z. 2013. 'Igal: The Traditional Performing Arts of the Bajau Laut in Semporna, Sabah', MA thesis. Kuala Lumpur: University Malaya.

Holt, C. 1967. *Art in Indonesia: Continuities and Change*. Ithaca, NY: Cornell University Press.

Hussin, H., and MCM Santamaria. 2008. 'Dancing with the Ghosts of the Sea', *Journal of Southeast Asian Studies, JATI* 13: 159–72.

Kealiinohomoku, J. 1974. 'Dance Culture as a Microcosm of Holistic Culture', in T. Comstock (ed.), *New Dimensions in Dance Research: Anthropology and Dance (The American Indian)*. New York: Committee on Research in Dance, pp. 99–106.

Kaeppler, A.L. 1967. 'The Structure of Tongan Dance', Ph.D. dissertation. Honolulu: University of Hawaii.

———. 1972. 'Method and Theory in Analyzing Dance Structure with an Analysis of Tongan Dance', *Ethnomusicology* 16(2): 173–217.

———. 1978. 'Melody, Drone and Decoration: Underlying Structures and Surface Manifestations in Tongan Art and Society', in M. Greenhalgh and V. Megaw (eds), *Art and Society; Studies in Styles, Culture and Aesthetics*. London: Duckworth, pp. 261–74.

———. 1983. *Polynesian Dance with a Selection for Contemporary Performances*. Honolulu, Hawai'i: Alpha Delta Kappa.

———. 1985. 'Structured Movement Systems in Tonga', in P. Spencer (ed.), *Society and the Dance: The Social Anthropology of Process and Performance*. Cambridge: Cambridge University Press, pp. 92–118.

———. 1986. 'Cultural Analysis, Linguistic Analogies, and the Study of Dance in Anthropology Perspective', in C.J. Frisbie (ed.), *Explorations in Ethnomusicology: Essays in Honor of David P. McAllester*. Detroit Monographs in Musicology 9. Detroit: Informations Coordinators, pp. 25–33.

———. 1991. 'American Approaches to the Study of Dance', *Yearbook for Traditional Music* 23: 11–21.

———. 1993. *Poetry in Motion: Studies on Tongan Dance*. Nuku'ulofa, Tonga: Vava'u Press.

———. 1999. 'Mystique of Fieldwork', in T.J. Buckland (ed.), *Dance in the Field: Theory, Methods and Issues in Dance Ethnography*. London: Macmillan Press, pp. 13–25.

———. 2007. 'Method and Theory in Analysing Dance Structure with an Analysis of Tongan Dance', in A.L. Kaeppler and E.I. Dunin (eds), *Dance Structures: Perspectives on the Analysis of Human Movement*. Budapest: Akademiai Kiado, pp. 53–102.

Malinowski, B. 1961 [1922]. *Argonauts of the Western Pacific*. New York: E.P. Dutton.

Merriam, A.P. 1974. 'Anthropology and the Dance', in T. Comstock (ed.), *New Dimensions in Dance Research: Anthropology and Dance (The American Indian)*. New York: Committee on Research in Dance, pp. 9–28.

Ness, S.A. 1992. *Body, Movement and Culture; Kinesthetic and Visual Symbolism in a Philippine Community*. Philadelphia: University of Pennsylvania Press.

Nor, M.A.Md. 1986. *Randai Dance of Minangkabau West Sumatra with Labanotation Scores*. Kuala Lumpur: University of Malay Press.

———. 1993. *Zapin: Folk Dance of the Malay World*. Singapore: Oxford University Press.

———. 2001. 'Dancing on the Proscenium: Re-constructing, Revitalizing and Appropriating Malay Folk Dances', in E.I. Dunin, T. Zebec et al. (eds), *Proceedings of the 21st Symposium of the ICTM Study Group on Ethnochoreology*. Zagreb, Croatia: Institute of Ethnology and Folklore Research, pp. 238–43.

———. 2003. 'Arabesques and Curvilinear Perimeters in the Aesthetics of Maritime-Malay Dances', *Yearbook for Traditional Music* 35: 179–81.

———. 2007. 'Structural Constructs in Indigenous Dances in Malaysia', in A.L. Kaeppler and E.I. Dunin (eds), *Dance Structures: Perspectives on the Analysis of Human Movement*. Budapest: Akademiai Kiado, pp. 357–62.

———. 2017a. 'Symbiotic Relationship of Igal and Pangalay in Semporna, Sabah', in M.A.Md. Nor (ed.), *Proceedings of the 2nd International Conference on Bajau-Sama' Diaspora and Maritime Southeast Asian Cultures*. Kuala Lumpur: Nusantara Performing Arts Research Center, pp. 136–45.

———. 2017b. 'Presentation and Representation of Igal in Semporna', in M.A.Md. Nor (ed.), *Perspectives of Bajau/Sama' Diaspora*. Sabah Museum Monograph 13. Kota Kinabalu, Dept. of Sabah Museum, pp. 85–91.

Nor, M.A.Md., and H. Hussin. 2011. 'Gendering Dance, Gazing Music: Dance Movements, Healing Rituals and Music Making of Sama Bajau and Sama Dilaut of East Malaysia and Southern Philippines', *Journal of Maritime Geopolitics and Culture* 2(1): 97–113.

———. 2012. 'Mag-igal and Igal-jin: Dancing the Spirits of the Ancestors in the Rituals of Magduwata of the Bajau Kubang in Bumbum Island, Semporna, East Malaysia', in E.I. Dunin, A. Giurchescu and C. Könczei (eds), *Proceedings of the 24th Symposium of the ICTM Study Group on Ethnochoreology*. Cluj-Napoca, Romania: The Romanian Institute for Research on National Minorities, pp. 143–48.

Paetzold, U., and P.H. Mason. 2016. *The Fighting Art of Pencak Silat and Its Music: From Southeast Asian Village to Global Movement*. Leiden, Netherlands: Brill Publishers.

Pike, K. 1954. *Language in Relation to a Unified Theory of the Structure of Human Behavior*. Glendale, CA: Summer Institute of Linguistics.

Quintero, D.A., and M.A.Md. Nor. 2016. 'The Curvilinear Ethnoaesthetic in Pangalay Dancing Among the Suluk in Sabah, Malaysia', *Wacana Seni Journal of Arts Discourse* 15: 1–25. http://dx.doi.org/10.21315/ws2016.15.1.

Rutnin, M.M. 1993. *Dance, Drama, and Theatre in Thailand*. Tokyo: The Toyo Bungko.

Saat, G. 2003. 'The Identity and Social Mobility of Sama-Bajau', *Sari* 21: 3–11.

Saleeby, N.M. 1905. *Studies in Moro History, Law and Religion*. Manila, Philippines: Bureau of Public Printing.

Santaella, M. 2016. 'Sounding Movement Extrinsically and Intrinsically: An Ethnochoreomusicological Analysis of Tarirai Among the Bajau Laut in Semporna, Sabah', *Musika Journal* 12: 70–90.

———. 2017. 'Shared Practices and Idiosyncrasies of the Bajau/Sama' Tagunggu' Ensemble', in M.A.Md. Nor (ed.), *Perspectives on Bajau/Sama' Diaspora*. Sabah Museum Monograph 18. Kota Kinabalu: Dept. of Sabah Museum, pp. 75–84.

Sather, C. 1997. *The Bajau Laut: Adaptation, History, and Fate in a Maritime Fishing Society of South-eastern Sabah*. South-East Asian Social Science Monographs. Singapore: Oxford University Press.

Saussure, F.d. 1972 [1916]. *Cours de Linguistique Générale*. édition critique préparée par Tullio de mauro. Paris: Payot.

Sheppard, M. 1969. *Joget Gamelan of Trengganu*. Straits Time Annual. Kuala Lumpur: New Straits Times Press.

———. 1983. *Taman Saujana; Dance, Drama, Music and Magic in Malaya Long and Not-so-Long Ago*. Petaling Jaya: International Book Service.

Sim, K. 1946. *Malayan Landscape*. London: Michael Joseph.
Small, C. 1998. *Musicking: The Meanings of Performing and Listening*. Middletown, CT: Wesleyan University Press.
Soedarsono, R.M. 1984. *Wayang Wong: The State Ritual Dance Drama in the Court of Yogyakarta*. Jogjakarta: Gadjah Mada University Press.
Stepputat, K. 2013. *Performing Arts in Postmodern Bali: Changing Interpretations, Founding Traditions*. Aachen, Germany: Shaker.
Sulehan, J., and G. Nurdin. 2017. 'Rituals, Magic and Sacred Places of the Pala'u Lepa Communities', in M.A.Md. Nor (ed.), *Perspectives on Bajau/Sama' Diaspora*. Sabah Museum Monograph 18. Kota Kinabalu: Dept. of Sabah Museum, pp. 219–28.
Swettenham, F. 1895. *Malay Sketches*. London: The Ballantyne Press.
Villaruz, B.E.S. 2007. *Treading Through: 45 Years of Philippine Dance*. Quezon City, Philippines: University of the Philippines Press.
Warren, J.F. 2007. *The Sulu Zone: The Dynamics of External Trade, Slavery and Ethnicity in the Transformation of a Southeast Asian Maritime State, 1768–1898*. 2nd edn. Singapore: National University of Singapore Press.
Wharton, A.v.B. 2009. 'Changes in the Transmission of Javanese Dance: A Case Study', in M.A.Md. Nor et al. (eds), *Proceedings 25th Symposium of the ICTM Study Group on Ethnochoreology*. Kuala Lumpur: ICTM Study Group on Ethnochoreology, pp. 140–45.
Van Zile, J. 2001. *Perspectives on Korean Dance*. Middletown, CT: Wesleyan University Press.

Chapter 7

Courting as Structured Movement in the Eastern Highlands of Papua New Guinea

Don Niles

I probably first met Adrienne Kaeppler in 1977, when I mumbled some shy introduction at the International Musicological Society congress in Berkeley, where she presented on a panel chaired by Trevor Jones with other luminaries in Pacific music and dance research: Wolfgang Laade, Mervyn McLean, Alice Moyle, Richard Moyle, Barbara Smith and Gordon Spearritt (Heartz and Wade 1981: 114–38).

This was followed most memorably by becoming her student in a class on Pacific dance, in the same year, when I visited Honolulu. While I clumsily attempted to do the Polynesian dances she was teaching, I imagine I fared better as a student in her lectures. She revealed that the best ethnographic study of dance she had read was Edward Schieffelin's *The Sorrow of the Lonely and the Burning of the Dancers* (1976). As I was leaning towards focusing my own studies on Papua New Guinea music and dance, I was thrilled to learn of her preference (but also rather alarmed that I had never heard of it).

Of course, it was well before 1977 that I had read some of her work. As Adrienne later told me, she originally intended to do research somewhere in New Guinea but was dissuaded from doing so after the 1961 disappearance of Michael Rockefeller; her PhD research in Tonga began in 1964. Nevertheless, one of her first publications was a review of a key disc of Papua New Guinea music (Kaeppler 1963). But even more important for me was her overview with Dieter Christensen of music and dance in Oceania in *Encyclopædia Britannica* (Christensen and Kaeppler 1974). I was encouraged by their efforts to see trends and contrasts over a very diverse region, such as that of dances of impersonation and of participation in Melanesia, and how they differed from dances in Polynesia and Micronesia and the sociopolitical structures there.

I was also to be inspired by her consideration of some dances as 'airport art' (Kaeppler 1977); work with artefacts collected by Captain Cook (Kaeppler 1978); promotion of a wide variety of sources as essential research documents (Kaeppler 1992, 2017); explorations of the use and origins of particular instruments and forms using such sources (Kaeppler 1993, 2001) and many other topics. She shaped my ideas about dance but also about how to do and write up research.

I helped with Papua New Guinea entries for her collaboration with Jacob Love on the Garland Encyclopedia of World Music's *Australia and the Pacific Islands* (Kaeppler and Love 1998), but I got to know Adrienne best through our work with the International Council for Traditional Music.[1] Quite coincidentally, her terms as president (2006–13) coincided with mine as general editor of the *Yearbook for Traditional Music*, and I served on the Executive Board with her beginning in 2007, where I saw her in quite a different role.

More than four decades on, Adrienne continues to teach me about dance, research, diplomacy and decision making. My contribution here honours that involvement as a scholar and a friend by following her lead in trying to recognize regionally characteristic elements from a mass of disparate sources. Furthermore, some of these elements are germane to considering what is dance.

Adrienne has often offered definitions of dance and music. One of the most recent is:

> In many societies there are no categories comparable to the Western concepts 'music' and/or 'dance'; thus analyses of sound and movement have been enlarged to encompass all structured sound and movement, including, but not limited to, those associated with religious and secular ritual, ceremony, entertainment, martial arts, sign languages, sports, and games. What these categories share is that they result from creative processes that manipulate (i.e. handle with skill) sounds and movements made by humans through time and space . . . Some categories of sound and movement may be further marked or elaborated culturally as 'music' (a specially marked or elaborated category of structured sound) and 'dance' (a specially marked or elaborated category of structured movement). (Kaeppler 2017: 430–31)

The idea of dance as a special type of structured movement is key to my discussion of courting that follows. Indeed, many of these structured movements would likely not be recognized as dance in more restrictive definitions.

General Features of Highlands Courting

The nation of Papua New Guinea is located north of Australia and east of Indonesia. It has been independent since 1975 and is known for its cultural diversity.

It is estimated that the population of 7.6 million people speak 841 languages, making it the most linguistically diverse country (Simons and Fennig 2018). Despite this diversity, in considering music and dance there are certain features that appear to transcend such boundaries and suggest more regional characteristics. One such example of this is the courting to be considered here: commonalities abound, but contrasts do as well, certainly confounding compact definitions.

The courting I am considering here, nevertheless, requires a definition. But because its forms are spread across a wide region, where people speak many different languages, and with variations in choreography, contextual details etc., such a definition is far from simple. Furthermore, many of the courting activities described here appear to be no longer performed due to various pressures from missionization, 'modernization', changing styles, etc.; however, as in so many cases in Papua New Guinea where generalizations are difficult at best, it is also true that some of them do exist, albeit in occasionally modified forms. Because of these uncertainties, I thought it safest to use the ethnographic present in my discussion.

The courting I am concerned with is one of the main socially acceptable ways to meet and interact with members of the opposite sex in much of the Highlands of Papua New Guinea. Many ethnographic reports emphasize that girls make many decisions regarding such courting: the time and place, whom to invite and to court, whether the relationship should continue, etc. Courting is almost universally for unmarried females, on the one hand, and unmarried or married males looking for additional wives, on the other. Deeper relationships can also form between unmarried pairs, but as marriage is a serious subject transcending the desires of individuals, marital decisions are often made by others. For unmarried participants, courting comes at a time of life when they have few major responsibilities.

Groups of males and females court together, forming couples who sit or lie down together. Partners change during the evening, while chaperones, often older women, watch over the activities. No instruments are used, but singing is commonplace. These courting occasions are done quite publicly; they are not clandestine liaisons.

Most courting is done indoors at night. Courting frequently involves dance or some sort of special body contact between those courting. This body contact is special because it is usually quite different from what would otherwise be deemed acceptable social behaviour. Exceptions to any of these generalizations will be noted in the appropriate places below. Much more highly variable elements relate to the type of movements used, any separation of dancers from singers and the numbers involved. After overcoming initial reluctance or shyness, most participants enjoy courting.

I am not concerned with individual flirting done privately or at other dance performances. Nor do I include courting solely through love magic that is done at a distance from the intended recipient. Love magic is often used before engaging in the courting dances discussed here, but the latter involve face-to-face interactions.

Reports of courting vary from detailed ethnographic descriptions to brief notes, photographs, paintings, films, novels etc.[2] Nevertheless, because of visitors' fascination with such dances and their contrast with dances in other areas, descriptions abound for many regions. In my doctoral dissertation, I focused on courting in the Mount Hagen area but also considered courting throughout the entire Highlands, particularly in relation to the treatment of space and choreography (Niles 2011: 158–83, 428–67).[3]

While such courting is found in all seven Highlands provinces (Southern Highlands, Hela, Enga, Western Highlands, Jiwaka, Chimbu and Eastern Highlands) and is a feature of most core Highlands groups, it is particularly varied and elaborate in Western Highlands, Jiwaka and especially Chimbu. Other studies generally focus on courting amongst particular groups. Aside from the Eastern Highlands area discussed below, works of particular importance for other parts of the region concern the Duna (Gillespie 2010: 157–81), Huli (Pugh-Kitingan 1981: 285–90), Enga (Kyakas and Wiessner 1992: 22–63; Talyaga 1973), Hagen (Pitcairn and Schleidt 1976; A. Strathern 1974; A. Strathern and M. Strathern 1971: 38–43; Vicedom and Tischner 1943–48: 1/244–45, 247, 2/190–97), Chimbu (Gende 1998; Nilles 1950: 33–35), Maring (Jablonko 1991: 372–74), Wahgi and North Wahgi (Luzbetak 1954: 73–75; O'Hanlon 1989: 40–41, 98; Simpson 1955: 174–76). Of course, many authors tend to prioritize their discussion on the songs, movements or sociocultural context of courting, according to their own particular interests and expertise. Other observations of courting in the Papua New Guinea Highlands abound, tending to be less detailed but nevertheless invaluable source materials.

Courting in the Eastern Highlands

The focus of my discussion is on Eastern Highlands Province, the easternmost Highlands province and easternmost extent of courting. These groups speak Kainantu-Goroka languages, a division of the huge Trans-New Guinea family (Simons and Fennig 2018). Kainantu-Goroka languages are subdivided into Gorokan languages in the western part of the province and Kainantu languages in the eastern (Figure 7.1.). Where names of groups used in the literature differ from those found in this linguistic classification, I have indicated the latter in parentheses following the name in the source. I realize that one group's practices within a language do not necessarily mean that they are found throughout that language, but for my purposes of overview and classification, using a standard, easily accessible reference work is quite adequate and advantageous.

I will be making use of all sources available to me, which, for the most part, are limited to written records: ethnographic reports but also travelogues, remi-

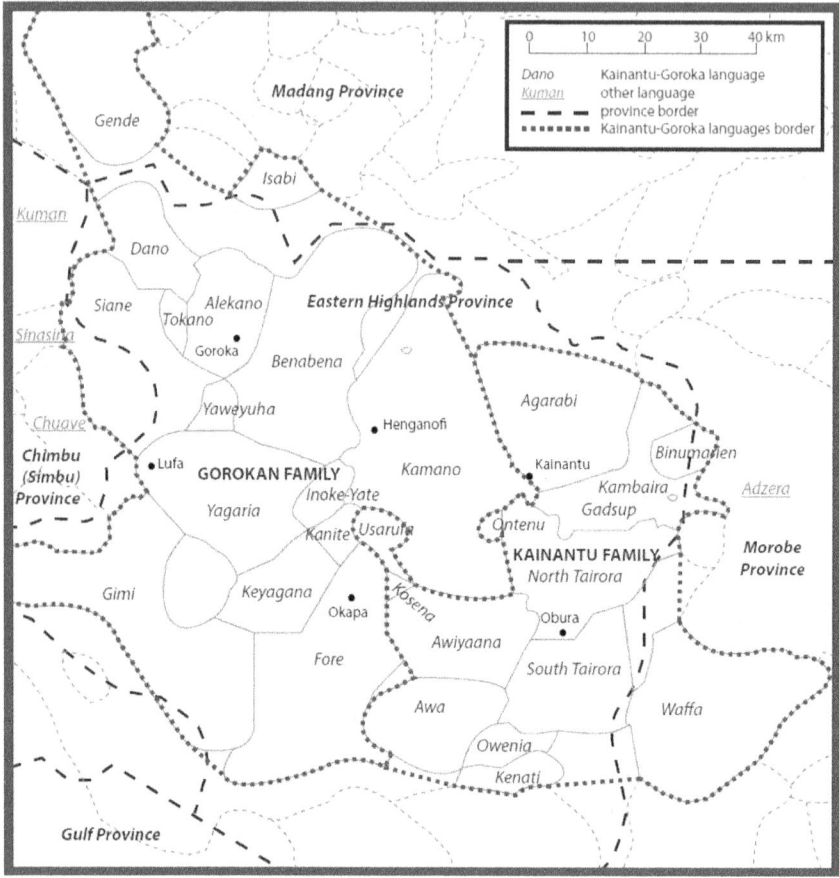

Figure 7.1. Languages of Eastern Highlands Province, Papua New Guinea. Map based on those in Simons and Fennig (2018). © Don Niles.

niscences, dictionaries, emails, interviews etc.[4] In the absence of photos or films from the areas concerned, these written sources have been visually evocative of the traditions described – certainly that is precisely what they were intended to do when originally published. I take repeated silence on courting in major ethnographic works as indicative of absence. I hope that further research will clarify some of the questions raised here.

My discussion of courting here proceeds from west to east and distinguishes three major styles, as shown in Figure 7.2. This map considerably simplifies the complexities of choreographic styles here, but I hope that it will also encourage refinements and improvements.[5]

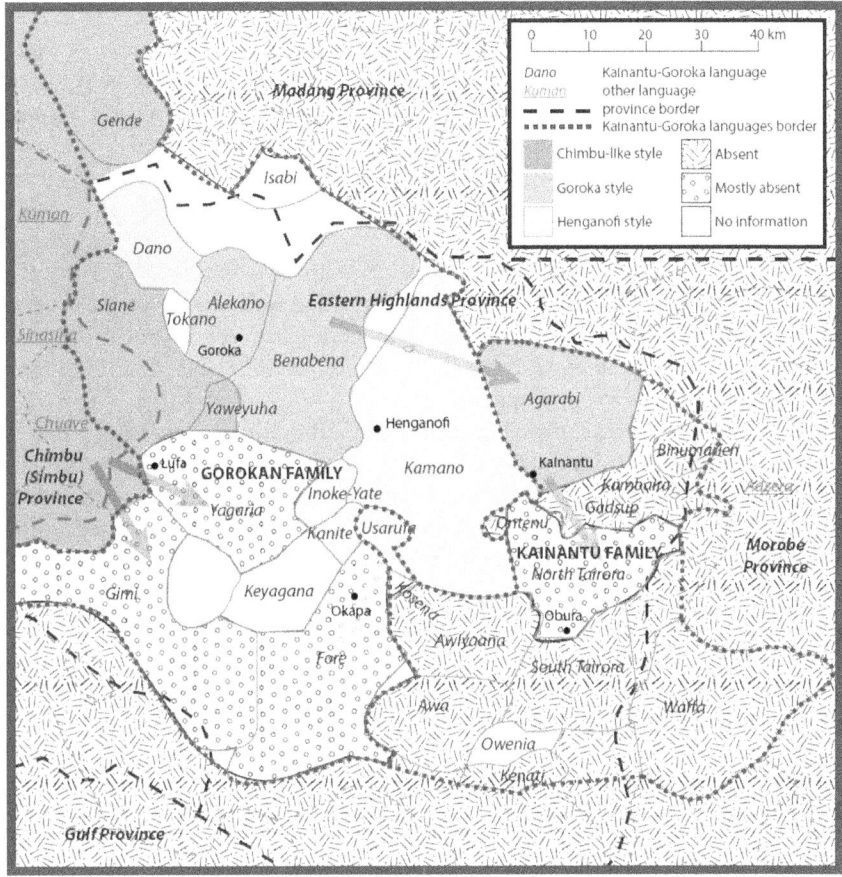

Figure 7.2. Courting styles in the Eastern Highlands. © Don Niles.

Chimbu-Like Style

Groups on or near the Chimbu-Eastern Highlands border sometimes have a number of different types of formal courting events involving performers sitting in circle formations and swaying or shaking their heads. Salisbury's writings on the Siane identify two types of courting that are distinguished by choreography and instigators.

About every three years, a clan prepares a large garden to make a huge distribution of food to another clan and to recognize the contribution of spirits to their gardening success. During the *ka mafo* (yam-taro) ceremony, boys and girls temporarily become spirits while dancing and during a type of courting called *gimagama*. The hosts invite another clan's unmarried girls to be their 'wives'; they are entertained as wives of men's houses, rather than individuals, for up to a week. They and unmarried men of the host clan perform *gimagama* at night, sleeping by rivers in the day, and dancing and watching pantomimes in evenings. *Gimagama* takes place inside the men's houses, from which all beds are removed. Girls squat in a circle around the fire; boys form a circle around them. Boy-and-girl pairs sway from side to side while singing, gradually moving towards each other when their noses meet and they sway in unison. Boys move to the right to change partners (Salisbury 1962: 33; 1965: 64–65; Salisbury-Rowswell 1957: 50).[6] The side-to-side swaying and the rubbing of noses (along with foreheads and cheeks) are characteristic of courting activities further west (e.g. see photos in Pitcairn and Schleidt 1976: plate v–vi; Baglin and De Courcy 1988: 41). The rubbing of facial parts also links with groups further east.

In contrast to such courting at clan-organized events, *awoiro* takes a different form and results from individual actions. A boy goes with age-mates to visit girls in other villages, providing a chance to make contact with clans other than his own or his mother's brother's. If the youths are successful in attracting the attention of girls, they are invited into the girls' clubhouse for a night of singing, talking and petting, although no dance is described. A boy's activities are not linked here to clan obligations and so serve as an introduction to the dangers and rewards of dealing other clans (Salisbury 1962: xix, 36; Salisbury-Rowswell 1957: 54–55). *Awoiro* is also performed at a girl's first menstruation, quite a different context. Small groups of older men from other villages are invited to sing *awoiro* songs in the outer room of the girl's house to protect her spirit with their noise. For five days this continues, and the girl sleeps behind a partition. On the sixth evening, she comes out to the fire when her own clan youths enter the house singing *awoiro*. She is instructed by her lineage head about proper behaviour with men (Salisbury 1965: 72–73).[7] Again, it is unclear if any dance is associated with such activities.

To the north of Siane, but actually in Madang Province, lies the most northern member of the Kainantu-Goroka languages: Gende (see Figure 7.1.). In courting, as in many cultural aspects, Gende have been considerably influenced by Chimbu practices to their south; indeed Gende youths may walk for days to court with Chimbu girls. Although terminology is not consistent between ethnographic reports, Gende generally distinguish at least two types of courting, one for male and female couples (*kango*) and another involving many girls and boys (big *kango*, *koanandi*). In the former, boys come to a girl's house, where they sit around a fire, chat, tell funny stories, the girls laugh, and they sing together. A girl may place her legs over her partner's, in a position very common further west in Chimbu and Jiwaka provinces (e.g. Reay 1959: ill. 17; Simpson 1955: opp. 126). *Koanandi* involves much larger groups, perhaps more than forty girls in a specially built house. Boys sit between the girls and sing, frequently changing places. Songs are passed around the circle like a wave, some dancers sway and shake their heads, always remaining seated; there are no reports of facial contact (Aufenanger and Höltker 1979: 121–23; Fitz-Patrick and Kimbuna 1983: 62–64 (photos), 77–80; Zimmer 1985: 161–63). Terms similar to *koanandi* commonly designate similar large-scale courting activities in parts of Chimbu.

Information on the Daulo (Yawehuya) is given by Sexton. Although lacking much detail, courting involves the singing of songs and swaying of heads from side to side, with this latter element suggestive of similar forms described for the Siane and Chimbu, hence its tentative inclusion here. Sexton's work notes the incorporation of such movements in activities of *wok meri* groups, organized by women as a savings and exchange system (Sexton 1982: 177, 194; 1995: 211–12).

The information available on the Gururumba (Dano) focuses particularly on the long, multiversed songs sung in a quavering falsetto with phonetic modification while sitting in circles. Between verses, there is audible inhalation by the boys to resemble a heart-rending sigh. Girls then reply in kind. One group of boys leaves, allowing another group to court the girls, continuing as such throughout the night. Upon a girl's subsequent betrothal, for each night over about ten days, the girl, her age-mates and her brothers go to different villages where she has invited boys to serenade her before. But this time, the young men sing as a farewell, as the girl will never again be able to participate in such events (Newman 1962: 186, 189–94, 275; 1965: 97–98). I can find no mention of any movements during such courting or the contact of facial parts. Considering contemporary reports from other areas about such activities, it would be surprising if Newman omitted these details. Because of the minimal information about such performances, it is tentatively included with others related to Chimbu courting but coloured slightly differently on the map to show this uncertainty.

The inclusion of other groups in this category is even more uncertain. Haiman's Hua (Yagaria) dictionary includes a number of terms suggesting inclusion here to be appropriate, for example: *gima hu-* 'shake head in mass courtship party'; *igua* 'kissing courtship'; *sava* 'song at mass courtship party where girls party visit boys' village'; *soisava* 'mass courting parties, occurred when surplus food available' (Haiman 1991: 67, 94, 96). Haiman had read reports about courting in other parts of the Highlands but knew little about Hua ethnography during his research (2011, pers. comm., 24 October); I assume he wrote what he was told.[8] Because of the type of movements described, I have included arrows to Yagaria from Chimbu Province, linking traits more recently or only very generally described for neighbouring areas where such features are distinctive.

Similarly, there appears to be nothing in writings about Gimi courtship in early ethnographic reports. Later, Bragginton (1975: 84) mentions youths engaged in courtship activities considered 'suitable', but without elaboration. Gillison, however, describes young men going to a woman's house to sing *aboE* courting songs. Men sit cross-legged on a platform at the rear with their backs to the fire, while women sit facing the flames. Male and female dancers shake their heads rhythmically, swaying in unison to the singing by both sexes that juxtaposes poetic images of wild taro (beautiful girls) and black birds-of-paradise or cordyline (fine men). Facial contact between dancers also takes place and partners change. Between songs, actors perform *harukaru* ritual theatre.[9] Gillison (1993: 254; 2018, pers. comm., 18 and 24 October) notes the presence of Chimbu words in lyrics, but these are not necessarily indicative of borrowing. Because of this sole reference and its similarity to Chimbu courting, an arrow connects Chimbu to the Gimi area to include it as a possible member of this style.

Goroka Style

To the east of Dano and Siane speakers are a number of groups that practise quite different forms of courting but still display western links. Perhaps the most well-known account of the style I label 'Goroka' is from anthropologist Kenneth Read, who first conducted research in the Gahuku (Alekano) area in 1950–52. Australian journalist Colin Simpson cites a meeting with Read during the final year of his fieldwork, quoting the anthropologist: 'during courtship a man and woman lie side by side and rub their chins together until the skin is broken and bleeds' (Simpson 1955: 139). This is the first published account of courting practices in the Eastern Highlands and highlights two distinctive features of this style: the couple lies down and rubs parts of their faces together. Read (1965: 192–93) notes that the courting at night is for ten to fifteen couples but without adult supervision. The boy lies facing the girl, who places her head on his forearm, and they rub chins and lips together aggressively. The courting also involves singing, laughter and petting. One of the pair cradling the head of the other is also a recurring feature of courting in this style.

Benabena formal courting parties are described by Langness. One clan goes to another's men's house for all-night sessions involving much singing, joking and excitement. The interior of the house is swept clean, and fresh banana leaves are spread on the floor. Girls of each clan lie down around a fire along opposite walls; they call for partners who lie down alongside them and all sing. Continuing for an hour or two, the behaviour changes from the girls kissing[10] the young men around the neck and lower jaw to more ardent love-making. After the fire is rekindled, the girls call for new partners and the activity repeats. Girls change partners three or four times. More informal events also occur, where girls from one clan sing special songs to lure young men out into the grass for courting, but little more is known about these (Langness 1967: 166–67, 172–73; 1969: 42–43; 1999: 140–41, 152).

In more recent research on the Benabena, Dickerson-Putman (1986: 97–98; 1996: 48, 58–59) mentions the invitation from young men to young women of another clan to sing and court in the men's house on banana leaves but provides no other details. Finally, Kimiafa (2012: 5–6) describes *zafa guna*, where participants move up and down in columns, singing and trading kisses, resulting in sore chins and cheeks.

Further to the east of the Benabena, but excluding Kamano in between (see Henganofi style below), Agarabi courting takes place at night in the girls' clubhouse or during the day in a secluded spot. The couple lies together, with the boy cradling his head on the girl's arm, and the two rub their faces together. It is not clear if singing is absent or just not mentioned (J.B. Watson 1960: 146).[11] Note that the Agarabi are in the Kainantu area, where courting parties are generally absent.

Another seeming anomaly in the Kainantu area is North Tairora speakers. Although no mention of courting is found in other ethnographies, Virginia Watson's *Anyan's Story* (1997) describes courting where couples move to the inner room of the girl's house to lie down and 'cuddle'; the girl may put her head on the boy's arm or vice versa. The couple then rub their cheeks and jaws together (V.D. Watson 1997: 40–41). On Figure 7.2., arrows link related traditions to the east.

Henganofi Style

Rubbing parts of the face, associated with Goroka style, is also a main feature of groups in the Henganofi region and to the south. Here, however, the chins and cheeks are rubbed together by seated couples. The most detailed descriptions of this courting are provided by Ronald Berndt, resulting from fieldwork between 1951 and 1953, particularly in two areas: Inoke-Yate and Usarufa.[12]

Berndt notes two types of courting. The more common type is arranged by older men, who invite girls and their brothers to visit the village for formal courting. Less commonly, groups of girls themselves go from village to village to court. As an example of the former, for Jate (Inoke-Yate) *ajafahawaise* (chin rubbing), visitors arrange themselves on elevated ground near the men's house or in a specially constructed shelter. Boys form one line, while girls form another opposite them, each facing a *nenafu* (cross-cousin). The pairs rub chins. Such activities continue for two days. Feasting takes place during the evening, while the daytime is for chin rubbing. On the third and final day, the boys give presents to the girls. There is no explicit mention of singing (Berndt 1962: 117–19).

Additionally, Berndt describes courting between the Usurufa (Usarufa) and Jate (Inoke-Yate). Love magic is prepared by Usurufa participants, who spray the mixture on cooked sweet potatoes. Boys bring their sisters to this place and perform nose bleeding by forcing small sticks smeared with magic into their noses to make them less shy and more desirous to rub chins. When the Jate are asleep, the Usurufa visitors surround their house and pull off the grass roof, while girls enter the house and remove the boys' possessions, leaving them naked. The girls give these items to their brothers. The naked boys then emerge from the house, singing. The Usurufa girls' brothers sing in response. The Usurufa boys then lead their sisters to the Jate house to rub chins with their cross-cousins. In the morning, they go to higher ground near the men's house and form two lines to sing. Rubbing chins is then repeated and partners exchanged. A girl shows her preference for a partner by placing her hands on his shoulders or thighs, or touching his penis. Genuine attachments may be made, possibly leading to betrothal (Berndt 1962: 119–20).

Ethnomusicologist Vida Chenoweth also worked among the Usarufa and wrote her dissertation, a book and articles concerning their music. Formal courting was performed until the mid-1950s and was known as *timaaíkaq tótó yareqtareq-yátááqá* 'chin-rubbing'.[13] Girls were taken to other villages by their brothers and seated in a line opposite the young men of that village. Couples rubbed their chins and cheeks together. The boys' line then shifted, creating new pairings. This continued for two days. Chenoweth notes that songs were not sung during chin rubbing but that there are songs about it. But she then observes that courting songs are songs sung in seclusion (*aúpáq-ímá*) and that *aaqebaamá* songs, which structurally contrast a base (text) and leaves (vocables), are sung at courting parties. Are these sung during courting or about courting?

Furthermore, Chenoweth notes that there are no courting songs composed by an Usarufa or in that language; courting was always done with the Kanite, never between two Usarufa villages. Hence she suggests that it is probably a Kanite custom borrowed by the Usarufa. Volume 2 of her dissertation includes three courting songs in Kamano language (rather than Kanite), with translations into Usarufa and English. While acknowledging the considerable musical exchange between Usarufa, Kosena, Kanite, Kamano and Fore, the details of these exchanges for courting are not clear. In a later article, Chenoweth omits any reference to an outside origin (Chenoweth 1974: vol. 1, 30–31, 173, 181, 185, 187; vol. 2, sect. 1–3; 1979: 16, 89, 93, 96; 1998: 528).

Chenoweth's mention of Kanite courting is the only information available for this group. Fortunately, there is more for the Kamano. In 1935, Reo Fortune conducted the first research in the Highlands by a professional anthropologist and returned in 1951–52. Although he published very little (Hays 1992: 13–14; McLean 1992), Terence Hays kindly shared with me relevant extracts from Fortune's unpublished manuscript. Fortune describes courting parties in Finintegu (Kamano), where girls invite boys to court in the house of a young married couple, the latter acting as chaperones. The boy sits still with his arms folded across his chest while his partner sits at some distance opposite him. At intervals, she approaches him, puts her chin on his and rubs it around his cheek bones. The couple does not talk, although the chaperones talk to each other all night as the courting continues (Fortune [n.d.]: [14]; McLean 1985: 25).

Writing about fieldwork much later among the Kafe (Kamano), Faithorn (1990: 134, 140–42) describes 'kissing parties', where young people engage in ritualized kissing during the dry season, arranged between two villages and lasting several days.

Figure 7.2. has arrows showing possible influences of Henganofi courting on the Fore. While there are no reports about courting in any ethnographic reports, in a Fore dictionary under 'petting, kissing (chinning)', two nouns are listed: *amagi'énawe* (North–Central dialect) and *amaginé* (Southern dialect) (Scott 1980: 191).

Absences and Lack of Information

Chenoweth (1966: 288) describes the music of Gadsup courting songs but otherwise reveals nothing about them. Ethnographic reports discuss liaisons in the bush, but public courting would cause great shame (Du Toit 1975: 59). Specific reports of absences of courting activities are noted for the Awa (D. Boyd 2012, pers. comm., 29 June), Kenati (P. Lemonnier 2018, pers. comm., 9 October),[14] Ontenu (Finch 1991: 46) and South Tairora (Johnson 1980; T. Hays 2012, pers. comm., 14 March). No information on courting can be found in reports on the Awiyaana (Robbins 1982), Binumarien (Hawkes 1976; Oates 1992)[15] and Waffa (Stringer et al. 1979).[16] Here, I interpret this as meaning an absence.

For some language areas, I simply lack any sources at all: Isabi, Keyagana and Tokano (Gorokan languages); Kosena, Owenia and Kambaira (Kainantu languages).

Considering the Data

I have considered types of courting activities in Eastern Highlands Province, focusing on whether the couple is sitting or lying down, their spatial arrangement and what movements and songs (if any) are involved.

The data suggest three styles. Not surprisingly, the westernmost style links to other practices in neighbouring Chimbu Province. But courting in the Goroka area, the second style, concerns couples lying down and rubbing parts of their faces together. For the third style, focused on the Henganofi area, the couple is seated, particularly rubbing their chins and cheeks together.

Interestingly, most of these groups with courting traditions speak Gorokan languages: the only Kainantu languages with evidence of such courting are among the Agarabi and Usarufa, with one report also for the North Tairora. Such a distribution suggests that courting in Eastern Highlands likely spread from west to east. This is not particularly surprising, since much more varied courting traditions are found to the west.

Yet are the courting movements to be considered 'a specially marked or elaborated category of structured movement' (Kaeppler 2017: 431) – that is, dance? Many of the movements, particularly the rubbing of facial parts of couples lying together, are certainly not types of everyday public activities for couples; indeed, such public interactions would otherwise be considered quite inappropriate. Yet in the context of courting, they become not only socially acceptable but required, movements that can be called dance. Hence, while courting in Eastern Highlands often seems to lack the more structured, coordinated movements of some courting in Chimbu, Jiwaka and Western Highlands, there is little question that the movements are very much specially marked, elaborated and highly enjoyable for the participants. I hope Adrienne would agree. If she does not, I am sure she will let me know why. As always, thank you, Adrienne.

Don Niles is acting director and senior ethnomusicologist of the Institute of Papua New Guinea Studies, where he has worked since 1979. He researches and publishes on many types of music and dance in Papua New Guinea, including traditional, popular and Christian forms. The author/editor of numerous books, articles and audiovisual publications on various aspects of music, dance and archiving, Don also edits the Institute's music monograph series (*Apwɨtɨhɨre: Studies in Papua New Guinea Musics*) and journal (*Kulele: Occasional Papers in Pacific Music and Dance*). He is a vice president of the International Council for Traditional Music and former editor of their journal, the *Yearbook for Traditional Music*. He is also honorary associate professor at the Australian National University. In 2016, he was invested as an Officer in the Order of Logohu.

Notes

1. For some reasons now forgotten, my visit to Honolulu did not extend to the world conference of what was then the International Folk Music Council, 13–18 August 1977. How unfortunate, considering the importance of the Council to both of our lives later on!
2. Extensive use of such varied materials is made in my dissertation (Niles 2011) and an article about confusion over initial reports of courting in the Hagen area (Niles 2017).
3. Stewart and A. Strathern (2002: 29–90) provide an invaluable overview of courting in the Highlands, albeit with different emphases from my own.
4. My knowledge of and accessibility to relevant sources for Eastern Highlands has greatly benefited from the kindness and generosity of Terry Hays. He has also freely shared his own insights about many aspects of courting. *Tenkyu tru, poro*. I have also learned from communications with David Boyd, Dalson Eriko, Gillian Gillison, John Haiman and Pierre Lemonnier. Of course, any misinterpretations are my own. I undertook brief research trips to Eastern Highlands in 1982, 2011, 2012 and 2016 and explored relevant resources at the University of Goroka and SIL in Ukarumpa. In all this work, I have been supported by the Institute of Papua New Guinea Studies. My attachment as honorary associate professor at the Australian National University enables access to many library resources that otherwise would have been unavailable to me. Editors Kendra Stepputat and Brian Diettrich helped me further refine and improve my presentation. My sincere thanks to all.
5. For me, mapping is an essential methodology in both presenting some idea of the complexity of the area under consideration (particularly for those unfamiliar with this part of Papua New Guinea), as well as helping to illustrate potential groupings based on certain

aspects of courting. Without such maps, I fear that the abundance of names would likely overwhelm the points I am trying to make.

6. Similar movements are also described in Bogner's biography of a Siane woman, although with contact of noses and heads, followed by kissing (Bogner 1984: 181–82, 188).
7. In discussing the first European patrols in the region, Salisbury notes that participants encountered courting practices in the Chimbu and Dene (Chuave) areas that were less restrained than *awoiro* (Salisbury-Rowswell 1957: 171; Salisbury 1962: 113). It is surprising he does not consider the more comparable *gimagama* instead.
8. The general features are confirmed by Yagaria speakers, who have heard about such courting from their elders (D. Eriko 2018, pers. comm., 22 October).
9. Although described by Berndt (1962), particularly see the rich photographic essay by Gillison (1983).
10. While I recognize that kissing can refer to different things in different cultures, as with most of the descriptions contained in this chapter, I generally follow the terminology in the sources consulted, as further information is presently unavailable.
11. The only other description of Agarabi courting is of a different kind: groups of boys singing on a hill to seduce the girl intended so that she will invite the boy to go to her house (Watson 1965: 117–18).
12. In their overview of Highlands courting, Stewart and A. Strathern (2002: 33–35) cite Berndt's work but erroneously attribute the courting to the Fore.
13. The name in a later publication (Chenoweth 1998: 528) is slightly different: *timaaíkaq tótó yareqtareq-yátááré*. Perhaps this is another grammatical form.
14. Although spending just a short time in this region, Lemonnier recalls that courting parties would have horrified the neighbouring Baruya and they would have informed him.
15. Hays (2011, pers. comm., 10 November) notes that anthropologist Kristin Hawkes told him that the Binumarien never had courting parties. He further reflects that as the Binumarien spent many years in the Markham Valley, only returning to the Kainantu area after Australian pacification, it is very hard to know what they did previously, what they learned in Markham, etc.
16. Hays worked with South Tairora people, who had close ties with the Waffa. They claimed there were no courting parties among the Waffa (2011, pers. comm., 10 November).

References

Aufenanger, H., and G. Höltker. 1979. 'The Gende of Central New Guinea, Part One', *Oral History* 7: 1–144. Translated by Philip Holzknecht (1st part of *Die Gende in Zentralneuguinea*. Wien-Mödling: Missionsdruckerei St. Gabriel, 1940).

Baglin, D., and C. de Courcy. 1988. *The Jimi River Expedition 1950: Exploration in the New Guinea Highlands*. Melbourne: Oxford University Press.

Berndt, R.M. 1962. *Excess and Restraint: Social Control among a New Guinea Mountain People*. Chicago: University of Chicago Press.

Bogner, P. 1984. *In der Steinzeit geboren: Eine Papua-Frau erzählt*. Lamuv Taschenbuch 35. Bornheim-Merten: Lamuv Verlag.

Bragginton, J. 1975. 'Patterns of Interaction in the Beha Valley: A Study of Social Organization in the Eastern Highlands of New Guinea', Ph.D. dissertation. Evanston: Northwestern University.

Chenoweth, V. 1966. 'Song Structure of a New Guinea Highlands Tribe', *Ethnomusicology* 10(3): 285–97.
———. 1974. 'The Music of the Usarufas', Ph.D. dissertation. Auckland: University of Auckland.
———. 1979. *The Usarufas and Their Music*, vol. 5, SIL Museum of Anthropology Publication. Dallas: SIL Museum of Anthropology.
———. 1998. 'Highland Region of Papua New Guinea: Eastern Highlands Province', in A.L. Kaeppler and J.W. Love (eds), *Australia and the Pacific Islands*, vol. 9, Garland Encyclopedia of World Music. New York: Garland Publishing, pp. 526–33.
Christensen, D., and A.L. Kaeppler. 1974. 'Oceanic Peoples, Arts of: III. The Performing Arts: Music and Dance', in *The New Encyclopædia Britannica, Macropædia*, vol. 13, 15th edn. Chicago: Encyclopædia Britannica, pp. 456–61.
Dickerson-Putman, J. 1986. 'Finding a Road in the Modern World: The Differential Effects of Culture Change and Development on the Men and Women of an Eastern Highlands Papua, New Guinean Community', Ph.D. dissertation. Bryn Mawr: Bryn Mawr College.
———. 1996. 'From Pollution to Empowerment: Women, Age, and Power among the Bena Bena of the Eastern Highlands', *Pacific Studies* 19(4): 41–70.
Du Toit, B.M. 1975. *Akuna: A New Guinea Village Community*. Rotterdam: A.A. Balkema.
Faithorn, E. 1990. 'The Female Life Cycle and Male-Female Relations among the Kafe of the Papua New Guinea Highlands', Ph.D. dissertation. Philadelphia: University of Pennsylvania.
Finch, J. 1991. 'Coffee, Development, and Inequality in the Papua New Guinea Highlands', Ph.D. dissertation. New York: City University of New York.
Fitz-Patrick, D.G., and J. Kimbuna. 1983. *Bundi: The Culture of a Papua New Guinea People*. Nerang: Ryebuck Publications.
Fortune, R.F. [n.d.]. *Men of Purari* [Manuscript]. [s.l.]
Gende, E. 1998. 'Highland Region of Papua New Guinea: Chimbu Province: Kuman', in A.L. Kaeppler and J.W. Love (eds), *Australia and the Pacific Islands*. The Garland Encyclopedia of World Music, 9. New York: Garland Publishing, pp. 522–26.
Gillespie, K. 2010. *Steep Slopes: Music and Change in the Highlands of Papua New Guinea*. Canberra: ANU E Press.
Gillison, G. 1983. 'Living Theater in New Guinea's Highlands', *National Geographic* 164 (August): 146–69.
———. 1993. *Between Culture and Fantasy: A New Guinea Highlands Mythology*. Chicago: University of Chicago Press.
Haiman, J. 1991. *Hua–English Dictionary with a English–Hua Index*. Wiesbaden: Otto Harrassowitz.
Hawkes, K. 1976. 'Binumarien: Kinship and Cooperation in a New Guinea Highlands Community', Ph.D. dissertation. Seattle: University of Washington.
Hays, T.E. 1992. 'A Historical Background to Anthropology in the Papua New Guinea Highlands', in T.E. Hays (ed.), *Ethnographic Presents: Pioneering Anthropologists in the Papua New Guinea Highlands*. Berkeley: University of California Press, pp. 1–36.
Heartz, D., and B. Wade (eds). 1981. *Report of the Twelfth Congress Berkeley 1977*. Kassel: Bärenreiter.
Jablonko, A. 1991. 'Patterns of Daily Life in the Dance of the Maring of New Guinea', *Visual Anthropology* 4: 367–77.

Johnson, R. 1980. '"Secret Knowledge": An Analysis of Ommura Ceremonies', Ph.D. dissertation. Oxford: University of Oxford.

Kaeppler, A.L. 1963. 'Music of New Guinea; the Australian Trust Territory', *Ethnomusicology* 7(1): 60–61.

———. 1977. 'Polynesian Dance as "Airport Art"', in A.L. Kaeppler, J. Van Zile and C. Wolz (eds), *Asian and Pacific Dance: Selected Papers from the 1974 CORD-SEM Conference*, vol. 8, Dance Research Annual. New York: Committee on Research in Dance, pp. 71–84.

———. 1978. *'Artificial Curiosities': Being an Exposition of Native Manufactures . . .*, vol. 65, B.P. Bishop Museum Special Publication. Honolulu: Bishop Museum Press.

———. 1992. 'The Use of Archival Film in an Ethnohistoric Study of Persistence and Change in Hawaiian Hula', in A. Marshall Moyle (ed.), *Music and Dance of Aboriginal Australia and the South Pacific*, vol. 41, Oceania Monograph. Sydney: University of Sydney, pp. 110–23.

———. 1993. *Hula Pahu: Hawaiian Drum Dances. Volume 1: Ha'a and Hula Pahu: Sacred Movements*, vol. 3, Bulletin in Anthropology. Honolulu: Bishop Museum Press.

———. 2001. 'Accordions in Tahiti—an Enigma', in H. Reeves Lawrence and D. Niles (eds), *Traditionalism and Modernity in the Music and Dance of Oceania: Essays in Honour of Barbara B. Smith*, vol. 52, Oceania Monographs. Sydney: University of Sydney, pp. 44–66.

———. 2017. 'Capturing Music and Dance in an Archive: A Meditation on Imprisonment', in K. Gillespie, S. Treloyn and D. Niles (eds), *A Distinctive Voice in the Antipodes: Essays in Honour of Stephen A. Wild*. Canberra: ANU Press, pp. 429–42.

Kaeppler, A.L., and J.W. Love (eds). 1998. *Australia and the Pacific Islands*, vol. 9, Garland Encyclopedia of World Music. New York: Garland Publishing.

Kimiafa, K. 2012. 'Traditions of the Bena Bena People of Eastern Highlands', in *Keith Jackson & Friends: PNG ATTITUDE* [online]. Retrieved 11 April 2019 from http://asopa.typepad.com/files/traditions-of-the-bena-bena.pdf.

Kyakas, A., and P. Wiessner. 1992. *From Inside the Women's House; Enga Women's Lives and Traditions*. Illustrated by A.W. Ipu. Buranda: Robert Brown and Associates.

Langness, L.L. 1967. 'Sexual Antagonism in the New Guinea Highlands: A Bena Bena Example', *Oceania* 37(3): 161–77.

———. 1969. 'Marriage in Bena Bena', in R.M. Glasse and M.J. Meggitt (eds), *Pigs, Pearlshells, and Women: Marriage in the New Guinea Highlands*. Englewood Cliffs: Prentice Hall, pp. 38–55.

———. 1999. *Men and 'Woman' in New Guinea*. Novato: Chandler and Sharp Publishers.

Luzbetak, L.J. 1954. 'The Socio-Religious Significance of a New Guinea Pig Festival', *Anthropological Quarterly* 2: 59–80, 102–28.

McLean, A. 1985. 'Fighting for Survival: A Study of Violence in the Eastern Highlands of Papua New Guinea', BLitt thesis. Australian National University.

———. 1992. 'In the Footprints of Reo Fortune', in T.E. Hays (ed.), *Ethnographic Presents: Pioneering Anthropologists in the Papua New Guinea Highlands*. Berkeley: University of California Press, pp. 37–67.

Newman, P.L. 1962. 'Supernaturalism and Ritual among the Gururumba', Ph.D. dissertation. Seattle: University of Washington.

———. 1965. *Knowing the Gururumba*. New York: Holt, Rinehart and Winston.

Niles, D. 2011. 'Structuring Sound and Movement: Music and Dance in the Mount Hagen Area', Ph.D. dissertation. Port Moresby: University of Papua New Guinea.

———. 2017. '"Never Seen It Before": The Earliest Reports and Resulting Confusion about the Hagen Courting Dance', in K. Gillespie, S. Treloyn and D. Niles (eds), *A Distinctive Voice in the Antipodes: Essays in Honour of Stephen A. Wild*. Canberra: ANU Press, pp. 407–28.

Nilles, J. 1950. 'The Kuman of the Chimbu Region, Central Highlands, New Guinea', *Oceania* 21: 25–65.

Oates, L. 1992. *Hidden People: How a Remote New Guinea Culture Was Brought Back from the Brink of Extinction*. Sutherland: Albatross Books.

O'Hanlon, M. 1989. *Reading the Skin: Adornment, Display and Society Among the Wahgi*. London: British Museum Publications.

Pitcairn, T.K., and M. Schleidt. 1976. 'Dance and Decision: An Analysis of a Courtship Dance of the Medlpa, New Guinea', *Behaviour* 58: 298–316.

Pugh-Kitingan, J. 1981. 'An Ethnomusicological Study of the Huli of the Southern Highlands, Papua New Guinea', 3 vols. PhD dissertation. Brisbane: University of Queensland.

Read, K.E. 1965. *The High Valley*. New York: Charles Scribner's Sons.

Reay, M. 1959. *The Kuma: Freedom and Conformity in the New Guinea Highlands*. Carlton: Melbourne University Press.

Robbins, S. 1982. *Auyana: Those Who Held onto Home*, vol. 6, Anthropological Studies in the Eastern Highlands of New Guinea. Seattle: University of Washington.

Salisbury, R.F. 1962. *From Stone to Steel: Economic Consequence of a Technological Change in New Guinea*. Melbourne: Melbourne University Press.

———. 1965. 'The Siane of the Eastern Highlands', in P. Lawrence and M.J. Meggitt (eds), *Gods Ghosts and Men in Melanesia*. Melbourne: Oxford University Press, pp. 50–77.

Salisbury-Rowswell, R.F. 1957. 'Economic Change among the Siane Tribes of New Guinea', Ph.D. dissertation. Canberra: Australian National University.

Schieffelin, E.L. 1976. *The Sorrow of the Lonely and the Burning of the Dancers*. New York: St. Martin's Press.

Scott, G. 1980. *Fore Dictionary*, vol. C 62, Pacific Linguistics. Canberra: Australian National University.

Sexton, L. 1982. '*Wok Meri*: A Women's Savings and Exchange System in Highland Papua New Guinea', *Oceania* 52(3): 167–98.

———. 1995. 'Marriage as the Model for a New Initiation Ritual', in N.C. Lutkehaus and P. B. Roscoe (eds), *Gender Rituals: Female Initiation in Melanesia*. New York: Routledge, pp. 205–16.

Simons, G.F., and C.D. Fennig (eds). 2018. *Ethnologue: Languages of the World*, 21st edn. Dallas: SIL International.

Simpson, C. 1955. *Adam in Plumes*, 2nd edn. Sydney: Angus and Robertson.

Stewart, P.J., and A. Strathern. 2002. *Gender, Song, and Sensibility: Folktales and Folksongs in the Highlands of New Guinea*. Westport: Praeger.

Strathern, A. 1974. *Melpa Amb Kenan: Courting Songs of the Melpa People*. Boroko: Institute of Papua New Guinea Studies.

Strathern, A., and M. Strathern. 1971. *Self-decoration in Mount Hagen*. London: Gerald Duckworth.

Stringer, M.D., J.M. Hotz and Sibaamo Punuqo. 1979. *Dictionary of Waffa, Tok Pisin, English*, vol. 3, Dictionaries of Papua New Guinea. Ukarumpa: Summer Institute of Linguistics.

Talyaga, K. 1973. *Enga Eda Nemago: Meri Singsing Poetry of the Yandapo Engas*. Papua Pocket Poets, 40. Port Moresby: [n.p.].

Vicedom, G.F., and H. Tischner. 1943–48. *Die Mbowamb: Die Kultur der Hagenberg-Stämme im östlichen Zentral-Neuguinea*. 3 vols. Monographien zur Völkerkunde. Vol. 1: Hamburg: Cram, de Gruyter, 1943–48; Vol. 2–3: Hamburg: Friederichsen, de Gruyter, 1943.

Watson, J.B. 1960. 'A New Guinea "Opening Man"', in J.B. Casagrande (ed.), *In the Company of Man: Twenty Portraits by Anthropologists*. New York: Harper and Brothers, pp. 127–73.

Watson, V.D. 1965. 'Agarabi Female Roles and Family Structure: A Study in Sociocultural Change', Ph.D. dissertation. Chicago: University of Chicago.

———. 1997. *Anyan's Story: A New Guinea Woman in Two Worlds*. Seattle: University of Washington Press.

Zimmer, L.J. 1985. 'The Losing Game: Exchange, Migration, and Inequality among the Gende People of Papua New Guinea', Ph.D. dissertation. Bryn Mawr: Bryn Mawr College.

PART III

Music and Dance as Agency in Power Struggles

Chapter 8

Disturbing Bodies

Danced Resistance and Imperial Corporeality in Colonial Micronesia

Brian Diettrich

Synchronized groups of young men and women in bright-coloured attire stepped from side to side and exuberantly clapped in time. One group processed in close arrangement, while bystanders adorned performers with shards of cloth and sprayed perfume. Unprompted bodies leapt up and moved to the beat with arms above heads amid outbursts of delight. People grooved together in the hot, raucous, celebratory gathering as a chorus of unified voices sang out over the heavily amplified keyboards, its rhythms encouraging participation from those stirred by the multisensory experience. This communal outpouring of corporeal joy celebrated the centennial Jubilee of the Catholic Church in the islands of Chuuk, in the Federated States of Micronesia. On the 4th and 5th of February 2011, the event brought together hundreds of Islanders from eleven parishes in Chuuk Lagoon and its outer atolls, to exuberantly celebrate the first arrival of their faith to the islands in 1911 (Figure 8.1). Chuukese Catholics commemorated the gathering with newly created songs and with choreographed dances. Today, as in the past, dance is an integral component of community performance spaces in Chuuk, and shared experiences in movement are integral to the celebratory fabric of society.[1]

In the colonial period that brought the first conversions to Christianity, however, dance was rarely integrated within the emerging Catholic or Protestant faiths in the islands. For the earliest Christian missionaries, dance was instead one of the most recognizably abhorrent practices, one that seemed antithetical to the church and its imported notions of civilization. American Protestant missionary Francis Price, for example, condemned Chuukese dancing as 'the most subtle device of Satan, and his most powerful weapon' (Price 1895a, 13 June), while the Catholic missionary Laurentius Bollig, known for his otherwise thoughtful writing about Chuukese culture, judged the dances he witnessed as a 'school

Figure 8.1. Dancers in formation at the centennial Jubilee of the Catholic Church in Chuuk; Weno, Chuuk, 4 February 2011. © Brian Diettrich.

for fornication' (Bollig 1927: 194). Missionaries recognized dancing in Chuuk as a source of influential power, and one they felt compelled to confront. But while missionary opposition to Indigenous dance is ubiquitous in the Pacific and elsewhere, what is much less known is the extent of how Chuukese collectively danced as a means of resistance to the imperialism of the new church. In the late nineteenth century, the moving body was at the centre of a series of cultural confrontations in which Islanders danced against the new faith and simultaneously promoted a shared choreography of Indigenous society as an alternative to the new way of the light (*saram*).

This chapter explores the power and politics of dance performance in cross-cultural ideology. I examine how dance became a primary impediment to mission attempts at domesticating and taming Indigenous bodies. In reflecting on the proliferation of dancing in the earliest period of Christian conversions in Chuuk, I narrate how for some Islanders dancing became a means to resist the mission. Through a close consideration of Chuukese practices of dance, representation by the mission and dance in early documentary film, I examine the interplay of Indigenous bodies, collective movement and colonialism. I especially aim to provide a cultural view of the place of dance in late nineteenth-century Chuuk, reading past the biases of the mission records as well as the absences of music and dance in historical accounts of Micronesia. Drawing on critical perspectives of the body and performance, I argue that the confrontations over dancing in Chuuk were a potent indication of the corporeality of imperialism in the northwest Pacific.

Understanding the emergent power of dance and performance in the Pacific Islands involves tracing the past politics of moving, social bodies over time (Giurchescu 2011). In doing so, this chapter builds on the extensive research and publications of Adrienne Kaeppler, and especially her long-spanning research on dance in Tonga and in Hawai'i, among other areas. While much of Kaeppler's work builds on ethnographic methods, she has also engaged deeply with the practice of history, and especially in tracing the manifestations of expressive practices over time, including music and dance, but also visual materials, both objects and photography (Kaeppler 1970, 1992, 2001, 2007). In bringing together anthropological and historical methods for Tongan dance, Kaeppler asks, 'how can bodies converse and convey history?' To this she offers an additional query, 'And how can history help us to understand dance and other structured movement systems in the present?' (Kaeppler 2007: 26). In Kaeppler's scholarship on the Hawaiian genre *hula pahu* and the Tongan dance type *lakalaka*, she examined historical transformation in style and meaning from Indigenous perspectives. In bridging anthropological and historical methods, Kaeppler's work also contextualized Indigenous agency in performance innovations over time in the Pacific. In this chapter, I take inspiration from Kaeppler's dance explorations to investigate the politics of dancing and missionization in colonial Micronesia.

Corporeality and Empire

Notions of the body as a realm of discourse has remained an integral component of cultural analysis (Kim and Gilman 2018; Lepecki 2004; Rao and Pierce 2006; Turner 2012). For Rao and Pierce, understanding the situated bodies of colonized Others reveals the intimate relationships of imperialism to ideas of cultural difference (Rao and Pierce 2006: 5). Similarly, for Ballantyne, in writing about New Zealand, colonization through missionary enterprises offered 'deep and recurrent concern for the body, its meaning, and its regulation' and resulted in projects of 'remaking Māori bodies' (Ballantyne 2014: 6). Balme, in his study of Pacific performance, further noted how colonialism 'acted on bodies' but added that 'bodies responded to these impositions more often in performance' (Balme 2007: 96). This efficacy of performance resonates across the Pacific Islands, where Indigenous peoples moved and danced through, past and sometimes around imperial impositions, or in the case of Pohnpei Island, what Petersen (1992) has termed 'dancing defiance'. Indeed, the Pacific is replete with examples of dances that were condemned and banned but also that persisted (Alexeyeff 2009: 36–4; Barrère, Pukui, Kelly 1980; McLean 1999: 421–25; Moyle 1988: 205–12). A reflection on these examples underscores the inherent corporeality of colonial discourse globally – a focused desire to objectify and regulate Indigenous bodies, particularly since they disrupt the colonizer ideals (Shea Murphy 2007) and what Brendan Hokowhitu (2014) explores as 'colonised physicality'. The politics of imperial confrontations in music and dance were often direct and traumatic, and examples in the Pacific stand in contrast to pervasive encounter narratives that have focused on mere cultural ambiguity (Agnew 2013). Viewing dance in imperial contexts suggest instead the lived yet contested implications of colonialism (Radano and Olaniyan 2016).

Building on critical and cultural perspectives, Indigenous dancing bodies in this chapter are a prime site for both the imperial gaze but also as an agency of resistance, a choreography between Islander and colonizer that simultaneously disrupted and re-enacted Indigenous society. As such, this chapter builds on critical work that has explored dancing as a strategic means of power in society and culture (Hokowhitu 2014; Knowles 2009; Kowal, Siegmund and Martin 2017; Shea Murphy 2007; Teaiwa 2012). In nineteenth-century Micronesia, dance was at the centre of confrontation about similarity and difference, but dance practices also transformed at the meeting point of imperial vision. In Chuuk, Islander bodies posed risks for disruption and disturbance of both sacred and secular empire, but at the same time new ideas about dance – including its cultural abandonment – offered novel pathways to engage with the modernity that was shaping island communities. In the in-between realm of late nineteenth-century Micronesia, dance was both a site of intense resistance and an Indigenous way of life, closely intertwined with ancestral reverence and community well-being. This chapter is part of a larger historical project focused on historical music and dance in the northwest Pacific, and based on research in the region since 2000, as well as a close examination of archive materials. In what follows, I provide a cultural narrative that has so far remained largely hidden in official Micronesian histories.[2] Telling stories of dance in Chuuk's past brings together strands of empire, corporeality and the cultural past and provides further evidence of how Micronesians were less 'strangers in their own land' (Hezel 1995) but more agents in their collective futures.

Movements of Resistance

Beginning in the mid nineteenth century, arrivals to Chuuk from Europe, America and later Japan brought new visions of dance and the body. Congregational missionaries of the American Board of Commissioners for Foreign Missions (ABCFM), in particular, saw Indigenous dance as particularly evil and largely representative of all that was uncivilized. In their formal reports and extensive personal letters written from the 1870s through the first decade of the twentieth century, the earliest ABCFM missionaries in Chuuk recorded the prominence of group dances in communal life, and they pervasively condemned them for perversions of sexuality and Indigenous religion.[3] At times they wrote obsessively about the bodies of those they encountered. They particularly condemned the long hair of men, the use of turmeric as regular cosmetic, what they viewed as improperly clothed bodies, as well as body adornments intricately fashioned from shell and inserted into pierced ear lobes and the hair. Of all practices, however, it was participation in 'the dance', as the Protestant missionaries often simplified it, that was a culmination of all that was wrong about the body, and more than anything, the ABCFM mission intended to remake Chuukese bodies in a vision of their own white American identity (Conroy-Krutz 2015: 5–6; Knoll 1997). But missionaries were not the only colonial figures who gave attention to dance. Officials of the German and Japanese administrative governments variously banned and yet promoted dancing, while early ethnographers described and recorded it (Bollig 1927; Krämer 1932; Tanabe 1968). From these colonial representations and transformations from the late nineteenth and early twentieth century, Chuukese bodies were a focal point of imperial corporeality in Micronesia. In their large-scale group dances, Chuukese bodies – adorned, painted with turmeric and moving in synchrony – were also a fulcrum for organized responses to the religious intrusions and conversions that appeared within island communities.

Dancing at Lemankok Meeting House, Weno Island 1895

By the late nineteenth century, the various villages that encircle Weno Island, today the capital of Chuuk, were engaged in breakouts of conflict. The political ramifications of these skirmishes saw that lineages from the southern villages on Weno, especially that of Mwáán, were pitted against villages to the north, especially those of Iras and Mechitiw (King and Parker 1984; Parker 1985). Into these local conflicts came additional pressures by the new Protestant mission – consisting of a few American men and women but also a cohort of Indigenous teachers – as well as the Spanish and subsequent German governments that vied for control of the region. Mwáán village could boast that it held the seat of the Protestant mission, called Anapau, which held the most influential foreigners in Chuuk, including the leading American missionary Robert Logan. By the mid-1880s, a small church also had been built in Tunnuk village to the north under chief Pokio, and by the early 1890s, an early church was also established in Mechitiw village. In Iras village to the northwest and under the shadow of mount Tonaachaw, chiefs repeatedly rejected offers to establish a church in the 1880s. Raaf, a powerful senior chief and spirit medium, was strongly opposed to the mission (King and Parker 1984: 93), and thus Iras was openly defiant toward the faith. But by late 1895, the Protestant missionary Francis Price happily reported in his letters that the first church in Iras was under construction (Price 1895a, 4 November) on a parcel of land called Fónnap and likely at the request of Raaf's chiefly son named Nikkichiinnap, who was open to the mission (Parker 1985: 232–33). The presence of the new faith on Weno in the late nineteenth century was thus precarious and entangled in lineage politics (Peter 1996), but it was also closely entwined with dance.

During the nineteenth century in Chuuk, dance (*pwérúk*) was practised for a wide variety of reasons, both large-scale in villages but also in private, by spiritual knowledge specialists. In public contexts, dance by groups was a primary means of social cohesion. Dances brought people together for important social functions and offered entertainment on a grand scale that broke from daily life; dances were also an important means of hosting visiting groups and a primary means of exchange between communities – across villages and separate islands, including the more distant atoll communities (Figure 8.2.). Chants and dances were newly learned and brought back home during these engagements. With dance songs that focused on play, banter and veiled sexuality, communities undertook social dances called *éwúwénú* for entertainment under the guidance of the female deity Inemes, especially in the non-breadfruit season of lean resources. Still another main context for dance was public spirit medium communications, in which a summoned spirit offered advice about conflicts, healing and future outcomes. At these events, dances called *tukuyá* (stick dances) and *pisimóót* (seated dances with handclapping) celebrated spiritual encounters for a particularly powerful and valued ancestral spirit (Bollig 1927; Goodenough 2002: 166–67; Tanabe 1968). Dances were thus intimately interwoven into everyday village life but also special festive occasions that brought people together across villages and islands. For the American Protestants, the dances were evidence of a debased sexuality and superstitious ignorance – roadblocks on the pathway to a Christian life. Everywhere the missionaries travelled around Chuuk's many islands they condemned all forms of *pwérúk*, and as Islanders were newly baptized, they were expected to refrain from dances. Even as their peers participated, new converts were expected to target dance as a Satanic practice.

In reaction to the continual prohibitions on dancing by the mission and joined by the small but emerging community of Islanders who saw value in abandoning *pwérúk*, at least temporarily, some villages seemed to hold dances on an increasingly large scale by the late nineteenth century, and this strongly suggests a strategic 'dancing defiance' (Petersen 1992) to the interventions brought by the mission. In 1894, missionary Francis Price and his wife first arrived at Anapau on Weno Island to assist the mission after the death of Robert Logan. Price quickly started to make regular excursions to Iras and other villages and wrote with confidence in 1895: 'I asked them if they were willing to give up the dance, their heathen practices, tobacco, and other things not allowed by the church and they answered that they were willing' (Price 1895a, 18 February). Given how dance was integral to society, Price's letters portray an over self-confidence if not naiveté, but certainly some Islanders saw opportunity in conversions in the form of new social recognition and material wealth and were thus willing to outwardly agree with the mission. By May 1895, Price believed that there was strong willingness to stop dance performances of Weno, and although his letters to the board offered hope for the new *lamalam* (religion), the events

Figure 8.2. Men from Chuuk adorned for a community celebration, c. 1910 (Krämer 1932: Plate 8c). Image courtesy of the Museum am Rothenbaum (MARKK), Hamburg, Germany.

that followed showed that the mission was rarely in control of its own destiny (Price 1895a, 17 May).

Sometime that same year, a former Christian convert named Levi (Newi), who formerly worked with the mission under Robert Logan, decided to break with the new faith (Price 1895a, 13 June). The Anapau mission at Mwáán at the time was undergoing extraordinary stress as a result of rogue missionary Alfred Snelling, and although it is possible Levi was influenced by these events, it is more likely that Levi's interventions came from his own personal and communal experiences.[4] Sometime before July, Levi received direction from an ancestral spirit (generally called *énúúsór*), and as a result he organized a series of extensive community dances. Price referred to Levi as a 'medicine man' of strong influence (Price 1895a, 13 June), and while it is difficult to understand Levi's exact position from mission letters, a corroboration with Indigenous spiritual practices in Chuuk suggests he was a spirit medium (*wáán énú* or *wáátawa*), and thus would have been understood as a source of great benefit and power within the broader population. Importantly, mediums conveyed new songs and dances from their encounters with ancestral spirits, and thus dance events were an important context for learning new song compositions and for the exchange of music and dance. For an especially charismatic and efficacious medium like Levi, dances offered wide participation, and they were quickly taken up by others.

Such was the influence of Levi and his spiritual encounters that in 1895 he constructed a new *wuut* (meeting house) at an area on Weno called Lemankok for the purpose of holding these group dances, perhaps as directed by the spirit. At Lemankok that year, Chuukese on Weno danced in open disregard and defiance of the mission's prohibitions. So influential were Levi's dance events, and likely the expressions and performances that came from them, that additional dances were begun by residents of neighbouring Mechitiw village, also on the northern tier of Weno. A chief of Mechitiw named Loi (Loyi) sanctioned these new dances, in part because of the influence of a wife of Levi, unnamed in the accounts, but who was from the same village (Price 1895a, 13 June). Price viewed Levi and the wave of dancing that he started on Weno in 1895 as a primary obstacle to God's work. He vented frustration with the resulting dances in a number of letters and reports to the board, and he characterized them variously as 'the source of great evil', 'a feast for the devil' and 'conducted with wild madness and most licentious practices' (Price 1895c: 51), as well as 'his [Satan's] most powerful weapon against the church' (Price 1895a, 13 June). Reading Price's condemnations reveals how dancing became a powerful means of opposition to the church, and particularly as led by practising spirit mediums. Writing later from his residency in Chuuk from 1913 to 1919, German Catholic priest Laurentius Bollig (1927: 63–64) explained that male and female spirit mediums were the cultural specialists most opposed to Christian conversion. Chuukese community engagement in large dance festivals in the late nineteenth century offered an alternative perspective to the new faith. By the late 1890s, those Chuukese opposed to the church had effectively rolled back Christianity on Weno. Communities eventually abandoned the churches formerly established at Iras and Mechitiw (King and Parker 1984: 83), and the ABCFM, consumed by internal strife, moved their main station to Tonoas Island at Kinamue (Kinamwmwe, meaning 'Peace') by 1896. Community dances continued, largely unabated, despite the mission.

The dancing in the late nineteenth century was not limited to Weno Island, and as the mission's letters reveal, dancing was practised at almost every island they visited, across Chuuk Lagoon and on the Mortlock atolls to the south. For example, when visiting Udot Island in central Chuuk Lagoon during the first half of 1895, Price witnessed the dances organized by chief Fetelaplap, who also sought interest in the new faith. In his letters, Price wrote of the dances on Udot with particular scorn:

> This dance is a most vile device of Satan, and his most powerful weapon and does far more harm than all the wars and other evils combined. It is exciting, furnishes the only opportunity that their natural vanity has for expressing itself in decorating the body, and is licentious through and through. (Price 1895a, 13 June)

Later in 1895 when visiting the Mortlock Islands, Price likewise found, to his dismay, that dancing was a regular activity. On Ta Island, where even the Deacon and his wife took part in the dances, Price and Moses – the Indigenous missionary who worked on Uman Island – gave a sermon before the fledgling congregation that specifically targeted the evils of the dance. After these public messages, Price tried to convince chief Boaz (Poas) of Ta to stop the dancing, but as he narrated: 'The old man seemed troubled, and after sometime said that it was impossible for him to stop the dance, for he said, "If I do, the people from the adjacent islands, where they have the dance and want it to continue, will come over and fight us, and we shall have a war on our hands"' (Price 1895b: 42–43). Chief Boaz knew the importance of dance exchanges to the social fabric of the islands, while Price merely saw a heathen offense that had to be torn down in the refashioning of Christian bodies. In the 1890s in Chuuk, dance was simultaneously an institution of communal society and a great disturbance on the pathway to 'civilization'.

Dancing for the Kaiser

Dancing in Chuuk was fully entangled in the ideology and efforts of the American mission, but by the first years of the twentieth century, dance also came to the attention of the German colonial government, which became more closely involved in Chuuk after it took over the administration of the Caroline Islands from Spain in 1899. In the first years of the new century, the German power would enter the fray over dance politics, and from the earliest period of their rule, the Germans who visited Chuuk were much more sympathetic to the dancing they witnessed. This is demonstrated in the first official German visit to Chuuk after succeeding the Spanish. In 1900, Rudolf von Bennigsen, the Governor of

German New Guinea, witnessed a grand seated dance of welcome by the men of Tonoas Island, then the centre of the American mission, and which would become the main station of the German administration in Chuuk Lagoon (Bennigsen 1900). Bennigsen's report does not provide much detail about the dance, but it is free of the condemnations so common in the missionary descriptions.

Under German rule, dancing also flourished in the Mortlock Islands. In 1903, the American Protestants led by Francis Price undertook one of their regular tours of these atolls, and there they found that dancing had not only continued in their absence but was widespread. In that year, a spirit medium, unnamed in the mission letters but from Nema Island in the northern Mortlocks, initiated new dances that lasted the whole night and due to their popularity were taken up on other atolls. Missionary Martin Stimson reported on these dancing exchanges: 'The young men of Lukunor [Lukunoch Island] go across the see [sic] to Etal [Ettal Island] for "puarik" and the Etal men come to Lukunor' (Stimson 1903, 15 June). By 1905, the dances that originated on Nema were practised in the lower Mortlock Islands and also in communities in Chuuk Lagoon to the north. In responding to these widespread dances that were seemingly sanctioned by the German government, Stimpson conveyed that Joni, a teacher on Lukunoch 'asked Mr. Higgins if it is true that the government wishes them to "puarik" [*pwérúk*]' (Stimson 1903, 15 June). According to mission letters, although the German government was at first opposed to regular dancing due to the negative effect on manual labour and thus the economy of the colony, they later emended this view of *pwérúk*, with apparent support from traders and other visitors, especially ethnographers (Tanabe 1968). The Germans believed that dances could be further transformed as an expression of colonial solidarity, and the mission letters even suggest there was talk of a fine for those not participating, though there is no evidence that this was initiated as policy (Jagnow 1906, 30 April). By the first years of the twentieth century, the German colonials came to view Chuukese dancing positively, and Chuukese in turn would use this support as validation for continuing the practice, despite the condemnation of the American mission. This colonial support for dance found expression in new imperial contexts. On 27 January 1907, near the meeting house (*wuut*) called Djonufar (Chonufar) in the village of Mwáán, former seat of the Protestant mission, and presided over by chief Takuraar, Chuukese danced for the birthday of Kaiser Wilhelm II. This dance was described in detail by German ethnographer Augustin Krämer (1932), and upon return in 1910, Krämer and the Hamburg Expedition recorded this and other dances as moving images, inscribing Chuukese bodies within the fledgling category of ethnographic film. Krämer found that dance was widespread in 1907, noting that 'The Trukese dance happily and often' (Krämer 1932: 278). Thus by the first decade of the twentieth century, dance in Chuuk not only survived eradication by Christianity but it was increasingly integrated into an emergent modernity and shifting way of life in the islands.

Moving Images of *Pwérúk* (1910): Beyond the Colonial Gaze

The politics of dancing in Chuuk between 1890 and the first years of the twentieth century are recorded in the historical archive, but these written records are much less transparent about the actual appearance of the dances. Missionary and colonial records reveal some detail about dance contexts and undertakings but almost nothing about dance movements; the Protestant mission offered more condemnation than description. While Augustin Krämer (1932) and Laurentius Bollig (1927) provided more detailed written examinations, visual access to Chuukese dance from this period is instead preserved by one of the earliest examples of filmed dances in Oceania. These moving images, made in Chuuk in 1910 by the Hamburg Expedition and collectively edited as *Völkerkundliche Filmdokumente aus der Südsee aus den Jahren 1908–1910* (Tischner 1939), not only reveal an unprecedented visualization of 'the dance' from this period, but they also expose another layer of imperial corporeality in the salvage documentation and staging of Indigenous dance as part of colonial ethnographic discourse (Weinstein 2010). But as I contend below, the Chuukese dancers that reach out to us over a century later through this film also reveal an embodied agency, as they disclose details of arrangement, movement, adornment and rhythm, all previously hidden within the colonial gaze.

The silent film titled *Völkerkundliche Filmdokumente* presents five short segments of dance from Chuuk and its outer islands, each segment under one minute in length. The first two dances are from the Mortlock Islands and include a mask dance (*tapwaanú*) and a stick dance (*tukuyá*) by men. The other three dances are from Chuuk Lagoon: a sitting dance, apparently by men and women, with two solo standing female dancers, a continuation of the sitting dance, and a standing line dance by women.[5] The Mortlockese mask dance, remembered but no longer performed in 1910, was a specialty dance for environmental management, and the expedition requested its performance; it would not have been a type usually viewed by missionaries. All the other dance genres filmed are performed today in some form, showing a remarkable resilience in traditional dance.[6] The final standing dance (generally termed *minen wúútá*) is rarely described in the colonial record, but it appears to be an early form of the marching dance, called *maas*, an innovation in 1910 and as reported by Bollig (1927: 200; Nagaoka and Konishi 2006).[7] The stick dance (*tukuyá*) in the film is regularly performed today at cultural events, but in the nineteenth century it was undertaken at spirit possession celebrations and would have been known by the missionaries. But of all the dances in the film, it is the sitting dances (generally termed *minen móót*) and their accompanying solo standing performers that were most likely the dances targeted by the mission. Below I provide a close reading of these segments of the film based on archival and cultural understandings of the dance.

Sitting dances followed two types of performance contexts with contrasting poetic conventions: one called *éwúwénú* was focused on socialization and sexuality, and one called *pisimóót* acknowledged spirits at possession events.[8] Though not confirmed, I suspect that both genres drew on similar motifs that emphasized body percussion. When discussing the 1910 film with the elders in Chuuk, all identified the segment as *éwúwénú*, and some linked it to performances by those on the western atolls of Chuuk State, where communities are especially known today for dancing. As displayed in the film, a tight circle of seated dancers with large feathered combs (*táf*) in their hair face inward and sit cross-legged. Performed in synchrony, they bend their upper bodies downward in the circle while seated, likely singing together (as in present-day practice), and then, after a pause, they sit up and begin to turn their upper bodies rhythmically from side to side and clap with hands flat (*pis*), slap thighs (also *pis*) and possibly strike their upper chests (*fáánaap*); not shown in the film, they would likely also strike the bent crook of the left elbow held against the body (*óónu*) and shout vigorously (*mweyir*) into their bent, raised right arms at the concluding section (*pwérúkún sópw*) of each dance chant. Within the seated group, a dance leader (*sowupwérúk*) remains standing in the centre of the performers but faces away from the camera; this person's movements are difficult to discern in apparently directing or encouraging the performance.

While some Chuukese communities still perform these seated dances, Chuukese eventually abandoned the accompanying standing dance shown by the female performers in the film. Dressed in hibiscus fibre skirts, with earrings and arm bands made from shell, they enter to the right of the seated performers, and only one is shown clearly, with the second dancer awkwardly half off to the side of the camera frame. According to accounts from the time, the female standing dance was called *maan* (bird) or *asaf* (frigate bird). The standing women remain stationary with knees bent and upper body held straight, with arms held down but slightly outward, away from the body, and with their wrists flexed upward. This position of arms and wrists was representative of the frigate bird wings. Occasionally, the main standing female in the film rotates both wrists in a quick flourish, and she periodically lowers herself as she dances. She employs a lateral hip movement, and then a horizontal, circular movement of the pelvis – a movement called *wusek* or *nek* (Goodenough 2002: 256; Goodenough and Sugita 1980: 233, 383). Throughout the film, the solo women dance rhythmically with the seated group of men in a clearly choreographed rather than spontaneous arrangement. Foreign male writers who witnessed the dance were particularly struck by the *maan* dance of women, perceiving them solely for sexual display. Jan Kubary, writing about the *wusek* he witnessed on Fefen Island in the 1880s, referred to the 'sensuous meaning of the movements' (Krämer 1932: 285; Goodenough 2002: 256), while Bollig (1927: 181) noted the 'erotic impression' and 'an appeal to sensual instincts', which he interpreted from the hip movements. The sung poetry of *éwúwénú* draws from experiences of unrequited love, intrigue of relationships and sexuality, and thus the performances were entertaining, fun and of wide interest, but they were predominantly a means of social cohesion through shared participation. The spatial and gendered politics of group dance at the time also offered deeper temporal and cosmological significance. Not shown in the film but as part of protocol for dance events, one of the observers might rise and recite a *pwelepwel* (protection chant) to offer safety from sorcery (*péwút*). Before some performances, dancers would drink a medicine called *pwó*, which further protected them and ensured a successful presentation but could also cause an opposing dance group to weaken (Goodenough 2002: 177). Like most aspects of performance, seated dances thus embodied social protocols, politics and hierarchies of corporeal engagement.

The 1910 film segments present a remarkable window into the visual aesthetics of the dancing body in early twentieth-century Chuuk, but the making of these images also conveys additional aspects of an imperial corporality. While descriptions of music and dance were often of lesser consideration in the published volumes of the expedition, through photography and film they were given prime place as visual markers of the Other. As Weinstein (2010: 236–38) has already described, the filmed dances would have underscored a dual vision of exoticism on one hand and a prime interest of salvage documentation on the other. All writers from the period lamented the decline of cultural practices in the face of colonial materiality, and in the film, Indigenous bodies disrupt these colonial ideas and ideals of cultural purity. The dancers from the Mortlock Islands, for example, wear pants and long dresses, clothing in fashion in Chuuk since the late nineteenth century and a marker first of Christianity in the Islands but gradually appropriated by the full population. But an imperial corporality is also apparent in how the Germans asked for dances to be performed for the camera that were already abandoned (such as the mask dance) or performed in new colonial contexts. While the American missionaries sought to erase the dancing bodies that they saw, the Germans promoted them as artefacts of primitive society to be salvaged. The dancing bodies, in their direct display of movement in the 1910 film, also move beyond mere colonial depiction. The dancers appear to us across time and onto our screens, and in doing so they disrupt the colonial gaze by their presence. From this perspective, the dancers, though unnamed and unattributed in the film, offer an agency behind the imperial lens, both in their direct visuality and their shared participation in the recorded cultural moment. For Chuukese viewers today, the filmed dances represent fragile links to a past, part recognizable and part indistinguishable. Viewing these dances over a century later, the participants reach out in their silent, embodied rhythms and in celebration of an Indigenous collective that moves them through the imperial turbulence of the time period.

Reflections: Agency, Imperialism, Dance

This chapter has examined dance as entangled in the imperial corporeality of Micronesia. This colonial vision that sought to control, regulate and remake

Chuukese bodies was deployed most forcefully in the late nineteenth century by American missionaries, for whom Indigenous dance was a primary site of cultural contestation. While a small number of new converts grappled with abandoning dance as directed by the church, most people continued to participate in danced exchanges, which were central to social and spiritual well-being. Spirit mediums and sometimes chiefs led dance practices both privately and publicly over missionary objections. The coming of the German Empire brought new contours in the imperial corporeality that played out in Micronesia, with colonial administrators eventually favouring and promoting Indigenous dance, as well as incorporating it into their research and political aims, in prioritizing the documentation of dance but also in encouraging dance celebrations for directly colonial contexts. While group dancing in late nineteenth-century Chuuk was a continuation and enactment of culturally ingrained practices, the historical record strongly suggests that dancing also became a means of social mobilization, of bodies moving together in time and rhythm as an alternative temporality to the emerging mission. I suggest that while colonialism in Chuuk was multisensorial, the visuality of empire was not a single, unified gaze but instead was nuanced through religious, political and cultural interests. Missionaries condemned in writing what they saw, but German ethnologists sought to salvage what they witnessed, most provocatively in moving images. I have argued that beyond this imperial gaze, Chuukese dance from 1910 in descriptions and in film presents a deployment of cultural agency – historical danced expressions that disrupt the colonial narrative and force us to engage with Chuukese bodies, rhythms, decorations and participation from across time and through the refraction of salvage aesthetics. From this perspective, the movements of Chuukese bodies disturb Indigenous pasts and presents.

In a seminal study of the visual arts, Adrienne Kaeppler (1996: 152) concluded with a declaration for future research: 'We must investigate the visual aspects . . . how sound and visual performances help to construct society.' In this chapter, I have taken up this challenge but expanded it to investigate not only visual performance as a means to enact society but how the politics of performances and of representation are a means of contestation in society. The study of Chuuk confirms how Indigenous bodies were at the centre of global imperialist projects in the Western Pacific in the late nineteenth and early twentieth centuries. Both missionary and colonial officials, two sides of an imperial vision, sought to remake Indigenous bodies through periods of control, conformation and restriction. I contend that dance and the spectacle of dancing bodies in solidarity was a primary cultural and political challenge to this colonial vision, and thus dance was especially disturbing and dangerous. Further exploration of such cases in Oceania and beyond might further affirm historical cultural practices such as music and dance not only as art but as modes of political power and resiliency through struggle.

Acknowledgements

It is with profound thanks that I acknowledge the generosity of time and support of many individuals in Chuuk State over many years of research. My understanding of dance in Chuuk has been deepened from knowledge shared with me by John Sandy, Fuchiko Pasen, Meichik Amon, Pedro Limwera, Rewi, and Joakim Peter (all now deceased), as well as Elias Sandy and Francie Wishim. My thanks also to Jane Freeman Moulin and Kendra Stepputat for expanding my understanding of the movements displayed in the 1910 film. I am grateful to Myjolynne Kim for a critical reading and comments on a draft of this chapter. I thank the Museum am Rothenbaum (MARKK) in Hamburg, Germany, for permission to use the image in Figure 8.2. Past research in Chuuk has been generously supported by the Wenner-Gren Foundation (Grant 7409), the University of Hawai'i at Mānoa, Victoria University of Wellington and the College of Micronesia-FSM.

Brian Diettrich (PhD, University of Hawai'i at Mānoa) is Senior Lecturer in Ethnomusicology at Victoria University of Wellington, New Zealand. His research has focused on Indigenous music and dance in Oceania and especially in the Federated States of Micronesia. Among his publications is the co-authored book *Music in Pacific Island Cultures: Experiencing Music, Expressing Culture*. Brian is an executive board member of the International Council for Traditional Music (ICTM), and he chairs the ICTM Study Group on Music and Dance of Oceania. Brian formerly taught music in the Federated States of Micronesia.

Notes

1. Chuuk State is a group of forty-one islands governed together and part of the Federated States of Micronesia (FSM), a culturally diverse Island nation in the north-western Pacific. The state of Chuuk is comprised of the high islands enclosed inside Chuuk Lagoon, as well as five groups of surrounding atolls.
2. The doctoral dissertation by Dernbach (2005) is one of the few sources that has examined the ABCFM letters in detail, and including the missionary focus on dance and its description in mission letters.
3. Protestant missionaries produced one of the earliest and largest corpuses of writing about Micronesia in their personal letters to the mission board. While these documents are deeply biased in their widespread condemnations of people and culture, their letters nevertheless display a marked consideration of ethnographic detail, including personal names of people, places, practices and events, which can be corroborated directly and indirectly.
4. As evidenced by missionary letters and reports from the time, Alfred Snelling became estranged from the ABCFM missionaries and eventually broke with them before leading some Chuukese to follow him against the other missionaries, thus creating a bitter rivalry within the early mission.
5. The seated dancers in the film segments from Chuuk are difficult to distinguish but appear to show men and women. The published records of the Hamburg Expedition do

not provide many details about the film or the recording of the individual segments. The expedition visited Chuuk Lagoon from 1–14 December 1909, 28 December to 14 January 1910, and 29 March to 4 April 1910 (Berg 1988). Much of the time was spent on Uman and Weno Islands, where the dances were likely recorded. The expedition visited Satawon Island in the Mortlock Islands from 25–27 March (Berg 1988), and according to Thilenius (1927: 337–341), this is when the masked dance was likely recorded. Hans Tischner assembled the film clips in 1939, together with other clips from Melanesia and accompanying notes from the various expeditions to produce the film compilation. As Weinstein surmised (2010), it is likely that additional recorded footage was lost or damaged. For example, in the published notes to the film, Tischner described a paddle dance (*kepir*) from Pohnpei not included in the footage segments.

6. In her study of the film, limited to an early twentieth-century German perspective, Weinstein did not investigate how the filmed dances might link with Indigenous practices from Chuuk, or how Chuukese audiences might understand the recorded performances. There is much meaning in the recorded film segments when they are considered from the viewpoint of Chuukese history and culture.
7. When I viewed this segment with elders in Chuuk, all identified it as the marching dance.
8. By the early twentieth century, the people of Chuuk lagoon called the *éwúwénú* dance: *pwérúkún fáán maram* ('dances under the moon').

References

Agnew, V. 2013. 'Encounter Music in Oceania: Cross-Cultural Musical Exchange in Eighteenth- and Early Nineteenth-Century Voyage Accounts', in P.V. Bohlman (ed.), *The Cambridge History of World Music*. Cambridge: Cambridge University Press, pp. 183–201.

Alexeyeff, K. 2009. *Dancing from the Heart: Movement, Gender, and Cook Islands Globalization*. Honolulu: University of Hawai'i Press.

Ballantyne, T. 2014. *Entanglements of Empire: Missionaries, Māori, and the Question of the Body*. Durham, NC: Duke University Press.

Balme, C. 2007. *Pacific Performances: Theatricality, Cross-Cultural Encounter in the South Seas*. New York: Palgrave Macmillan.

Barrère, D.B., M.K. Pukui and M. Kelly. 1980. *Hula, Historical Perspectives*. Honolulu: Dept. of Anthropology, Bernice Pauahi Bishop Museum.

Bennigsen, R. 1900. 'Bericht über seine Reise zum Zwecke der Übernahme des Inselgebietes der Karolinen, Palau und Marianen in deutschen Besitz', *Deutsches Kolonialblatt* XI: 100–12.

Berg, M.L. 1988. 'The Wandering Life Among Unreliable Islanders: The Hamburg Südsee Expedition in Micronesia', *The Journal of Pacific History* 23(1): 95–101.

Bollig, L. 1927. *Die Bewohner der Truk-Inseln*. Munster: Aschendorffsche Verlagsbuchhandlung. [Unpublished translation by the Yale Cross Cultural Survey in Connection with the Navy Pacific Islands Handbook Series, 1967. New Haven: Human Relations Area Files.]

Conroy-Krutz, E. 2015. *Christian Imperialism: Converting the World in the Early American Republic*. Ithaca, NY: Cornell University Press.

Dernbach, K. 2005. 'Popular Religion: A Cultural and Historical Study of Catholicism and Spirit Possession in Chuuk, Micronesia', Ph.D. Dissertation. Iowa City: University of Iowa.

Giurchescu, A. 2011. 'The Power of Dance and Its Social and Political Uses', *Yearbook for Traditional Music* 33: 109–121.

Goodenough, W.H. 2002. *Under Heaven's Brow: Pre-Christian Religious Tradition in Chuuk*. Philadelphia: American Philosophical Society.

Goodenough, W., and H. Sugita (comps). 1980. *Trukese-English Dictionary*. Memoir 141. Philadelphia: American Philosophical Society.

Hezel, F.X. 1995. *Strangers in Their Own Land: A Century of Colonial Rule in the Caroline and Marshall Islands*. Honolulu: University of Hawai'i Press.

Hokowhitu, B. 2014. 'Haka: Colonized Physicality, Body-Logic, and Embodied Sovereignty', in L.R. Graham and H.G. Penny (eds), *Performing Indigeneity: Global Histories and Contemporary Experiences*. Lincoln, NE: University of Nebraska Press, pp. 207–9.

Jagnow. 1906. *Annual Report of the ABCFM Mission in Truk and the Mortlocks*. 30 April. Micronesian Mission. 1900–1909. Harvard University, Houghton Library, Cambridge, Massachusetts.

Kaeppler, A.L. 1970. 'Tongan Dance: A Study in Cultural Change', *Ethnomusicology* 14(2): 266–77.

———. 1992. 'The Use of Archival Film in an Ethnohistoric Study of Persistence and Change in Hawaiian Hula', in Alice Marshall Moyle (ed.), *Music and Dance of Aboriginal Australia and the South Pacific: The Effects of Documentation on the Living Tradition: Papers and Discussions of the Colloquium of the International Council for Traditional Music (ICTM) held in Townsville, Queensland, Australia, 1988* (Oceania Monograph 41). Sydney: University of Sydney, pp. 110–29.

———. 2001. 'Accordions in Tahiti – An Enigma', in Helen Reeves Lawrence (ed.), *Traditionalism and Modernity in the Music and Dance of Oceania: Essays in Honour of Barbara B. Smith* (Oceania Monograph 52). Sydney: University of Sydney, pp. 45–66.

———. 1996. 'The Look of Music, the Sound of Dance: Music as a Visual Art', *Visual Anthropology* 8: 133–53.

———. 2007. 'Dances and Dancing in Tonga: Anthropological and Historical Discourses', in T.J. Buckland (ed.), *Dancing from Past to Present: Nation, Culture, Identities*. Madison, WI: University of Wisconsin Press, pp. 25–51.

Kim, Y., and S.L. Gilman (eds). 2018. *The Oxford Handbook of Music and the Body*. New York: Oxford University Press.

King, T., and P.L. Parker. 1984. *Archaeology in the Tonaachaw Historic District, Moen Island*. Carbondale, IL: Center for Archaeological Investigations, Southern Illinois University.

Knoll, A.J. 1997. 'Zealotry among the Converted: American Board Missionaries in Micronesia, 1852–1919', in H.J. Hiery and J.M. MacKenzie (eds), *European Impact and Pacific Influence: British and German Colonial Policy in the Pacific Islands and the Indigenous Response*. London: Tauris Publishers, pp. 100–18.

Knowles, M. 2009. *The Wicked Waltz and Other Scandalous Dances: Outrage at Couple Dancing in the 19th and Early 20th Centuries*. Jefferson, NC: McFarland & Company.

Kowal, R.J., G. Siegmund, and R. Martin. 2017. 'Introduction', in R.J. Kowal, G. Siegmund and R. Martin (eds), *The Oxford Handbook of Dance and Politics*. New York: Oxford University Press, pp. 1–26.

Krämer, A. 1932. 'Truk', in *Ergebnisse der Südsee-Expedition 1908–1910*. Part II. Ethnographie, B. Mikronesien, vol. 5. Hamburg: Friederichsen, de Gruyter. [Unpublished translation by the Yale Cross Cultural Survey in Connection with the Navy Pacific Islands Handbook Series, 1968. New Haven: Human Relations Area Files.]

Lepecki, A. 2004. 'Introduction: Presence and Body in Dance and Performance Theory', in A. Lepecki (ed.), *Of the Presence of the Body: Essays on Dance and Performance Theory*. Middletown, CT: Wesleyan University Press, pp. 1–9.
McLean, M. 1999. *Weavers of Song: Polynesian Music and Dance*. Auckland: Auckland University Press.
Moyle, R. 1988. *Traditional Samoan Music*. Auckland: Auckland University Press.
Nagaoka, T., and J. Konishi. 2006. 'Western Culture Comes from the East: A Consideration of the Origin and Diffusion of the Micronesian Marching Dance', *People and Culture in Oceania* 22: 107–36.
Parker, P.L. 1985. 'Land Tenure in Trukese Society: 1850–1980', Ph.D. Dissertation. Philadelphia: University of Pennsylvania.
Peter, J.M. 1996. 'Eram's Church(Bell): Local Appropriations of Catholicism on Ettal', *ISLA: Journal of Micronesian Studies* 4(2): 267–87.
Petersen, G. 1992. 'Dancing Defiance: The Politics of Pohnpeian Dance Performances', *Pacific Studies* 15(4): 13–28.
Price, F. 1895a. Letters. 18 February, 17 May, 13 June, 4 November. Letters and Papers of the ABCFM: Mission to Micronesia, 1852–1909. Harvard University, Houghton Library, Cambridge, Massachusetts.
———. 1895b. 'Journal of Voyage to Mortlock Is', *The Friend* 53(6): 41–45.
———. 1895c. 'Ruk and Mortlock Islands', *The Friend* 53(7): 50–51.
Radano, R., and T. Olaniyan. 2016. 'Introduction: Hearing Empire – Imperial Listening', in R. Radano and T. Olaniyan (eds), *Audible Empire: Music, Global Politics, Critique*. Durham, NC: Duke University Press, pp. 1–22.
Rao, A., and S. Pierce. 2006. 'Discipline and the Other Body: Humanitarianism, Violence, and the Colonial Exception', in S. Pierce and A. Rao (eds), *Discipline and the Other Body: Correction, Corporeality, Colonialism*. Durham, NC: Duke University Press, pp. 1–35.
Shea Murphy, J. 2007. *The People Have Never Stopped Dancing: Native American Modern Dance Histories*. Minneapolis, MN: University of Minnesota Press.
Stimson, M. 1903. Letters. 15 June. Letters and Papers of the ABCFM: Mission to Micronesia, 1852–1909. Harvard University, Houghton Library, Cambridge, Massachusetts.
Tanabe, H. 1968. *Nan'yo, Taiwan, Okinawa Ongaku Kikō*. Tokyo: Ongaku no Tomosha. [Unpublished translation of chapter five, 'The Truk Islands', by Yoko Kurokawa, 2006, 50 pages. Personal collection of Brian Diettrich.]
Teaiwa, K. 2012. 'Choreographing Difference: The (Body) Politics of Banaban Dance', *The Contemporary Pacific* 24(1): 65–94.
Thilenius, G. 1927. 'Plan der Expedition', in *Ergebnisse der Südsee-Expedition 1908–1910*. Part I. Allgemeines. Hamburg: L. Friederichsen & Co.
Tischner, H. 1939. *Völkerkundliche Filmdokumente aus der Südsee aus den Jahren 1908–1910* [Ethnological Film Documents from the Pacific from the Years 1908–1910]. Berlin: Reichsanstalt für Film und Bild in Wissenschaft und Unterricht (RWU). Retrieved 4 February 2019 from https://av.tib.eu/media/22265.
Turner, B.S. (ed.). 2012. *Routledge Handbook of Body Studies*. New York: Routledge.
Weinstein, V. 2010. 'Archiving the Ephemeral: Dance in Ethnographic Films from the Hamburg South Seas Expedition 1908–1910', *A Journal of Germanic Studies* 46(3): 223–39.

Chapter 9

Greek Politicians' Dancing

Theatrical Representations of Political Power

Irene Loutzaki

This chapter provides an interpretation of Greek politicians dancing in public settings. It focuses on brief snapshots of dance drawn exclusively from prime-time private Greek television news programmes and during the period when the Panhellenic Socialist Movement (or PASOK) was in its political heyday, between 1981 and 2011. The chapter accepts the premise that the main component of modern politics is the dependence of politics itself upon the immediate and mass communication put forward through media. In addition to analysing specific dance snapshots at the choreographic level, the study's theoretical approach focuses on the usage of televised images as historical testimony, as well as the structural analysis of narrational and musical texts. From a methodological perspective, Kaeppler's approach to dance structure (1972) is useful in understanding the individual units of mobility in a multimodal practice, as well as the relationships found between units of movement.

In the case of Greek politicians dancing, the moving images, the accompanying music and the journalistic discourse about them all create a coherence and flow. This empirical material about dance is useful as data for analysis and validation of the results. In focusing on the way that Greek politicians are exposed to the public in interpreting dance forms on televised media, the relationship between the dance itself, on the one hand, and the political history of a particular era, on the other, unavoidably emerges. In the political contexts of this chapter, the dance in question is the popular *zeibekiko*, whose perpetrator and protagonist is Andreas Papandreou, the founder and head of PASOK and later Prime Minister of Greece (1981–1989).

The *zeibekiko* is a dance genre of public display for men and has been a significant practice for socialist politicians who want to prove they are real men in front of the cameras. In this chapter, *zeibekiko* refers to three different means by which the art form addresses politics. The first is that dance through the moving body comments directly on political issues. The second is how theatrics are mobilized to convey political messages, and the third means is how politicians seek to make a point through dramatic delivery. This chapter's task is guided by the following question: In what ways is dance a tool for politics? In this study, I have chosen to understand representative government and some aspects of socialism from the viewpoint of dance.

Dance Anthropology in Greece as Influenced by Adrienne L. Kaeppler

After two years of studies at the Social Anthropology Department [Ethnomusicology] at Queen's University of Belfast [Northern Ireland], I return to my country, from where I begin the second phase of my field study among the refugees of Eastern Romelia, who are now settled in three villages in Northern and Central Greece. What hurdles will I encounter when inspecting my own field of study [villages that I had already visited and whose dances had already been recorded before I was a student] through the eyes of an anthropologist? Will I see dance differently from what I perceived it to be before I became entangled in the cogs of anthropology? Would the undertaking be easier or more difficult for me? Would I be able to implement everything that I learnt throughout my studies in my own field, in my own material? (Loutzaki 1983–1986)

The questions in the logbook extract above are those I considered as I prepared to undertake fieldwork in my home country of Greece, to illuminate the structure of Northern Thracian dance and to contribute a definition of style in dance. My thesis, supervised by Dr Adrienne L. Kaeppler, grew from a paper (Loutzaki 1984) that focused on dance in the rite of marriage in a complex village in Northern Greece. The thesis also provided a general description and analysis of the structured movement system of this ethnographic area. The theoretical model developed by Kaeppler (1972) was in fact the impetus for my study of dance style among Greek refugees from Northern Thrace, now residing in Greece (Loutzaki 1989, 2007).

Adrienne Lois Kaeppler, an American anthropologist, curator of Oceanic Ethnology at the Smithsonian Institution in Washington, D.C., and a specialist on material culture, as well as the visual and performing arts, arrived in Belfast at the Ulster Museum in November 1982. She was there to search for ethnographic specimens from the voyages of British explorer Jame Cook, among which was a tapa cloth figure from Rapanui (Easter Island), for which she had a special interest. During this same period, Professor John Blacking, the head of the Social Anthropology department at Queen's University of Belfast, extended Kaeppler an invitation to give an open lecture on a subject of her expertise, at the anthropology seminar of the department. It was following that lecture that Professor

Blacking invited three students from the MA programme who were interested in dance, and including myself, for a social gathering with Kaeppler. It was then that we learned that she was appointed to teach dance anthropology at Queen's. Two months later, I received a response from Kaeppler in which she agreed to supervise my MA thesis. As I set up and designed my own research topic, Kaeppler devoted a great deal of effort to assist me. Under her guidance, I completed my MA thesis in 1984, and I successfully defended my doctoral dissertation in December 1989 (Loutzaki 1984, 1989).

Serious and well-spoken, strict and particularly demanding, Kaeppler was engaged in explaining and interpreting cultural worlds, as well as developing theoretical paradigms, large and small, for making sense of art and culture. She was an avid supporter of dance anthropology, in which researchers who have the background knowledge help to appreciate and understand dance and other structured movement systems in the larger scheme of cultural forms. For Kaeppler, descriptions of dances are data to be analysed in ways that are anthropologically meaningful in both theory and method. She was opposed to the old classical methods and techniques concerned with description and comparison; those techniques were often applied by specialists who saw dance as a thing in itself, to be studied in isolation from its cultural context. In nearly no text that she produced during her early period did she neglect to highlight the difference between these two approaches, one considered American and another European in conception. However, as stressed by Professor Grau (1993: 66–70) in her critical essay on issues of theory and method in what was the state of dance research in 1991, the question was not one of geography but rather one of method and background knowledge, a position with which I fully identify.

Specialized in thick description, and like a storyteller with her steady and clear voice in the classroom, Kaeppler narrated experiences drawn from her years-long research regarding dance events from Hawai'i and greater Polynesia, Australia and New Zealand. As an empirical example, she often brought up the birthday of the King in the islands of Tonga to demonstrate every form of action that entailed a structured movement; in this case, the presentation of pigs, the enumeration of foodstuffs, kava mixing and drinking, as well as group speeches with choreographed movements, but also the *lakalaka* dance, a national genre of local performance (Kaeppler 1985: 92–118). She described and interpreted dance cultures that were very different from European practice, and thus her work disrupted established positions but also opened new avenues of theoretical reflection on themes such as museums, cultural heritage, art, visual culture and politics. Although her engagement with dance has been but a small part of her broader interests, the results were so significant for dance research that she was hailed from the outset as one of the pioneers of the field, contributing to the emergence of dance as a noteworthy element of study. In this manner, her contribution led to the establishment of dance anthropology internationally.

Since my initial work with her, I have met with Kaeppler on several additional occasions. Our first meeting, however, was at a time when the anthropology of dance was entirely unknown in Greece. My memories of her are closely intertwined with my memories of the introduction of the theoretical and methodological framework of systematic dance research in my own country.

Dance and Anthropology in Greece Today

A starting point for the systematic study of dance in Greece occurred in 1989, with the publication of the first doctoral theses produced in foreign (and later Greek) universities by researchers who mostly had in-depth knowledge of dance practice (see Loutzaki 2004). These theoretical works, which referred to dance as an example of the implementation of anthropological theories, provoked various reactions and contradictory comments, while creating ripples for the future study of dance in Greece. They were published during the development of critical approaches in the broader discipline of anthropology. In this regard, the most pioneering and influential work of that time, from a theoretical and methodological perspective, was the Greek language edition of Cowan's (1998) work, which combined the theories of phenomenology, practice and hegemony. Inspired by postmodernism, scholars during this period questioned and re-examined previously accepted concepts related to the 'why' and the 'how' of research, the procedures of fieldwork, as well as the final results and the ethnographic text of a study. Thus, in anthropological works on dance, writers re-examined and contested the analytical tools used in dance research. This included, for instance, previous assumptions regarding similar views of dance among members of a society, and also the functions of dance, which were hitherto considered to be a given. This new work questioned whether the notion of 'dance' has a common meaning, or whether this was an issue that must be further investigated globally. These issues found fertile ground in the initial investigations by Greek dance researchers.

Although some of Kaeppler's works on dance are not particularly well-known in Greece, three of her foundational texts on methodology (Kaeppler 1972, 1978, 1992) were all translated into Greek and are always included in the bibliography of students who study at undergraduate or graduate level with dance as an object of study, such as at the School of Physical Education and Sport Science at the National and Kapodistrian University of Athens (EKPA). Kaeppler herself, as a renowned ethnographer, was well-known among my students, since the work that she undertook on Tonga was part of the regular class 'Dance, Music and Cultures' as part of the MA programme 'Musical Culture and Communication: Anthropological and Communicative Approaches to Music' at the same university from 2000 to 2013.

Today, thirty years on, the new generation of Greek anthropologists of dance, having followed research developments and having adopted new methods and techniques through their experience at university, does not content itself with brief visits and fragmentary records from the field. Rather, they yearn to live for a prolonged period within communities they study, observing and taking part in the daily lives of people in an effort to comprehend their world 'from the inside'. While exploring dance as a structured system of movement, as a language of communication, as a performance, as bodied speech, as a social act, or as a ritual or a political act, researchers of dance examine the conditions from which dance in Greece is actuated. These include its cultural and social space, the people involved and the public, which at times appears to be the final recipient of dance experience and behaviour. I refer to a growing number of researchers of dance who engage in the study of their own societies and who frequently write in their mother tongue, usually turning to a local audience.[1]

As an anthropologist with a special interest in investigating new trends, I was particularly attracted to Kaeppler's idea that 'dance is visual manifestations of social structure through movements and expresses political and social reality' (Kaeppler 1985: 114). This notion helped me to extend my ability to recognize key features about time that I might have otherwise overlooked, but it also shone a light on transient data that can reveal patterns, prompt questions and, most importantly, tell stories. Kaeppler's approach, central to her distinct mode of intellectual inquiry, is the practice of participant observation, whether her field site is the islands of Tonga, Hawai'i or elsewhere. Being trained in structural functionalism in the same manner that Kaeppler used it, I believe, as did she, that traditional societies were discrete entities whose social organization could be explained through the analysis of the separate but interrelated institutions of kinship, religion, economic and political systems (see Loutzaki 1984, 1989). In the following case example, I build on these ideas to focus on the relationship between dance and politics in Greek society.

Television News in Greece: Orchestrating Dance in a Mediated World

The 1989 advent of the first two private television channels in Greece, called MEGA and ANTENNA, brought about many changes to the style, form and content of the news, which became more dramatized and visually sophisticated during this time. One significant change was the duration of news programmes, which have been notably prolonged. Another feature is the extended use of live links to cover events as they unfold. As a consequence, and in order to fill the gap, news corporations report what Boorstin (1961) called 'pseudo-events', which resemble a political spectacle organized to tell a certain narrative.[2] From these changes, the modern media landscape has reshaped our collective sense of reality to produce scripted and time-released 'news' in the form of press releases, public relations, advertising and more.

My field site for the present project is dancing, as it is tied to issues of representation in political media. The research is based on the examination of press extracts such as articles, photographs and films. The objective of this process is the visual reporting of newsworthy events (Caple 2013: 3), and while this kind of material is socially constructed, it is also a window on the world that captures reality. As a dance researcher, by using media artefacts like news storytelling, my gaze and interpretations are embedded in my positionality, which is neither neutral nor objective.

The impetus for my preoccupation with an object whose protagonists were high-profile individuals on the political scene was entirely a result of chance, when on the front-page cover of the weekly periodical *Tachydromos* (13 March 1986, issue 11) I found a picture of a minister of the socialist government in a dance-like pose suggestive of the *zeibekiko*. This instance was only the beginning of my interest, and I subsequently found the subject of dancing politicians not only in the printed press but across media in live presentations about the events of the day. Thus, my simple curiosity was transformed into a research focus that originated in the observation of two media-related transformations in Greece. The first was the deregulation and commercialization of the broadcasting system.[3] The second was the growing exposure in the press and in news broadcasts of well-known figures in public life (such as ministers and members of parliament of the Socialist Movement), who would shed before the lens the character of the politician to take on a role more familiar to the average Greek, which practically meant someone who dresses as he pleases, drinks and has fun with friends on Greek dance floors and stage fronts, all the while breaking political protocol.

Until the 1980s in Greece, the private side of a politician's life was traditionally regarded as a restricted journalistic subject. In the 1980s, however, many cases demonstrated the abandonment of this taboo. The most popular explanation for what seemed to be a new development was the spectacular victory of the Panhellenic Socialist Movement (PASOK), who marched to power in October 1981 under the powerful slogan of 'Allaghi' (Change). The movement's flamboyant and charismatic leader Andreas Papandreou, the complete antithesis to the austere leader of the conservative political party of Nea Dimokratia Konstantinos Karamanlis, began to promise everything to almost everyone, and therefore whipped up a frenzy of social expectations. It is no exaggeration to say that the PASOK really put its stamp on Greek politics and society during the post-transition era. No other party was able to channel successfully the aspirations of Greek society and mould it in its own image as did the PASOK. Its ascent to power was a milestone in Greek politics. The PASOK's success rested on its ability to propose an attractive political package expertly tailored to fit a society dominated by civil servants, small business owners, independent professionals and small farmers – what could be described as a petty bourgeois social constellation, which Papandreou inventively labelled as 'non-privileged' Greeks.

At that time, politicians were under increasing pressure to display their real selves, to prove their authenticity, to prove that they were ordinary enough to be representative of their electorates. They also invested emotionally in their messages to make visible those aspects of their lives that were once strictly private. With these political approaches, it was a case of one social class viewing another without dependencies or exclusion while entering into the spirit of what Herzfeld (1997) dubbed 'cultural intimacy'. The twin political approaches were connected when private television stations worked to reveal the private lives of politicians, highlighting their personal moments, and thereby playing a determining role in the rebroadcasting of events that exemplify a particular way of living.

Politicians, as media stars, are exposed to a vast volume of representations – by policymakers, photo reporters, journalists and cartoonists – which exceed their temporal and often cognitive capacity for critical reflections. In this sense, the media representations contribute to the constitution of the political realm that they seek to observe. Thus, whenever a high-profile person such as a politician or celebrity appears in a cabaret or tavern, in which the goal is entertainment through dance, this immediately attracts the gaze of those attending. And when this same instance of dancing finds its way into televised appearances – meaning that the TV camera invades a personal space – it is understood that the high-profile person represented is aware that certain viewers are watching the dance.[4]

What is conveyed through the news broadcasts of such filmed dances is a product that is visualized and branded, such as the famed *tsifteteli*, and the *zeibekiko* dance of politicians Andreas Papandreou, Akis Tsochatzopoulos and Yiorgos Papandreou, among others.[5] The dance surprises and draws attention while garnering enthusiasm and reaching large numbers of onlookers. By use of the vehicle of dance, the representatives of the Greek parliaments enter 'un-invited' into people's homes through news broadcasts and print journalism to promote personal images of themselves.

These occurrences in turn raise the question of how a viewer (or a reader) might perceive the icon of a 'great dancer' as the 'guy next door'. While accepting the idea that society and politics are interpreted and thus may potentially be used along with their representations, the image itself – still or moving – has earned an important position as an object of study in the social sciences. Considering this, I will focus below on the figure of Yiorgos Papandreou, the Minister of Foreign Affairs (1993–1994 and 1999–2004), son and grandson of Prime Ministers, and who was a dancer of the *zeibekiko*, a dance that has long contributed to an image of Greek culture in the Western mind.[6]

The *zeibekiko* is a solo dance, commonly performed in confined spaces, such as between tables in small cafes and taverns, in hashish dens and, perhaps, as a consequence, even when more space is available, the dancer tends to move within a very restricted area of the floor. The steps of the dance follow a basic circling pattern, punctuated by the dancer's leaping, crouching, spinning and kneeling, and his striking the ground with the palms of his hands. The style offers a fine opportunity for the dancer to display his physical prowess and agility. Being idiorhythmic as a 9/8 metered dance, the *zeibekiko* has several musical organizations and varies according to thematic content, the place of origin and the period during which it was created. It is classified as a *rebetiko* dance, from the period 1850 to 1953, insofar as its social dimension is concerned (Damianakos 1987; Gauntlett 2001). In the years prior to 1980, the developments and transformations of Greek society brought *zeibekiko* to the fore as a popular dance. From 1980 onwards, it transformed into a genre that is integrated within the context of contemporary Greek modernity. For as long as the tradition of the *zeibekiko* was limited to an indoor, private space, it bothered none. In fact, it was considered to be a form of bravery and manliness for the performer, who with slow and heavy moves and occasional pauses (for focus) would direct himself to the centre of the space in order to initiate the dance. The few patrons watching would be entertained with the simplicity of the undertaking. This context is the world reflected by *rebetiko* researchers such as Ilias Petropoulos (1968), Butterworth and Schneider (1975) and Panayiotis Kounadis (1979) in works in which they note that some people dance in order to glorify the fringes to which they belong, whereas others do so in order to drive away their longing, in tandem with substances, noting that in this space the code of expression is the *zeibekiko*. It is a dance of mysticism, with no clapping, showing off or gymnastic or showy moves but undertaken with bravado. The *zeibekiko* is often described as a metaphor for 'Greekness', encompassing a culture 'that resists the perceived negative forces of Europeanization, capitalization and globalization' (Stamatis 2011: XV).

From a technical perspective, dance, song and music are substantial parameters that contribute to the formation of specific aesthetic conventions, preferences and particularities that are projected onto the television screen. Through televised projection, the imaging of dance in various contexts such as family gatherings, on the occasion of the opening of an exhibition, during the presentation of the work of the government, or even in a pre-electoral period, is a feature of representation during news broadcasts. More specifically, the combination of image and sound recalls memories and signals sets of circumstances, with their interrelation with the text (word on image) allowing for a complementary, multi-perspectival 'reading' of important moments of an event.

While aiming not only to delimit but chiefly to evaluate the dance event that is being reproduced in the context of the news, I examine scenes of entertainment in which a public figure avails himself to recognition. With the help of technology, this now-recorded dance event transforms the intangible aspect of its parts into a tangible composition. Through film, a dance event displays established characteristics while offering a comparison on the most recent or older styles of dance as well as public life and political history in Greece.[7]

In viewing a politician dancing on television, I was in fact watching a theatrical performance, but this 'watching' is a performance too. As an analytical category, the word 'performance' (Kavouras 1997: 57) is not a typical interpretation of a dance, or an aesthetic expression of a given unit of movement, but rather a construction of a reality that includes the actors (i.e. dancers and audience) and their relationship to the construction itself. My emphasis here lies in the multifarious dance actions, as these are understood through performed knowledge. By watching a dance from this perspective, my interest lies in what the actors of the tradition in question recognize as movement differences, which as unrelated kinetic units 'are combined into meaningful motifs and further into recognized dances according to a specific group of people at a specific time' (Kaeppler 1998: 47). I argue that in every dance event people express their intentions by reproducing important identities and relationships in order to communicate with the audience. Thus in this chapter, the analysis of dance style (as the way one performs) relies on the kinetic behaviour of dancing politicians, who in accordance with unwritten rules try to promote prestige, power, status and social distancing. Today, the *zeibekiko* dance has an added political dimension, in that knowledge and understanding of this cultural form are valued as ingredients of ethnic identity (Kaeppler 1993: 234), or as Stamatis (2011) phrased it, as a counter-hegemonic practice within the context of national identity politics in Greece.

The *Zeibekiko* of Yiorgos Papandreou: A Family Tradition?

The *rebetiko* enjoyed one last charisma-fuelled political fling in 2001, when the last active member of the Papandreou dynasty, Yiorgos Papandreou (at the time Foreign Minister of Greece), performed at a media event a transcultural *zeibekiko* for his Turkish counterpart Ismail Cem, as a way of cementing the Greco-Turkish rapprochement. Though the coverage of the dancing by the networks was extensive, it helped to turn public sentiment against him. Was this situation a political move, a dance tradition or non-reciprocation by Cem? In any case, the opposition press reacted in a dual manner: Yiorgos Papandreou's dance was deemed to be either submissive to Turkey or anti-Greek.

> In five topics of those that are considered to be 'low politics', Greece and Turkey agreed to cooperate, through the foreign ministers of both countries, Yiorgos Papandreou and İsmail Cem. The decision was made yesterday afternoon at Kuşadası in Turkey (ancient Ephesus) where both ministers flew following their visit to Samos, where Ismail Cem had planted an olive tree in Iraio. (*Apogevmatini tis Kyriakis*, 25 June 2001: 10)

The quotation above is from the article titled '"Open Channel" for ... Olives and zeybekika!' and covered three quarters of page ten of the *Apogevmatini tis Kyriakis* daily newspaper of 25 June 2001. The article is split into two parts: first the political aspects, which appear in summary and refer to what was agreed and achieved through the meeting, and second the 'moving' part, which alludes to the *zeibekiko* that Yiorgos Papandreou and his two brothers, Nikos and Andrikos, along with the Foreign Minister of Turkey, danced on the anniversary of their father's memory and to the song 'Sinefiasmeni Kyriaki' (Cloudy Sunday). The article is illustrated with a picture of Greece's Foreign Minister in the foreground and in a dancing pose. Around the dancing figure, and at a great distance, men and women – some sitting, some standing – are gathered in a semicircle. In the dance scene, the Turkish Minister, though he appears to be clapping to the tune – as is mentioned in the reportage – did not reciprocate, as is customary in official events in his own country. The interpretation of this non-reciprocation was that the dance was organized in memory of Andreas Papandreou, or so it was presented by various media. The dance was thus not portrayed as a counter-gift to the Turkish counterpart for sealing the agreement set to be achieved between the two countries, and in fact no such gift was expected in return.

Of the documentaries about this day, the most controversial was about Yiorgos Papandreou's *zeibekiko*. Removed from the context of his meeting with Cem in 2001 and titled 'Y. Papandreou: Zeibekia for Father and Lost Ideals', the short colour film was posted online. It was accompanied by two songs 'Aftos o Anthropos, aftos pou perpataei panta skyftos' (This Man, this, that Walks Always with His Look Down), sung by Rita Sakellariou (his father's favourite singer), and 'Sinefiasmeni Kyriaki' (Cloudy Sunday), sung by Vasilis Tsitsanis. The documentary was also illustrated with photographs of the arrival of Yiorgos Papandreou, one of which shows several boys and girls, members of some dance group, performing what Kaeppler (1977) calls 'airport art-art', a special version of the dance for tourists.

One year later, another occasion of dancing politicians occurred in Iraklio (Crete), where Yiorgos Papandreou also danced *zeibekiko*. This event was reported in the following way:

> The impressive move of the Minister of Foreign Affairs Y. P., as it was immortalized by the lens, was witnessed at a party gathering, following the consumption of delicious Cretan meze and washed down with local wine. All of this led to a spike in the entertainment 'thermometer', and at one point he found himself in the center, where he displayed his dancing skills in zeibekiko, a dance which of course he has come to love, as it is part of the . . . tight Greek-Turkish rapprochement, which he pushes for vehemently. What matters of course is to dance it wherever, with style, and not . . . at whatever rapprochements are attempted with 'neighbours', rapprochements unfolding at a dizzying pace, if one considers that just after the elections a Greek frigate will participate for the first time in a NATO exercise. And let us see still if the Foreign Ministry continues with its own dance moves in the new crisis that is uncontrollably unfolding in long-suffering Kosovo. ('The Zeibekiko of Yiorgos!', *Apogevmatini tis Kyriakis*, 5 March 2002)

From this fragment, it appears that the *zeibekiko* is contested when Yiorgos uses it to express sentiments of Greek-Turkish friendship; meanwhile, it might also be said that foreign policy is marked by submissiveness. What dominates is the image of familiarity, which cannot be reciprocated (Figure 9.1.).

The social collective, represented by traditional circle dances in which everyone makes the same steps, does not entirely apply to the *zeibekiko*. The *zeibekiko* is a lone dance and as such does not require the presence of other individuals, something that applied during what Damianakos dubs the 'first phase' of the *rebetiko*, when it was performed in places such as the hashish den. There, the dancer did not communicate with the environment, and he was not interested in whether he was being watched or his movements scrutinized. The cases I examined, however, were precisely the opposite. The folk-like *zeibekiko* that is found in dance halls is performed in the presence of an audience who critically observes the dancer and his interpretation. The dancer dominates the space, imposing his presence; at times he is juxtaposed with some of the attendees, and at others he is more introverted and focused within himself. In any case, the juxtaposition or the dialogue is dynamic and determines the evolution of the plot of the dance. With the austere or minimal choreographic language and the emotional fluctua-

ΣΚΙΤΣΟ ΑΝΔΡΕΑΣ ΠΕΤΡΟΥΛΑΚΗΣ

Figure 9.1. Translation of Dialogue: 'The President [with his dancing] supports his friendship to Turkey.' / 'He danced the zeibekiko . . .'. Andreas Petroulakis, O Kosmos tou ependyti, 21–22 January 2006. Image used by permission.

tions as a vehicle, the movement and the pathos of the male body are highlighted through live music that accompanies the dance.

Technically, the dancing image of Yiorgos Papandreou did not correspond to the criteria mentioned above. The potentialities for expression that improvisation offered often led him to the uncontrolled violation of the given limits. Besides, in the course of the evolution of the dance form, personal style, the special stamp that marks every cultural product of individual habit, is nothing more than a variation in relation to the style of a specific era or social class. When Yiorgos Papandreou was on the dance floor, bearing his identity as an official figure, the protocol of the dance form dictated that he must not share this space with others. As a *zeibekiko* dancer, he was elevated to the status of protagonist yet without always succeeding in eliciting admiration, and with the choice of the particular dance not always being successful or appropriate, as characteristically described by one critic:

> As for the dance of Yiorgos Papandreou, it is the first time in my life that I witnessed a zeibekiko with no meraki.[8] The fact is that there were some who liked it. As for myself, the Minister of Foreign Affairs Yiorgos Papandreou, whether he sits or stands, has lost his physical elegance by dancing this zeibekiko. He should choose tango next time. (Vasilakaki 2001)

In what was categorized first as form but was also political content, the two dances, tango and *zeibekiko*, were juxtaposed, with the commentary highlighting the role of the bourgeois Westerner versus the village Easterner. While conducting her critique, Vasilakaki welcomed what Boorstin (1961: 253) dubbed the 'news behind the news' and focused on the dance and its origins with the Zeybeks while highlighting that the Minister of Foreign Affairs of Turkey would have no problem in supporting Papandreou dancing while clapping.

Yiorgos was not, however, the only member of the Papandreou family to dance. His mother, Margarita Papandreou, also danced the *zeibekiko*, as did his father, Andreas, and his brothers too. Thus it appears that the *zeibekiko* is generational and a tradition that somehow extends to members of the government, to ministers and other members of parliament of the PASOK.

Sporadically at first, but more frequently with the turn of the millennium and as a result of the political hue that the *zeibekiko* began to take on, and even more systematically from the end of 2003 with the looming of elections, Yiorgos Papandreou who followed his father into politics, decided to use *zeibekiko* as an additional means to claim the party presidency. Newspapers and supplements started to sing the praises of the new leader of the PASOK, not least after February 2004, when Papandreou took on the leadership of the party, and his life was then intensely scrutinized. From this period onward, publications abounded that addressed the following: his professional background, his professional activities, his performance as a dancer, his skills and hobbies, his political action, his personal and private moments (at home and overseas) and topics that concerned his sartorial choices. With his choice of the *zeibekiko*, the continuation of the family tradition was dynamically visualized – a confirmation of Papandreou-*ness* – as was his succession to the leadership of the PASOK.

Whether as signifier (as a form) or signified (as content), dance does not cease to preoccupy current political affairs in Greece, whether in printed publications, televised, in online media or in news broadcasts. As stressed by Chaniotis (2009: 73), the observer highlights and comments on the theatricality of the behaviour of public figures when it is clearly visible and exceeds boundaries and norms.

Epilogue

Much like any performer who interprets a form, the dancer of the *zeibekiko* may function without rules though never without a framework. For those who know the dance from 'within', the view that elevates arbitrariness to improvisation – the dancer on the stage doing as he pleases – is entirely false. The notion of 'improvisation' presupposes the complete knowledge of rules and particular features, as well as the means and manners with which these features are reconstituted into a form at the moment of dancing. In this kind of dance in particular, all is taken for granted (steps, formations, rhythm, framework), and thus the only possibility that is granted to the dancer, as Kaeppler (1987: 13–22) mentions, is the spontaneous resynthesis of given elements, not the conception of novel ones.

How is Yiorgos Papandreou using dance today? His statement was very clear in response to certain hostile comments about his dance performance in Samos in 2001: 'I will dance more *zeibekika* if necessary. . .' (*Apogevmatini*, 1 October 2007).[9] He also made another statement in front of the cameras the day he left the PASOK leadership: 'Now – as a citizen . . . I will have the time to be hunted down by the media, who will seek to criminalize everything; I will continue to work out, swim, canoe and dance a *zeibekiko* every now and then' (*Ethnos*, 20 March 2012). That day marked his last appearance in the offices of the PASOK.

From the moment that the *zeibekiko* travelled from the *rebetis* to the politicians, the cultural contexts changed, and the symbolism of the dance changed too.[10] In the new context, the performance of the dancer-politician, even where the latter does not respond to the mood of the dance, appears to be authentic only where the moment of the execution is authentic. However, just as important to consider is the role of the media and how a performance is promoted by the newspapers and on television, where, in addition to the image, we have a journalistic discourse that guides the average viewer away from the mere moving body. In this manner, from the viewer's perspective, the object of dance, together with its properties, recedes – that is, whether the dance is authentic or not, or if the politician is dancing well or not – and in its place we see instead how dance is presented as something above current political life. In this transformation, dance offers an expression of politics.

Irene Loutzaki is Associate Professor in Dance Anthropology at the National and Kapodistrian University of Athens, Greece. As Research Fellow, she collaborated with the Peloponnesian Folklore Foundation Ethnographic Museum and Research Centre (1974–1995) and taught Dance Anthropology in the Faculty of Music Studies at the University of Athens (1996–2013). She has carried out fieldwork in Greece, among the refugees from Eastern Romelia, and in Western Thrace and on the island of Crete. Her research interests include dance history and historiography; theory of dance anthropology, and ethnography. Her current writing engages with issues of cultural policy, cultural management and the political dimension of dance. She has published – in Greek, English and French – in academic and professional journals within the fields of dance, material culture, technology and ethnography.

Notes

1. See case examples on Greek dance in Loutzaki (1992) and Avdikos, Loutzaki and Papakostas (2004), as well as the work *Archaeology and the Arts* (2004).
2. For example, when the Prime Minister cut the ribbon at the reopening of a historic Library, or when the Ministry of Culture represents the government at social meetings and on special occasions.
3. After the deregulation of television in 1989, private terrestrial channels proliferated to create a chaotic broadcasting environment with no regulations in the beginning. Until 1989, Greek television was under state monopoly with two public channels, ERT 1 and 2 (now renamed ET-1 and NET). Since then, there has been a gradual proliferation of channels, both national and local, peaking to 150 in the mid-1990s. This is a large number for a small market of eleven million inhabitants and confirming Papathanassopoulos' view that there is an excess of supply over demand (Papathanassopoulos 1999: 381). The deregulation of the Greek broadcasting system was, as Papathanassopoulos (1990: 387) has noted, a political and contingent decision rather than the product of planning and public policy. This, along with the symbiotic relationship between the media and politicians, explains the loosely regulated broadcasting system.
4. The dancing politician is an event that draws attention and cannot be ignored by newspapers, TV stations and online outlets. 'It was the owner of the cabaret who called the reporters to cover the event. For publicity. You know,' said Demetris, a bouzouki player. And he continued, 'Every Saturday evening, you could see politicians on the floor. Every Saturday the same figures. They usually come three of four of them, only men, without their wives. They eat, drink, shout, and dance. This event is a good news for reporters to cover, as they help them to tell an interesting trend and newsworthy story. Mostly, it is the owner of the cabaret who call the reporters. For publicity. You know! Occasionally the politicians were followed by their reporters' (Loutzaki 1983–1986).

5. Andreas Papandreou, Prime Minister; Akis Tsochatzopoulos, Minister of Defence; Yiorgos Papandreou, Ministry of Culture (and son of Andreas).
6. Belonging to a political dynasty of long standing, Yiorgos Papandreou served under his father, then-prime minister Andreas Papandreou, as Minister for National Education and Religious Affairs (1988–1989 and 1994–1996) and Minister for Foreign Affairs from 1999 to 2004. He also served as Prime Minister of Greece from 2009 to 2011 (Wikipedia [n.d.]).
7. A comparison can be made with Kaeppler's ideas on the use of archival film in ethnographic research (1988: 110–29).
8. The word *meraki* comes from the Turkish word *merak*, which translated meanspassion, curiosity.
9. *Zeibekika* (sing. and pl.), the name for a generic dance in a 9/8 rhythm.
10. *Rebetis*: a member of a subculture comprising the lowest socio-economic class; specifically a member of the underworld.

References

Archaeology and the Arts. 2004. Special Issue 92 (September 2004), https://www.archaiologia.gr/wp-content/uploads/2011/07/92-4.pdf.

Avdikos, E., I. Loutzaki and C. Papakostas (eds). 2004. *Χορευτικά Ετερόκλητα* [Dance Miscellany]. Athens: Ellinika Grammata.

Boorstin, D.J. 1961. *The Image: A Guide to Pseudo-Events in America*. New York: Harper Colophon.

Butterworth, K., and S. Schneider. 1975. *Rebetika, Songs of the Old Greek Underworld*. Athens: Komboloi.

Caple, H. 2013. *Photojournalism: A Social Semiotic Approach*. New York: Palgrave McMillan.

Chaniotis, A. 2009. *Θεατρικότητα και δημόσιος βίος στον ελληνιστικό κόσμο* [Theatricality and Display in Hellenistic Cities]. Irakleio: Panepistimiakes Ekdoseis Kritis.

Coleman, S. 2007. 'Mediated Politics and Everyday Life', *International Journal of Communication* 1: 49–60.

Cowan, J. 1998. *Η πολιτική του σώματος. Χορός και κοινωνικότητα στη Βόρεια Ελλάδα* [Dance and the Body Politic in Northern Greece]. Athens: Alexandreia.

Damianakos, S. 1987. 'Το ρεμπέτικο τραγούδι: εθνολογικές και ταξικές συνιστώσεις' [The Rebetiko Song: Ethnological and Class-Related Components], in S. Damianakos (ed.), *Παράδοση ανταρσίας και λαϊκός πολιτισμός* [Popular Culture and the Tradition of Insubordination]. Athens: Plethron, pp. 169–81.

Gauntlett, S. 2001. *Ρεμπέτικο τραγούδι: Συμβολή στην επιστημονική του προσέγγιση* [Contribution to a Scientific Approach to the Rebetiko Song]. Athens: Ekdoseis tou Eikostou Protou.

Grau, A. 1993. 'Reviewed Work: Yearbook for Traditional Music', *Dance Research: The Journal of the Society for Dance Research* 11(2): 66–70.

Herzfeld, M. 1997. *Cultural Intimacy: Social Poetics in the Nation-State*. New York and London: Routledge.

Kaeppler, A.L. 1972. 'Method and Theory in Analyzing Dance Structure with an Analysis of Tongan Dance', *Ethnomusicology* 16(2): 173–217.

———. 1977. 'Polynesian Dance as Airport Art', in A.L. Kaeppler et al. (eds), *Asian and Pacific Dance: Selected Papers from the 1974 CORD Conference*. CORD Annual VIII. New York: Committee on Research in Dance, pp. 71–84.

———. 1978. 'Dance in Anthropological Perspective', *Annual Review of Anthropology* 7: 31–49.

———. 1985. 'Structured Movement Systems in Tonga', in P. Spencer (ed.), *Society and the Dance*. Cambridge: Cambridge University Press, pp. 92–118.

———. 1987. 'Spontaneous Choreography: Improvisation in Polynesian Dance', *Yearbook for Traditional Music* 19: 13–22.

———. 1988. 'The Use of Archival Film in an Ethnohistoric Study of Persistence and Change in Hawaiian Hula', in A.M. Moyle (ed.), *Music and Dance of Aboriginal Australia and the South Pacific: The Effects of Documentation on the Living Tradition. Papers and Discussions of the Colloquium of the International Council for Traditional Music Held in Townsville, Queensland, Australia 1988*. Australia: University of Sydney, pp. 110–29.

———. 1992. 'Σκέψεις για τη θεωρία και τη μεθοδολογία της ανθρωπολογικής μελέτης του χορού και των συστημάτων της ανθρώπινης κίνησης' [Theoretical and Methodological Considerations for Anthropological Studies of Dance and Human Movement Systems], *Ethnographica* 8: 17–26.

———. 1993. *Poetry in Motion: Studies of Tongan Dance*. Tongatapu: Vava'u Press.

———. 1998. 'Dance and the Concept of Style', in Theresa Buckland and Georgiana Gore (eds), *Dance, Style, Youth, Identities*. Keynote address for the 19th Symposium of the International Council of Traditional Music (ICTM) Study Group on Ethnochoreology. Prague: Czech Academy of Sciences, pp. 45–56.

Kavouras, P. 1997. 'Δρώμενα από εθνογραφική σκοπιά. Μέθοδοι, τεχνικές και προβλήματα καταγραφής' [Dromena from Ethnographic Perspectives: Methods, Techniques and Issues of Inscription], in *Dromena: Moyens modernes et techniques d' enregistrement. Proceedings of the 1st International Conference, 4–6 October 1996*. Komotini, pp. 45–78.

Kounadis, P. 1979. *Εις ανάμνησιν στιγμών ελκυστικών: κείμενα γύρω από το ρεμπέτικο* [Memories of Appealing Moments: Texts on the Rebetiko]. Athens: Katarti.

Loutzaki, I. 1983–1986. Personal Notebook.

———.1984. 'Dance and Society in a Complex Greek Peasant Community', Master's thesis. Belfast: Queen's University of Belfast.

———. 1989. 'Dance as a Cultural Message: A Study of Dance Style among the Greek Refugees from Northern Thrace in Micro Monastiri, Neo Monastiri and Aeginion', Ph.D. dissertation. Belfast: Queen's University of Belfast.

———. 1992. Special Issue: The Dance in Greece. *Ethnographica* 8. Nafplion: Peloponnesian Folklore Foundation.

———. 2004. 'Εισαγωγή' [Introduction], in E. Avdikos, I. Loutzaki and C. Papakostas (eds), *Χορευτικά Ετερόκλητα* [Dance Miscellany]. Athens: Ellinika Grammata, pp. 13–38.

———. 2007. 'Understanding Style in Monastiri Dance, Greece', in A.L. Kaeppler and E.I. Dunin (eds), *Dance Structures: Perspectives on the Analysis of Dance*. Budapest: Akademiai Kiado, pp. 303–30.

Papathanassopoulos, S. 1990. 'Broadcasting, Politics and the State in Socialist Greece', *Media, Culture and Society* 12: 387–97.

———. 1996. *Η δυναμική της τηλεόρασης* [The Power of Television]. Athens: Kastaniotis.

———. 1999. 'The Effects of Media Commercialisation on Journalism and Politics in Greece', *The Communication Review* 3(4): 379–402.

Petropoulos, E. 1968. *Ρεμπέτικα τραγούδια* [Rebetika Songs]. Athens: Kedros.

Robertson, R. 2011. 'Seeing is Believing', *Journal of Media Practice* 3(2): 85–95.

Stamatis, Y. 2011. 'Rebetiko Nation: Hearing Pavlos Vassiliou's Alternative Greekness through Rebetiko Song', Ph.D. dissertation. Ann Arbor, MI: University of Michigan.
Vasilakaki, F. 2001. 'Why Didn't You Choose the Tango?', *Kyriakatiki Eleftherotypia*, 1 July 2001.
Wikipedia. [n.d.]. 'George Papandreou', in *Wikipedia: The Free Encyclopedia* [online]. Retrieved 2 September 2019 from https://en.wikipedia.org/wiki/George_Papandreou.

Chapter 10

Lalåi

Somatic Decolonization and Worldview-Making through Chant on the Pacific Island of Guåhan

Ojeya Cruz Banks

> It was the night when the gods sang the world into being,
> the world of light to the world of music.
> —Hirini Melbourne in 'Te Hekenga-a-rangi'

The proverb above, signalling that music gave birth to Indigenous Māori world(s), is echoed across Oceania. On the Pacific island of Guåhan (Guam), *lalåi* or the act of chanting sings into being somatic worldviews that are embodied, felt and revelatory but often invisible to the eye. For this reason, Kaeppler's emphasis on the importance of 'the visual dimension' (Kaeppler 1996: 133) of Pacific music is paradoxical. While her critique on the overemphasis of sound analysis is imperative for understanding music's multidimensionality; Kaeppler's examples of the 'the visual' aspects focus on optical observations. This can be a minor element for Indigenous music-making traditions. For instance, Flintoff (2004: 14), discussing Māori music, wrote the spiritual dimension 'transcends the sounds' created. Few studies have examined the distinct somatic or sensuous political role chant can play in a colonial climate. In Guåhan, *lalåi* 'nurture(s) intellectual and sensory acuity' (Perez 1997: 10) by grounding singers in their Indigenous Chamoru/Chamorro[1] language, cultural memory and genealogy. Hence, the focus of this chapter is to articulate chant as a practice of somatic restitution of oral history and a critical Chamoru ancestral worldview. A decolonial project that restores Indigenous language and spirituality, singing is shown to bring to light visions of the past and future.

To explore this topic, the voice and work of Mr Leonard Iriarte (Figure 10.1.) are examined. He is an esteemed Chamoru chant composer in Guåhan and a co-founder of the highly regarded chant group on the island called I Fanlalai'an

Figure 10.1. Mr. Leonard Iriarte (holding the staff) and I Fanlalai'an members at the grand opening of the 2016 Festival of Pacific Arts in Guåhan. © Ojeya Cruz Banks.

(A Place for Chant). The group has made an enormous contribution towards invigorating knowledge that became inactive as a consequence of Spanish and American colonialism (Clement 2011; Cruz Banks 2013; Flores 1999, 2002; Leon-Guerrero 2014). The cultural work done by I Fanlalai'an elucidates an Indigenous sensory activism that is visionary work vital to the Chamoru worldview and spirituality. The significance of chant according to Iriarte and his group I Fanlalai'an is emphasized in this chapter.

Across the Pacific, chant has a somatic advantage because of its several symbiotic relationships. Kaeppler (1996: 140) explains that performing arts in Oceania are interdependent systems that 'combine visual, aural, kinesthetic and esthetic considerations with culturally understood symbols'. For example, Pacific island chant is an amalgam of oration, song gesture, facial expressions, body percussion, rhythm and movement for total embodiment of Indigenous subjectivities (Condevaux 2011; Cruz Banks 2013; Kaeppler 2004, 2013; Royal 2010, 2014; Shennan 1977; Teaiwa 2008). Chanting is not just about voice; it involves the whole body functioning as a resonating cavity of song. A multifaceted embodied experience, chant inherently cultivates somatic consciousness and intelligence.

This chapter begins with an overview of the research context, methodology and my research positionality. Then, a literature review on the importance of chant around the Pacific is briefly summarized. In this section, I articulate how chant in Guåhan is a process of somatic transformation that enlivens *kåna*: spiritual energy for tapping into networks of ancestral knowledge. I call this process decolonization of the soma or body in the way I Fanlalai'an utilizes chanting to create robust sensory embodiments of the Chamoru worldview. The sociocultural and biophysical effects of chants are discussed in this chapter. In the last section, I discuss the distinct politics of chant revitalization work done by I Fanlalai'an, including why they specifically sing in *fino' håya*, an older Chamoru language that fell out of practice due to colonialism. Two portraits of I Fanlalai'an are described: a practice session and a performance. To conclude, the I Fanlalai'an depictions provide insights into their sensory activism and the multidimensional ways Indigenous worlds are activated through chant.

Defining Somatics and Worldview

Two key concepts in this chapter are somatics and worldview. First, somatics means 'of the body', a term coined by Thomas Hanna (2004) to refer to the body from a subjective, qualitative perspective that often equates to exercises that enhance body awareness. Somatics is a field of movement studies that emphasizes internal physical perception and experience or the body as perceived from within. While North American and European trajectories of somatics tend to dominate (Eddy 2009; Green 2002), this study articulates a Chamoru notion of somatics. I am interested in how *lalåi* enlivens in-bodied cultural restoration and activates a critical Chamoru worldview through chant. Second, worldviews, as defined by Hart (2010: 2), 'are cognitive, perceptual, and affective maps that people continuously use to make sense of the social landscape and to find their ways to whatever goals they seek. Indigenous worldviews emerged as a result of the people's close relationship with the environment'. Both concepts are important because Indigenous knowledge is embodied, and decolonization involves reclaiming bodily, psychological and spiritual perceptions and experiences (see Cruz Banks 2009; Tuhiwai-Smith 1999).

Research Context, Methodology and Indigenous Diaspora Positionality

I met Iriarte and other members of I Fanlalai'an in 2010 at a Micronesia Studies postgraduate gathering in Hågatna, Guåhan. The isle is a member of an archipelago of fifteen called the Mariana Islands, located in the north-western Pacific Ocean. Guåhan is an astonishingly beautiful rainforest surrounded by the most sublime turquoise waters. For some time now, the island has been treated as a 'lynchpin in the United States' strategy to assert influence in the Pacific' (Crisostomo 2013: 7). Bevacqua (2009: 120) resentfully describes the island as 'one big American footnote' and with good reason because Guåhan (often called 'Guam USA') has a global reputation as a US military base. Guåhan was one of the first Pacific isles to be colonized in the fifteenth century and is still the longest-standing colony in the region. The continued United States military expansion across the Mariana Islands is labelled by many Indigenous island activists as profane and environmentally devastating (see Marsh and Taitano 2014). Hence, the resurgence of chant by I Fanlalai'an is fuelled by an aspiration to protect the Chamoru worldview, ancestral land and stories.

Using ethnographic principles,[2] information was collected through informal conversations with Leonard Iriarte and field notes of participant observations of I Fanlalai'an practices and performances during my visits to Guåhan in 2010, 2011, 2014 and 2016. The research reflects a relationship and collaboration between myself and Mr Leonard Iriarte that has been cultivated over the years. He provided constructive feedback on early drafts and supported the publication of this research. Additionally, the Human Ethics Committee at the University of Otago in Aotearoa/New Zealand, where I served as a senior lecturer in dance for a decade also granted approval. The central idea explored in this study is how *lalåi* brings about sensuous orientation to history and ancestral spirit.

I draw from my standpoint as a person of Chamoru diaspora descent and family experiences in Barrigada, Guåhan and in San Diego, California (Cruz Banks 2017; Cruz Banks and Marler 2019). The research is also informed by practice as a singer, songwriter and dancer along with dance anthropology fieldwork undertaken in Africa, the Pacific and in the USA. For almost two decades, I have used singing to understand dance culture in locations such as Uganda, Mali, Guinea, Aotearoa/New Zealand and Guåhan. Chant has offered emotionally felt experiences that have immersed me in my native tongue, melodic and rhythmic soundscapes, proverbial meaning and ritual. I can testify that singing can bring about musical sensations that have an effective power on the mind, body and soul (see also Grünhagen 2012). Chanting can evoke somatic resonance that brings about cultural astuteness. However, a limitation of the study is that I do not speak the Chamoru Indigenous language, so there are natural epistemological limitations in attempting to describe the significance of chant.

Articulating Chant as Somatic Transformation

Chanting in Oceania is heralded for spiritual currency, oral history, political messaging, peace and conflict resolution, Indigenous pedagogy, language revitalization, sung poetry, ceremonial purpose and ecological knowledge (Cruz Banks 2013; Diettrich 2017, 2018; Kaeppler 2013; Matthews 2004; Moulin 1994; Perez 2014; Silva 1989). The research signals that music is more than sound, as Kaeppler (1996) argues. My research agrees that music does in fact have many dimensions with a multiplicity of meanings. However, the terming of music as a 'visual art' sits uneasy for me. For one, the emphasis on the visual is a European performing arts preoccupation and a spectator trajectory. While I agree dance, regalia, the look of instruments and ritual events have visual symbolic significance, the importance of 'visuality' for I Fanlalai'an has more to do with a somatic reimagining of history, language and identity.

Chants confront postcolonial power by asserting what Hokowhitu (2014: 295–96) calls 'embodied sovereignty', which transcends colonial space by invoking a 'multidimensional way of being indigenous'. He is referring to the sociopolitical and physiological effect of chant. I would add that chant can bring about a somatic transformation of a worldview and a felt sense of self-determination. While Hokowhitu was referring to Māori *haka* (posture dance), the idea applies in Guåhan, where *lalåi* is understood to summon Chamoru states of being and experiencing the world.

For example, Iriarte has mentioned that an important objective for I Fanlalai'an is the cultural production of *kåna* or spiritual energy. He says that they believe chant generates *kåna* through breath and intonation. Therefore, chant members are trained to exude *kåna* in order to exude the 'appropriate energy so our ancestors will recognize us' (Iriarte 2011, pers. comm., 2 July). Ancestral connection and appeasement is everything to Chamoru culture. Likened to a somatic state, *kåna* boosts specific sensorial experiences that set in motion ancestral knowledge remembrance, affection and respect through *lalåi*.

Flores (1996, 1999, 2002; Leon-Guerrero 2014) chronicles the chant and dance revitalization – what she calls a cultural reinvention – that peaked in the 1980s in Guåhan: 'artists reinvented traditions from the vestiges of their pre-contact Chamorro heritage' (Flores 1996: 103). The Chamoru arts renaissance was built on a passion to connect with ancestral knowledge (Flores 1999; Leon-Guerrero 2014). I have described what was going on in Guåhan as an example of 'critical postcolonial dance recovery' (Cruz Banks 2009: 357). This was about the invigoration of cultural expressions, such as song and dance, that have spiritual currency and are helpful for fertilizing Indigenous ways of seeing and being in the world and that were deliberately oppressed. Bevacqua (2014) asserts that the search for ancient ancestry through chant and dance has helped to shatter the blinding screen over the Chamoru sense of the past. The rise in chant and dance groups has activated 'virtuous energies' needed for the project of safeguarding Indigenous Chamoru knowledge (Aguon 2013). Chant rituals are also articulated as 'gestures of Chamorro defiance against colonial power' (Farrer and Sellmann 2014: 128); these authors go on to say chant is a recovery of magical powers and 'spiritual resistance' to the fanatical Americanization and militarization of the island.

Given that chants invoke Indigenous language, they have somatic and epistemological power for hitting the mute button on colonial mentalities. Singing can be a therapy for filling a historical void, identity anxiety and emotional insecurity brought upon by colonialism. In Guåhan, chant is a practice of ancestral respect, Indigenous dignity and land sacredness, which are the very things that colonialism desecrates. Hence, to chant is a means of cultural repair and activation of vital Chamoru ontological protocols, which are about acknowledging the spiritual dimensions of life.

For instance, chants can usher in psychological shifts that unfurl and transcend colonial logics. Neuroscientists Jamshed Bharucha and Daniel Levitan assert music has an instinctive effect on the central nervous system (World Science Festival 2014 video; see also Grünhagen 2012). And Royal (2014: 10) argues new expressions of Indigeneity such as chant are not merely about colonial resistance or decolonization but instead 'challenge[s] us to re-centre, to reground, to reindigenise' our way of life. Hence, I argue chanting can be a practice of somatic decolonization for generating essential Indigenous cultural production. The upcoming portrait of I Fanlalai'an will show this group working to somatically (re) engineer Chamoru identity, history and their worldview through chant.

I Fanlalai'an

I Fanlalai'an has become one of the featured groups representing the Guåhan delegation at the quadrennial Festival of Pacific Arts. The group was founded by Iriarte, his sister Juanita Iriarte Sgambelluri and wife Lynn Iriarte in 1998. They named the group I Fanlalai'an, from the root word *lalåi* (to chant, to sing). The songs they perform are written by Iriarte and his family and colleagues. Together they write the lyrics and harmonies and devise choreographies of the chants. I Fanlalai'an's distinct approach to chant composition is to use older Chamoru concepts and the language *fino' håya*. This is a native tongue not laden with Spanish vocabulary and is rarely spoken. The group is dedicated to revitalizing *fino' håya* through chant. *Fino' håya* started to fall out of practice in the 1500s, and during the Spanish colonial era, the Chamoru language was creolized with Spanish, and this adaptation is widely spoken today. Even more severe language loss occurred during the American colonization, beginning in 1898. Language oppression got worse, for instance, in 1912, when the US Naval government banned the Chamoru language and later implemented a 'No Chamoru Policy' in public spaces such as schools and playgrounds (Hattori 2011; Underwood 1984). Therefore, chanting in *fino' håya*, Iriarte (2010, pers. comm., 6 November) argues, reinforces language acquisition and unique Chamoru cultural concepts that foster linguistic, historical and educational corrections. In short, Iriarte believes the revival of this older language is essential to strengthening Chamoru Indigenous identity.

The I Fanlalai'an chant compositions have stirred orthographic queries and debates about language, words and pronunciation on the island (Cruz 2016). Many of the historical Chamoru documents often consulted were written by earlier explorers and had inaccurate spelling and descriptions, which has led to cultural and linguistic confusion (Cruz 2016). This problem encouraged Iriarte to do an etymological analysis of Indigenous word forms and existing practices found in neighbouring Micronesian islands to gain clues into ancient Chamoru ways of life (Flores 1996, 1999). Jeremy Cepeda, a former senior tutor of the group, described the revitalization of the older language as 'cracking the codes of history' (in Cruz 2016: video). In other words, chants provide allegoric and metaphorical information and insights into pre-contact Chamoru life. The language research is a project of divesting the deleterious effects of colonialism and territorialism. More importantly, chant ushers in a somatic (re)centring and reclamation to see the world through Chamoru eyes.

I Fanlalai'an uses chant as a principle method of teaching and learning. Iriarte (2010, pers. comm., 9 November) calls chants critical thinking tools for breeding Chamoru cultural perception and recovering important ancestral visions of the world. The chant work submerges the group in a practice of *kåna* and *fino' håya*. At one of the group's weekly evening practices at the University of Guam, I observed an exercise led by senior tutor Carlos Laguåña. When I entered the room, the entire group was in a circle formation undertaking breath and chant synchronization training, their heads slightly bowed and eyes closed. There was a quiet and otherworldly energy in the space. I found the group's concentration incredibly diligent and undisturbed as if they were filtering out white noise. They were completely rapt in the moment and devoted to the exercises. Later, Iriarte explained they had been cultivating a sense of *kåna* individually and within the group. Iriarte (2011, pers. comm., 2 July) noted that this is achieved through proper pronunciation of *fino' håya* and learning how to stand with grace, composure and to emanate Indigenous conviction as you sing and dance.

In this exercise, I Fanlalai'an had the goal to fine-tune consciousness through cultivating *kåna*. I noticed there was a stillness and an undeniable energy that was spiritually charged and radiating from the circle. The group seemed to be collectively decompressing through sound and breath. As Iriarte articulates, the breath and chant work facilitated by Laguåña provides psychological preparation for reinforcing the acquisition of *fino' håya*. Emphasis is put on intonation of language and spiritual energy. The exercise is a strategy for enhancing somatic awareness of the sonic textures and rhythms of the native tongue. The 'tapping into *kåna*' exercise is vital to learning the songs and their meanings because it prepares the body for a sensory download of allegory and historical narratives. Chanting with *kåna* is believed to enhance receptivity to ancestral networks of knowledge and spirit.

Iriarte (2010, pers. comm., 6 November) describes I Fanlalai'an as an 'ongoing oral history programme that seeks to secure a traditional depository for archaic terminology and language through the creation of chants and dances fashioned after a seventeenth-century model'. The chants they sing are about the 'old ways . . . about the matrilineal heritage, deceased family members, the Chamoru genesis, legendary sea voyages, and more'. According to the liner notes of I Fanlalai'an's first released music CD, 'the purpose of singing this song is to unify the minds of the chanters' in a Chamoru worldview (Iriarte, Manibusan and Santos [n.d.]).

On 24 June 2012, I attended an I Fanlalai'an performance preview held at the University of Guam's Fieldhouse in preparation for the Showcase for the Festival of the Pacific Arts, hosted by the Solomon Islands. I Fanlalai'an performed a selection described as 'precontact cultural material' in the performance programme. To commence their performance, the group of about twenty-five chanters patiently walked in unison up to the elevated stage, which was lit with purple-blue hues. Everyone was dressed in black and orange and wearing yellow crowns made of flowers. The young men led the way, moving in multiple single-file lines and singing the chant 'I Acho' Åtte' (The Magic Stone). Iriarte sang the opening call. The *lalåi* invokes the genealogy of a legendary sea voyager, and the lyrics included information about what was taken on canoe voyages. Behind the chanters was a painted mural depicting the island's tropical landscape and massive latte or limestone pillars. The men paced ceremonially with paddles in their hands as they sang, and then the entire assembly began to undulate gently. With their right hand, the men extended their paddles outward, while their left hand kept the pulse of the chant with body percussion; they slapped their thighs four times and their hips thrusted like turbulent wind blowing through the water. In contrast, the women's arms floated, hands flexed away from their hips, while their whole body swayed; their feet shifted carefully as calm as water. The song had a deep register and poignantly blended the female and male voices, which exuded a sensuous and meditative energy. The vibe was not a staged performance; it felt like a ritual. Their performance embodied qualities of physical strength, assurance, groundedness, tranquillity and dignity.

I Fanlalai'an's performance represented an ongoing Chamoru somatic transformation occurring in Guåhan. They embody distinct movement that emerges from chanting in *fino' håya* and the aspiration to permeate *kåna*. There was a razor-sharp focus in their eyes as if they had psychically catapulted themselves into a canoe voyage and were carefully reading the ocean swell. Their movement was oceanic. I could see the ripples, the tides and the ginormous wave crests in their dancing. I could hear the sound of a canoe slapping against the surface of water. The performance gave me goosebumps. For the chanters and the audience, the chant created a sensorial experience of oral history about the journey of our seafaring ancestors. From my observations, I Fanlalai'an's performance spiritually transported everyone. Through a smooth combination of *kåna*, song and dance, revelations of a Chamoru worldview and topographical connections are cultivated. The chants transcend and transfigure colonial space through language reclamation and a profound somatic embodiment of Indigenous dignity.

Through performance, I Fanlalai'an divests the colonization of the senses and reboots the Chamoru mental landscape with *fino' håya*. Former principal chanter,

Cepeda (2013) has called their songs 'vocal literature', providing important information and snapshots of time, and should be sung across the generations. He describes chant as a somatic depository and a heart and soul elixir. The chants render embodied experiences that are aural, visual, tactile and kinetic; they are spiritually felt storyboards of a Chamoru worldview and heritage.

In contemporary Guåhan, chant according to the work of I Fanlalai'an is a project of decolonial revisioning and a form of sensorial Indigenous activism. This is why I think Kaeppler's (1996) description of music as 'visual art' is paradoxical. Chant is involved in the making of Chamoru people from the inside out, through nurturing embodied knowledge and spiritual experiences. For I Fanlalai'an, *lalåi* trains the body to be a somatic vessel of genealogy, language and history. *Lalåi* can actuate revelations of a Chamoru worldview and strengthen cultural memory endangered by colonialism, militarization and US territorialism. Chanting in Guåhan (re)indigenizes the soma.

Concluding Thoughts

I Fanlalai'an is on a mission to activate the Chamoru worldview through somatic means. For them, chanting is not in spite of colonial dilemmas but an act of Indigenous sensory activism for propagating *kåna* and *fino' håya*. There is an emphasis on somatic embodiments of Chamoru spirituality and language. By re-establishing oral tradition through chant, I Fanlalai'an capitalizes on somatic techniques for archiving genealogy, history and important words. They understand people to be ultimate storehouses of worldview and Indigenous epistemologies. Hence, *lalåi* reinforces a somatic attention on revisioning what it means to be Chamoru and discovering the world through Chamoru eyes. I would argue the *lalåi* work in Guåhan, from an Indigenous perspective, is visionary work, not 'visual art'. The chanting strengthens Chamoru futures with ancestral memory and connection instead of being threatened by US territorialism. I call *lalåi* somatic decolonization because it invigorates full-bodied sensibilities of identity and culture. I Fanlalai'an portraits reveal that chanting invokes embodied ancestral worldviews that have epistemological and spiritual power. More research featuring song compositions and group member voices are needed to understand the multidimensional ways Indigenous worlds are activated through chant in Guåhan.

Acknowledgements

I want to say *si yú os måase* to Leonard Iriarte, Jeremy Cepeda, I Fanlalai'an, Fanai Castro and Dakota Alcantara-Camacho for their constructive feedback towards developing this chapter. Also, big thanks to Dr Robert Underwood and Dr Troy McVey at the University of Guam for supporting research seminars at the University of Guam. Thank you to family in Barrigada, Yigo and San Diego for their support and love.

Ojeya Cruz Banks (PhD) is an Associate Professor of Dance at Denison University. Her research combining African and Pacific lineages is inspired by her identity as a Pacific Islander (Guåhan/Guam) and African American with roots in Alabama, Kentucky and Louisiana. For over a decade, she worked as a Senior Lecturer at the University of Otago in Aotearoa/New Zealand. This is where she developed an interest in Indigenous somatic practices and Black Pacific dance intersections. Her choreographies and publications include topics such as West African dance (Guinea and Senegal), Pacific Island dance as critical spiritual and cultural health, and Indigenous education and performance. Ojeya's short dance film titled *Tåno/Land* premiered at the 2016 Pacific Arts Festival, and in 2018, her dance film collaboration *Original Spaces: Black/African/Pacific Intersections* was curated at the Gibney Center in New York City. She recently performed with the acclaimed Philadelphia-based dance company FlyGround.

Notes

1. Chamoru or Chamorro refers to a native person of Guåhan/Guam and the Northern Mariana Islands.
2. Dunham (1942); Kaeppler (2000); Denzin, Lincoln and Smith (2008).

References

Aguon, J. 2013. 'Julian Aguon-interview', *Moana Nui Action Alliance* [online]. Retrieved 18 August 2019 from http://mnaa-ca.org/moananui2013/open-discussion-new-ideas/julian-aguon-interview/.

Bevacqua, M. 2009. 'My Island is One Big American Footnote', in A.M. Tamaira (ed.), *The Space Between: Negotiating Culture, Place, and Identity in the Pacific*. Honolulu: University of Hawai'i at Mānoa, pp. 120–22.

———. 2014. 'When the Moon Waxes: Dancing Pasts, Dancing Futures', *Mariana Variety Guam Edition*, 9 July.

Clement, M.R. 2011. '*Kustumbre*, Modernity and Resistance the Subaltern Narrative in Chamorro Language Music'. Doctoral dissertation, Honolulu: University of Hawai'i at Mānoa, December 2011.

Condevaux, A. 2011. 'Contextualisation of Dances in Tourism: A Tongan Case Study', *The Journal of the Polynesian Society* 120(3): 269–91.

Crisostomo, R.A. 2013. 'Strategic Guam: Past, Present and Future', Master's thesis. Carlisle, PA: United States Army War College.

Cruz, B.L. 2016. 'I Tinituhon: Rediscovering Fo'na & Ponta', *YouTube* [online video]. Retrieved 22 January 2019 from https://www.youtube.com/watch?v=yQPM1Iayq7s.

Cruz Banks, O. 2009. 'Critical Postcolonial Dance Recovery and Pedagogy: An International Literature Review', *Pedagogy, Culture & Society* 17(3): 355–67.

———. 2013. 'Espritu tasi/the Ocean Within: Critical Dance Revitalization in the Pacific', *Dance Research Aotearoa* 1(1): 24–36.

———. 2017. 'Black Chamoru Dancing Self-Revelation', *Amerasia Journal* 43(1): 147–56.

Cruz Banks, O., and M. Marler. 2019. 'Soil, Soul and the Somatic Senses: Memoirs of Dance in Japan and Guam/Guåhan in Postcolonial Times', in A. Williamson and B. Sellers-Young (eds), *Soulful and Spiritual Research in Dance Studies: Bodily Inscription, Self-Narrative and Auto-ethnography*. Bristol: Intellect Books, pp. 348–65.

Denzin, N.K., Y.S. Lincoln and L.T. Smith (eds). 2008. *Handbook of Critical and Indigenous Methodologies*. Los Angeles: Sage.

Diettrich, B. 2017. 'Chanting Diplomacy: Music, Conflict, and Social Cohesion in Micronesia', in K. Gillespie, S. Treloyn and D. Niles (eds), *A Distinctive Voice in the Antipodes: Essays in Honour of Stephen A. Wild*. Canberra: ANU Press, pp. 195–218.

———. 2018. '"Summoning Breadfruit" and "Opening Seas": Toward a Performative Ecology in Oceania', *Ethnomusicology* 62(1): 1–27.

Dunham, K. 1942 [2006]. 'The Anthropological Approach to the Dance', in V. Clark and S.E. Johnson (eds), *Kaiso! Writings by and about Katherine Dunham*. Madison: University of Wisconsin Press, pp. 508–13.

Eddy, M. 2009. 'A Brief History of Somatic Practices and Dance: Historical Development of the Field of Somatic Education and its Relationship to Dance', *Journal of Dance and Somatic Practices* 1(1): 5–27.

Farrer, D.S., and J.D. Sellmann. 2014. 'Chants of Re-enchantment: Chamorro Spiritual Resistance to Colonial Domination', *Social Analysis* 58(1): 127–48.

Flintoff, B. 2004. *Taonga Puoro: Singing Treasures*. Nelson: Craig Potton Publishing.

Flores, J. 1996. 'Reinventing Artistic Traditions: The Chamoru Search for Identity', Master's thesis. Hagatna: University of Guam.

———. 1999. 'Art and Identity in the Mariana Islands: Issues of Reconstructing an Ancient Past', Ph.D. dissertation. Norwich: University of East Anglia.

———. 2002. 'The Re-creation of Chamorro Dance as Observed through the Festival of Pacific Arts', *Pacific Arts* 2002(25): 47–63.

Green, J. 2002. 'Somatic Knowledge: The Body as Content and Methodology in Dance Education', *Journal of Dance Education* 2(4): 114–18.

Grünhagen, C. 2012. 'Healing Chants and Singing Hospitals: Towards an Analysis of the Implementation of Spiritual Practices as Therapeutic Means', *Scripta Instituti Donneriani Aboensis* 24: 76–88.

Hanna, T. 2004. *Somatics: Reawakening the Mind's Control of Movement, Flexibility, and Health*. Boston: Da Capo Press.

Hart, M.A. 2010 'Indigenous Worldviews, Knowledge, and Research: The Development of an Indigenous Research Paradigm', *Journal of Indigenous Voices in Social Work* 1(1): 1–16.

Hattori, A.P. 2011. 'Teaching History through Service Learning at the University of Guam', *The Journal of Pacific History* 46(2): 221–27.

Hill, K. 2011. '"Te Hekenga-a-rangi" (Excerpt 1) – Hirini Melbourne and Richard Nunns', *YouTube* [online video]. Retrieved 18 August 2019 from https://www.youtube.com/watch?v=FaH6s-twdzU.

Hokowhitu, B. 2014. 'Colonized Physicality, Body-Logic, and Embodied Sovereignty', in L.R. Graham and H.G. Penny (eds), *Performing Indigeneity: Global Histories and Contemporary Experiences*. Lincoln: University of Nebraska Press, pp. 273–304.

Iriarte, L.Z, V.R. Manibusan and M.A. Santos. [n.d.]. *Guma Pålulie/ I Linalai Fino' Håya Siha: Chamorro Chants of Guma Pålu lie (Guåhan)* [compact disc]. [s.l.]: [s.n.].

Kaeppler, A.L. 1996. 'The Look of Music, the Sound of Dance: Music as a Visual Art', *Visual Anthropology* 8(2–4): 133–53.

———. 2000. 'Dance Ethnology and the Anthropology of Dance', *Dance Research Journal* 32(1): 116–25.
———. 2004. 'Recycling Tradition: A Hawaiian Case Study', *Dance Chronicle* 27(3): 293–311.
———. 2010. 'The Beholder's Share: Viewing Music and Dance in a Globalized World. (Charles Seeger Lecture Presented at the 51st Annual Meeting of the Society for Ethnomusicology, 2006, Honolulu)', *Ethnomusicology* 54(2): 185–201.
———. 2013. 'Chanting Grief, Dancing Memories: Objectifying Hawaiian Laments', *Humanities Research* 19(3): 71.
Leon-Guerrero, J. 2014. 'Dr. Judy Flores, PhD', *Vimeo* [online video]. Retrieved 18 August from https://vimeo.com/94122782.
Marsh, K.G., and T.J. Taitano. 2014. 'Guam', *The Contemporary Pacific* 26(1): 170–77.
Matthews, N. 2004. 'The Physicality of Māori Message Transmission: "Ko te tinana, he waka tuku kōrero"', *Junctures: The Journal for Thematic Dialogue* 3: 9–18.
Moulin, J.F. 1994. 'Chants of Power: Countering Hegemony in the Marquesas Islands', *Yearbook for Traditional Music* 26: 1–19.
Natividad, L., and G. Kirk. 2010. 'Fortress Guam: Resistance to US Military Mega-Buildup', *The Asia-Pacific Journal* 8(19): 1–17.
Olvera, A.E. 2008. 'Cultural Dance and Health: A Review of the Literature', *American Journal of Health Education* 39(6): 353–59.
Perez, C.C. 1997. 'Signs of Being: A Chamoru Spiritual Journey', Ph.D. dissertation. Honolulu: University of Hawai'i.
Perez, C.S. 2014. 'Singing Forward and Backwards: Ancestral and Contemporary Chamorro Poetics', in J.H. Cox and D.H. Justice (eds), *The Oxford Handbook of Indigenous American Literature*. Oxford: Oxford University Press, pp. 152–66.
Quiroga Murcia, C., et al. 2010. 'Shall We Dance? An Exploration of the Perceived Benefits of Dancing on Well-Being', *Arts & Health* 2(2): 149–63.
Routhan, T., and S. Ruhela. 2014. 'Chanting: A Therapeutic Treatment for Sports Competitive Anxiety', *International Journal of Scientific and Research Publications* 4(3): 1–5.
Royal, T.A.C. 2010. 'Whakaahua: An Approach to Performance', *Dancing Across the Disciplines: Cross Currents of Dance Research and Performance throughout the Global Symposium, 29 June 2010*. Dunedin, New Zealand: University of Otago Press.
———. 2014. 'Indigenous Ways of Knowing', *Argos Aotearoa: The University Beside Itself* [online]. Retrieved 18 August 2019 from https://issuu.com/argosaotearoa/docs/argos-aotearoa_issue-1_the-universi.
Shennan, J. 1977. 'Waiata-a-Ringa: A Movement Study of Action Song, the Dance Genre Developed in the Twentieth Century by the Maori People of New Zealand', Ph.D. dissertation. Auckland: University of Auckland.
Silva, K. 1989. 'Hawaiian Chant: Dynamic Cultural Link or Atrophied Relic?', *The Journal of the Polynesian Society* 98(1): 85–90.
Smith, L.T. 2013. *Decolonizing Methodologies: Research and Indigenous Peoples*. Moorpark: Cram101 Inc.
Teaiwa, K.M. 2008. 'Saltwater Feet: The Flow of Dance in Oceania', in S. Shaw and A. Francis (eds), *Deep Blue: Critical Reflections on Nature, Religion and Water*. London: Equinox, pp. 107–26.

Tuhiwai, S.L. 1999. *Decolonizing Methodologies: Research and Indigenous Peoples*. London: Zed Books. Ltd.
Underwood, R. 1984. 'Language Survival, the Ideology of English and Education in Guam', *Educational Research Quarterly* 8(4): 72–81.
World Science Festival. 2014. 'Notes and Neurons: In Search of the Common Chorus', *YouTube* [online video]. Minutes 18:00–30:00. Retrieved 18 August 2019 from https://www.youtube.com/watch?v=S0kCUss0g9Q.

PART IV
Significance of the Tangible

Chapter 11

Intangible Dancing as Tangible Museum Exhibits

Elsie Ivancich Dunin

Extensions of the dancer's body such as footwear, masking, dress and held items, for example swords or sound-making instruments, are some of the tangible items that are part of intangible dancing contexts. Those in scientific or artistic disciplines unfamiliar with dancing bodies produced most early twentieth-century museum displays. Tangible spatial items directly contacting or influencing the movement of the dancer, such as specially made flooring or ground covers like Pacific Island barkcloth, are tangible conditions for dancing bodies. Some barkcloth examples were acquired by European travellers in the late nineteenth and early twentieth century and placed as art objects for preservation in newly established museums. Such is the case with Tongan items uncovered by Adrienne Kaeppler in a relatively unknown Pacific collection of an ethnographic museum founded in the early twentieth century in Zagreb, Croatia.

This chapter, about my own museum displays, was inspired by the scholarship of Adrienne Kaeppler. At the end of the symposium in 2000 of the Study Group on Ethnochoreology, part of the International Council for Traditional Music, and held on Korčula Island in Croatia, Adrienne mentioned to me that she was travelling to the capital city Zagreb to look at Tongan items in the Ethnographic Museum. She had been visiting museums in Europe and Australia to compile information about Oceanic artefacts such as Tongan barkcloths and *moai kavakava* (wooden figures from Rapa Nui), and the Museum in Zagreb happened to have both such objects. At this time, I had no knowledge about barkcloths that were part of the Tongan *lakalaka* (sung poetry with choreographed movements) until Adrienne's keynote presentation two years later for the 'Dance and Aesthetics' panel at the Study Group on Ethnochoreology symposium held in 2002 in Szeged, Hungary. For the symposium proceedings (I was an editor), she included photographs of barkcloths, with one so large that it was carried by at least ten men and women.

Figure 11.1. Photograph of barkcloth by Adrienne Kaeppler, 1975. Image used by permission.

Writing about the tangible and material links to dance in Tonga, Kaeppler (2005: 213–214) stated:

> Tongan *lakalaka* share their underlying structure and aesthetic evaluative ways of thinking with Tongan social structure and other expressive forms, such as barkcloth design. . . . A large piece of barkcloth may be presented to the central dancer to acknowledge the aesthetic performance of the *lakalaka*, and here the aesthetics of presentation can be seen. . . . The barkcloth is unfurled to show the design motifs, straight lines, and the craftsmanship.

In a 2003 article (written after her visit to Zagreb and keynote presentation in Szeged), Kaeppler described motifs on barkcloth examples found in museums worldwide, emphasizing that '[o]bjects cannot be understood simply through visual examination, but must be related to the social and cultural contexts in which they were used and evaluated according to Polynesian aesthetic principles' (Kaeppler 2003: 12).

Due to my own exhibition at the same museum in Zagreb in 2018, I visited the Oceanic permanent exhibition, where I saw three Oceanic items: two Tongan barkcloths[1] and a black-coloured wooden *moai kavakava* statue from Rapa Nui that Adrienne identifies in her 2003 article as being part of the founding collection of the Zagreb museum. As a viewer of these preserved artefacts with no hint of their social or dance-related context in the display, I was reminded of a change in attitude and greater recognition of a dancer's perspective toward displaying intangible contexts through tangible objects. This transformation appears to have come after the establishment of UNESCO's 2003 Convention for the Safeguarding of Intangible Cultural Heritage.

At the Ethnochoreology Study Group's 2008 symposium in Kuala Lumpur, Adrienne discussed in her keynote address the significance of UNESCO's Intangible Cultural Heritage proclamation that year for the *lakalaka*, which is considered by the Tongans as the living cultural history of the community. After 2008, the subject of captured intangible dancing held in archival holdings and museum exhibits was more evident in literature, such as with Anette Rein's article, 'Flee(t)ing Dances! Initiatives for the Preservation and Communication of Intangible World Heritage in Museums' (Rein 2011). In 2014, the Ethnochoreology Study Group's second symposium on Korčula Island proposed as a research theme 'Dance as Tangible and Intangible Cultural Heritage', and furthermore, the Korčula Town Museum featured for the first time an exhibit on the island's sword-dance.[2] Recently, in 2017, Adrienne Kaeppler again returned to this topic with the article 'Capturing Music and Dance in an Archive: A Meditation on Imprisonment', which explored the issue of saving captured intangible culture and the question of its use and for what appropriate purposes (Kaeppler 2017: 430).

Inspired by Adrienne Kaeppler's work on museum exhibits holding 'culturally dance-related' artefacts far from their Oceanic source, this chapter describes two of my museum exhibits, each with a differing purpose. Both were multi-week exhibits organized from a dancer's perspective. The first was held in 1984 at the University of California at Los Angeles (UCLA), during the Olympic Games year in both Yugoslavia (Sarajevo) and the United States. This exhibit was called 'Dance Occasions and Festive Dress in Yugoslavia' and used tangible body extensions and slide film projections to educate those not familiar with the cultural dancing contexts in Yugoslavia. My dance research at the time was focused on South Slavs who had emigrated from south-eastern Europe to California. In addition, I was teaching a course in the UCLA Department of Dance that featured learning dances from Yugoslavia. With the understanding that body movements are influenced by what is worn, I regularly introduced costumes to my students from my own collection. In addition, I was aware of many costumes from Yugoslavia that had been donated to the Museum at UCLA since the 1950s. The second exhibit was held in 2018 in Skopje, Macedonia, and displayed fifty years of a Romani George's Day/Erdelezi ('coming of summer') celebration in photographs, documentary film projections and two fifty-year-old festive outfits.[3] In contrast to the earlier one, the 2018 exhibition was designed for a community already intimately familiar with this holiday event. The chapter compares the design of the 1984 and 2018 exhibits relative to the audiences and to changing technologies of visual documentation.

Planning and Designing the 1984 Exhibition

After the two-country USA and Yugoslavia Olympic combination was announced to take place in 1984, I informally suggested to the directors and curator of folk art and textiles of UCLA's Museum of Cultural History that an exhibit might be planned along with ethnographic film showings. Overseen by the Center for Russian and East European Studies, UCLA had recently received through a newly established UCLA Yugoslav Exchange Program library requests and ethnographic television programmes produced in Zagreb. In exchange, Yugoslavia requested and received English-language literature for their American studies university classes. My intent at UCLA was simply to offer my suggestions and assistance to the museum. The thought was to assemble costumes from Yugoslavia that were already in the holdings of the museum, supplemented by my own collection and those from the South Slavic immigrant communities in the Los Angeles area. The suggestion was very enthusiastically received, and on the spot, I was asked to be the 'visiting curator' of the exhibit! Up to this moment in my professional life, I had only visited and appreciated a number of ethnographic museums in each country of my research travels. With great hesitation, I accepted the challenge, realizing that I was to present a relatively unknown culture area to the United States and from a dance ethnologist's perspective of Yugoslavia. The museum staff was put at my disposal, while photographs would be taken of the display items for the catalogue, and professional editing would be provided for the accompanying monograph/catalogue. Research funds were also made available to the Department of Dance graduate students to assist both with the preparation of the exhibit and for parts of the publication.

Until this co-Olympics hosting, the American public at large was not familiar with the Socialist Federal Republic (SFR) of Yugoslavia, bordered by seven European countries (Italy, Austria, Hungary, Romania, Bulgaria, Greece and Albania). During the late nineteenth century, South Slavs (Croatians, Slovenians, Serbs and Montenegrins) who were then under Austrian rule immigrated to the Los Angeles area as Austrian citizens. After the First World War, South Slavic populations became unified under the Kingdom of Serbs, Croats and Slovenes, which in 1929 officially changed its name to the Kingdom of Yugoslavia, a name literally meaning the South Slavs. After the Second World War, Yugoslavia became aligned with Socialist Communist countries, but by 1948 it had split from this Soviet-controlled Eastern European block of countries. SFR Yugoslavia became the only independent communist country in Europe until its own break up into six independent democratic countries during the 1990s. My intent in the auspicious year of 1984, therefore, was double-edged. On one hand, it was to recognize the ongoing South Slav communities in the Los Angeles area through a visualization of their emigrant locations and to make a point of their communities and continuing dance events in my opening lecture about the exhibit. On the other hand, I was to educate a public unfamiliar with Yugoslavia through dance zones that did not coincide with Yugoslavia's six federated republics of Slovenia, Croatia, Bosnia and Herzegovina, Serbia, Montenegro and Macedonia.

The 1984 UCLA museum space preceded the internationally known Fowler Museum, which opened in 1992 with wonderfully planned multi-use display spaces. The UCLA Museum of Cultural History in the 1980s was otherwise known in the United States for holding one of the largest collections of African and South Pacific art. For the Yugoslav exhibit, I encountered a large blank room with entrance and exit doors, a space that heretofore had exhibited colourful pieces from Africa and the South Pacific, accompanied with combined monographs/catalogues authored by visiting curators.

My earliest tasks were to assess the Yugoslav holdings in the museum alongside my personal costume pieces that I used in my classes. What items needed to be solicited from personal collections among South Slav emigrants and their descendants in the greater Los Angeles area? Since my approach to teaching about dances and dancing in my courses was through dance zones of Yugoslavia, it was a natural decision on my part to select and display the costumes by zones. Thirty-six festive outfits worn for dance occasions were selected. Some of the costumes were completely handmade, from the weaving of the cloth to the final stitching. Others were made from commercially prepared materials. Some were highly embroidered, highly ornate, while others seemed relatively simple at first glance but were actually intricate in their detail. The designs of the outfits were believed to be quite old, but the garments on display were largely from the early twentieth century.

My vision was to display the outfits on 'dancing bodies' rather than showing selected pieces of fabrics pinned to a board or laid out horizontally. But the museum was not equipped with freestanding mannequins, and the cost of acquiring new ones, such as those used in fashion store display windows, could not be handled within the budget. Therefore, the staff constructed bodies made of crossbars for the shoulders; plastic bags filled with paper were taped into body shapes and attached to the posts. Each bag-body post had to be carefully attached to the floor so that stockings and footwear could properly show a leg gesture. Acid-free tissue paper filled the sleeves and shaped the arms and other body parts. In order to show headwear, faceless heads were attached to each body post. There were many decisions to make from head to toe with regards to garment placement, in order to show an accurate dancing position.

The 1984 Exhibition

In the 1984 exhibit, the festive dress outfits were displayed in groups corresponding to the six 'dance zones' proposed in 1964 by Dr Ivan Ivančan, pioneer Croatian ethnochoreologist: the Adriatic, the Alpine, the Dinaric, the Morava, the Pannonian and the Vardar (Ivančan 1964–65). These zones do not directly coincide with the borders of the six federated republics. Within these groupings, the dressed mannequins in the exhibit were arranged as much as possible into dancing formations and positions relative to the characteristics of the 'zones' (see Figure 11.2.).

Figure 11.2. The Vardar dance zone. © E. Dunin, 1984.

Each zone of costumes was lit with special lighting from above to distinguish it from others and to highlight colour in the fabric, and each costume was identified with a label showing the year, place of origin and donor.

In a darkened corner of the museum space, there was a continuous projection from a slide carousel that presented visuals taken by the author from 1967 to 1983. These images showed dance zone locations with distinctive features of geography, and the festive dress in dancing contexts especially, featuring a Dubrovnik area traditional wedding, Romani dancing occasions of the Vardar zone, festival occasions in the Pannonian zone, and dancing of the Konavle's Čilipi village dance group near Dubrovnik as an example of the Adriatic zone. The colourful slide projections corresponded to the four articles of dance occasions in the exhibit's accompanying monograph. From a private collection of hundreds of slides, the discretionary viewing limit was ten minutes, meaning four seconds per slide from a 140-slide tray of images.

Distinctive dance music accompaniment at each zone could not be accommodated by separate sound systems. The decision, therefore, was to have an overall soundscape of music that included typical examples from each zone: button accordions with a polka example and a sample of clanging bells worn by winter carnival fur-covered *kurenti* of the Alpine zone; the sound of plucked mandolins by *tamburica* bands with various sizes of guitar-shaped instruments of the Pannonian zone; *gajda* (bagpipe) sounds for dance in the Vardar zone, compared with *duda* (bellow bagpipes) of the Pannonian zone; beating on a *tapan* (large double-head drum) struck on one side with a mallet and a twig on the other accompanied with *zurla* (two oboe-type double-reeds) of the Vardar zone; and the sound of three-string, pear-shaped *lijerica* with rhythmic foot-stamping for the Adriatic zone. Upon entering the museum space, visitors heard these changing soundscapes but low enough in volume to allow conversations.

Accompanying the museum exhibit was a weekly Sunday showing of Yugoslav ethnographic documentaries produced between 1948 and 1979. These 16 mm film and television documentaries on video format were produced by ethnographer directors for Croatian Television in Zagreb and acquired by the UCLA Library through the Yugoslav Exchange Program.[4] The seven weekly showings – different each week – were in a space separated but nearby to the exhibition space. South Slavic communities many miles distant in greater Los Angeles visited the displays, and overall the exhibit was the most successful in visitation numbers that had been held to that date at UCLA's Museum of Cultural History.

Monograph with Catalogue of the Exhibition

The tangible outcome of the multimedia and multi-week museum exhibit and ethnographic film showings was the 72-page book *Dance Occasions and Festive Dress in Yugoslavia*, published 1984 as the UCLA Museum of Cultural History (monograph series 23). The contents of the monograph/catalogue included a map of the dance zones, four illustrated articles of dance occasions with distinctive festive dress, Labanotation scores of dances from a southern Adriatic coastal area that has a high number of immigrants in California, and a complete bibliographic listing of sources about dance and costume available in the UCLA Library. The four articles were related to dance occasions from my research of dancing and festive dress in social contexts: the Skopje Gypsy St. George's Day in 1967; Dubrovnik area weddings in 1977 and 1979; several folk festival and professional ensemble programmes observed and documented since 1957; and Čilipi village dance events from 1976 to 1977. The dances of the touristic Čilipi programme were videotaped on 17 April 1977, and this video documentation offered a tangible form for a dance ethnology graduate student[5] to prepare Labanotation of five dances to be included in the museum publication. During my research of the South Slavic dancing occasions in California, as compared with source areas of their emigration, I learned that every village in the Dubrovnik area in the southern Adriatic dance zone had family members in California, so it was appropriate to highlight dances from this area in the monograph/catalogue. In addition, the bibliographic listing in the museum publication includes every published source for dance and costume in the UCLA Library holdings.[6]

The catalogue section made note of each costume in the exhibition, and photographs showed complete outfits where possible. All pieces that comprise an outfit were identified and described with meticulous measurements made by one of the dance ethnology graduate students.[7] The catalogue was divided into geographic areas that share common dance and costume characteristics and that coincided with Dr Ivančan's dance zones. Slavic terms and descriptions for costume pieces were determined through field interviews where possible; and when this could not be accomplished, a thorough examination of the literature was conducted by dance ethnology graduate student assistants.[8]

The Romani (Gypsy) costume from the urban city of Skopje did not fit easily into the dance zone categories. I donated it in 1969, and it was the first 'Romani' outfit to be part of a museum collection and exhibit in the United States. This Romani outfit and article 'A Gypsy Celebration of St. George's Day in Skopje' in a 1984 monograph (Dunin 1984: 24–27) became significant thirty years later for another UCLA museum exhibit, when this same Romani costume was shown comparatively with a Romani costume acquired for the Fowler Museum in 2011 (Dunin 2013a, 2013b).

My acceptance of a visiting curator position for the 1984 exhibition with author responsibilities for *Dance Occasions and Festive Dress in Yugoslavia* offered exceptional learning experience that led to another museum project thirty-four years later in 2018. The 1984 exhibit was designed to educate a public about Yugoslavia with festive costumes from ethnographically recognized dance zones. The tangible results of this temporary 'intangible showing' were the monograph/catalogue from a dancer's perspective and artefacts in the museum's collection that became more carefully identified and left for further study of textiles within the Museum of Cultural History at UCLA.

Planning the Design of the 2018 Exhibition

The 2018 exhibit 'Fifty Years of the Romani George's Day / Erdelezi 1967–2017' was produced in Skopje's Museum of Macedonia, in the Republic of Macedonia. During the last decade of a fifty-year longitudinal study of a rich communal dance and annual event celebrated by the Roms (Gypsies) in Skopje, Macedonia, I had been planning a monograph. Covering multiple generations of dancers and musicians, I noted continuities, changes and discontinuities of the event parallel to sociocultural lifestyle contexts. Skopje's Romani population is very sizeable,[9] being the third largest after Macedonians and Albanians in the capital city and the fourth in population numbers in the Republic of Macedonia. However, as an outsider to the community, and writing in English about 'their' event, I felt that an academic approach in writing for 'others' was selfishly one-sided. As a retired professor, I carefully stored my thousands of photographs and movement documentations with 16 mm film, video and now smartphone records of the event. My 1967 memories and written notes of the George's Day multi-day event climaxing on 9 May offered vivid accounts. Describing the event to academic colleagues and students, stating that at least ten thousand Gypsies were assembled on a hillside, dressed colourfully for the holiday occasion, hundreds dancing to several music bands in a cacophony of sounds, were thought to be exaggerated statements. Finally in 2017, the fiftieth year of documenting this 'coming of summer' event by decades, I was able to digitize the 1967 16 mm films, the later 1977 and 1987 video recordings and the hundreds of slides spanning 1967 to 2007.[10] This visual documentation can now be accessed easily in digital format, and the photographs can be reproduced into large-size images on lightweight forex boards, canvases and roll-up banners. Before completing a diligently written opus covering a half-century, I decided to share the visual documentation of an extraordinary Romani holiday with communal dancing through a museum exhibition in Skopje. For safekeeping, some of the original film materials were transferred from my private collection to the Cross-Cultural Dance Resources (CCDR) Collections located in the Arizona State University in Tempe.[11]

A multimedia exhibit in an ethnographic museum context for a local Romani population not familiar with the concept of such displays makes for a challenging project. Furthermore, within the last decade, this holiday with its public communal dancing has become a point of much contention due to restrictions imposed by outsider institutionalized evangelical Christian sects and fundamentalist Islamic leadership. Within a ten-year period, the event declined as an outdoor public celebration. However, the historical documentation reveals the extent of the event, which is still remembered by the oldest generations as occurring at a time when 'outside' religions and politics did not interfere with 'their' holiday traditions.

Acquiring permission in 2017 from the director[12] of the Museum of Macedonia for a month-long exhibition to be held in 2018 was a major first step toward an exhibit with a Romani theme. Up to this time, there had not been a representative display of the Romani culture in any museum in Macedonia. Setting the dates to overlap with the holiday period, from 11 April into 11 May, offered the possibility to share long-term visual materials with Skopje's Romani population. The museum's location is near the old historic (*čaršija*) centre of Skopje, where Roms were active for generations as merchants, tradesmen and musicians for hire. Importantly, the exhibit became a cooperative venture between the Museum of Macedonia and the Romano Ilo – Skopje Association that is the prime promoter of cultural manifestations for the local and other Romani populations in cities of Macedonia.

The Romano Ilo – Skopje Association is an active non-governmental organization formed twenty years ago in 1998 as *Udruženje ljubitelja romske folklorne umetnosti 'Romano Ilo' – Skopje* (Association of Admirers of Romani Folklore Art 'Gypsy Heart' – Skopje). In 1998, they sponsored my thirty-year exhibit (1967–97) of sixty framed photographs in an art gallery in central Skopje and in the Romani Šuto Orizari municipality. With a local grant, Romano Ilo – Skopje published the monograph/catalogue entitled: 'Gypsy St. George's Day – Coming of Summer 1967–1997' in three languages (English, Macedonian, Romani). All sixty colour photographs of the exhibit in an art gallery were identified by years and locations and showed the customs, vitality and public communal dancing associated with the multi-day holiday.

But in contrast to the 1984 Los Angeles museum exhibit, where the intent was to educate visitors about Yugoslavia, then a mostly unknown country, this 2018 exhibit was to share fifty years of a single event with a Romani community intimately familiar with the location and traditions. Planning and designing a museum exhibit based on fifty years of visual documentation of 'their' event creates challenges in sharing an outsider's perspective.

I acknowledge the assistance of a young Rom, Daniel Petrovski, the son of the director of Romano Ilo – Skopje Association, and a university-level ethnology student. He understood my approach to documentation of the event in relation to the continuities and changes of the sociocultural contexts. He is a younger generation Rom familiar with social media and has experience as a journalist and recorder of Romani social issues in his community. With an insider's perspective, he assisted in selecting photographs, setting the sequence and spatial arrangement of the themes, and deciding appropriate colours for their background, all to highlight the relevancy of the event. We discussed the issue of maintaining rights to the photographic images when sharing them on social media. We also had many discussions on the making of the two documentary films based on the digitized visuals: one a six-minute film showing the continuities and changes of festive dressing and communal dancing across five decades, and the second, a twenty-minute film explaining how the fifty-year documentation began, the continuities and changes of the event, and my offering of the tangible museum exhibit and film as gifts to *Sa o Roma* (all Gypsies) of the two (old and new) Romani communities of Skopje.

The exhibit was designed for two rooms at the Museum of Macedonia. The smaller room was delegated to an earlier exhibit, with sixty framed photographs showing thirty years of the event, 1967 to 1997, sponsored by Romano Ilo – Skopje in 1998. Each photo was identified with a caption stating year and location in three languages (Macedonian, Romani and English). In the other, large room, six themes with forty panels displayed sixty-six large photos, large enough for those with age-related deteriorating eyesight to view the illustrations without glasses. There were six themes relative to the event, each identified with a different colour panel: the cycle of the lambs, from their arrival into the Romani community with *tapan* and *zurla* music on 2 May through to their sacrifice on 5 to 6 May and marking children's foreheads with dots of blood, sharing liver with neighbours, and outdoor lamb-meat feasting by families on 9 May. The second theme featured the morning hours of dancing on 5 May at the site of spring waters and poplar trees; the third theme, hanging green poplar branches at the entries of homes; the fourth theme, 9 May as the day of socializing and dancing on a hillside, which by 2017 was taken over by the US Embassy, causing a cessation of the celebration on this hillside; the fifth theme, in the Šuto Orizari municipality, showing the takeover of the event by annual Luna Park amusements; and the sixth theme, the comparative continuities of the event relative to festive dressing, communal dancing, music groups and traditional food preparations. In addition, there were five vertically shaped panels with text (in Macedonian and English) that pointed out significant social events and changes, such as the introduction in 1967 of the Đelem Đelem Romani hymn, the first Yugoslav Romani census in 1971, the first Romani language grammar book in 1980, the independence of Macedonia from SFR Yugoslavia in 1991, and the establishment of Romani television stations introducing a standardization of spoken Romani language; in the first decade of the twenty-first century, the proclamation of 8 April, the Romani International Day as a national holiday in Macedonia; and finally the inscription of Erdelezi (Hıdrelez) in Macedonia and Turkey as intangible cultural heritage by UNESCO in 2017.

The Skopje-based Romano Ilo Association, established twenty years ago, continues to sponsor cultural, theatrical and educational projects and manifestations for the Roms in Macedonia. As the insider and culturally based extension of the Romani communities, the Romano Ilo Association promoted the museum exhibit to the local Roms by organizing with leaders of the Romani preschool classes and teachers in local schools to bring students to visit the exhibit; connecting with the Romani university student group; and by organizing Romani senior citizen groups. Young children in school groups excitedly recognized family members and neighbours in photographs, as well as themes of the exhibit, such as the Luna Park amusements. They certainly told their parents and grandparents about the exhibit, but the older generation did not necessarily understand the extent of the visuals and so did not take time to come to the Museum. Daniel Petrovski suggested posting the twenty-minute documentary film on his personal Facebook account temporarily (overlapping with the holiday dates). The *Sa o Roma* film produced immediate commentary, which was overwhelmingly positive; people recognized 'their' Romani identity that many felt had been 'lost' in recent years. Response in the Romani and Macedonian languages also came from families that had migrated to European countries and Australia. I was truly amazed at the Facebook response, which showed over 12,000 'hits' in three weeks before the film was removed.

The museum exhibition with its two documentary films was so positively received that there was strong support for the exhibit to travel internationally to other museums, therefore extending its purpose (See Figure 11.3., a poster for the exhibition in Zagreb).

The Romano Ilo Association reached out for support from Romani civic leaders in Zagreb to accept the Romani Skopje-based museum exhibition to be shown in Croatia. The exhibit became formally and diplomatically opened in Zagreb's Ethnographic Museum by the Ambassador of Macedonia, the Director

Figure 11.3. Poster for the Romani exhibition in Zagreb's Ethnographic Museum. Image used by permission.

of the Museum and local Zagreb-based Romani leaders. For the opening, there was also national television coverage.

Reflections

This is the same museum where Adrienne Kaeppler had uncovered Tongan barkcloths in the year 2000. The barkcloth is a tangible artefact, but its permanent display is disconnected to its meaningful cultural context. The travelling Skopje Romani exhibition shows continuities and changes of an annual cultural event, visually designed through themes and its communal dance perspective. A temporary exhibit of photographs and the accompanying documentary film is in itself intangible in nature. However, both multimedia museum exhibits – Dance Occasions and Festive dress in Yugoslavia in 1984 and George's Day / Erdelezi 50 years of research 1967–2017 – are preserved through accompanying catalogues of their entire exhibits – a longer-lasting tangible outcome. In 2018, there were three additional showings of the exhibit reaching other Romani communities in Macedonia and Croatia. Catalogues and a DVD of the *Sa o Roma* documentary were left behind in these communities. Furthermore, Petrovski's Facebook page announced the dates (and subsequent outcome) of the travelling exhibit to his local Skopje Romani population. In answer to Adrienne's question in 2017 about the purpose of archival materials, I can report that my longitudinal documentation was gifted back to its community in a tangible form of a museum exhibit and documentary films.

Elsie Ivancich Dunin is Professor Emerita, University of California Los Angeles (UCLA) and external dance research associate, Institute of Ethnology and Folklore Research (IEF) in Croatia. She is an advisory member of Cross-Cultural Dance Resources (CCDR) Collections at Arizona State University, was the local organizer with IEF of two ICTM Study Group on Ethnochoreology symposia on Korčula Island in Croatia and was past chair of the Publication Committee of ICTM Study Group on Ethnochoreology. Fifty years' (1967–2017) documentation of Skopje's Romani George's Day/Erdelezi annual event was displayed in the touring multimedia museum exhibit with its accompanying award-winning documentary film. Her research continues to focus on social dance changes in relation to sociocultural transformations.

Notes

1. According to the museum's inventory file, barkcloths from Tonga were donated to the Museum in 1932 by a professional Croatian violinist.
2. Kumpanjija sword dance group in Pupnat village on Korčula island, an exhibit authored by Elsie Ivancich Dunin and installed with Marija Hajdić (museum director) and Sani Sardelić (curator).

3. Although the 'coming of summer' holiday was safe-guarded in Macedonia and Turkey as Intangible Cultural Heritage (UNESCO 2017), I had already completed tangible documentation of the event spanning a half-century.
4. The Yugoslav Exchange Program, established in 1981, was associated with UCLA's Center for Russian and East European Studies.
5. Delores Crawford was challenged with many questions on what movements to notate from a group of dancers in the same dance.
6. This rich listing was made possible through two library acquisitions programmes. During the 1960s, UCLA was selected as a recipient of materials from Yugoslavia under the US Public Law 480 Program, in which a developing nation could repay its debts to the US in the form of library materials. In the 1980s, the UCLA Yugoslav Exchange Program facilitated additional acquisitions from Yugoslavia to the UCLA Library.
7. Nadine Dougan, who later completed a thesis based on fieldwork in Yugoslavia.
8. Edith Greenblatt, who had pre-Second World War family connections in Yugoslavia, and Allison Kaplan, who combined dance ethnology with her Library School studies.
9. From the census for Macedonia in 2002, Roms are in the range of 54,000, but higher numbers in the range of 200,000 are estimated.
10. After 2007, photographs were already available in digitized format.
11. Tempe in Arizona also happens to be a sister city of Skopje.
12. Mr Gordon Nikolov, who studied anthropology at the University of Belgrade before Macedonia became independent from SFR Yugoslavia.

References

Dunin, E.I. 1984. *Dance Occasions and Festive Dress in Yugoslavia*. Museum of Cultural History UCLA monograph series 23. Los Angeles: Regents of University of California. [Monograph with four dance occasion articles, catalogue of museum exhibits, Labanotation of Čilipi dances, bibliographic sources in UCLA libraries, map of Yugoslav dance zones.]

———. 2013a. 'After the Ashes of War: Continuity and Change in the Costume, Music, and Dance of a Croatian Village', in E.W. Barber and B.B. Sloan (eds), *Resplendent Dress from Southeastern Europe: A History in Layers*. Fowler Museum Textile Series 11. Los Angeles: Fowler Museum at UCLA, pp. 195–206.

———. 2013b. 'Festive Dress and Dance Events in the Romani Community of Skopje, Republic of Macedonia, 1967 and 2011', in E.W. Barber and B.B. Sloan (eds), *Resplendent Dress from Southeastern Europe: A History in Layers*. Fowler Museum Textile Series 11. Los Angeles: Fowler Museum at UCLA, pp. 207–16.

———. 2018. *Fifty Years of Research 1967–2017 Ѓурѓовден/Erdelezi/George's Day*. Skopje: Romano Ilo Association.

Ivančan, I. 1964–65. 'Geografska podjela narodnih plesova u Jugoslaviji' [Geographic Classification of Folk Dances in Yugoslavia], *Narodna umjetnost* 3: 17–38. Zagreb: Zavod za istraživanje folklora.

Kaeppler, A.L. 2003. 'Sculptures of Barkcloth and Wood from Rapa Nui: Symbolic Continuities and Polynesian Affinities', *RES: Anthropology and Aesthetics* 44 (Autumn): 10–69. [*Moai kavakava* wooden statue artefact identified as part of Zagreb Ethnological Museum's founding collection.]

———. 2005. 'An Introduction to Aesthetics (Keynote)', in E.I. Dunin, A.v.B. Wharton and L. Felföldi (eds), *Dance and Society: Dancer as a Cultural Performer*. Budapest: Akadémiai Kiadó, European Folklore Institute, pp. 207–15.

———. 2009. 'Lakalaka and Mak`yong: A Story of Two Masterpieces', in M.A.Md. Nor, E.I. Dunin and A.v.B. Wharton (eds), *Transmitting Dance as Cultural Heritage & Dance and Religion: Proceedings of the 25th Symposium of the ICTM Study Group on Ethnochoreology*. Kuala Lumpur, Malaysia: Cultural Centre University of Malaya, pp. 1–7.

———. 2017. 'Capturing Music and Dance in an Archive: A Meditation on Imprisonment', in K. Gillespie, S. Treloyn and D. Niles (eds), *A Distinctive Voice in the Antipodes: Essays in Honor of Stephen A. Wild*. Canberra: ANU Press, pp. 429–42.

Rein, A. 2011. 'Flee(t)ing Dances! Initiatives for the Preservation and Communication of Intangible World Heritage in Museums', in G. Klein and S. Noeth (eds), *Emerging Bodies: The Performance of Worldmaking in Dance and Choreography*. Bielefeld: Transcript Verlag, pp. 93–106.

UNESCO United Nations Educational, Scientific and Cultural Organization – Intangible Cultural Heritage. 2017. 'Spring Celebration, Hıdrellez, the Former Yugoslav Republic of Macedonia and Turkey, inscribed in 2017 (12.COM) on the Representative List of the Intangible Cultural Heritage of Humanity', *UNESCO United Nations Educational, Scientific and Cultural Organization – Intangible Cultural Heritage* [online]. Retrieved 30 May 2019 from https://ich.unesco.org/en/RL/spring-celebration-hdrellez-01284.

Chapter 12

Creativity and Ceremony in the Repatriation of King Ng:tja

Kirsty Gillespie

Prelude

The museum curator is constantly called upon to traverse disciplinary boundaries in their work; to move between multiple bodies of knowledge and methods. Throughout her career, Adrienne Kaeppler has done this in an exemplary fashion, being recognized as a leading scholar in fields as diverse as ethnomusicology, ethnochoreology, Pacific studies, Pacific history, museum studies and material culture.

I first came to know Adrienne through the International Council for Traditional Music's Study Group on the Music and Dance of Oceania. I first attended the study group in the Republic of Palau in 2004 and directly after the 9th Festival of Pacific Arts, which was held there. As a new postgraduate student, I was impressed with the expertise in the room and the opportunity to be a part of it; much later I was to have the honour of chairing the study group (from 2013 to 2015). Adrienne was to go on to become the President of the International Council for Traditional Music (from 2005 to 2013), during which time she graciously launched my first book *Steep Slopes: Music and Change in the Highlands of Papua New Guinea* (Gillespie 2010) at the Australian National University in 2011. Adrienne continues to be an inspiration to generations of scholars and curators, in academia, museums and beyond.

Introduction

Repatriation has been a growing concern for museums across the world for several decades. It involves the return of items in museum collections – including human remains – to individuals or communities of origin. As Kaeppler has illustrated through her own experiences, repatriation is often a highly complex and contested activity, especially when items may have an association with more than one group of people, or when repatriation is motivated by particular political agendas (Kaeppler 2005). In Australia, the repatriation of the human remains of Aboriginal Australians and Torres Strait Islanders is an important concern. Different museums have different approaches to this activity; however, it is generally acknowledged that the remains of Indigenous Australians that are currently held in museums should be returned to their relatives (or communities, where direct relatives cannot be identified) where possible and desirable.[1] Repatriation is seen by many as part of the process of reconciliation between Indigenous and non-Indigenous Australians (see Batty 2006; Lambert-Pennington 2007). The repatriation process can be long and complex, especially in the case of returning remains held in international institutions. It involves ongoing engagement with family and community, who by and large respond to the event of a repatriation with ritual, ceremony and cultural practices adapted for the purpose.

This chapter takes inspiration from Kaeppler's research in art, creativity and performance to present the repatriation of Ngadjon[2] elder King Ng:tja from Berlin to North Queensland in 2017. This repatriation was facilitated by the Indigenous Repatriation Program, a programme administered by the Australian Government Department of Communications and the Arts. I was involved with this repatriation as a representative of the receiving museum, the Museum of Tropical Queensland in Townsville (part of the Queensland Museum Network, Australia). At the time of writing, King Ng:tja rests in the care of the Museum of Tropical Queensland as he awaits return to Country.[3]

In this chapter, I describe the life and death of King Ng:tja and his removal to Germany. I consider the ceremonies surrounding his return – held in Berlin and Townsville – and present the elements of visuality, smoking and sound as they have been creatively expressed by family members during these events. I show how the repatriation of King Ng:tja has facilitated a re-engagement by some family members with cultural practices of both local and national origin, and argue that repatriation provides a unique space for the reinvigoration of tradition in a new context. In this vein, I explore Kaeppler's assertion that '[l]ike all symbolic systems, art creates new meanings by combining old forms in new ways. Product and process, verbal and visual, interact dialogically, relying on shared understandings among artists, performers, and viewers' (Kaeppler 2008: 38).

The Story of King Ng:tja

King Ng:tja ('Narcha'), also known as Barry Clarke, was a prominent figure amongst the Ngadjon-Jii,[4] whose Country centres around the town of Malanda, in Far North Queensland, Australia. Born around 1840,[5] Ng:tja was one of many Aboriginal elders identified as leaders in their communities by the European colonizers and bestowed with a breastplate, also known as a king plate, due to the incorporation of royal titles; this is how Ng:tja obtained the title of 'King'.[6] Ng:tja's breastplate reads 'NARCHA – King of Boonjie'. The name Clarke came to be attached to Ng:tja and his family due to their association with prominent European settler and founder of the Boonjie goldfields George Clarke (see Govor 2000: 161–62; Daley 2017).

Ng:tja passed away in May 1904 and was mummified in a way that was customary for 'very distinguished males' (Roth 1907: 393). Roth writes that 'after being disembowelled and dried by fire on a grid or platform, the corpse is tied up and carried about for months' (Roth 1907: 393). He adds of the area closest to Ng:tja's country in his documentation that '[o]n the Russell River, this desiccation process appears to be highly developed, the "mummy" being ornamented' (Roth 1907: 393).

In 1904, the time of Ng:tja's passing, Hermann Klaatsch, the German comparative anatomist and physical anthropologist, was in the first year of a three-year expedition in Australia, conducting his own research into the evolution of humankind whilst also collecting for German museums. In December 1904, Klaatsch visited the area and procured Ng:tja's mummified body and his breastplate from his relatives.

In Klaatsch's account, documented in a letter to his colleague Otto Schoetensack and dated 10 January to 20 January 1905, he describes taking possession of the mummy in exchange for food, tobacco and clothing; hence he is described as having 'purchased' Ng:tja (Erckenbrecht 2010: 100; Erckenbrecht and Klaatsch 2010: 124). He documented that the morning after this exchange Ng:tja's relatives changed their minds and appealed to have the mummy back. Klaatsch declined to return it; he was later offered two skulls in exchange for the mummy, which he accepted without returning the mummy (see also Turnbull 2017: 272–73). Klaatsch then left the following morning.

In early January 1905, Klaatsch brought the mummy to Cairns, packed it and sent it on to Germany (Erckenbrecht 2010: 101–2). In the same letter, Klaatsch describes the mummy as 'a first class attraction. It is in amazing condition even through the mummy was preserved by smoke only' (Klaatsch, cited in Erckenbrecht and Klaatsch 2010: 124). His comments solidify his reputation as a collector at all costs (see also Turnbull 2008) and reveal his drive to procure specimens not only for scientific research but for museum display. This approach to collecting, typical for the period, was highly traumatic for indigenous communities.[7]

Ng:tja remained in Germany for over a hundred years. Meanwhile, he was not forgotten in Australia. His relatives continued to speak about him, about his life when he was alive and about the removal of his body prior to the completion of the mourning process. The wish to have him returned home to Country was always apparent. Research conducted by various family members gained pace in the 1990s, and the exact location of Ng:tja became known to them around this time. Still, relatives were not able to proceed with the repatriation until making contact with the Federal Government's Indigenous Repatriation Program around 2015. From then on, the financial and logistical way to proceed became clear.

In March 2017, two of Ng:tja's descendants travelled with Federal Government representatives to Berlin to retrieve Ng:tja. A ceremony took place at the Australian Embassy in Berlin on 23 March 2017, where the body of Ng:tja (and his breastplate) were officially handed over by the Berlin Society for Anthropology, Ethnology and Prehistory (Berliner Gesellschaft für Anthropologie, Ethnologie und Urgeschichte).[8] Together with Ng:tja, the delegation travelled back to Australia a few days later (the breastplate was to follow once paperwork for its return had been completed).

Ng:tja arrived in Townsville on 30 March 2017; the museum could not receive him from Sydney on 27 March as planned due to the approaching Cyclone Debbie, which had shut down the museum.[9] Ng:tja rested in Sydney, his point of arrival into the country, until another flight could be arranged. Once Ng:tja arrived in Townsville, he rested in the quarantine area of the museum until 28 April 2017, when family members gathered at the museum for a ceremony prior to his being brought into the museum and unpacked. This occasion would be the first time any of Ng:tja's living relatives had seen his body in person.

King Ng:tja's Return: The Need for Ceremony

Ceremony is an important part of the process of repatriating the remains of indigenous ancestors. In the words of Yorta Yorta man Henry Atkinson:

> Indigenous people must be allowed to have this spiritual connection with their ancestors – beginning with the performance of ceremonies by Indigenous custodians when their remains are released from their obscene holding areas before they commence the long journey home, where they can be joined by the waiting Indigenous community before – after due traditional customs – they are returned to the earth of their beginning. (Atkinson 2010: 19; see also Pickering 2010: 170)

Prior to taking part in the Berlin ceremony, the attending family members were encouraged by members of the Indigenous Repatriation Program to think of ways they could commemorate this event. Considerable creativity was apparent in both the official handover ceremony in Berlin and the later ceremony in Townsville, when Ng:tja was taken from the quarantine area into the main museum building. Three core elements in both ceremonies were apparent: the use of visuals, a smoking ceremony and the use of sound. I will explore each of them in turn here.

Visuality

For both occasions, perhaps the most striking visual was the use of the Aboriginal flag, draped over the box holding the remains. The incorporation of the Aboriginal flag in the ceremonies clearly places Ng:tja within a historical present and within a broader national identity; the Aboriginal flag did not yet exist at the time of Ng:tja's death, being designed in the early 1970s, and was not officially recognized by the state until 1995. The reclaiming of Ng:tja's body becomes a political act, and by implication the handing over of his remains evokes an act of reconciliation, of righting past wrongs. In Berlin, the Aboriginal flag was also present as part of the Embassy's backdrop, alongside the Australian, German and Torres Strait flags, and evident in the colours of the scarf worn by a member of the delegation.

In conjunction with the Aboriginal flag, a calico cloth was placed over the box holding Ng:tja's remains. Upon this cloth, ochre handprints were made; inspired, it was said, by handprints seen on the backs of Aboriginal dancers from other parts of Australia, which had been placed to show support, encouraging them to move forward (V. Ketchell 2017, pers. comm., 30 March). This incorporation of elements from elsewhere further places the ceremony within a broader frame of reference. Handprints were intended for the box itself; however, due to international travel requirements, such markings on the box were not permitted. Instead, handprints were made on the fabric at the ceremony in Berlin; the same fabric, with handprints already made, covered the box in the Townsville cere-

Figure 12.1. Vera Ketchell making handprints on the box containing Ng:tja. Repatriation handover ceremony at the Australian Embassy in Berlin, Germany, March 2017, facilitated under the Australian Government's Indigenous Repatriation Program. Photograph courtesy of the Department of Communications and the Arts.

mony. It was important that these handprints were placed, as it were, on Ng:tja's back; as such, the box was marked to indicate where Ng:tja's back would be. In Townsville, care was made to place the fabric in the same orientation over the box while it was in the museum quarantine area and later during the ceremony there.

Smoking Ceremony

The smoking ceremony was a key part of both the Berlin and Townsville ceremonies and indeed has featured in repatriation ceremonies across the country; Martin Thomas has written that '[s]moke and fire have a purgative effect' (Thomas 2015: 151). As detailed in the Berlin ceremony programme notes, the smoking ceremony 'cleanses away any evil spirits that may have attached themselves to the ancestors over the years. It prepares the ancestors for their journey back to Country. The smoke will also cleanse everyone present of any unwanted spirits' (Australian Government [2017]).

Due to quarantine restrictions, the delegation were unable to take the traditional foliage used for smoking ceremonies to Berlin for the ceremony; instead, plants were sourced within Germany. In Townsville, there were no such restrictions, and a large bag of leaves was brought down from the Tablelands for the ceremony.

The smoking ceremony was performed twice; in Berlin to cleanse Ng:tja of his experiences to date, and in Townsville to cleanse Ng:tja after his travels from Germany to Australia, in readiness to enter the museum in a neutral state. The smoking ceremonies also served to cleanse those present and/or involved with the repatriation, as described above. Contemporary methods of fire-making were incorporated into both these ceremonies; artificial fire-starters were used, and in the case of the Townsville ceremony, the leaves were burnt inside a mosquito coil burner with a lid for safety.

Sound

For music to accompany the Berlin ceremony, family members selected a recording by Spider Henry, an elder of the neighbouring Jirrbal group. The recording was made in 1982 by R.M.W. Dixon and the text and its translation published in the monograph *Dyirbal Song Poetry: The Oral Literature of an Australian Rainforest People* (Dixon and Koch 1996: 119–20). The recordings from this book were later made publicly accessible via the website of the Languages and Cultures Research Centre at James Cook University.[10] It was from this website that family members accessed the recording, downloading it to play at the ceremony.[11]

Dixon writes that the song is 'performed as if sung by the spirit of a recently deceased man who has come down from the tablelands and calls out to find where his people are' (Dixon and Koch 1996: 119). In this recording, Spider Henry accompanies himself by clapping two boomerangs together, as is typical for this song genre, known as *gama*, and described by Dixon and Koch as being 'performed at corroborees' (Dixon and Koch 1996: 13).

The original text and free translation of this song appear in Dixon and Koch's volume as follows:

munamadalmi jawurr gambil-barra
ŋaja ŋunyiny-ju gunmi-n banagay-mba-n

I, who come from Munamadalmi, in a gorge on the tablelands
I, the spirit of a departed one, return and call out to locate my own people.
(Dixon and Koch 1996: 119)

The song was interpreted for the Berlin handover ceremony as 'singing the spirits of the ancestors back to Country' (Australian Government [2017]), according to the programme notes. This interpretation represents a shift in perspective; from the voice of a lost ancestor looking to locate his people, to the people themselves using the song and its/their agency to unite the ancestor with his people and his Country. The agency of the song is harnessed and repurposed for the repatriation.

In the Townsville ceremony, the Spider Henry recording was not played, but a relative was invited to play the didjeridu. Although the didjeridu is not an instrument traditionally used by the rainforest peoples of North Queensland, it has been incorporated into contemporary performance practice as a signifier of a national Aboriginal identity (see Neuenfeldt 1996) so was considered an appropriate choice. A general preference for live music over a recording played a part in the decision-making.

Conclusion

Historian Paul Turnbull has written that the return of remains 'as ancestors, not specimens, attests to the continuing vitality of Aboriginal culture in Queensland' (Turnbull 2008: 35). In the words of the Honourable Leeanne Enoch, proud Quandamooka (Indigenous Australian) woman and Queensland State Government Minister of the Arts, 'culture heals everything' (L. Enoch 2019, speech at the launch of the Queensland Museum's first Reconciliation Action Plan, 20 November). In this chapter, I have explored some of the ways in which culture has been creatively and publicly expressed by some of the relatives of Ng:tja during the process of his return. It should be noted that every repatriation is unique, and while some activities such as smoking ceremonies, the use of handprints and the didjeridu might be seen across the country, there is important local differentiation as well. Similarly, there is not always consensus on a local level as to what methods should be used to commemorate a repatriation. In Kaeppler's words, '[a]rt and society are ... surface manifestations of the underlying structure and philosophy of a particular culture or subculture at a particular point in time. This ever-changing entity is a complex of contested and uncontested ways of living, thinking, and evaluating' (Kaeppler 1997: 22). Kaeppler's words here help us in thinking about creativity in performance and ceremony but also about the activity of repatriation itself. The processes involved in a repatriation – and their contestation – deserve much more scrutiny than is possible here.

As seen in the case of Ng:tja's return, repatriation can provide a place for people to re-engage with past practices and to reinvent new ones, drawing upon local and national identities. Recognizing the creative space that repatriation engenders is important; such recognition may lead to more financial support from the government for families and communities to perform the return of their ancestors. As it stands, there are limited government funds available for repatriation beyond the actual transportation of remains, which can hinder the progress of repatriations.

Ng:tja's relatives continue to discuss and explore the way forward for his repatriation to Country. There are many challenges as relatives face this experience of repatriation for the first time. It is not considered desirable to inter Ng:tja in the bush where he might have been interred in the past, due to the inaccessibility of the country and the possible risk of theft and vandalism.[12] The Malanda Cemetery, however, is seen by some as a suitable contemporary interment place; it has a patch of rainforest vegetation adjacent to the cemetery and a view towards Mount Bartle Frere, a significant feature in the landscape and home to Choorechillum, the ancestral place to which the spirits of the deceased return to rest. However the final leg of Ng:tja's journey is commemorated, there seems no doubt that a considerable display of creativity will be utilized, drawing on past and present practices, and local and national frames of reference, in order to commemorate the unique life and history of the man known as Ng:tja.

Acknowledgements

I wish to convey my thanks to Vera Ketchell and to colleagues at James Cook University and the University of Sydney for their comments on this chapter in draft form, and to the Australian Government Department of Communications and the Arts for permission to use their photograph in this chapter. Where possible, I have avoided using the names of individual family members in order to protect their privacy and to respect the different perspectives that surround this repatriation.

Kirsty Gillespie received her PhD from the Australian National University in 2008 for research into the music of the Duna people of Hela Province, Papua New Guinea. She has conducted research into the performance traditions of Papua New Guinea since 2003; her latest book is *Pil: Ancestral Stories of the Lihir Islands* (Institute of Papua New Guinea Studies, 2018). Kirsty has served as the Chair of the International Council for Traditional Music's Study Group on Music and Dance of Oceania (2013–2015) and as Audio Reviews Editor for the *Yearbook for Traditional Music* (2015–2019). She is currently an Honorary Research Fellow with the Queensland Museum Network, Australia.

Notes

1. There continues to be contention and controversy both within institutions and amongst communities regarding the repatriation of human remains (see, for example, Lambert-Pennington 2007; Turnbull 2002). It should be noted that according to the *Aboriginal Cultural Heritage Act 2003* (Qld), section 16, museums are obliged to continue to look after the human remains of Indigenous Australians in their care, should those identified as the owners of those remains wish for them to do so. For some background on previous repatriation activities within the Queensland Museum Network, see Aird (2002).
2. According to linguist R.M.W. Dixon, the correct spelling of this language group is 'Ngajan', as there is no 'o' in the language (R.M.W. Dixon 2018, pers. comm., 27 April). In this chapter, however, I will continue to use the more commonly accepted term 'Ngadjon'.
3. The term 'Country' as it is used in this context in Australia refers not only to the physical landscape. 'Country' is a difficult concept to define; the following description by Kwaymullina proves useful: 'For Aboriginal peoples, country is much more than a place. Rock, tree, river, hill, animal, human – all were formed of the same substance by the Ancestors who continue to live in land, water, sky. Country is filled with relations speaking language and following Law, no matter whether the shape of that relation is human, rock, crow, wattle. Country is loved, needed, and cared for, and country loves, needs, and cares for her peoples in turn. Country is family, culture, identity. Country is self' (Kwaymullina 2005: 12). Ng:tja's return to Country was initially scheduled for 21 March 2020, but, due to the COVID-19 pandemic, was postponed.
4. As 'Jii' means 'people', 'Ngadjon-Jii' translates to mean 'Ngadjon people'.
5. Ng:tja was estimated by Klaatsch to be around 60 to 70 years of age when he died (Erckenbrecht and Klaatsch 2010: 122).
6. For more on breastplates as both a form of colonial control and an expression of Aboriginal resilience, see Darian-Smith (2015).
7. Fitzpatrick (2019) provides an in-depth analysis of Klaatsch's collecting and the return of Ng:tja in the context of 'decolonization'.
8. This ceremony also included the handover of remains from the Clarence River area in New South Wales.
9. The significance of this climatic event occurring at the time of Ng:tja's return generated considerable discussion among Ngadjon people; ultimately the cyclone bypassed both the museum and Townsville.
10. James Cook University [n.d.].
11. The availability of these recordings and the subsequent use of them in this repatriation ceremony puts forward a strong case for open access publication in academia.
12. Thomas (2015: 164) describes similar limitations for the interment of human remains of the Gunbalanya community of Arnhem Land.

References

Aboriginal Cultural Heritage Act 2003 (Qld).
Aird, M. 2002. 'Developments in the Repatriation of Human Remains and Other Cultural Items in Queensland, Australia', in C. Fforde, J. Hubert and P. Turnbull (eds), *The Dead and Their Possessions: Repatriation in Principle, Policy and Practice*. New York and London: Routledge, pp. 303–11.

Atkinson, H. 2010. 'The Meanings and Values of Repatriation', in P. Turnbull and M. Pickering (eds), *The Long Way Home: The Meaning and Values of Repatriation*. New York and Oxford: Berghahn, pp. 15–19.

Australian Government. [2017]. *Ceremony for the Repatriation of Australian Indigenous Ancestral Remains*. Unpublished programme.

Batty, P. 2006. 'White Redemption Rituals: Reflections on the Repatriation of Aboriginal Secret-Sacred Objects', in T. Lea, E. Kowal and G. Cowlishaw (eds), *Moving Anthropology: Critical Indigenous Studies*. Darwin: Charles Darwin University Press, pp. 55–63.

Daley, P. 2017. 'Narcha's Remains Have Been Repatriated But Colonialism's Malevolence Lingers', *The Guardian*, Monday 3 April [online]. Retrieved 5 February 2018 from https://www.theguardian.com/australia-news/postcolonial-blog/2017/apr/03/narchas-remains-have-been-repatriated-but-colonialisms-malevolence-lingers.

Darian-Smith, K. 2015. 'Breastplates: Re-Enacting Possession in North America and Australia', in K. Darian-Smith and P. Edmonds (eds), *Conciliation on Colonial Frontiers: Conflict, Performance and Commemoration in Australia and the Pacific Rim*. New York: Routledge, pp. 54–74.

Dixon, R.M.W., and G. Koch. 1996. *Dyirbal Song Poetry: The Oral Literature of an Australian Rainforest People*. St Lucia: University of Queensland Press.

Erckenbrecht, C. 2010. *Auf der Suche nach den Ursprüngen: Die Australienreise des Anthropologen und Sammlers Hermann Klaatsch 1904–1907*, vol. 27, Ethnologica Neue Folge. Köln: Wienand Verlag.

Erckenbrecht, C., and H.H. Klaatsch. 2010. 'Mummies in Australia – A Special Form of Aboriginal Burial Rites', in A. Wieczorek and W. Rosendahl (eds), *Mummies of the World*. Munich and London: Prestel, pp. 121–25.

Fitzpatrick, M.P. 2019. 'Indigenous Australians and German Anthropology in the Era of "Decolonization"'. *The Historical Journal* 1–24. https://doi.org/10.1017/S0018246X19000384.

Gillespie, K. 2010. *Steep Slopes: Music and Change in the Highlands of Papua New Guinea*. Acton, ACT: ANU E Press.

Govor, E. 2000. *My Dark Brother: The Story of the Illins, A Russian-Aboriginal Family*. Sydney: University of New South Wales Press.

James Cook University. [n.d.]. 'Australia: Dyirbal Song Poetry', *James Cook University Language and Culture Research Centre*. Retrieved 20 November 2020 from https://www.jcu.edu.au/language-and-culture-research-centre/resources/language-archives.

Kaeppler, A.L. 1997. 'Polynesian and Micronesian', in A.L. Kaeppler, C. Kaufmann and D. Newton, *Oceanic Art*. New York: Abrams, pp. 21–155.

———. 2005. 'Two Polynesian Repatriation Enigmas at the Smithsonian Institution', *Journal of Museum Ethnography* 17: 152–62.

———. 2008. *The Pacific Arts of Polynesia and Micronesia*. Oxford: Oxford University Press.

Kwaymullina, A. 2005. 'Seeing the Light: Aboriginal Law, Learning and Sustainable Living in Country', *Indigenous Law Bulletin* 6(11): 12–15.

Lambert-Pennington, K. 2007. 'What Remains? Reconciling Repatriation, Aboriginal Culture, Representation and the Past', *Oceania* 77(3): 313–36.

Neuenfeldt, K. 1996. *The Didjeridu: From Arnhem Land to Internet*. Sydney: John Libbey.

Pannell, S., and Ngadjon-Jii Traditional Owners. 2006. *Yamani Country: A Spatial History of the Atherton Tableland, North Queensland*. Cairns: Rainforest Collaborative Research Centre.

Pickering, M. 2010. 'Despatches from the Front Line? Museum Experiences in Applied Repatriation', in P. Turnbull and M. Pickering (eds), *The Long Way Home: The Meaning and Values of Repatriation*. New York; Oxford: Berghahn, pp. 163–74.

Roth, W.E. 1907. 'North Queensland Ethnography. Bulletin No. 9. Burial Ceremonies, and Disposal of the Dead', *Records of the Australian Museum* 6(5): 365–403.

Thomas, M. 2015. 'Bones as a Bridge between Worlds: Responding with Ceremony to the Repatriation of Aboriginal Human Remains from the United States to Australia', in K. Darian-Smith and P. Edmonds (eds), *Conciliation on Colonial Frontiers: Conflict, Performance and Commemoration in Australia and the Pacific Rim*. New York: Routledge, pp. 150–68.

Turnbull, P. 2002. 'Indigenous Australian People, their Defence of the Dead and Native Title', in C. Fforde, J. Hubert and P. Turnbull (eds), *The Dead and Their Possessions: Repatriation in Principle, Policy and Practice*. New York and London: Routledge, pp. 63–86.

———. 2008. 'Theft in the Name of Science', *Griffith REVIEW Edition 21: Hidden Queensland* Spring (2008): [227–35].

———. 2017. *Science, Museums and Collecting the Indigenous Dead in Colonial Australia*. Cham, Switzerland: Palgrave Macmillan.

Chapter 13

The Weave Within

Being, Seeing and Sensing in *Barasili* – Solomon Islands

Irene Karongo Hundleby

Introduction

Woven through Adrienne Kaeppler's substantial scholarship are all the elements of Pasifika art: artefacts, dance, laments, songs, space and the environment, as well as reflections on the participants, the creators, the audiences and the specific forms themselves. Her 'leave no stone unturned' approach to Pacific anthropology and the arts is both overwhelming and inspiring. Kaeppler's comprehensive writing investigates numerous themes that are familiar and pertinent to any discussion of Solomon Islands arts, music and dance. Thus, for this chapter I have selected two themes that are fundamental to Solomon Islands artistry: firstly, the concept of 'art'; and secondly, spirituality as art. In a Pacific context, these ideas are interrelated.

The Solomon Islands archipelago lies to the east of Papua New Guinea in western Oceania. Solomon Islands is a nation of cultural and geographic diversity:[1] our peoples are estimated to speak more than seventy languages and populate over 900 islands covering 27,986 square kilometres of land and 910 square kilometres of water (Worldatlas [n.d.]). This diversity is perceptible in the arts – a variety of distinctive practices and vibrant performances are prominent in each of the nine provinces. Alas, to date, few scholars have explored Solomon Islands art forms in any detail (Burt and Bolton 2014; Firth and McLean 1990; Howarth and Waite 2011; Rossen 1978, 1987a, 1987b; Zemp 1978), and only a handful of art forms have been interpreted by Indigenous Solomon Islanders themselves (Henry and Foana'ota 2015; Hundleby 2013, 2017; Pollard 2000; Suri 1976, 1980, 1991). This gap in Solomon Islands research inspired me to begin work with my own peoples in the Lau-Mbaelelea region of North Malaita. Since 2014, our family members have worked together to collect, record and document our dance, music and art practices as a way to sustain our cultures and histories for future generations. This chapter draws on our collective research experiences as well as my own life experiences – the ways of thinking and being I have learnt from my elders since I was born. This Indigenous perspective offers deep meanings about the context, function and purpose of Lau-Mbaelelea art.

Applying an Indigenous lens, this chapter aims to elaborate further on Kaeppler's detailed scholarship: Solomon Islands cultural ways of thinking bear similarity to other Oceania cultures (Hauʻofa 1994, 1998; Kaʻili 2012; Walker 2004: 10–23). Significantly, however, this research is the first study to examine the arts using collaborative methods that incorporate North Malaitan ways of thinking and being (Hundleby 2017: 49–84, 193–231). For clarity, this discussion is divided into two parts: the first section introduces North Malaitan philosophies central to artistry and explores aesthetics and visuality from a local perspective. Section two describes the *barasili* art form and explains how Indigenous knowledge and values are embedded within our art practices.

What Is Art?

An appropriate place to begin a discussion of North Malaitan art is with the following definition provided by Kaeppler (1985: 109–10):

> The arts are cultural forms that result from creative processes that use or 'manipulate' words, sounds, movements, or materials in such a way that they formalise the nonformal. Aesthetics is defined here as ways of thinking about these cultural forms. Art, in the Western sense of the word, was not a conceptual category of traditional Hawaiian culture, but *noʻeau* 'skilfulness' or 'cleverness' was a part of all activity. One could argue that art did not exist or that art as *noʻeau* was all pervasive. The resulting products might be passed as heirlooms from generation to generation, and the occasions on which they were used became part of them. They became chronicles of social relationships objectified in visual form and were inherited not only as products made with skilfulness, i.e., works of art, but also as information. The skilful process of an object's manufacture and later repair or refurbishing, in addition to its objectified social relationships and changing symbolism, were aspects of an aesthetic system concerned with ongoing process and use.

While Kaeppler used this definition in relation to Hawaiian art and society, she makes several points that parallel North Malaitan thinking in terms of our arts and cultures. Firstly, the concept of 'art' in its Western sense is a foreign one. Perhaps it would be simpler to denounce the word 'art' and negate the difficulties this complex term poses cross-culturally. However, rather than shy away, I have chosen to redefine this word in a way that is meaningful for our people.

In a North Malaitan context, art, creation and expression are viewed as an integral part of everyday living and are interwoven with *kastom* (cultural) and spiritual practices. Similarly, our art forms are shared from generation to generation, and expertise is commonly learnt via apprenticeship-style teaching (Gegeo and Watson-Gegeo 2001; Hundleby 2017). Art in our region includes performance art forms such as *kastom* dance, *nguu* (songs) and *unuunu* (storytelling); and visual art forms such as carving and weaving used in artefacts, adornments, valuables and as part of structural design for houses, sanctums and canoes.

In Lau-Mbaelelea societies, we make and create useful and practical items as a necessary part of daily life: stores only carry basic necessities, we do not have wired electricity in our homes and we are less reliant on bought goods, home appliances and devices. The arts entertain us and participation strengthens our familial and community relationships. Furthermore, oral traditions and art-making practices are precious as they perpetuate Indigenous knowledge and *kastom*: '*Kastom* . . . embraces culture, tradition, norms and modes of behaviour; ways of thinking, doing, and creating; and, of course, Indigenous epistemology. Anything born of the land and passed from generation to generation is part of *kastom*' (Gegeo and Watson-Gegeo 2001: 59).

North Malaitan descendants communicate *kastom* knowledge through the arts. In Lau-Mbaelelea, art engages with both the natural and the supernatural: physical and spiritual planes are deeply integrated. Similarly, Kaeppler (2007: 97) observed that religion is a fundamental component in the art cultures of our Pasifika neighbours: 'In Polynesia, as in many cultural traditions, religion was (and is) the progenitor of important works of art.' Expanding on Kaeppler's observation, in a Solomon Islands context, the word 'spirituality' is more appropriate and definitive than the word 'religion'. We do not necessarily think of ourselves as being spiritual peoples – rather, our spiritual ways of thinking and being are simply who we are.[2] The concept of spiritual synthesis is an inherent part of many, if not all, Solomon Islands identities:

> 'We, the people of Solomon Islands, have *toba ruka* (two bellies or divided belly):[3] one for the gospel (Jesus and Christianity) and one for the beliefs of our ancestors' (Dominic Alebua,[4] as told to my father Peter Hundleby ca. 1959, Avuavu, Guadalcanal).

In recent fieldwork experiences, this core concept has been referred to time and time again as a key Malaitan philosophy. Numerous descriptions of our dual belief systems have been presented to me with persistence and rigour. It is important to understand the significance and longevity of this cultural concept. This learning has been taught to me informally by my Malaitan family since I was a young child (i.e. for a period of over forty years), and Alebua first described this idea to my father over sixty years ago. However, this way of thinking cannot be regarded as a mere relic of the past; Alebua's statement still has strength and validity in present day Solomon Islands. Whether one's home is North Malaita, within another district of Malaita or in other regions of Solomon Islands, a mix of spiritual ways of thinking, being and feeling prevails today (Hundleby 2017: 267).

In North Malaita, art forms are viewed in an integrated way: art practices are rarely thought of as individual stand-alone processes. Rather, they are considered interrelated practices centred on *kastom*, family and community. Being connected is fundamental to who we are: we value being connected to the land, to the ocean, to our environments, to our ancestors and each other.[5] It is important to nurture the bonds we have – as family members, between clans and within our larger communities. Being cohesive and interdependent within a collective has many social benefits, and connection is considered the foundation for a healthy, happy and successful life. Hence, connectivity is a fundamental concept in North Malaitan aesthetics – a thread that pervades our art-making practices (Hundleby 2017: 105–19, 317–25).

The Malaitan psyche is inclined towards connection. In my opening paragraph, I consciously chose the word 'element' to list various kinds of Pasifika art. This was a considered choice, to avoid words that might infer an art form as separate or independent. Classification terms such as genre, class, object or type cast a foreign lens over our art forms – such classifications are considerably removed from Malaitan cultural thinking. On the contrary, if we consider an art form as an element, the form is no longer viewed as an independent separate entity; rather, each form becomes a part of something more holistic and much greater than itself. The art form becomes connected.

Kaufe and Aesthetics

As Kaeppler (1985: 109) expresses, aesthetics are ways of thinking about the arts – cultural forms. Kaeppler (2003: 153–55) also points out that aesthetics and the paradigm of 'beauty' in art is a mental construct that differs from culture to culture: 'If we are to understand (rather than just appreciate) an aesthetic, or a society's cultural forms, it is essential to grasp the principles on which such an aesthetic is based, as perceived by the people of the society which holds them' (Kaeppler 2003: 154). In North Malaita, we keep and create art forms for their designated function(s) and cultural purpose, and strong emphasis is placed on spiritual value. While tangible items often find their way into international collections, our communities rarely keep *do abu* (sacred things) solely for their visual design aesthetics. The things we create contain symbols that refer to our ancestors, to our continuous living history and to our people and our places.

In Lau-Mbaelelea, ornaments, clothing and artefacts have a function, and any aesthetic beauty is significant for its ability to please and to evoke emotion. Shared emotion further reinforces togetherness, family and community. Furthermore, North Malaitan art-making processes are often communal. The cultural significance of these processes becomes amplified through the shared experience. For example, dance group practices prior to a *barasili* performance are deemed important not only for the skills involved in creating the end product but also for the opportunities to make memories, to learn, teach, share and bond as relatives and community members (Hundleby 2017: 123–51). The primary focus in performance practice, ceremony and all associated art forms is to establish and to nurture harmonious relationships – between the living and also with our deceased ancestors.

As an example, consider *kaufe*, otherwise known as a 'home umbrella'. *Kaufe* is considered by my family to be one of our most significant artefacts. Found in most Lau-Mbaelelea homes, it is imbued with cultural importance as a profoundly functional and symbolic device. This multifaceted artefact has no less than six applicable functions including: sleeping mat, umbrella shelter, burial cloth, backpack to carry firewood, large carrying basket and small carrying basket (or internal pocket). *Kaufe* is most commonly used as a practical sleeping mat that is portable[6] for travel and for use during our most significant cultural occasions – a necessity for *maea* (funeral occasions) or *dao urii geni* (marriage ceremonies) (Hundleby 2017: 243–44).

Kaufe is an object unlikely to be on display or to be valued as an important artefact outside of our own cultural contexts. Outwardly, its appearance may suggest simple tailoring. In actuality, the creator requires skill, and they must pay attention to detail in order to construct it correctly – the process is deemed as important as the final product. The pandanus leaves are collected, cut, dried, sun bleached and then hand sewn together. The duration of the process is irrelevant; rather more critical is the care taken throughout the process and the intent of the maker. The result is a multifaceted artefact that enables the maker/user to adapt, fold and transform the *kaufe* to suit the occasion.

Beyond its many functions and uses, *kaufe* is most significant as a valuable link to our traditional ceremonies (*maea, dao urii geni*), ancestors and to our collective histories. Furthermore, *kaufe* is fashioned from natural materials within our environment, and its attributes complement our North Malaitan identities: *kaufe* is adaptable, durable, ever present and resilient.[7] Despite its modest appearance as an everyday object, it has been held in high regard for generations. *Kaufe* is symbolic for who we are, our Lau-Mbaelelea environments, histories and values. The aesthetics of *kaufe* are not limited to visual characteristics; rather, its aesthetics are more intangible and experiential than visual.

Visuality and the Malaitan Senses

Visuality in a Western sense is commonly viewed as a response to the physical and material. However, for a Malaitan, visuality can also reference the spiritual. The question, 'What do you see?' can invoke a response that refers to sight in its physical sense as well as its non-physical sense – that is, the viewer or audience senses the metaphysical as well as the physical.

In North Malaita, that which may be seen is as important as that which cannot be seen. Ways of sensing the world include feeling sensations within the body, hearing sounds that nobody else may hear, psychic dreaming, seeing spirits[8] and receiving premonitions or messages (Gegeo and Watson-Gegeo 2001: 63–66). Each way of sensing is considered a sign that conveys important information from the ancestors and the spirit world. These signs offer knowledge beyond what we deem to be physically true. Spiritual knowledge and the presence of our ancestors and spirits within our physical world are best likened to the presence of air. While air cannot easily be seen with the naked eye, it may be physically felt and heard in a variety of ways, and we cannot disregard its presence as part of our world. We do not need to see the air to believe that it exists. In a North Malaitan context, we connect to our ancestors and the spirits. They are as real to us as our family members that stand alive and breathing. The spirits impact our physical world; they surround us, affect us, live through us and are part of our lives (Hundleby 2017: 115).

Performance is commonly viewed as a way to connect to the spiritual veil – a temporal bridge between the worlds of the living and the dead. When we sense and express emotion, we are able to connect – the spiritual component in visuality. In performance, visuality also includes the physical facade – clothing, dance ornaments, decorative body ornaments, plants, physical body movements and instruments. The next section introduces *barasili* and discusses visuality – the physical and the spiritual – in twenty-first-century *barasili* performance.

Barasili

In 2012, the Takwa Barasili Dance Group participated in the Festival of Pacific Arts and Culture (FestPAC) in Auki, Malaita, Solomon Islands.[9] The Takwa women presented the *barasili* dance form and explained cultural practices specific to women. A few years prior, Lucy Bakale, Matilda Adu and Kii formed the Takwa Barasili Dance Group to teach the *barasili* art form to our women and youth. They hoped to reinvigorate the form, to preserve cultural traditions and to empower our women through performance. As one of only two female performing groups in Auki, our Takwa women received accolades for the unique performances and cultural heritage they brought to the festival.

Te Te (Mum) Lucy Bakale is the sister of my birth Mum – Modesta Masiala, who died when I was in my early twenties. Since Mum's passing, all of her sisters have continued to teach me our cultural ways of thinking and being. Whenever I am home, I live with *Te Te* Lucy in Takwa Village in Lau-Mbaelelea, North Malaita. From dawn till nightfall, she continues to teach me the details of our oral traditions, arts and history.

The information that follows is derived from years of conversations with *Te Nau* (my Mum), *Te Te* Lucy and our prominent *kastom* group leaders, as well as conversations and recordings made with family and community members. From these discussions, I explore our ways of thinking and the significance behind the artefacts, instruments and performance styles prevalent in contemporary *barasili* dance today.

Over the years, people have suggested to me several definitions for *barasili*. These can be summarized as follows: *barasili* is an art form incorporating narrative, song and dance, performed by groups of ideally eight to twelve or more, within public spaces. Although *barasili* includes both dance and song, in a Malaitan context, dance and song are not thought of as separate entities. In *barasili*, movement is integral to the music, and the music is reliant on movement. *Te Te* Lucy's definition expands on this definition further: '*Barasili* are *kastom* songs from the ancestors, from *long taem bifo – go kasim nao*' – from our ancestral past to now (*Te Te* Lucy Bakale 2015, pers. comm., 15 March). Our *barasili* songs are looked upon as gifts from our ancestors; they are familial gifts that connect us to our past (*taem bifo*) and continue our traditions into contemporary, twenty-first century Malaita (*go kasim nao*). Lucy Bakale's definition hints at the history and genealogical information inherent in our *barasili* dances and the most common method of transmission: oral tradition (Hundleby 2017: 193–94).

A Brief History

During our recording sessions around Takwa Village, countless discussions centred on the history and context of *barasili*. Prior to the introduction of Christianity in the twentieth century, songs and dances were performed by men as part of Indigenous spiritual worship or for community feasting events such as *maoma* (Burt 2015: 113–15), which also held spiritual significance. Each were performed in public for a common sociological purpose: 'Dances were held to entertain the guests and the ghosts' (Burt 2015: 104). In the 1930s, a To'amba'ita[10] descendant discussed the concept of 'pleasing the ghosts' (*akalo* or *agalo*) to Hogbin (1939: 107):

> In the hills we carry out funeral rites, sacrifices, and dances to please the *akalo*. We exchange weeping, pigs, and dancing for their good will. Then they give us what we ask.[11] Just as in theory people do not weep because they are sorry, so also they do not dance for enjoyment: they weep and rejoice only to please the spirits.

Historically, women were prohibited from dancing, as dancing was a spiritual act performed to please the *agalo* (spirits) and influence *mamana* (spiritual protection). This was due to the belief that women were *sua* (had feminine power): the ability to give birth and shed menstrual blood gave women the power to neutralize all things sacred. In contrast, men – in particular *fata'abu* (high priests) – were able to communicate directly with the spirits and were considered to be *abu* (ritually clean) through communication with *agalo*, who were also considered *abu* (sacred)[12] (Hundleby 2017: 196–97).

All across North Malaita, this tradition was prominent until the latter half of the twentieth century. By this time, Christianity had become the most prominent religion, and many of our *fata'abu* leaders no longer practised our traditional Indigenous religion, had converted to Christianity, or had passed on. With Christianity's rise in popularity, North Malaitan communities began to allow more freedom and relaxed *tabu kastom* (sacred ritual/boundaries/culture), instead praying to their Christian God rather than their Indigenous God for *mamana* protection (Hundleby 2017: 196–97).

Contemporary Barasili

Performance is still an essential part of *barasili* artistry. Spiritual dance of the past had rigid rules and boundaries that focused on presenting a pleasing performance to the spirits. Dance of today – while still keeping in mind a supernatural audience – is no longer performed as part of Indigenous ceremonial rituals. Instead, there is greater focus on entertaining the living in a variety of contexts and spaces. Today in North Malaita, *barasili* may be performed by anyone – men, women and youth – and an increasing number of groups are engaged in the teaching, learning and performance of the genre. In contemporary settings, these dances are performed for special school or church occasions such as cultural days, graduations and religious feast days, as well as for national or regional celebrations and fundraising events (Hundleby 2017: 197–98).

There are three performance art forms that are fundamental to contemporary *barasili*: songs, stories and body movements. While an in-depth discussion on each form is beyond the scope of this chapter, their significance can be summarized as follows: *Nguu* (songs) and *unuunu* (stories) are integral to our dance forms – each cannot exist without the other.

At the heart of any dance or song is a *kastom* story or narrative. The *kastom* story is always connected to a particular clan, and significantly, clan members collectively own their stories. Details within a clan story will usually pertain to family members or ancestors and describe historical memories and specific geographical landmarks (land or sea). Therefore, clan stories can be sensitive due to the private knowledge contained within (Hundleby 2017: 138–40).

Songs may be thought of as short, abbreviated stories that suggest or point to the underlying meanings. Songs summarize our clan stories and protect clan information: public messages can be shared with a broader audience, while private messages are masked using metaphor. Similarly, our dancers express our stories using emotion and body movement as a metaphoric device. Informed listeners and audience members can decipher the symbols and reflect meaningfully on the details (Hundleby 2017: 138–40). As Kaeppler (2003: 157) also noted in Tongan dance culture: 'One is "inwardly warm or exhilarated" by an understanding of the metaphors created through references.' In *barasili*, our songs elicit emotion and invite connection; our stories share cultural messages and our body movements reinforce these messages using visual impact and drama.

Barasili is a versatile platform that combines the material (instruments, body ornaments, dance ornaments and the human form) with the intangible (music, stories, dance, knowledge) to communicate across physical *and* spiritual planes. In contemporary *barasili*, performers make a concerted effort to honour the legacy of the art form: the traditional melodies, dance costuming and accompanying instrumentation such as *falake* (ankle rattles), *kisi kisi* (hand rattles) and *o'o* (slit drum) are exhibited and performed in a similar manner to *kastom* performances of the past. Indigenous instruments[13] and costumes visually emulate and pay homage to our ancestors and our collective histories.

Indigenous Instrumentation
Falake (Ankle Rattle)

In North Malaitan dance music, the *falake* is an ankle bracelet made from seed pods of the *falake* plant (*Pangium edule*)[14] and woven *sule* plant rope (*Trichospermum psilocladum*). The rattle is usually worn around the right ankle and used as percussive accompaniment. Hence, the *falake* has dual purpose: as part of *kastom* dress costuming and as an essential dance instrument. Our dance group leaders explained to me that *falake* are part of all contemporary dances and were traditionally used in our older sacred dance practices as part of *fa-ta'abu* spiritual worship (Suri 1991: 31). Late nineteenth-century and early twentieth-century photos (Burt 2015: 17; Hogbin 1939: 69) provide evidence of their long-standing use. Walter George Iven's (1930: 215) description is likely to be one of the earliest documents of North Malaitan pan-pipe playing and dancing using the *falake*:

> On the right ankle they wear rattles made of a strong seed, and these are rattled with regular stamping of the foot when stationary, and at every other movement of the foot when they are on the move. Much energy is put into the playing, and the best players bend down over their pipes and blow and stamp with surprising energy, turning and twisting from side to side.

The repetitive rhythms performed with the *falake* provide a rhythmic anchor to *barasili a cappella* melodies. Aside from the natural materials the *falake* are made from, *falake* rhythms have a relationship to the natural rhythms that permeate our bushland environments, in particular the *angi* (crying) of the *keke* (cricket) (Hundleby 2017: 199–200).

The *keke* cries at specific intervals during the day and night. However, the most significant *keke angi angi*[15] for our mainland people is the cry that starts as the evening sun begins to go down. The reverberant sound is all-pervasive as every *keke* in the vicinity joins together in rhythmic unison. When the sun is completely gone, the crying ceases. Their communal cry acts like a clock, reminding us that night is drawing closer. Their rhythms mark the arrival of our ancestors, who are more spiritually available to us in the night (Hundleby 2017: 199–200).

Keke Angi Angi (Cricket Cry)

Figure 13.1. Keke angi angi *(cricket cry) rhythm. Transcribed by I.K. Hundleby.*

In *barasili* dance, the *falake* foot strikes the ground and engages the ankle rattle with emphasis. This movement is followed by a much less emphatic step with the other foot. If dancing in one place, the dancer will stamp the right foot and immediately slide the plantar surface of the foot against the ground with continued force to engage the rattle for a longer duration. The left foot follows with a lighter, less pronounced step. Generally, these movements are repeated throughout the duration of a song to create a rhythm that directly resembles the *keke* rhythm notated above (Figure 13.1.). In North Malaita, as documented in South Malaita (Zemp 1978: 63), sound forms and patterns within our natural environments (for example, birds) are often mimicked or referred to in song (Hundleby 2017: 133–34, 151). In Lau-Mbaelelea, our ancestors and the spirits are thought to communicate to the living through birds, animals and marine life. Thus, the relationship between *falake* and *keke* rhythms is not only one of rhythmic similarity: significantly, both the *falake* and the *keke* evoke and herald the arrival of the spirits (Hundleby 2017: 200–1).

The intrinsic reason for dancing has always been and still is to call the ancestors, to entertain our living people and, most importantly, to communicate with the spirits. Even though contemporary performances are not always specifically linked to spiritual rituals, dance is always for both the living and the dead (Burt 2015: 104; Maranda 1975: 487). The *keke* call that pre-empts nightfall simultaneously heralds the arrival of the ancestors and greater accessibility to the spirit world, and so the *keke* purpose parallels that of the *falake* in song: the rhythm calls to the spirits and encourages them to be present (Hundleby 2017: 199–201).

Kisi Kisi (Hand Rattle)

The *kisi kisi* is a hand rattle made from *ruri* (*Planchonella grayana*) seed pods. Groups of *ruri*[16] pods are attached with woven *sule* (*Trichospermum psilocladum*) plant rope to the top end of a small piece of wood, leaving enough space for the hand to grasp the other end of the wood as a handle. Unlike the *falake*, the *kisi kisi* instrument is only used by the leader(s) of the dance group (Suri 1991: 31). At the outset of a performance, the *kisi kisi* is shaken to signal to both the audience and other performers that a dance is about to begin (Hundleby 2017: 201–2).

Figure 13.2. Kisi kisi *(hand rattle) rhythm to signal the beginning of a dance. Transcribed by I.K. Hundleby.*

The introductory tremolo-like shake of the *kisi kisi* call ends abruptly with a sharp punctuated movement (Figure 13.2.). At times, the initial call of the *kisi kisi* may also be reinforced by a vocal call that will mimic the sharp punctuation of the rattle. Often, a brief pause will ensue before the dance leader commences the song and dance. As the dance progresses, the *kisi kisi* is used to augment the *falake* and vocal rhythms and to pre-empt dance changes such as shifts in melodic structure or in dance direction and movement. Tremolo-like ornaments highlight particular parts of the song or are used to add excitement (Hundleby 2017: 201–2).

The persistent rattling draws attention and evokes an appropriate atmosphere – one of respect, focus and presence. Today, the call of the *kisi kisi* in contemporary *barasili* dance bears a direct relationship to the call of the *kisi kisi* used in pre-Christianity prayer, when the rattle was used to signal the ancestor spirits. In a similar way, the *o'o* is also used as an instrument that communicates and 'calls' (Hundleby 2017: 201–2).

O'o (Wooden Slit Drum)

The *o'o* is a wooden slit drum traditionally made from a local hardwood such as *fata* (or *fasa*; *Vitex cofassus*) or *ligi* (*Pterocarpus indicus*) (Suri 1991: 32). The middle portion of the drum is struck using two short sticks, one held in each hand. These sticks are sometimes made from *koa* mangrove wood (*Bruguiera gymnorrhiza*). While contemporary *o'o* vary in size, *kastom* drums used for sacred purposes were prominent in size – up to three or four feet in length and up to two feet deep, as filmed in 'Are'are (Burt 2015: 123) by Hugo Zemp et al. (1979).

Like the 'Are'are, our *o'o*, as sacred objects, held magical power and were consequently subject to traditional *tabu*. To this day, sacred *o'o* passed on from relatives and ancestors who practised our traditional religion must continue to be treated with special reverence. Women cannot touch or play them because they would defile them with *sua* (neutralize with female power). The instrument should not be defiled in other physical ways; one must walk around the drum rather than step over it,[17] and the *oʻo* must be stored in a proper place – preferably a *mana beu* or sacred men's space.

Oʻo were historically used for two purposes: for religious prayer and dance to please the *agalo* (spirits) and to communicate significant messages or to call people across long distances. Ivens (1930: 211–12) describes the use of *oʻo* in 1920s sacred *maoma* (memorial) feasts:

> Gongs[18] are beaten every day from now on to announce the maoma, and the sound of them goes rolling up into the hills. . . . The date of a maoma is indicated by the number of single beats on the gongs which follow a continuous roll, the number being decreased by one each day. . . . The gongs also are a guide to the hill people as to the day on which they are to bring down the taro which they have grown for the feast, and for which they are to be paid.

Until very recently (the late twentieth century), chiefs would use specific drum rhythms to communicate, signal to, and inform people across distant villages; 'it was never beaten without some definite motive or meaning' (Suri 1991: 32). One rhythm might symbolize the death of a chief or *fataʻabu*; a different pattern could communicate a special meeting or war victory; yet another could signify the beginning of a *maea* funerary process (Hogbin 1939: 103).

Contemporary *oʻo* have no sacred attachment and can be played by anyone. The *oʻo* today is used to help maintain the beat and to unify the dancing and singing of group members. This instrument has a variety of specific signals that have different meanings. Typically, the *oʻo* player will drum a short burst to call the dancers to attention prior to beginning a performance. They may also perform a short drum rhythm for the performers to dance into position on the stage at the beginning of a performance, or off the stage at the conclusion of dance performances. The drummer may at times use an ornamented change in rhythm to signal a section change or to pre-empt the conclusion of a performance. The *oʻo* has physical design similarities to slit drums of other Pasifika nations (Hundleby 2017: 204–7).

Today, *oʻo* is often used as an instrumental accompaniment to non-sacred *barasili* tunes, and women's use of *falake* and *kisi kisi* as part of costuming and instrumentation is widespread. While contemporary *falake*, *kisi kisi* and *oʻo* are precious for their physical attributes as skilfully made objects, these instruments are considered most valuable for their ancestral attributes (Hundleby 2017: 204–7). Likewise, the Indigenous art forms and designs used in Lau-Mbaelelea dance costuming are considered significant for similar reasons.

Costume Dress

Contemporary women's dance attire and body decoration is imbued with North Malaitan history. Costuming places a visual emphasis on identity and connections to family. It is a tribute to men's *kastom* dance attire, *maoma ni geni* (sacred women's festival) and *dao urii geni* (wedding) attire commonly used over the last two centuries. For us, the inherent symbolism in our dance attire is meaningful, heart-warming and aesthetically pleasing. Despite changes in clothing during this time, both men and women have continued to decorate their bodies with meaningful ornaments for special and sacred events. As per earlier styles of traditional dress, the body ornaments used in *barasili* dance performances are gender specific. The next section details contemporary examples of costuming for women's *barasili* dance performance[19] (Hundleby 2017: 212–15).

Body Ornaments

Women who are comfortable doing so may choose to perform bare-breasted, and although this practice is increasingly rare, in the minds of many, bare breasts are still considered an integral part of traditional dance attire. Those who are not

Figure 13.3. Takwa Women's Barasili Group, September 2012. Kokosi and Adu wear tafuli'ae *across their breasts and* fo'odara *across their brows. Upper arms are adorned with* 'abagwaro *and* rii *plants. Wrists are decorated with* obi aba. *Photograph by S. and P. Hundleby.*

comfortable without covering instead wear a plain bra or a small bare-shouldered crop top – sometimes woven from plant materials, or sewn from blue calico. Across her breasts, a female dancer is layered with the criss-cross design of *tafuli'ae* shell money, a fathom-long, ten-string construction fashioned from hundreds of handworked shell pieces (Burt 2009: 61; 2015: 117).[20] The lower body is clothed with a blue calico skirt or a plain skirt layered beneath a grass skirt. The length of the grass skirt is usually to just below the knees (Hundleby 2017: 210).

Until the early to mid-twentieth century, Lau-Mbaelelea men and women wore very little in everyday life. *Kastom* dress required no clothing, only natural bare skin and specific traditional belts for males, married women and young maidens (Burt 2009: 23, 53, 144–50). By the mid-twentieth century, in our part of North Malaita some women were using *kapilato* (loin cloths or aprons), but eventually knee-length skirts made from blue calico became the norm. As our Takwa people converted to Christianity, the local Catholic missionaries provided calico at the Parish store to make clothing.[21] Once introduced, blue calico also became significant as part of *kastom* dress[22] (Hundleby 2017: 208–9).

The *tafuli'ae* and *rere* (dolphin teeth money) are undoubtedly the most valuable items we wear in performance practice. Our shell money, *tafuli'ae*, is most commonly given as part of bride wealth rituals (*dao urii geni*) and currently valued between SBD$1000 and SBD$2000. They are often kept as family possessions and passed from generation to generation. *Tafuli'ae* is still used as a form of currency in place of Solomon Islands dollars. If available, shell money should be worn for performance as it is considered an essential component of *kastom* dress.

Around a dancer's upper arms are *'abagwaro* (arm bands) patterned from plastic beads into traditional designs (Burt 2009: 132–33) or *gwaroa'adi'adi* (arm bands) fashioned from woven vine strips, *adi* (yellow orchid; *Dendrobium solomonense*) and *taketake niu* (red coconut; *Cocos nucifera*) into recognizable local designs. Alternatively, women performers may be decorated with *fa'ikome* (*conus* ring made from *Tridacna* clam shell), sometimes also in addition to *gwaroa'adi'adi* or *'abagwaro* armbands. The wrists are adorned with *obi aba* (a woven band of rattan for the wrist) and the ankles with *obi ae* (woven band of rattan for the ankle). Traditionally, these were woven from red-dyed (*dilo*) rattan (Burt 2009: 128). These days, a cheaper version is made from red plastic bags and braided into a long rope that is wrapped several times around the wrists and fastened. Finally, in addition to the *obi ae*, the legs are decorated with *ma'e'ae*, a leglet that is tied onto the upper calves just below the knee (Figure 13.4.). *Ma'e'ae* are made from plastic beads or shell beads and may be further ornamented with dolphin teeth or *ruri* pods and coloured wool (Burt 2009: 155). A *falake* ankle rattle is also affixed to the dancer's right ankle (Hundleby 2017: 201–11).

Across the female dancer's brow is an intricate shell-money decoration called *fo'odara*. In Lau, these are commonly ornamented with *rere*; in Mbaelelea bush

Figure 13.4. Ma'e'ae made from plastic beads by Lawrence Fadaua, a respected designer and creator of traditional body ornaments. They rest upon a copy of Ben Burt's (2009) book, which family members use as a reference guide when ordering dance costume pieces. Photograph by I.K. Hundleby, 2014.

areas, *fo'odara* are often adorned with *ruri* seed pods (Burt 2009: 81). Modern variations may also include coloured wool or coloured plastic beads. The final touches to a dance costume include *bala alingia* (ear decorations), usually made from a combination of turtle shell, dolphin teeth and plastic beads, which are attached to and hang from the earrings (Burt 2009: 90), and/or *mu'u alingia*, a beaded ear-fringe ornament that hangs from the brow to the ear commonly made with *rere* (Burt 2009: 89).

Contemporary arm, leg and brow ornaments vary in design, materials and colour. Bright colours and introduced materials are more common in modern variations, and new patterns can also feature contemporary emblems, such as the Solomon Islands flag (Figure 13.4.). The designs and the materials used are identity markers. They are particular to specific geographical places. For example, *ruri* seed pods reference bush/forest environments, and *rere* dolphin teeth reference ocean environments. Generally, Lau-Mbaelelea elders can visually assess an ornament and know its place of origin. In contrast, plant ornamentation tends to be more uniform across clans and geographical areas (Hundleby 2017: 208–15).

Natural Plant Ornamentation

The female dancer's costume is not complete until she has been adorned with two spiritually important local plants: *rii* (*Euodia hortensis*) and *hango* (*Cordyline fruticosa*). The arm is further decorated by sliding branches of fragrant *rii* leaves between the *fa'ikome* ornament and the arm (Figure 13.3.). Some women will also adorn their hair with branches of *rii* in the style of women's ornamentation for *dao urii geni*. *Rii* is a particularly fragrant plant that is not only pleasing to smell but also acts to spiritually protect those who wear it. *Rii* was documented by Ivens (1930: 221) as being much loved by women and thought to possess magical qualities. Finally, as she dances, the *barasili* dancer holds a branch of *hango* upright in her left hand. This practice emulates historic men's sacred dance performance of our past, as seen in Maranda's photographs of my Ganomela relatives in the late 1960s (Burt 2015: 113, 116). *Hango* has spiritual properties and was/is commonly used in rituals for casting out 'demons' and for returning spirits to their proper places. In the past, as detailed by Ivens (1930: 222), both the green and bright red varieties of *hango* have been used in spiritual practice (Hundleby 2017: 212–15).

The presence of *hango* and *rii* in modern *kastom* dancing shows the ongoing reverence North Malaitan men and women still hold for spiritual dance traditions and confirms that underlying attitudes towards old religious *kastom* practice still prevail (Hundleby 2017: 212–15).

Dancing Ornaments

In addition to natural plants and *kastom* body ornaments, dance ornaments are fashioned for use in dance performance. Two common accessories used by the Takwa Women's Barasili Group are *fote* paddles (Lau) and *kidi* bamboo sticks. *Kidi* were historically used as rhythmic accompaniment in men's *ainimae* narrative dance. *Ainimae* is still viewed as one of our most sacred art forms – significant for the historical details contained within each narrative. The use of *kidi* in *barasili* is a nod to our ancestral past (Hundleby 2017: 216–17).

Fote (paddles) are a vital part of Lau living. Canoes are used on a daily basis to transport our family members between our artificial islands[23] and the mainland. They are especially important for fishing, collecting seafood and carrying crops from mainland-based gardens. *Fote* and *kidi* serve as identity markers. However, most importantly these dance accessories add an element of visual impact and dramatization to dance performance. The North Malaitan sense of humour is quick, witty and light, and these qualities are highly valued in dance performance. Dance props are often used for comedic effect (Hundleby 2017: 216–17); for example, the strike of a *fote* paddle can be over-acted, the movements deliberate and exaggerated; the dancer's face might flitter between amusement and theatrics while the right leg simultaneously stamps the ground with force to raise the *falake* rattle. Meanwhile, the march and pivot of each foot engages the hip swing and accentuates the swish and sway of grass skirts as voices cry out to all who can hear, sense and see.

Conclusion

In the analysis of an art form such as *barasili*, it is tempting to concentrate solely on one individual element, such as the dance movements or the music. However, when we extricate an individual strand and only investigate one aspect, we risk overlooking the significance, the overall construction and the beauty of the weave in which that strand exists.

Barasili dance is a synthesis of the arts.[24] The composite art form is a weave of cultural art expressions: the tangible (material and visual art forms) and the intangible (performance art forms) are interlinked experiences of being Malaitan. In order to be truly understood, each facet must be considered in relation to the other. If we consider the art forms collectively, the weave is purposeful, valuable and powerful:[25] the prime function of *barasili* is to nurture, support and facilitate healthy relationships. It brings us together as family members and communities and brings us closer to our ancestors and the generations that came before us. Our art forms are not only 'chronicles of social relationships objectified in visual form' (Kaeppler 1985: 110) – they are the threads that nurture and sustain our family and ancestral relationships.

The cultural arts represented in *barasili* fit precisely with Kaeppler's (1985: 109–10) aforementioned statement on the arts: as creative processes they '"manipulate" words, sounds, movements, or materials . . . to formalise the nonformal'. Kaeppler's definition, the example of *kaufe*, and Malaitan views on visuality and aesthetics provide a framework for understanding North Malaitan *barasili*. To summarize: art is useful, it evokes emotion – we laugh, we cry, we remember – and it is meaningful. Significantly, through art we become connected. The descriptions in section two show how each thread of the *barasili* form is intrinsically connected to key aspects of Malaitan being: who we were and who we are, our environment and our cultures. Products are 'not only works of art, but also contain information' (Kaeppler 1985: 109–10): our Lau-Mbaelelea creations are living archives that contain Indigenous knowledge and our ways of being.

The composite art form is spiritually meaningful to us. The spiritual intentions of the artist/maker and the active contemplation of the musicians, the dancers and the audience are imperative. Whenever we place *tafuli'ae* on our bodies, rattle a *kisi kisi* high in the air or foot-strike the ground with *falake*, we are acting with spiritual intent: we share emotion and we sense for a response. Above all, the process or performance is a shared experience – we act together, as family, as community.

Barasili, like *kaufe*, is a metaphor for how we view the world: we choose connection over isolation.[26] The Lau-Mbaelelea notion of being connected is spiritual: it extends beyond the living to include our ancestors, the land, the sea, all creatures and our environments. Relationships are continuous and last beyond the grave. Our art forms build and strengthen these connections: in art, we create, we sense and we see the sacred.

Irene Karongo Hundleby is a bicultural (Solomon Islands, New Zealand) ethnomusicologist and independent researcher. Her doctoral thesis 'Kwaimani Ana Liohaua Gia (The Heart of Us)' (2017, University of Otago, New Zealand) reflects on knowledge, relationships and the importance of expression within North Malaitan music, arts and culture. Irene's study focused on ethnographic experiences as an apprentice learning intangible cultural heritage from her elders. In 2019, Irene began work on a book dedicated to Lau-Mbaelelea culture bearers and the collaborators involved in her doctoral music research. Irene continues to focus on collaborative grassroots projects. Current projects present Indigenous Pasifika and Māori perspectives in education and research. Irene and her husband Dave James own and operate Relics Music, an independent record store and Relics Hifi, an audio store established in 2013. Irene also provides health support through her neuromuscular therapy practice in Ōtepoti, Aotearoa.

Notes

1. While the majority of cultural groups in Solomon Islands identify as Melanesian, there are also groups that identify as Polynesian and Micronesian as well as Chinese-descendant and expatriate migrant communities.
2. Agnosticism and atheism are unfamiliar, foreign concepts that do not feature in our traditional teachings or Indigenous philosophies. When we have discussed these concepts, family members have expressed to me that these ideas are baffling and incomprehensible – some have posed that these ideas could lead to mental illness. In the last full census conducted in 2009, 'persons with no religion comprised less than 1% of the population' (Solomon Islands National Statistical Office 2009: 81).
3. *Toba ruka* means two bellies or divided belly. When I discussed this saying with my father, he explained to me that in this translation the English 'two bellies' infers two separate ideas that never meet; while the divided belly suggests a vessel that holds both ideas. He insisted the 'divided belly' translation to be a more accurate depiction of both Guadalcanal and Solomon Islands thinking (Hundleby 2017: 267).
4. Dominiko Alebua was a respected elder of the Avuavu region in Guadalcanal and the father of Solomon Islands third Prime Minister Ezekiel Alebua. Dominiko educated my father Peter in Guadalcanal cultures and languages when he first arrived in Solomon Islands. For more information on Alebua, see the book by Tarcisius Tara Kabutaulaka (2002): *Footprints in the Tasimauri Sea: A Biography of Dominiko Alebua*.
5. The ideas contained within Māori oral stories that I grew up learning in New Zealand have many similarities to the Malaitan values I also grew up with. Ideas regarding the connection of people to the land (*tangata whenua*) and to the environment, and to one another as family and clan (*hapū* and *iwi*, *kotahitanga*), and the importance of genealogy (*whakapapa*) and our life forces/spirits (*wairua*), which upon death return to the land of the spirits

(*Ana Gwou* for Malaitans, *Te Po/Hawaiki* for Māori), are kindred philosophies (see Walker 2004: 10–23). These ideas also extend to other Pasifika/Oceania nations. Metaphor as an important device for expression is also prevalent throughout the Pacific. As an example, refer to the academic writings of Hauʻofa (1994, 1998) and Kaʻili (2012) and their use of metaphorical examples in regard to knowledge and Indigenous philosophies.

6. *Kaufe* can be folded, tucked under the arm during travel and, when needed, opened up to become a single bed mat.
7. In North Malaita, power – physical and spiritual strength – is highly valued. The characteristics describing *kaufe* relate to *ramo* (warrior) characteristics. *Ramo* refers to a warrior who is physically strong, an adversary in physical combat and notorious. The word *ramo* is commonly used to refer to Malaitan identity and also refers to resilience as a Malaitan characteristic (Hundleby 2017: 102–4).
8. In this chapter, I make multiple references to spirits – in these contexts (unless stated otherwise) I am referring to the spirits (plural) of our ancestors and those that have died rather than the 'shade', spirit or soul of an individual.
9. Two Lau-Mbaelelea cultural groups participated in the Festival of Pacific Arts and Culture (FestPAC) held in 2012 – the Takwa Women's Barasili Group and the Adaua Cultural Group of Mbaelelea. Both groups performed alongside thirty other Malaitan groups and international performers at the Auki (Malaita) venue. The Adaua performance group demonstrated the making of various cultural items, such as dyeing materials for weaving and costuming, as part of their performances, and also received accolades for sharing their traditional knowledge and performance practices. The Forest Lake Village in the Auki region of Malaita was one of four satellite venues. These venues enabled local performers to showcase their arts without the hefty cost of inter-island group travel. The majority of FestPAC 2012 performances were staged in Honiara (Teaiwa 2014: 348).
10. The five languages and regions of North Malaita are: Toʻambaʻita, Mbaelelea, Lau, Baegu and Fataleka.
11. The word 'they' refers to the *akalo*, the spirits, who are thought to provide whatever it is the people need, when the *akalo* are honoured through ritual rites, sacrifices and dances.
12. Note there are several differing contextual meanings for the word *abu*. Furthermore, definitions that apply to the living, do not always apply to the spiritual. For example, *agalo* (the spirits) cannot be considered spiritually/ritually unclean.
13. These instruments are often sold to Solomon Islands visitors as artefacts in Honiara artefact stores. They are also kept as artefacts in museums. If they are considered spiritual, our people continue to keep them in sacred storage spaces. Though modern instruments are sometimes made using modern materials, the production style is usually close to or identical to older traditional versions.
14. Latin plant names kindly provided by ethnobotanist Matthew Bond, who has carried out research in Baegu, North Malaita.
15. Repeated words are common to our languages, and this is an example of the linguistic process called reduplication – the repetition of syllables or, in this case, words, for added emphasis.
16. *Ruri* seeds are commonly used across North Malaita as shell-money necklace decorations and also in traditional body ornamentation.
17. This *tabu* is related to the sacredness of the pelvic region and genitalia, and the perceived power of genitalia.

18. *O'o* are commonly referred to as 'wooden gongs' or abbreviated as 'gongs' in historical literature written about Malaitan people and cultures.
19. While there are similarities between men's and women's costuming, attire can vary between men and women, as the attire is related to other sacred and traditional ceremony costuming that is gender specific.
20. The British administration introduced common unit measures such as the fathom during the early part of the twentieth century. Throughout my lifetime, all of my relatives, including my Mum, have described the *tafuli'ae* shell money measurement as one fathom long.
21. Knowledge transmitted via oral tradition: Mum first recounted these experiences to me when I was a young child. Throughout my lifetime, her sisters and other relatives have reiterated their own experiences as young children. Mum (Modesta) was born in 1939 to parents that practised our Indigenous religion – often referred to as 'pagans'. Mum recalled the introduction of calico from the late 1940s onwards, when the local Catholic mission station in Takwa started a mission store. The mission itself was officially established in 1935. During the late 1930s to 1940s, many babies and children were baptized. Over time, parents became more trusting of the church and open to Christian conversion. In our family, it was many years before our grandparents converted – although all of their children attended the Catholic school for an education. Our family/clan baptism records confirm these stories.
22. Local Christian churches encouraged our people to be 'modest' and to cover their bodies. Over many years, the use of more clothing became popularized. However, elder family members (my aunts and uncles currently in their seventies and eighties) have recounted that in their youth introduced clothing such as shirts, pants and skirts were only worn when they had to attend church or the mission schools. As soon as they left the buildings, the clothes would be discarded.
23. In Lau Lagoon, artificial islands have been built by our ancestors over hundreds of years – and as recently as the 1960s. At low tide, builders take canoe loads of coral reef rock, dive to the ocean floor and build layers of coral rock until the island is several metres above the high tide mark. This can take a considerable amount of time to achieve. Reinforcement and maintenance are a regular part of artificial island upkeep.
24. Similarities to this way of thinking and being may be drawn in Wagner's *Gesamtkunstwerk* concept – though in addition, for many North Malaitans, the art synthesis is as much metaphysical as it is physical.
25. For discussion on Malaitan notions of power, see 'Kwaimani Ana Liohaua Gia' (Hundleby: 2017: 102–4).
26. We are connected to the environment through the materials we use. We are connected to the ancestors through their compositions and oral histories. We are connected to our family members through the instruments and ornaments we pass from generation to generation.

References

Burt, B. 2009. *Body Ornaments of Malaita, Solomon Islands*. Honolulu: University of Hawai'i Press.
———. 2015. *Malaita: A Pictorial History from Solomon Islands*. London: British Museum.
Burt, B., and L. Bolton. 2014. *The Things We Value, Culture and History in Solomon Islands*. London: Sean Kingston Publishing.

Firth, R., and M. McLean. 1990. *Tikopia Songs: Poetic and Musical Art of a Polynesian People of the Solomon Islands*. Cambridge: Cambridge University Press.
Gegeo, D.W., and K.A. Watson-Gegeo. 2001. '"How We Know": Kwara'ae Rural Villagers Doing Indigenous Epistemology', *The Contemporary Pacific* 13(1): 55–88.
Hau'ofa, E. 1994. 'Our Sea of Islands', *The Contemporary Pacific* 6(1): 148–61.
———. 1998. 'The Ocean in Us', *The Contemporary Pacific* 10(2): 392–410.
Henry, R., and L. Foana'ota. 2015. 'Heritage Transactions at the Festival of Pacific Arts', *International Journal of Heritage Studies* 21(2): 133–52. doi: 10.1080/13527258.2014.915870.
Hogbin, H.I. 1939. *Experiments in Civilization: The Effects of European Culture on a Native Community of the Solomon Islands*. London: G. Routledge.
Howarth, C., and D. Waite. 2011. *Varilaku: Pacific Arts from the Solomon Islands*. Canberra: National Gallery of Australia.
Hundleby, I.K. 2013. 'Kastom lo las yesterdae go kasim nao: Case Studies in Women's Music, Malaita, Solomon Islands 1969–2012', BMus Honours dissertation. Dunedin: University of Otago.
———. 2017. 'Kwaimani Ana Liohaua Gia – The Heart of Us', PhD dissertation. Dunedin: University of Otago.
Ivens, W.G. 1930. *The Island Builders of the Pacific: How and Why the People of Mala Construct Their Artificial Islands, the Antiquity & Doubtful Origin of the Practice, With a Description of the Social Organization, Magic, & Religion of Their Inhabitants*. London: Seeley, Service & Co.
Kabutaulaka, T.T. 2002. *Footprints in the Tasimauri Sea: A Biography of Dominiko Alebua*. Suva, Fiji: Institute of Pacific Studies, University of the South Pacific.
Kaeppler, A.L. 1985. 'Hawaiian Art and Society: Traditions and Transformations', in A. Hooper and J. Huntsman (eds), *Transformations of Polynesian Culture*. Auckland: The Journal of the Polynesian Society, pp. 105–32.
———. 2003. 'An Introduction to Dance Aesthetics', *Yearbook for Traditional Music* 35: 153–62. doi: 10.2307/4149325.
———. 2007. 'Containers of Divinity', *The Journal of the Polynesian Society* 116(2): 97–130. www.jstor.org/stable/20707389.
Ka'ili, T.O. 2012. 'Felavai, Interweaving Indigeneity and Anthropology', in J. Hendry and L. Fitznor (eds), *Anthropologists, Indigenous Scholars and the Research Endeavour: Seeking Bridges Towards Mutual Respect*. New York: Routledge, pp. 21–27.
Maranda, E.K. 1975. 'Lau Narrative Genres', *The Journal of the Polynesian Society* 84(4): 485–91.
Pollard, A.A. 2000. *Givers of Wisdom, Labourers Without Gain: Essays on Women in the Solomon Islands*. Suva, Fiji: Honiara, Solomon Islands.
Rossen, J.M. 1978. 'The Suahongi of Bellona: Polynesian Ritual Music', *Ethnomusicology* 22(3): 397–439. doi: 10.2307/851194.
———. 1987a. *Songs of Bellona Island (Na Taungua o Mungiki), Volume 1*. 2 vols. Copenhagen: Forlaget Kragen ApS.
———. 1987b. *Songs of Bellona Island (Na Taungua o Mungiki), Volume 2*. 2 vols. Copenhagen: Forlaget Kragen ApS.
Solomon Islands National Statistical Office. 2009. *National Report (Volume 2): 2009 Population & Housing Census*. Honiara: Ministry of Finance and Treasury.

Suri, E. 1976. 'Music in Pacific Island Worship, with Special Reference to the Anglican Church in Lau, Malaita, Solomon Islands'. Unpublished B.D. Thesis. Suva, Fiji: The Pacific Theological College.

———. 1980. *Ten Traditional Dances from Solomon Islands*. Honiara, Solomon Islands: University of the South Pacific, Solomon Islands Centre.

———. 1991. 'Indigenizing Christian Forms in Worship: A Perspective from the Lau Region of Malaita, Solomon Islands', Master's thesis. Dunedin: University of Otago.

Teaiwa, K. 2014. 'Reflections on the 11th Festival of Pacific Arts Honiara, Solomon Islands, 1–14 July 2012', *The Journal of Pacific History* 49(3): 347–53. doi: 10.1080/00223344.2014.953665.

Walker, R. 2004. *Ka whawhai tonu mātou: Struggle Without End*. Auckland: Penguin Books.

Worldatlas. [n.d.]. 'Solomon Islands', in *Worldatlas* [online]. Retrieved 18 August from https://www.worldatlas.com/webimage/countrys/oceania/sb.htm.

Zemp, H. 1978. ''Are'are Classification of Musical Types and Instruments', *Ethnomusicology* 22(1): 37–67. doi: 10.2307/851365.

Zemp, H., et al. 1979. *Are'are Music* [VHS]. Watertown: Documentary Educational Resources (DER).

PART V
Perspectives from Adrienne L. Kaeppler

Interview with Adrienne L. Kaeppler
A Conversation with the Kupuna

Ricardo D. Trimillos and Adrienne L. Kaeppler

On 1 November 2018, Adrienne Kaeppler and I met at the Tangö Café, one of the intimate upscale local restaurants in the burgeoning Ward Village area of the Kakaʻako district just ewa (west) of Waikiki. In her usual jet-set fashion, Adrienne was touching down in Honolulu to open an exhibition at the Bishop Museum on Rapa Nui (Easter Island) en route to Rapa Nui for a conference.[1] Over designer sandwiches and glasses of Pinot Grigio, we enjoyed a couple of hours of 'talk story' among the lunch crowd. Under the guise of interviewing her for a retrospective about the Study Group on Music and Dance of Oceania (SGMDO) of the International Council for Traditional Music (ICTM), I craftily interviewed this kupuna[2] about her life for this volume.
(Ric Trimillos, 7 March 2019 in Honolulu)

Ric Trimillos (RT): What they want is to contextualize the SGMDO in terms of everyone's career. So the first question is how you became interested in the Pacific as a career area and came to the University of Hawaiʻi?

Adrienne Kaeppler (AK): OK I'll tell you. I went to the University of Wisconsin Milwaukee, and I was walking down the street one day in 1959 and it was 20° below 0. And I said, I'm outta here. I'd taken anthropology, but I was really majoring in English literature. I also went to the Wisconsin Conservatory of Music, where I studied mainly voice and also some piano. So anyway I had this mixed bag.

RT: I've never heard you sing, so I can't imagine your singing voice.

AK: I was a coloratura soprano. And I remember just before I left to come to Hawaiʻi I was in a little opera. I can't even remember what the opera was.[3] Anyway, there were three witches. I remember doing my big part as the first witch.

RT: But how did you pick Hawai'i out of all these places you could go to?

AK: It was warm! I came to the University of Hawai'i because I had taken some anthropology of the Pacific and Africa, but I decided not to go to Africa. I was always interested in various kinds of music. I met Barbara Smith,[4] and she told me about the *gagaku* [Japanese court music] class. I met Rev. Shamoto,[5] and there were three of us. One played flute, one played *hichiriki* [double-reed instrument] and I played *shō* [free-reed mouth organ]. We had, you know, a great time together. Then as things moved on in *gagaku*, more people started playing. I started taking dance of various kinds. I took Korean dance and Japanese dance.

RT: Speaking about that, how did you get involved with *nihon buyo*, with Japanese dance? Was that before or after you got interested in *gagaku*?

AK: Actually, it was before. I remember going to a Japanese concert and seeing the *shamisen* [three-stringed plucked lute] players. The *shamisen* players: that's really cool. I want to do that. I used to play violin in my other life. So I asked Barbara Smith where I could learn to play *shamisen*, and she gave me the name of Mikayoshi Bando. I went to Bando-*sensei* and said, I want to learn how to play the *shamisen*. She didn't have any haole[6] students – I was the new anomaly. We sat down; I could sit on the floor with no problem. And she said, 'OK you put your fingers like this.' OK and so it goes [Adrienne hums first phrase of 'Sakura']. So I came back for my second lesson and I could play it. And she said, 'how did you figure out how to do that?' I said, because I play the violin; it's the same thing. What I really found difficult in the *shamisen* was changing the tuning during playing. I just could never do it. [Repeats] I just could never do it. That's the one thing that defeated me. That's really difficult. But I really wanted to learn how to play *shamisen*. I just liked the sound.

RT: But you also learned to dance; you also took dancing.

AK: After I took *shamisen* for about a year, she said, 'you know in this studio we'd like to have our students doing two things – [among] singing, dancing, *shamisen*', I said, well I can't sing – I'm not going to be able to sing – and I do know how to dance. So how about dance? She brought me into the dance part because she liked to have people do two things, not just one.

Were you in the group that we did *noh* [Japanese musical drama]? Remember we did *noh* [she sings a phrase of *su-utai*]. So we did *noh* too. I took a lot of Asia. With playing *shamisen*, doing Korean dance I almost became an Asian person as you probably realized by now!

RT: How did you get involved in Tongan dance?

AK: I was just at the right place at the right time. In Hawai'i I met this Tongan woman. Her name was – it'll come to me – Kalo Mataʻele. Anyway, she taught me some Tongan dancing. At the time I belonged to a group called the Pan-Pacific and Southeast Asian Women's Association. In 1964, we were invited by the Queen of Tonga to come to a meeting of the Pan-Pacific and Southeast Asian Women's Association in Tonga. Most of the people in the Hawai'i group were ancient [laughs]. Not really. But they were, shall we say, grown-ups. There were two of us who were not grown-ups yet. Every delegation – one from Korea, one from Japan, one from wherever – had to present a couple of dances. And so the two who were not grown-ups yet, we were designated to dance. I had actually learned a couple of hulas at the Y[7] because I always do that. We did two Hawaiian dances in proper missionary garb! I also gave a paper on various Hawaiian things – music, dance, whatever. The next morning, the Queen of Tonga – this was Sālote – came in and said to me, 'oh you made such a nice performance last night. And your [paper] presentation was good. So I want you to stay and do the same thing for Tonga.' Just like that. So instead of going home after the conference, I had to stay for the whole summer.

She sent me to all of the most important old dance teachers. I had the Queen's imprimatur. I actually lived with Kalo Mataʻele's grand aunt. She was a friend of Queen Sālote and a high- ranking lady. Anytime I wanted to go anywhere I'd just say, Halaevalu, take me to such and such. So we'd go. And Queen Sālote, you know, she was the nicest person you could possibly imagine. She just took me under her wing. Anything that included dancing, I was there. I was also interested in things that women made – barkcloth and mats and so forth. She always sent me to places where things were happening.

Then I came back to Hawai'i, and Carl Wolz[8] was here so I decided I really had to do something with dance. Carl taught Labanotation. I think you were in the same class. Remember how difficult it was? When I had Carl by myself I would say, how do you do this? How do you write that? [she performs Tongan wrist movement] And he'd say, 'that's difficult'.

RT: You mean the rotation of the wrist?

AK: The hand and arm movements. For most dance, you use your body and your feet. I went back for my year of fieldwork. It was 1965–66. But in the meantime I had taken linguistics. So I came up with this system as you probably know using linguistic analogies to study motion. I went back to my old teachers from the year before and said, OK can you tell me – is this the same or different? That's one and that's two [she gestures]. Is it the same or different? They'd look at me and go, 'Oookaaay, who's this crazy wahine[9] who wants to know if things are the same or different?' But I had by that time figured out which was the same and different. That's how I came up with my system.

RT: Seriously did they think you were crazy or did they just humour you?

AK: They humoured me. My main teacher was a man named Vaisima Hopoʻate, who descended from Tupou I through all these high-ranking people. Vaisima just took me under his wing too. And he said, 'OK, I'll go over all these things with you.' He taught me the men's dances; he taught me the women's dances; he taught me everything. Vaisima's sister taught me the old ladies' dances. The ancient ladies' dances, which were *ula*, *fahiaʻiula*. I was learning to speak Tongan by that time. She wasn't too keen on the 'same or different', but she did teach me the dances. But Vaisima, he was fine with it. He also showed me all the old texts; he had texts from his ancestors. 'Is this the same or different?' was good for him.

Then the Queen of Tonga died in 1965 in December. I had been there six months, and there was no dancing because of the period of mourning. But my 'is this the same or different?' didn't matter, because we weren't actually dancing. I wrote my first article on funerals. Because I was close to the Queen I was included in everything. No dancing, but there was all the tapa making, mat making and presentation of the tapas and so forth. So that's how I got interested in tapa.

RT: So was that your maiden article for Tonga?

AK: That was my first Tongan article, 'Meʻa fakaʻeiki: Tongan Funerals in a Changing Society'. (1973). It is actually still used by the Tongans because it was about the last traditional Tongan funeral. When King Tupou IV died in 2006, they used my article to figure out how to re-assemble this in their minds because nobody of high rank had died between 1965 and 2006. But I was still there, you know, ticking along [laugh].

RT: They accepted the fact that whatever you had written was accurate and everything?

AK: Of course. I was there looking at what was happening with the Queen. The lady I stayed with was Halaevalu; she was from one of the other lines of chiefs. They always brought the presentations of food to our house before they went to the palace. So I was counting all the pigs . . .

RT: Talk about serendipity. You were in the right place at the right time.

AK: Absolutely. And it was year after year I was in the right place at the right time . . . I went back and I finished writing my PhD. I wanted to put it off for another year because I wanted to go back so I could see the year-end ceremonies for the Queen. But they wouldn't let me.

RT: Who was 'they'?

AK: All the people on my dissertation committee. I was in the anthropology department, not the music department. So I finished my PhD, but I did go back so I could see the end of the funeral ceremonies for the Queen. And they could start dancing again.

The coronation – this was for Tupou IV – was going to be in 1967. Sālote was Tupou III. At that point I decided, OK I have to take part in the *lakalaka* [Tongan group dance]. Somebody I knew was dancing with the Ha'ateiho *lakalaka*. I asked if I could learn. I mean I didn't want to perform. They said, 'Oh yes you could listen and learn.' So I learned all the *lakalaka* from Ha'ateiho. I already knew how to do the motifs and so forth, so I just saw how they were structured together and how they went with the poetry. I had no expectation of dancing in the coronation. But they said, 'well we taught you all this, so you have to perform'. So I went, oookay, okay I'll perform. The way the *lakalaka*-s are laid out in a big line, the high-ranking person stands in the middle, and then the second one is ceremonial attendant, and then the third one, for men and women, to the right; I was on the women's side. And the third one is the best dancer. The chief of the village decided who was going to stand in these positions. He said, '. . . and Uli'afu is going to stand in the third position.' Uli'afu is my Tongan name. But actually the person who stood fourth was the best dancer. He just put me there because I had learned. I couldn't let them down. So, I performed for the coronation. We performed about eight times including for the Duke and Duchess of Kent. We had to go to their house.

RT: What did they say about seeing this haole lady in the group?

AK: Nobody said anything. They probably thought, OK maybe this is normal. It was anything but normal!

RT: In 2017, at your invitation, Queen Nanasipau'u of Tonga brought a Tongan dance group to the Asian Pacific Dance Festival in Honolulu. The present Queen is what relationship to Sālote? A granddaughter?

AK: This queen is actually a close relative to her. One of Tupou I's descendants was Vaea, a grandson of Tupou II, who had three children – Queen Sālote, a son with another high-ranking female chief, and a son with a high-ranking Fijian chiefess. The second son was the father of Vaea, and his daughter is the present Queen Nanasipau'u.

The oldest son of King Tupou IV (son of Queen Sālote, Tupou III) became Tupou V, but he never married and did not have descendants. His younger brother, the present King, married Vaea's daughter, became Tupou VI. He is the son of Tupou IV and brother to Tupou V, who died shortly after he became King.

RT: How do you know all this stuff?!

AK: I am an anthropologist [laughs]. Anthropologists learn these things!

RT: How was it that you decided to concentrate on dance and not music?

AK: Because of the Queen. But also, you know, in Tonga there are no musical instruments – it's all vocal. Singing Tongan vocal things – I mean I could do it, but I didn't really want to concentrate on it. I sang with the choir in the big church.[10] When we sang the 'Hallelujah Chorus', the director said, 'please don't sing the high notes'[laughs]. I had a high coloratura soprano, and I could not sing the high notes because they said, 'you stick out [in] the high part'.

RT: I am surprised they would say that. Because when I hear Tongans sing they are quite piercing. That timbre is the one that stands out.

AK: Somehow my timbre was not correct and mine stood out more. So they didn't want me to sing the high notes, the real high notes.

RT: Did you learn to read that Tongan notation?[11]

AK: It's the British tonic sol fa. But instead of singing do re mi, you start with number 3, because the word for 3 is 'tou' (tolu), so the whole thing is skewed. Anyway I learned to do it.

RT: I don't know if you ever met Lasinga Koloamatangi; he was at the University in the 1970s. He was a classically trained tenor and from the First Methodist Church Tongan congregation, so he knew how to read that notation too. He took some of my courses. He read a couple of your articles on Tonga and he said, 'She knows too much!'

AK: Oh really. [Adrienne role playing] 'She's not supposed to know this – she's not Tongan.' Actually, it was interesting. When I taught the Polynesian dance class, the ensemble, there were two Tongans. I'd say something about Tonga, and then I'd ask them, is that the way you understand it? After the second time I did that, one of them said, 'Please don't ask me . . . I don't know the answers to that. Please don't ask me. I am here to learn.'

In our naiveté, we expect every Tongan to know everything about their music. Of course, they don't, just as I do not know everything about Western music, and I am sure that Lasinga Koloamatangi knew much more about that than I did!

I learned one of the old dances, the *me'etu'upaki* – the one with the paddle from the people who lived in that village. They told me I could not teach anybody that was not from that village. The Polynesian Cultural Center at one point asked me if I would come and teach the *me'etu'upaki*, and I said, no. I was told I could not teach anyone who wasn't from that village. And I didn't teach them.

RT: Did you have any relations with the Polynesian Cultural Center professionally?

AK: Never. For fear they would want me to do something, like teach.

RT: In your identity of identities, do you consider yourself first an anthropologist and then a dance ethnologist?

AK: I consider myself an anthropologist who uses music and dance as data. For example, how people stand in the *lakalaka*; if you don't know the social structure, you won't understand why they're standing there. And when you get to the end of the line that's the second ranking person in the village. And if I hadn't asked anthropological questions . . .

RT: There are very few anthropologists who really mined the performance area. Why don't they? Because particularly in Pacific and Asia . . .

AK: . . . it's so important. Right. First of all most anthropologists are men – Western men. You say something about 'Why don't you ever look at anything about dance?' [They say] 'I don't dance.'

RT: Do you think it's a gender thing? One of the major themes for the Pacific is the whole aspect of gender construction. Do you see that as an area that for the Pacific is being more researched than before?

AK: Well in some areas. In Tonga, gender is not a problem because women are considered higher than men. So sisters always outrank their brothers. In New Guinea I think there are problems with that. There is a young woman from New Guinea; I think she's in New Zealand right now working on a PhD.[12] And so women are starting. In traditional society, they are not expected to go on. And if they do, it's usually in education, teaching the next generation.

RT: Are you not considered a woman in the same way?

AK: I am not considered a woman. And certainly when I first went to learn Tongan dances. They taught me all the men's parts. I was never considered . . . 'oh this female, we can't tell her anything'. That was never a problem for me, which was lucky.

RT: Probably because you are an outsider. You don't come under the gender role for them.

AK: But remember when we went to Japan with *gagaku* they wouldn't let the girls play *hichiriki*?[13] . . . I had learned to play *hichiriki*, but they wouldn't let me play *hichiriki* because they didn't want to see . . . [she puffs cheeks].

RT: But talk about field research for ethnomusicology. Sometimes the gender of the researcher doesn't come under the Indigenous system, and sometimes it does.

AK: Sometimes it is irrelevant. Sometimes, you know, it is helpful to be a woman.

RT: Aren't there any next-generation type anthropologists you know of who are taking the performance aspect more seriously? I mean, are there any of your disciples, as it were, in anthropology?

AK: Well, when I taught at Belfast with John Blacking from 1982–1987 (part time), the students were primarily music students in the social anthropology department. There were a few of them but not that many [interested in dance]. I had a couple of students: Irene Loutzaki from Greece.[14] She's an anthropologist, but she worked on dance. There are a number of them, but they aren't anthropologists. They are mostly dancers.

RT: I mean, I'm thinking of women anthropologists. Even Margaret Mead didn't talk about dance. Of course she was really like a man, wearing men's clothing.

AK: Yeah. But she dressed in Samoan clothes, sometimes with a mat [*'ie tōga*]. But as far as I know, she never learned how to do the dancing. Ric, you know, anthropologists were never taught to do that.

RT: Even as an anthropologist, you became president of ICTM.[15]

AK: Which was a big surprise to me. I never thought I was going to be elected. How I actually got elected I'll still never know.

RT: I voted for you.

AK: Thank you.

RT: Of course, you are most remembered for your ICTM dance.

AK: [laughs] That was the first time I became president (2005). [Adrienne re-enacts her opening speech] 'Now it is my pleasant duty to open the I-C-T-M' [Adrienne sings the letters and does the arm movements based on the Village People's 'YMCA']. Everyone was surprised. They weren't offended. People afterwards said, 'how did you do that again?' And it even became a performance at one of the meetings of the Study Group on Ethnochoreology!

RT: In a way, it's a famous first in terms of ICTM. You were the first dance person who was president.

AK: . . . and the first female.

RT: Were you the first female? Wow!

AK: I was the first female and the first dancer.

RT: What are your thoughts about the fact that ICTM doesn't have a D [for Dance]. . . . Do you feel it has to be or is it OK the way it is?

AK: It was always a problem, and actually Dieter[16] tried to change it, to get music and dance. But he was told that within UNESCO there's already a dance group, CID,[17] so we couldn't – it was a UNESCO thing. And as far as I know that still stands.

When I was president of ICTM, my whole focus was that we should have an international way of doing things, not just Eurocentric. When I was president, our meetings were in Vienna (2007), South Africa (2009), Newfoundland (2011) and Shanghai (2013). We also organized Kazakhstan (2015). We didn't even have a member from that area until I insisted that Razia[18] become a member of the Executive Board, and now she's vice president. I really thought it was important. And then when we went to China for the second time other people on the Board said, 'but we've been to China already'. And I said, and we've been to Europe too.

RT: Getting back to your career . . . what do you consider your most important contribution or articles or things that you should 'be remembered for' in terms of you know . . .

AK: Well as far as dance goes, my system of using linguistic analysis for analysing dance movement – my kinemes, morphokines, and so forth. That was probably my [greatest] contribution – I invented it.

RT: Yes, a structuralist approach.

AK: Actually, people in Europe still use it. In [the] US, the dance departments just dance. They don't do the academic. Which is a pity.

RT: Why do you think that is?

AK: Maybe the way university is structured. Because dance is never thought to be important. Music probably wasn't thought to be important a long time ago, but it became important. But dance never really arrived.

RT: But you say in Europe . . .

AK: That's because it came out of folklore. It didn't come out of anthropology. They have more of a separation – we do dance, we do music. But never part of anthropology.

RT: Here you are at the 'sunset of your career' as it were. What do you see as directions for dance ethnology ethnomusicology in the Pacific? Where do you see it going, or where do you want to see it go, or do you have any reservations as to where it's going? You know – that whole thing of looking toward the future.

AK: Of course it's always wonderful to have Indigenous people. That's really important. I have failed with the Tongans. I've never been able to get any Tongans interested academically – they do a lot of singing and dancing and music and so forth, but I have failed to find a Tongan, for example, to do the networking for ICTM. I mean, I'm the representative for Tonga. I would so love to have a Tongan.

RT: There's no one in the museum or anything?

AK: They don't have a museum. We've got Samoans, we've got Fijians. Just thinking about people that are in ICTM. It's not that we haven't looked or tried, but there's just nobody. I really think it would be great to have more Indigenous people, except they're interested in their own thing. They're not so interested in conferences.

RT: You would think maybe that for the Tongan thing there would be what you would call diasporic Tongans that, say, grew up in the States or something, who understand the value of academic stuff. But you haven't run across anybody?

AK: I haven't run across anyone in music. I'm looking for the Tongan. But I can't find anybody.

RT: But what about like in Samoa – are there other people? In the rest of Polynesia, are there up-and-coming ones?

AK: There are, right. There are Samoan people. Yes, Kuki Tuiasosopo, who was Barbara's student.

RT: He's doing pretty well. He's organizing things. He's at that community college,[19] where he holds symposia and stuff.

AK: He has done a lot of things with Christian music. That's his thing. He's the Liaison Officer for ICTM.

RT: . . . for American Samoa. What about the Cooks. Is there anybody?

AK: I know somebody who'd like to be. Jean Mason. She told me once, she said, 'I really hate the way dance is going in the Cooks. You know when I grew up we were learning it this way and so forth.' She was even thinking of going off to New Zealand and getting a degree now. But she hasn't done it.

RT: . . . You know Kirk[20] is doing the Cooks. I guess he found some young people who are interested in the research part.

AK: The last time I was in contact with him we were talking about the words for aesthetics, *heliaki* and things like that, Indigenous terms for aesthetics.

RT: Is it [*heliaki*] the same word in Tongan?

AK: That's Tongan. But I was saying, I'm sure they have concepts – we've got *kaona* [Hawaiian], we've got *heliaki* [Tongan]. I even found a word in Easter Island.

RT: Oh speaking of that, I saw that they have you listed as [author for] a book, the tattooed something.

AK: It's *The Iconic Tattooed Man of Easter Island* (2019). It follows illustrations of a Rapa Nui man from a carte de visite of c. 1870 to the famous well-known illustration of him by Knut Hjalmar Stolpe of 1884. We figured out who he is, the actual person.

RT: How did you do it?

AK: We traced back. We went through all the documents. Unbelievable. Actually Jo Anne[21] and I have been working on this for ten years. And we're giving a paper together on Easter Island. On Saturday, I'm going to Easter Island.

RT: We talked about how you see the field and where it's going. You stated the importance of trying to get Indigenous people involved.

AK: To get somehow involved. It's an amazing thought that Indigenous people are interested in playing violin, but they're not interested in talking about their own traditions. In Hawai'i, a lot of things got lost. And so now people are very interested.

What else do I need to talk about?

RT: You sort of covered everything, I think. Oh, I guess the last question is specifically about the study group.

AK: That's why we're here, right.

RT: Where do you see it going, and what direction do you see it should be going?

AK: The study group[22] I think is really important because it keeps us together, and it gives us a focus. I don't do a lot of music any more, but I am still interested in the study group because I like the information, the focus and so forth. I do think the study groups are important. When I was president, I was all for study groups – more and more study groups – because that's how people actually interact. In the dance study group,[23] we used to have sub study groups. We got together in various places and talked about whatever the subject was. We don't do that with the Pacific one because there's not enough people.

I don't know where the SGMDO (the Study Group on Music and Dance of Oceania) is going, but I think Brian[24] is doing an excellent job. Brian is really into keeping people informed, and that's how it should be. May it live forever! May it live forever!

RT: Thank you, Adrienne Kaeppler.

As closure and in celebration of the interview, we sipped coffee in decadent combination with strawberry mango crumble and blueberry bread pudding. Adrienne was none the wiser!

Welina e Adrienne, he noio ʻaʻe ʻale no ke kai loa!
(Greetings to Adrienne, the tern that treads upon the waves of a distant sea)

Ricardo D. Trimillos is Professor Emeritus in Ethnomusicology and Asian Studies at the University of Hawaiʻi at Mānoa in Honolulu, Hawaiʻi. His research and teaching focus on the expressive arts (music, dance, theatre) in their cultural context. He is recognized both nationally and internationally; he has been consultant to a number of governments, including Poland, Malaysia, the Philippines and Hong Kong for arts and public policy. His research topics include Hawaiian music and dance, the music of Muslim groups in the Southern Philippines, Catholic folk music in the Lowland Philippines and the traditional music of Japan. His theoretical emphases encompass music and ethnic identity, issues of cultural representation, and aspects of gender in the arts of the Pacific and Asia. He has taught Filipino *rondalla* and *kulintangan* and Japanese *koto* and *gagaku*.

Notes

1. 'Rapa Nui: The Untold Stories of Easter Island'; 3 November 2018 to 5 May 2019 at the Castle Memorial Building of the Bishop Museum.
2. Hawaiian word for a respected elder, commonly used in spoken English in Hawaiʻi.
3. Probably *Macbeth* by Verdi.
4. Founder of the ethnomusicology programme at the University of Hawaiʻi at Mānoa (UH).
5. Reverend Masatoshi Shamoto, *gagaku* teacher at UH.
6. Hawaiian term that denotes a White person, commonly used in spoken English in Hawaiʻi.
7. Richardson Young Women's Christian Association (YWCA) in downtown Honolulu.
8. At the time an East–West Center grantee and graduate student; Carl later was on the UH dance faculty and founded the World Dance Alliance in 1990.
9. Hawaiian term that denotes a female, commonly used in spoken English in Hawaiʻi.
10. The Wesleyan Methodist Centenary Church (Saione Foʻou) in Nukuʻalofa is known as 'The King's Church'.
11. The *tuʻungafasi* notation system was developed by missionary James Moulton in the nineteenth century and is still widely used in Tonga.
12. Naomi Faik-Simit, ICTM Liaison Officer for Papua New Guinea.
13. Double-reed instrument that carries the basic melody.

14. Irene Loutzaki authored Chapter 9 of the present book.
15. The International Council for Traditional Music, a non-governmental organization in formal consultative relations with UNESCO.
16. Dieter Christensen was Secretary General for ICTM from 1981–2001.
17. Conseil International de la Danse/International Dance Council.
18. Razia Sultanova.
19. American Samoa Community College.
20. Kirk Sullivan is a PhD candidate at the University of Hawai'i; Adrienne is on his dissertation committee.
21. Jo Anne Van Tilburg is an archaeologist specializing in rock art of Rapa Nui and is co-author of *The Iconic Tattooed Man of Easter Island*.
22. The ICTM Study Group on Music and Dance of Oceania.
23. The ICTM Study Group on Ethnochoreology.
24. Brian Diettrich (Victoria University of Wellington) is currently Chair of the Study Group on Music and Dance of Oceania.

Publications by Adrienne L. Kaeppler

Jess Marinaccio (compiler)

'Melanesian Masks in the Bishop Museum'. Master's thesis, University of Hawai'i, 1961.
Compiled with Robert N. Bowen. *Pacific Anthropologists 1962*. Honolulu: Pacific Scientific Information Centre, Bishop Museum, 1962.
'Ceremonial Masks: A Melanesian Art Style'. *The Journal of the Polynesian Society* 72(2) (1963): 118–38.
Review of the record *Music of New Guinea; The Australian Trust Territory, an Introduction. Ethnomusicology* 7(1) (1963): 60–61.
'Papuan Gulf Masks from the Village of Muru'. *Baessler-Archiv* 11 (1963): 361–73.
Compiled with Robert N. Bowen. *Pacific Anthropologists 1964*. Honolulu: Pacific Scientific Information Centre, Bishop Museum, 1964.
'Preservation of the Arts in Hawaii'. *The Delphian Quarterly* 48(3) (1965): 1–7 and 36.
Review of the record *Music of the Magindanao in the Philippines*, by Jose Maceda. *Ethnomusicology* 9(1) (1965): 78–79.
'Sunday in Tonga'. *The Delphian Quarterly* 49(4) (1966): 8–11 and 15.
'Folklore as Expressed in the Dance in Tonga'. *The Journal of American Folklore* 80(316) (1967): 160–68.
'Preservation and Evolution of Form and Function in Two Types of Tongan Dance', in Genevieve A. Highland, Roland W. Force, Alan Howard, Marion Kelly and Yosihiko H. Sinoto (eds), *Polynesian Culture History: Essays in Honor of Kenneth P. Emory* (Bernice P. Bishop Museum Special Publication 56) (Honolulu: Bishop Museum Press, 1967), 503–36.
'The Structure of Tongan Dance'. PhD diss., University of Hawai'i, 1967.
'Coronation Week in Tonga'. *The Delphian Quarterly* 51(1) (1968): 8–12.
With W.H. Fitzgerald and Roland W. Force. *Directory of Asian-Pacific Museums*. Honolulu: Bishop Museum Press, 1969.

'Tongan Dance: A Study in Cultural Change'. *Ethnomusicology* 14(2) (1970): 266–77.

'Feather Cloaks, Ship Captains, and Lords'. *Bishop Museum Occasional Papers* 24(6) (1970): 92–114.

'Aesthetics of Tongan Dance'. *Ethnomusicology* 15(2) (1971): 175–85.

'Regional Report: Hawaii', in Australian National Advisory Committee for UNESCO (eds), *Meeting on Studies of Oceanic Cultures* (Canberra: Australian National University, 1971), 87–111.

'Subject Survey: Dance in the Pacific', in Australian National Advisory Committee for UNESCO (eds), *Meeting on Studies of Oceanic Cultures* (Canberra: Australian National University, 1971), 131–38.

'Rank in Tonga'. *Ethnology* 10(2) (1971): 174–93.

'Eighteenth Century Tonga: New Interpretations of Tongan Society and Material Culture at the Time of Captain Cook'. *Man* 6(2) (1971): 204–20.

Review of *Traditional Maori Clothing: A Study of Technological and Functional Change*, by Sidney M. Mead. *American Anthropologist* 73(4) (1971): 887–88.

'Method and Theory in Analyzing Dance Structure with an Analysis of Tongan Dance'. *Ethnomusicology* 16(2) (1972): 173–217.

'The Use of Documents in Identifying Ethnographic Specimens from the Voyages of Captain Cook'. *The Journal of Pacific History* 7 (1972): 195–200.

'Acculturation in Hawaiian Dance'. *Yearbook of the International Folk Music Council* 4 (1972): 38–46.

'The Decorative Arts in the Marshall Islands', in E.H. Bryan, Jr. (ed.), *Life in the Marshall Islands* (Honolulu: Pacific Scientific Information Centre, Bishop Museum, 1972), 164–72.

'A Comparative Note on Anutan Social Organization', in D.E. Yen and Janet Gordon (eds), *Anuta: A Polynesian Outlier in the Solomon Islands* (Pacific Anthropological Records, No. 21) (Honolulu: Department of Anthropology, Bishop Museum, 1973), 21–24.

'Music in Hawaii in the Nineteenth Century', in Robert Günther (ed.), *Musikkulturen Asiens, Afrikas und Ozeaniens im 19. Jahrhundert* [Music Cultures of Asia, Africa and Oceania in the 19th Century] (Regensburg: Gustav Bosse Verlag, 1973), 311–38.

'Tonga', in John Clammer (ed.), *Peoples of the Earth, Vol. 8: The Pacific: Polynesia and Micronesia* (Danbury, CT: Danbury Press, 1973), 54–61.

Review of the record *Musique Polynésienne Traditionnelle d'Ontong Java (Iles Salomon)*, by Hugo Zemp. *Ethnomusicology* 17(1) (1973): 146–47.

'Pottery Sherds from Tungua, Ha'apai: And Remarks on Pottery and Social Structure in Tonga'. *The Journal of the Polynesian Society* 82(2) (1973): 218–22.

Review of *Music and Dance of the Tewa Pueblos*, by Gertrude Prokosch Kurath and Antonio Garcia. *American Anthropologist* 75(4) (1973): 1065–66.

'A Study of Tongan Panpipes with a Speculative Interpretation'. *Ethnos: Journal of Anthropology* 39(1–4) (1974): 102–28.

'Cook Voyage Provenance of the "Artificial Curiosities" of Bullock's Museum'. *Man* 9(1) (1974): 68–92.

With Dieter Christensen. 'Oceanic Peoples, Arts of (The Performing Arts: Music and Dance)', in *The New Encyclopaedia Britannica (15th Edition), Vol. 13* (Chicago: Encyclopaedia Britannica Inc., 1974), 456–61.

Review of the record *Musique de Guadalcanal: Solomon Islands*, by Hugo Zemp. *Ethnomusicology* 18(3) (1974): 477–78.

'An Eighteenth Century Kahili from Kauaʻi'. *Archaeology on Kauaʻi* 4(2) (1975): 3–9.

The Fabrics of Hawaii (Bark Cloth) [with 55 plates by Peter Gilpin] (World's Heritage of Woven Fabrics, Vol. 14). Leigh-on-Sea: F. Lewis Publishers Limited, 1975.

Review of the records *Traditional Music of Tonga*, by Richard M. Moyle, and *Tongan Festival Contingent*. *Ethnomusicology* 20(3) (1976): 612–15.

Edited with H. Arlo Nimmo. *Directions in Pacific Traditional Literature: Essays in Honor of Katharine Luomala* (Bernice P. Bishop Museum Special Publication 62). Honolulu: Bishop Museum Press, 1976.

With H. Arlo Nimmo. 'Preface', in Adrienne L. Kaeppler and H. Arlo Nimmo (eds), *Directions in Pacific Traditional Literature: Essays in Honor of Katharine Luomala* (Bernice P. Bishop Museum Special Publication 62) (Honolulu: Bishop Museum Press, 1976), xi–xvi.

'Dance and the Interpretation of Pacific Traditional Literature', in Adrienne L. Kaeppler and H. Arlo Nimmo (eds), *Directions in Pacific Traditional Literature: Essays in Honor of Katharine Luomala* (Bernice P. Bishop Museum Special Publication 62) (Honolulu: Bishop Museum Press, 1976), 195–216.

'Art', 'Art of Oceania: Polynesia and Micronesia' and 'Dance', in David E. Hunter and Phillip Whitten (eds), *Encyclopedia of Anthropology* (New York: Harper & Row, 1976), 20–21, 33–34, 113–14.

Edited with Judy Van Zile and Carl Wolz. *Asian and Pacific Dance: Selected Papers from the 1974 CORD-SEM Conference (Dance Research Annual VIII)*. New York: Congress on Research in Dance, Inc., 1977.

'Polynesian Dance as "Airport Art"', in Adrienne L. Kaeppler, Judy Van Zile and Carl Wolz (eds), *Asian and Pacific Dance: Selected Papers from the 1974 CORD-SEM Conference (Dance Research Annual VIII)* (New York: Congress on Research in Dance, Inc., 1977), 71–84.

'Polynesian Music, Captain Cook, and the Romantic Movement in Europe'. *Music Educators Journal* 65(3) (1978): 54–60.

'Dance in Anthropological Perspective'. *Annual Review of Anthropology* 7 (1978): 31–49.

'Exchange Patterns in Goods and Spouses: Fiji, Tonga and Samoa'. *Mankind* 11(3) (1978): 246–52.

'Melody, Drone and Decoration: Underlying Structures and Surface Manifestations in Tongan Art and Society', in Michael Greenhalgh and Vincent Megaw (eds), *Art in Society: Studies in Style, Culture and Aesthetics* (London: Duckworth, 1978), 261–74.

'Artificial Curiosities': Being an Exposition of Native Manufactures Collected on the Three Pacific Voyages of Captain James Cook, R.N. at the Bernice Pauahi Bishop Museum, January 18, 1978–August 31, 1978, on the Occasion of the Bicentennial of the European Discovery of the Hawaiian Islands by Captain Cook – January 18, 1778 (Exhibition Catalogue; Bernice P. Bishop Museum Special Publication 65). Honolulu: Bishop Museum Press, 1978.

(Editor) *Cook Voyage Artifacts in Leningrad, Berne, and Florence Museums* (Bernice P. Bishop Museum Special Publication 66). Honolulu: Bishop Museum Press, 1978.

'Preface', in Adrienne L. Kaeppler (ed.), *Cook Voyage Artifacts in Leningrad, Berne, and Florence Museums* (Bernice P. Bishop Museum Special Publication 66) (Honolulu: Bishop Museum Press, 1978), vii–x.

'The Cook Voyage Collection in Leningrad: Introduction', in Adrienne L. Kaeppler (ed.), *Cook Voyage Artifacts in Leningrad, Berne, and Florence Museums* (Bernice P. Bishop Museum Special Publication 66) (Honolulu: Bishop Museum Press, 1978), 1–2.

'The Cook Voyage Collection in Berne: Introduction', in Adrienne L. Kaeppler (ed.), *Cook Voyage Artifacts in Leningrad, Berne, and Florence Museums* (Bernice P. Bishop Museum Special Publication 66) (Honolulu: Bishop Museum Press, 1978), 18–24.

'The Cook Voyage Collection in Florence: Introduction', in Adrienne L. Kaeppler (ed.), *Cook Voyage Artifacts in Leningrad, Berne, and Florence Museums* (Bernice P. Bishop Museum Special Publication 66) (Honolulu: Bishop Museum Press, 1978), 71–74.

'*Me'a faka'eiki:* Tongan Funerals in a Changing Society', in Niel Gunson (ed.), *The Changing Pacific: Essays in Honour of H.E. Maude* (Melbourne: Oxford University Press, 1978), 174–202.

'"L'Aigle" and HMS "Blonde": The Use of History in the Study of Ethnography'. *The Hawaiian Journal of History* 12 (1978): 28–44.

Review of *The Dance in the Pacific: A Comparative and Critical Survey of Dancing in Polynesia, Micronesia and Indonesia*, by W.A. Poort. *American Anthropologist* 80(1) (1978): 152.

Edited with Douglas Newton and Peter Gathercole. *The Art of the Pacific Islands* (Exhibition Catalogue). Washington, D.C.: National Gallery of Art, 1979.

'Aspects of Polynesian Aesthetic Traditions', in Douglas Newton, Adrienne L. Kaeppler and Peter Gathercole (eds), *The Art of the Pacific Islands* (Exhibition Catalogue) (Washington, D.C.: National Gallery of Art, 1979), 77–95.

'A Survey of Polynesian Art', in Sidney M. Mead, assisted by Isabelle Brymer and Susan Martich (eds), *Exploring the Visual Art of Oceania: Australia, Melanesia, Micronesia, and Polynesia* (Honolulu: The University Press of Hawai'i, 1979), 180–91.

Review of *An Annotated Bibliography of Oceanic Music and Dance*, by Mervyn McLean. *Ethnomusicology* 23(1) (1979): 142–43.

With Judith Lynne Hanna, Roger D. Abrahams, N. Ross Crumrine, Robert Dirks, Renate Von Gizycki, Paul Heyer, Alan Shapiro, Yoshihiko Ikegami, Joann W. Keali'inohomoku, Gerhard Kubik, Roderyk Lange, Anya Peterson Royce, Jill Drayson Sweet and Stephen A. Wild. 'Movements Toward Understanding Humans through the Anthropological Study of Dance [and Comments and Reply]'. *Current Anthropology* 20(2) (1979): 313–39.

'Tracing the History of Hawaiian Cook Voyage Artefacts in the Museum of Mankind', in T.C. Mitchell (ed.), *Captain Cook and the South Pacific* (The British Museum Yearbook 3) (London: British Museum Publications Limited, 1979), 167–97.

Eleven Gods Assembled: An Exhibition of Hawaiian Wooden Images, Bernice Pauahi Bishop Museum, Honolulu, Hawaii, April 6–June 10, 1979 (Exhibition Catalogue). Honolulu: Bishop Museum Press, 1979.

Pahu and Puniu: An Exhibition of Hawaiian Drums: Bernice Pauahi Bishop Museum, Honolulu, Hawai'i, March 1–July 1, 1980 (Exhibition Catalogue). Honolulu: Bishop Museum Press, 1980.

'The Persistence of Tradition', in Roger G. Rose (ed.), *Hawai'i, The Royal Isles* (Exhibition Catalogue; Bernice P. Bishop Museum Special Publication 67) (Honolulu: Bishop Museum Press, 1980), 53–62.

Kapa: Hawaiian Bark Cloth. Hilo Bay: Boom Books, 1980.

'Hawaiian Art: An Anthropological Perspective'. *Educational Perspectives* 19(1) (1980): 10–15.

'Polynesian Music and Dance', in Elizabeth May (ed.), *Musics of Many Cultures: An Introduction* (Berkeley: University of California Press, 1980), 134–53.

'Pacific Islands: 2. Dance', in Stanley Sadie (ed.), *The New Grove Dictionary of Music and Musicians, Vol. 14* (London: Macmillan, 1980), 57–62.

'Polynesia: 7. Tonga', in Stanley Sadie (ed.), *The New Grove Dictionary of Music and Musicians, Vol. 15* (London: Macmillan, 1980), 68–69.

Review of *Master Mariner: Capt. James Cook and the Peoples of the Pacific*, by Daniel Conner and Lorraine Miller. *Man* 15(1) (1980): 214–15.

Review of *Introduction to Dance Literacy: Perception and Notation of Dance Patterns*, by Nadia Chilkovsky Nahumck. *Ethnomusicology* 24(2) (1980): 308–9.

'Observations on Jonathan King's Review of "Artificial Curiosities"'. *Newsletter (Museum Ethnographers Group)* 9 (1980): 10–13.

Review of the record *Polynesian Dances of Bellona (Mungiki) Solomon Islands*, by Jane Mink Rossen and Hugo Zemp. *Ethnomusicology* 25(1) (1981): 177–78.

'Further Observations on Jonathan King's "Further Comments . . . ."'. *Newsletter (Museum Ethnographers Group)* 11 (1981): 55–56.

Review of *To Dance is Human: A Theory of Nonverbal Communication*, by Judith Lynne Hanna. *American Ethnologist* 8(1) (1981): 218–19.

'Reply to Hanna'. *American Ethnologist* 8(4) (1981): 810.

'The Performing Arts of Papua New Guinea', in *The Sixth Festival of Asian Arts* (Hong Kong: Hong Kong Urban Council, 1981), 130–35.

'From the Guest Editor'. *Ethnomusicology* (Pacific Issue) 25(3) (1981): v.

Review of *The Nobility and the Chiefly Tradition in the Modern Kingdom of Tonga*, by George E. Marcus. *American Anthropologist* 84(3) (1982): 714–15.

'Genealogy and Disrespect: A Study of Symbolism in Hawaiian Images'. *RES: Anthropology and Aesthetics* 3 (1982): 82–107.

'Dance in Tonga: The Communication of Social Values through an Artistic Medium'. *Journal for the Anthropological Study of Human Movement* 2(3) (1983): 122–28.

Polynesian Dance: With a Selection for Contemporary Performances. Honolulu: Alpha Delta Kappa, 1983.

'A Further Note on the Cook Voyage Collection in Leningrad'. *The Journal of the Polynesian Society* 92(1) (1983): 93–98.

Review of *The Performing Arts: Music and Dance*, by John Blacking and Joann W. Kealiʻinohomoku, and *The Anthropology of the Body*, by John Blacking. *Ethnomusicology* 27(2) (1983): 359–60.

'Dance as Myth – Myth as Dance: A Challenge to Traditional Viewpoints (Keynote Address)', in Betty True Jones (ed.), *Dance as Cultural Heritage, Vol. 1: Selected Papers from the ADG-CORD Conference 1978 (Dance Research Annual XIV)* (New York: Congress on Research in Dance, Inc., 1983), 5–8.

Review of 'Future Directions in the Study of the Arts of Oceania', *The Journal of the Polynesian Society* 90(2). *Pacific Arts Newsletter* 17 (1983): 32–34.

Review of *The Performer-Audience Connection: Emotion to Metaphor in Dance and Society*, by Judith Lynne Hanna. *Anthropologica* 26(1) (1984): 61–63.

'Foreword', in Mary J. Pritchard (ed.), *Siapo: Bark Cloth Art of Samoa* (Pago Pago: American Samoa Council on Culture, Arts and Humanities, 1984), vi–vii.

Review of *Grass Huts and Warehouses: Pacific Beach Communities of the Nineteenth Century*, by Caroline Ralston. *Ethnohistory* 31(2) (1984): 149–50.

'Traditional Transmission and Transmission of Tradition in Polynesian Dance', in David McAllester (ed.), *Becoming Human through Music: The Wesleyan Symposium on the Perspectives of Social Anthropology in the Teaching and Learning of Music* (Reston: Music Educators National Conference, 1985), 29–42.

Compiled with Amy Kuʻuleialoha Stillman. *Pacific Island and Australian Aboriginal Artifacts in Public Collections in the United States of America and Canada.* Paris: UNESCO, 1985.

'Structured Movement Systems in Tonga', in Paul Spencer (ed.), *Society and the Dance: The Social Anthropology of Process and Performance* (Cambridge: Cambridge University Press, 1985), 92–118.

'Anthropology and the U.S. Exploring Expedition', in Herman J. Viola and Carolyn Margolis with the assistance of Jan S. Danis and Sharon D. Galperin (eds), *Magnificent Voyagers: The U.S. Exploring Expedition, 1838–1842* (Exhibition Catalogue) (Washington, D.C.: Smithsonian Institution Press, 1985), 119–47.

'Hawaiian Art and Society: Traditions and Transformations', in Antony Hooper and Judith Huntsman (eds), *Transformations of Polynesian Culture* (Memoir of The Polynesian Society, No. 45) (Auckland: The Polynesian Society, 1985), 105–31.

'Movement in the Performing Arts of the Pacific Islands', in Bob Fleshman (ed.), *Theatrical Movement: A Bibliographical Anthology* (Metuchen, NJ: The Scarecrow Press, 1986), 586–600.

'Cultural Analysis, Linguistic Analogies, and the Study of Dance in Anthropological Perspective', in Charlotte J. Frisbie (ed.), *Explorations in Ethnomusicology: Essays in Honor of David P. McAllester* (Detroit: Information Coordinators, 1986), 25–33.

With Olive Lewin. 'Fourth International Colloquium "Traditional Music and Tourism", Held at Kingston, and Newcastle, Jamaica, July 10–14, 1986'. *Yearbook for Traditional Music* 18 (1986): 211–12.

'Fourth Festival of Pacific Arts, Tahiti, June 29th to July 15, 1985'. *Pacific Arts Newsletter* 22 (1986): 3–5.

Review of *Hula Kiʻi: Hawaiian Puppetry*, by Katharine Luomala. *Pacific Studies* 11(1) (1987): 149–53.

'Spontaneous Choreography: Improvisation in Polynesian Dance'. *Yearbook for Traditional Music* 19 (1987): 13–22.

'Concerning a Maori Shell Trumpet from Cook's Second Voyage and Some Implications [Shorter Communication]'. *The Journal of the Polynesian Society* 96(2) (1987): 243–49.

'Response to David Simmons [Correspondence]'. *The Journal of the Polynesian Society* 96(4) (1987): 497–98.

'Polynesian Religions: Mythic Themes', in Mircea Eliade (ed.), *The Encyclopedia of Religion, Vol. 11* (New York: Macmillan, 1987), 432–35.

'Pacific Festivals and Ethnic Identity', in Alessandro Falassi (ed.), *Time Out of Time: Essays on the Festival* (Albuquerque: University of New Mexico Press, 1987), 162–70.

'Pacific Culture History and European Voyages', in William Eisler and Bernard Smith (eds), *Terra Australis: The Furthest Shore* (Exhibition Catalogue) (Sydney: International Cultural Corporation of Australia Limited, 1988), 141–46.

Review of *Half a Century of Dance Research*, by Gertrude Prokosch Kurath. *Dance Research Journal* 20(1) (1988): 47–48.

Review of *Bikmaus: A Journal of Papua New Guinea Affairs, Ideas and the Arts*, by Don Niles. *Ethnomusicology* 32(2) (1988): 154–55.

'She Writes the Songs that Make the Whole World Sing'. Review of the book and record *Songs of Love*, by Tu'imala Kaho. *Matangi Tonga* 3(4) (1988): 37–39.

'Four Entries (Hawaiian "Lei niho palaoa", Fijian or Tongan "Kali", Marquesan "'U'u" and "Pu")', in Suzanne Greub (ed.), *Expressions of Belief: Masterpieces of African, Oceanic, and Indonesian Art from the Museum voor Volkenkunde, Rotterdam* (Exhibition Catalogue) (New York: Rizzoli, 1988), 114–21.

'Hawaiian Tattoo: A Conjunction of Genealogy and Aesthetics', in Arnold Rubin (ed.), *Marks of Civilization: Artistic Transformations of the Human Body* (Los Angeles: Museum of Cultural History, UCLA, 1988), 157–70.

(Editor) *Come Mek Me Hol' Yu Han': The Impact of Tourism on Traditional Music, Papers Presented at the International Council for Traditional Music (ICTM) Colloquium in Jamaica, 1986.* Kingston: Jamaica Memory Bank, 1988.

'Introduction', in Adrienne L. Kaeppler (ed.), *Come Mek Me Hol' Yu Han': The Impact of Tourism on Traditional Music, Papers Presented at the International Council for Traditional Music (ICTM) Colloquium in Jamaica, 1986* (Kingston: Jamaica Memory Bank, 1988), xiii–xvi.

'Pacific Festivals and the Promotion of Identity, Politics, and Tourism', in Adrienne L. Kaeppler (ed.), *Come Mek Me Hol' Yu Han': The Impact of Tourism on Traditional Music, Papers Presented at the International Council for Traditional Music (ICTM) Colloquium in Jamaica, 1986* (Kingston: Jamaica Memory Bank, 1988), 121–38.

'Museums of the World: Stages for the Study of Ethnohistory', in Susan M. Pearce (ed.), *Museum Studies in Material Culture* (London: Leicester University Press, 1989), 83–96.

'Dance', in Erik Barnouw (ed.), *International Encyclopedia of Communications, Vol. 1* (New York: Oxford University Press, 1989), 450–54.

Review of *Nā Mele Hula: A Collection of Hawaiian Hula Chants. Volume 1*, by Nona Beamer. *Folk Music Journal* 5(5) (1989): 653–55.

Review of *Tongan Music*, by Richard Moyle. *Ethnomusicology* 33(2) (1989): 354–58.

'Art and Aesthetics', in Alan Howard and Robert Borofsky (eds), *Developments in Polynesian Ethnology* (Honolulu: University of Hawai'i Press, 1989), 211–40.

'A Report on the Fifth Festival of Pacific Arts'. *Pacific Arts Newsletter* 28 (1989): 1–3.

'Cook's Feathered Cape'. *Australian Natural History* 22(12) (1989): 548–50.

'Art, Aesthetics, and Social Structure', in Phyllis Herda, Jennifer Terrell and Niel Gunson (eds), *Tongan Culture and History: Papers from the 1st Tongan History Conference Held in Canberra 14–17 January 1987* (Canberra: Department of

Pacific and Southeast Asian History, Research School of Pacific Studies, Australian National University, 1990), 59–71.

'Musicology Plus (Or Minus) Anthropology Does Not Equal Ethnomusicology. Adrienne Kaeppler's Response to Richard Moyle's Response'. *Ethnomusicology* 34(2) (1990): 275–79.

'Hawaiian Art and the Communication of Social Values', in Dan Eban with Erik Cohen and Brenda Danet (eds), *Art as a Means of Communication in Pre-Literate Societies: The Proceedings of the Wright International Symposium on Primitive and Precolumbian Art, Jerusalem, 1985* (Jerusalem: The Israel Museum, 1990), 259–70.

'The Production and Reproduction of Social and Cultural Values in the Compositions of Queen Sālote of Tonga', in Marcia Herndon and Susanne Ziegler (eds), *Music, Gender, and Culture* (Wilhelmshaven: F. Noetzel, 1990), 191–219.

'Role of the Museum in a Changing Pacific: Development, Use, and Conservation of Collections'. *Pacific Arts* 1/2 (1990): 6.

'Me'etu'upaki and Tapaki, Paddle Dances of Tonga and Futuna, West Polynesia'. *Studia Musicologica Academiae Scientiarum Hungaricae* T. 33, fasc. 1/4 (1991): 347–57.

Guest edited with Anca Giurchescu and Lisbet Torp. *Yearbook for Traditional Music* 23 (1991).

With Anca Giurchescu and Lisbet Torp. 'Guest Editor's Preface'. *Yearbook for Traditional Music* 23 (1991): x.

'American Approaches to the Study of Dance'. *Yearbook for Traditional Music* 23 (1991): 11–21.

Review of *The Russian Discovery of Hawai'i: The Ethnographic and Historic Record*, by Glynn Barratt. *Man* 26(4) (1991): 750–51.

'Memory and Knowledge in the Production of Dance', in Susanne Küchler and Walter Melion (eds), *Images of Memory: On Remembering and Representation* (Washington, D.C.: Smithsonian Institution Press, 1991), 109–20.

Review of the exhibit *Traveling the Pacific*, by Phyllis Rabinow. *American Anthropologist* 93(1) (1991): 269–70.

'Samoan Material Culture in the 1980s'. *Pacific Arts* 3 (1991): 17–20.

'Taonga Maori and the Evolution of the Representation of the "Other" (Keynote Address)', in Mark Lindsay (ed.), *Taonga Maori Conference, New Zealand, 18–27 November 1990* (Wellington: Cultural Conservation Advisory Council, Department of Internal Affairs, 1991), 11–21.

'Epilogue: States of the Arts'. *Pacific Studies* 15(4) (1992): 311–18.

'*Ali'i* and *Maka'āinana*: The Representation of Hawaiians in Museums at Home and Abroad', in Ivan Karp, Christine Mullen Kreamer and Steven D. Lavine (eds), *Museums and Communities: The Politics of Public Culture* (Washington, D.C.: Smithsonian Institution Press, 1992), 458–75.

'The Use of Archival Film in an Ethnohistoric Study of Persistence and Change in Hawaiian Hula', in Alice Marshall Moyle (ed.), *Music and Dance of Aboriginal Australia and the South Pacific: The Effects of Documentation on the Living Tradition: Papers and Discussions of the Colloquium of the International Council for Traditional Music (ICTM) Held in Townsville, Queensland, Australia, 1988* (Oceania Monograph 41) (Sydney: University of Sydney, 1992), 110–29.

'Poetics and Politics of Tongan Laments and Eulogies'. *American Ethnologist* 20(3) (1993): 474–501.

Poetry in Motion: Studies of Tongan Dance. Nukuʻalofa: Vavaʻu Press, 1993.

With Christian Kaufmann and Douglas Newton. *L'art Océanien (Oceanic Art)*. Paris: Citadelles and Mazenod, 1993.

'La Polynésie et La Micronésie [Polynesia and Micronesia]', in Christian Kaufmann, Adrienne L. Kaeppler and Douglas Newton (eds), *L'art Océanien (Oceanic Art)* (Paris: Citadelles and Mazenod, 1993), 21–155.

Haʻa and Hula Pahu: Sacred Movements (Hula Pahu: Hawaiian Drum Dances, Vol. 1). Honolulu: Bishop Museum Press, 1993.

'Melody, Drone and Decoration: Underlying Structures and Surface Manifestations in Tongan Art and Society', in Janet Catherine Berlo and Lee Anne Wilson (eds), *Arts of Africa, Oceania, and the Americas: Selected Readings* (Englewood Cliffs: Prentice Hall, 1993), 36–47. [Reprinted from *Art in Society: Studies in Style, Culture and Aesthetics*, edited by Michael Greenhalgh and Vincent Megaw (London: Duckworth, 1978), 261–74.]

With assistance from Paula Rudall and Dorota Starzecka. 'Wood Analysis and Historical Contexts of Collecting Hawaiian Wooden Images: A Preliminary Report', in Philip J.C. Dark and Roger G. Rose (eds), *Artistic Heritage in a Changing Pacific* (Honolulu: University of Hawaiʻi Press, 1993), 41–46.

Review of *The Spirited Earth: Dance, Myth, and Ritual from South Asia to the South Pacific*, by Victoria Ginn. *Dance Research Journal* 25(1) (1993): 41.

'Rembrandt Peale's Hawaiian Ethnographic Still Life'. *The Hawaiian Journal of History* 27 (1993): 227–38.

'Festivals Past, Present and Future', in David Arnell and Lisette Wolk (eds), *Visions of the Pacific* (Rarotonga: Ministry of Cultural Development, Cook Islands, South Pacific, 1993), 130–31.

Review of *Tikopia Songs: Poetic and Musical Art of a Polynesian People of the Solomon Islands*, by Raymond Firth and Mervyn McLean. *Man* 29(3) (1994): 720–21.

'Paradise Regained: The Role of Pacific Museums in Forging National Identity', in Flora E.S. Kaplan (ed.), *Museums and the Making of 'Ourselves': The Role of Objects in National Identity* (London: Leicester University Press, 1994), 19–44.

'Music, Metaphor, and Misunderstanding'. *Ethnomusicology* 38(3) (1994): 457–73.

Review of *The Apotheosis of Captain Cook: European Mythmaking in the Pacific*, by Gananath Obeyesekere, and *Imagining the Pacific: In the Wake of the Cook Voyages*, by Bernard Smith. *Eighteenth-Century Studies* 28(1) (1994): 158–61.

'Theoretical and Methodological Considerations in the Study of Dance in Omani Folklore', in Issam El-Mallah (ed.), *The Complete Documents of the International Symposium on the Traditional Music in Oman: October 6–16, 1985, Part 2* (Wilhelmshaven: F. Noetzel and Heinrichshofen, 1994), 37–66.

'Dance and Dress as Sociopolitical Discourse', in Irene Loutzaki (ed.), *Study Group on Ethnochoreology, 17th Symposium, Nafplion, Greece, 2–10 July 1992, Proceedings, Dance and Its Socio-Political Aspects, Dance and Costume* (Nafplion: Peloponnesian Folklore Foundation, 1994), 45–52.

'Die ethnographischen Sammlungen der Forsters aus dem Südpazifik: Klassische Empirie im Dienste der modernen Ethnologie [The Forster Ethnographic Collections from the South Pacific: Science in the Service of Ethnography]', in Claus-Volker Klenke, Jörn Garber and Dieter Heintze (eds), *Georg Forster in interdisziplinärer Perspektive: Beiträge des Internationalen Georg Forster – Symposions in Kassel, 1. bis 4. April 1993* [Georg Forster in Interdisciplinary Perspective: Contributions to the International Georg Forster Symposium in Kassel, 1–4 April 1993] (Berlin: Akademie Verlag, 1994), 59–75.

With Christian Kaufmann and Douglas Newton. *Ozeanien: Kunst und Kultur* [Oceania: Art and Culture]. Freiburg: Herder, 1994. [German translation of *L'art Océanien (Oceanic Art)*. Paris: Citadelles and Mazenod, 1993.]

'Polynesien und Mikronesien', in Christian Kaufmann, Adrienne L. Kaeppler and Douglas Newton (eds), *Ozeanien: Kunst und Kultur* [Oceania: Art and Culture] (Freiburg: Herder, 1994), 21–151. [German translation of 'La Polynésie et La Micronésie (Polynesia and Micronesia)', in Christian Kaufmann, Adrienne L. Kaeppler and Douglas Newton (eds), *L'art Océanien (Oceanic Art)* (Paris: Citadelles and Mazenod, 1993), 21–155.]

'Poetics and Politics of Tongan Barkcloth', in Dirk A.M. Smidt, Pieter ter Keurs and Albert Trouwborst (eds), *Pacific Material Culture: Essays in Honour of Dr. Simon Kooijman on the Occasion of his 80th Birthday* (Leiden: Rijksmuseum voor Volkenkunde, 1995), 101–21.

'They Seldom Dance on Star-Trek: A Cautionary Tale for the Study of Dance and Ritual', in Grażyna Dąbrowska and Ludwik Bielawski (eds), *Dance Ritual and Music: Proceedings of the 18th Symposium of the Study Group on Ethnochoreology, The International Council for Traditional Music (ICTM), August 9–18, 1994, in Skierniewice, Poland* (Warsaw: Polish Society for Ethnochoreology, Institute of Art, Polish Academy of Sciences, 1995), 105–10.

'The Paradise Theme in Modern Tongan Music', in Linda Barwick, Allan Marett and Guy Tunstill (eds), *The Essence of Singing and the Substance of Song: Recent Responses to the Aboriginal Performing Arts and Other Essays in Honour of Catherine Ellis* (Oceania Monograph 46) (Sydney: University of Sydney, 1995), 159–83.

'Visible and Invisible in Hawaiian Dance', in Brenda Farnell (ed.), *Human Action Signs in Cultural Context: The Visible and the Invisible in Movement and Dance* (Metuchen: The Scarecrow Press, 1995), 31–43.

'Eduard Arning's Hawaiian Collections'. *The Hawaiian Journal of History* 29 (1995): 179–83.

'The Look of Music, the Sound of Dance: Music as a Visual Art'. *Visual Anthropology* 8(2–4) (1996): 133–53.

'The Great Adze in the Smithsonian Institution: History and Provenance'. *Rapa Nui Journal* 10(4) (1996): 89–92.

'Tonga', in Jane Turner (ed.), *The Dictionary of Art, Vol. 31* (New York: Grove's Dictionaries Inc., 1996), 142–44.

'The Investiture of 'Ulukālala VII: A Moment in History', in Janet Davidson, Geoffrey Irwin, Foss Leach, Andrew Pawley and Dorothy Brown (eds), *Oceanic Culture History: Essays in Honour of Roger Green* (Dunedin: New Zealand Journal of Archaeology, 1996), 475–89.

'Dance', in David Levinson and Melvin Ember (eds), *Encyclopedia of Cultural Anthropology, Vol. 1* (New York: Henry Holt and Company, 1996), 309–13.

With Christian Kaufmann and Douglas Newton. *Oceanic Art*. Translated by Nora Scott and Sabine Bouladon with the collaboration of Fiona Leibrick. New York: Harry N. Abrams, 1997. [English translation of *L'art Océanien (Oceanic Art)*. Paris: Citadelles and Mazenod, 1993.]

'Polynesia and Micronesia', in Christian Kaufmann, Adrienne L. Kaeppler and Douglas Newton (eds) and translated by Nora Scott and Sabine Bouladon with the collaboration of Fiona Leibrick, *Oceanic Art* (New York: Harry N. Abrams, 1997), 21–155. [English translation of 'La Polynésie et La Micronésie (Polynesia and Micronesia)', in Christian Kaufmann, Adrienne L. Kaeppler and Douglas Newton (eds), *L'art Océanien (Oceanic Art)* (Paris: Citadelles and Mazenod, 1993), 21–155.]

'La vie sociale d'un masque des îles Mortlock (The Social Life of a Mortlock Island Mask)', in Annick Notter (ed.), *La découverte du paradis: Océanie: Curieux, navigateurs et savants* (Lille: Association des conservateurs des musées du Nord-Pas-de-Calais; Paris: Somogy Éditions d'art, 1997), 197–201.

'Tongan Kava Bowls as Centerpieces for Performance'. *Baessler-Archiv* 45 (1997): 47–61.

'Reading V: Reprint of Structured Movement Systems in Tonga, 1985', in Drid Williams (ed.), *Anthropology and Human Movement: The Study of Dances* (Lanham: The Scarecrow Press, 1997), 87–122. [Reprinted from *Society and the Dance: The Social Anthropology of Process and Performance*, edited by Paul Spencer (Cambridge: Cambridge University Press, 1985), 92–118.]

'From the Temple to the Festival Stage: Pacific Festivals as Modern Rituals', in Crusader Hillis and Urszula Dawkins (eds), *New Dance from Old Cultures: Green Mill Papers 1996* (Braddon: Ausdance, 1997), 15–20.

Edited with Amy Henderson. *Exhibiting Dilemmas: Issues of Representation at the Smithsonian*. Washington, D.C.: Smithsonian Institution Press, 1997.

With Amy Henderson. 'Introduction', in Amy Henderson and Adrienne L. Kaeppler (eds), *Exhibiting Dilemmas: Issues of Representation at the Smithsonian* (Washington, D.C.: Smithsonian Institution Press, 1997), 1–11.

'The Göttingen Collection in an International Context/Die Göttinger Sammlung im Internationalen Kontext', in Brigitta Hauser-Schäublin and Gundolf Krüger (eds), *James Cook: Gifts and Treasures from the South Seas – The Cook/Forster Collection, Göttingen/James Cook: Gaben und Schätze aus der Südsee – Die Göttinger Sammlung Cook/Forster* (Munich: Prestel, 1998), 86–93.

'Tonga – Entry into Complex Hierarchies/Tonga – Eintritt in Komplexe Hierarchien', in Brigitta Hauser-Schäublin and Gundolf Krüger (eds), *James Cook: Gifts and Treasures from the South Seas – The Cook/Forster Collection, Göttingen/James Cook: Gaben und Schätze aus der Südsee – Die Göttinger Sammlung Cook/Forster* (Munich: Prestel, 1998), 195–220.

'Hawai'i – Ritual Encounters/Hawai'i – Die Begegnung als Ritus', in Brigitta Hauser-Schäublin and Gundolf Krüger (eds), *James Cook: Gifts and Treasures from the South Seas – The Cook/Forster Collection, Göttingen/James Cook: Gaben und Schätze aus der Südsee – Die Göttinger Sammlung Cook/Forster* (Munich: Prestel, 1998), 234–48.

'Airplanes and Saxophones: Post-War Images in the Visual and Performing Arts', in Deryck Scarr, Niel Gunson and Jennifer Terrell (eds), *Echoes of Pacific War: Papers from the 7th Tongan History Conference Held in Canberra in January 1997* (Canberra: Target Oceania, 1998), 38–63.

Edited with J.W. Love. *The Garland Encyclopedia of World Music, Vol. 9: Australia and the Pacific Islands*. New York: Garland Publishing, 1998. [Kaeppler contributed to many of the articles in this volume.]

'Dance and the Concept of Style', in Theresa Buckland and Georgiana Gore (eds), *Dance, Style, Youth, Identities: 19th Symposium of the Study Group on Ethnochoreology, 1996 Proceedings* (Strážnice: Institute of Folk Culture, Strážnice, Czech Republic, 1998), 45–56.

Review of *In Oceania: Visions, Artifacts, Histories*, by Nicholas Thomas. *The Journal of the Polynesian Society* 107(4) (1998): 432–33.

'La Danse Selon Une Perspective Anthropologique'. *Nouvelles de Danse* 34–35 (1998): 24–46. [French translation of 'Dance in Anthropological Perspective'. *Annual Review of Anthropology* 7 (1978): 31–49.]

From the Stone Age to the Space Age in 200 Years: Tongan Art and Society on the Eve of the Millennium (Exhibition Catalogue). Nuku'alofa: Tongan National Museum in conjunction with Vava'u Press, 1999.

'Tonga and Samoa', in Douglas Newton (ed.), *Arts of the South Seas: Island Southeast Asia, Melanesia, Polynesia, Micronesia – The Collections of the Musée Barbier-Mueller* (Munich: Prestel, 1999), 306–13.

'*Kie Hingoa*: Mats of Power, Rank, Prestige and History', *The Journal of the Polynesian Society* 108(2) (1999): 168–232.

'The Mystique of Fieldwork', in Theresa J. Buckland (ed.), *Dance in the Field: Theory, Methods and Issues in Dance Ethnography* (Basingstoke: Macmillan, 1999), 13–25.

Review of *The Halla Huhm Dance Collection: An Inventory and Finding Aid*, by Judy Van Zile. *Dance Research: The Journal of the Society for Dance Research* 18(1) (2000): 103–7.

Sculpture de Nukuoro and Sculpture d'Hawaii. Paris: Musée de quai Branly, 2000.

'Material Matters – in Tonga'. *The Smithsonian Material Culture Forum's Grapevine* 35 (2000): 1–3.

Review of *Maori Art and Culture, 2ⁿᵈ Edition*, by D.C. Starzecka. *The Journal of the Polynesian Society* 109(2) (2000): 209–11.

Review of *Queen Sālote of Tonga: The Story of an Era 1900–1965*, by Elizabeth Wood-Ellem. *The Journal of the Polynesian Society* 109(2) (2000): 213–15.

'Dance Ethnology and the Anthropology of Dance'. *Dance Research Journal* 32(1) (2000): 116–25.

'The Feather Cape Enigma: English or American Indian?' *Museum Anthropology* 23(3) (2000): 97–103.

'Ethnochoreology', in Stanley Sadie (ed.), *The New Grove Dictionary of Music and Musicians (2ⁿᵈ Edition)* (London: Macmillan, 2001). http://www.oxfordmusiconline.com/grovemusic/view/10.1093/gmo/9781561592630.001.0001/omo-9781561592630-e-0000040752.

With Barbara B. Smith, Osamu Yamaguti, Junko Konishi, Mary E. Lawson Burke, Michael Clement and Cynthia B. Sajnovsky. 'Micronesia', in Stanley Sadie (ed.), *The New Grove Dictionary of Music and Musicians (2ⁿᵈ Edition)* (London: Macmillan, 2001). http://www.oxfordmusiconline.com/grovemusic/view/10.1093/gmo/9781561592630.001.0001/omo-9781561592630-e-0000018608.

With Barbara B. Smith, Kevin Salisbury, Mervyn McLean, Amy Kuʻuleialoha Stillman, Jane Freeman Moulin, Richard M. Moyle, Thomas Allan and Dieter Christensen. 'Polynesia', in Stanley Sadie (ed.), *The New Grove Dictionary of Music and Musicians (2ⁿᵈ Edition)* (London: Macmillan, 2001). http://www.oxfordmusiconline.com/grovemusic/view/10.1093/gmo/9781561592630.001.0001/omo-9781561592630-e-0000041191.

With Barbara B. Smith, Artur Simon, Don Niles, Hugo Zemp, Jane Mink Rossen, Mervyn McLean, Peter Crowe, Derek A. Rawcliffe, Jean-Michel Beaudet and Kaye Glamuzina. 'Melanesia', in Stanley Sadie (ed.), *The New Grove Dictionary of Music and Musicians (2ⁿᵈ Edition)* (London: Macmillan, 2001). http://www.oxfordmusiconline.com/grovemusic/view/10.1093/gmo/9781561592630.001.0001/omo-9781561592630-e-0000041208.

(Guest Editor) *Yearbook for Traditional Music* 33 (2001).

'Guest Editor's Preface'. *Yearbook for Traditional Music* 33 (2001): xiii.

'Dance and the Concept of Style'. *Yearbook for Traditional Music* 33 (2001): 49–63.

'Encounters with Greatness: Collecting Hawaiian Monarchs and Aristocrats'. *History of Photography* 25(3) (2001): 259–68.

'Rapa Nui Art and Aesthetics', in Eric Kjellgren (ed.), *Splendid Isolation: Art of Easter Island* (Exhibition Catalogue) (New York: Metropolitan Museum of Art, 2001), 32–41.

'Accordions in Tahiti – An Enigma', in Helen Reeves Lawrence (ed.), *Traditionalism and Modernity in the Music and Dance of Oceania: Essays in Honour of Barbara B. Smith* (Oceania Monograph 52) (Sydney: University of Sydney, 2001), 45–66.

With Helen Reeves Lawrence and assistance from Jane Freeman Moulin. 'Appendix: Barbara Barnard Smith: A Sketch of Her Professional Life and Work', in Helen Reeves Lawrence (ed.), *Traditionalism and Modernity in the Music and Dance of Oceania: Essays in Honour of Barbara B. Smith* (Oceania Monograph 52) (Sydney: University of Sydney, 2001), 251–53.

'Tattooed Beauty: A Pacific Case Study'. *AnthroNotes* 22(2) (2001): 9–13.

'At the Pacific Festivals of Art: Revivals, Inventions, and Cultural Identity', in Elsie Ivancich Dunin and Tvrtko Zebec (eds), *Proceedings. 21st Symposium of the International Council for Traditional Music (ICTM) Study Group on Ethnochoreology, 2000, Korčula, Sword Dances and Related Calendrical Dance Events, Revival: Reconstruction, Revitalization* (Zagreb: Institute of Ethnology and Folklore Research, 2001), 192–96.

'Festivals of Pacific Arts: Venues for Rituals of Identity'. *Pacific Arts* 25 (2002): 5–19.

Review of *Hawaiki, Ancestral Polynesia: An Essay in Historical Anthropology*, by Patrick Vinton Kirch and Roger C. Green. *Journal of Anthropological Research* 58(4) (2002): 565–66.

'The Structure of Tongan Barkcloth Design: Imagery, Metaphor and Allusion', in Anita Herle, Nick Stanley, Karen Stevenson and Robert L. Welsch (eds), *Pacific Art: Persistence, Change and Meaning* (Adelaide: Crawford House Publishing, 2002), 291–308.

'The Tahitian Fête of 1937 Revisited in 1979', in Gabriele Berlin and Artur Simon (eds), *Music Archiving in the World: Papers Presented at the Conference on the Occasion of the 100th Anniversary of the Berlin Phonogramm-Archiv* (Berlin: VWB, 2002), 91–100.

'Hawaiian Art: From Sacred Symbol to Tourist Icon to Ethnic Identity Marker', in William L. Merrill and Ives Goddard (eds), *Anthropology, History, and American Indians: Essays in Honor of William Curtis Sturtevant* (Washington, D.C.: Smithsonian Institution Press, 2002), 147–59.

'Metafora e messaggio nelle arti dello spettacolo (Asia, il Pacifico e Broadway) [Metaphor and Message in the Performing Arts (Asia, the Pacific and Broadway)]', in Jean-Jacques Nattiez (ed.), *Enciclopedia della Musica, Vol. 3: Musica e Culture* [Encyclopedia of Music, Vol. 3: Music and Culture] (Turin: Einaudi, 2003), 925–43.

'Sculptures of Barkcloth and Wood from Rapa Nui: Symbolic Continuities and Polynesian Affinities'. *RES: Anthropology and Aesthetics* 44 (2003): 10–69.

'An Introduction to Dance Aesthetics'. *Yearbook for Traditional Music* 35 (2003): 153–62.

'La danza y el concepto de estilo'. *Desacatos* 12 (2003): 93–104. [Spanish translation of 'Dance and the Concept of Style'. *Yearbook for Traditional Music* 33 (2001): 49–63.]

'A Royal Wedding in the Kingdom of Tonga, June 2003'. *Anthropolog: Newsletter of the Department of Anthropology, National Museum of Natural History* (2003): 1–4.

'Recycling Tradition: A Hawaiian Case Study'. *Dance Chronicle* 27(3) (2004): 293–311.

'Hawaiian Treasures at the Smithsonian Institution'. *AnthroNotes* 25(2) (2004): 9–10.

'Appreciation and Challenge: Remarks for the Launch of the Oldman Catalogues, 3 November 2004'. *The Journal of the Polynesian Society* 113(4) (2004): 325–29.

'Queen Sālote's Poetry as Works of Art, History, Politics, and Culture', in Elizabeth Wood-Ellem (ed.) and translated by Melenaite Taumoefolau, *Songs & Poems of Queen Sālote* (Nukuʻalofa: Vavaʻu Press, 2004), 26–65.

'Notation, Texts, Translation and Interpretation', in Elizabeth Wood-Ellem (ed.), and translated by Melenaite Taumoefolau, *Songs & Poems of Queen Sālote* (Nukuʻalofa: Vavaʻu Press, 2004), 342–45.

'Ethnographic Results of Cook's Voyages', in John Robson (ed.), *The Captain Cook Encyclopaedia* (Auckland: Random House, 2004), 93–97.

'Report from the ICTM Study Group on Ethnochoreology: Roundtable at the ICTM 37th World Conference Report'. *Bulletin of the International Council for Traditional Music (ICTM)* 104 (2004): 45–46.

'Shielding in Micronesia and Polynesia: A Different Approach to Warfare', in Harry Beran and Barry Craig (eds), *Shields of Melanesia* (Honolulu: University of Hawaiʻi Press; Sydney: Oceanic Art Society, 2005), 259–61.

'Two Polynesian Repatriation Enigmas at the Smithsonian Institution'. *Journal of Museum Ethnography* 17 (2005): 152–62.

'Polynesian Religions: Mythic Themes', in Lindsay Jones (ed.), *Encyclopedia of Religion (2nd Edition), Vol. 11* (Detroit: Macmillan Reference USA, 2005), 7312–15.

'Animal Designs on Samoan *Siapo* and Other Thoughts on West Polynesian Barkcloth Design'. *The Journal of the Polynesian Society* 114(3) (2005): 197–225.

'The Tongan *Lakalaka* as Sociopolitical Discourse', in Ian Campbell and Eve Coxon (eds), *Polynesian Paradox: Essays in Honour of Professor 'I. Futa Helu* (Suva: Institute of Pacific Studies, University of the South Pacific, 2005), 154–67.

'Méthode et Théorie Pour L'analyse Structurale de la Danse Avec une Analyse de la Danse des îles Tonga', in Andrée Grau and Georgiana Wierre-Gore (eds), *Anthropologie de la Danse: Genèse et Construction d'une Discipline* [Anthropology of Dance: Genesis and Construction of a Discipline] (Pantin: Centre National de la Danse, 2005), 189–220. [French translation of 'Method and Theory in Analyzing Dance Structure with an Analysis of Tongan Dance'. *Ethnomusicology* 16(2) (1972): 173–217.]

'An Introduction to Aesthetics (Keynote Address)', in Elsie Ivancich Dunin, Anne von Bibra Wharton and László Felföldi (eds), *Dance and Society: Dancer as a Cultural Performer: Re-Appraising Our Past, Moving into the Future: 40th Anniversary of Study Group on Ethnochoreology of International Council for Traditional Music (ICTM): 22nd Symposium of the ICTM Study Group on Ethnochoreology, Szeged, Hungary, 2002* (Budapest: Akadémiai Kiadó and European Folklore Institute, 2005), 207–15.

'Dance, Dancing and Discourse', in Mohd Anis Md Nor and Revathi Murugappan (eds), *Global and Local Dance in Performance* (Kuala Lumpur: Cultural Centre, University of Malaya and Ministry of Culture, Arts and Heritage of Malaysia, 2005), 293–302.

'Art and Aesthetics in Tonga (South Pacific): An Integral Association of Visual and Performing Arts', in Michèle Coquet, Brigitte Derlon and Monique Jeudy-Ballini (eds), *Les Cultures à L'oeuvre, Rencontres en art* [Cultures at Work, Encounters in Art] (Paris: Maison des sciences de l'homme, 2005), 249–70.

'Ballet, Hula, and "Cats": Dance as a Discourse on Globalization', in Karen Rose Cann (ed.), *Dance/Diversity/Dialogue: Bridging Communities and Cultures: World Dance Alliance Global Assembly 2006 Proceedings* (Toronto: World Dance Alliance Global Assembly, 2006), 251–59.

'Tonga', in Sean Williams (ed.), *The Ethnomusicologists' Cookbook: Complete Meals from Around the World* (New York: Routledge, 2006), 216–19.

'Dances and Dancing in Tonga: Anthropological and Historical Discourses', in Theresa Buckland (ed.), *Dancing from Past to Present: Nation, Culture, Identities* (Madison: The University of Wisconsin Press, 2006), 25–51.

'La Danse Polynésienne, Dialogue Interculturel [Polynesian Dance, Intercultural Dialogue]', in Yves Le Fur (ed.), *D'Un Regard L'Autre: Histoire des regards européens sur l'Afrique, l'Amérique et l'Océanie* [Looking at Each Other: History of European Views of Africa, America and Oceania] (Exhibition Catalogue) (Paris: Musée du quai Branly, 2006), 116–21.

'The Pacific Islands', in Stephanie Burridge (ed.), *Shifting Sands: Dance in Asia and the Pacific: In Honour of Carl Wolz Founder of the World Dance Alliance* (Braddon: Ausdance, 2006), 77–81.

'Life in the Pacific in the 1700s and Today', in Stephen Little and Peter Ruthenberg (eds), *Life in the Pacific of the 1700s: The Cook/Forster Collection of the Georg August University of Göttingen, Vol. 2: European Research, Traditions, and Perspectives* (Exhibition Catalogue) (Honolulu: Honolulu Academy of Arts, 2006), 9–19.

'The Göttingen Collection: A Cook-Voyage Treasure', in Stephen Little and Peter Ruthenberg (eds), *Life in the Pacific of the 1700s: The Cook/Forster Collection of the Georg August University of Göttingen, Vol. 2: European Research, Traditions, and Perspectives* (Exhibition Catalogue) (Honolulu: Honolulu Academy of Arts, 2006), 49–53.

'Dance'. *Journal for the Anthropological Study of Human Movement* 14(2) (2006): 99–105.

'Containers of Divinity'. *The Journal of the Polynesian Society* 116(2) (2007): 97–130.

Edited with Elsie Ivancich Dunin. *Dance Structures: Perspectives on the Analysis of Human Movement*. Budapest: Akadémiai Kiadó, 2007.

'Method and Theory in Analyzing Dance Structure with an Analysis of Tongan Dance', in Adrienne L. Kaeppler and Elsie Ivancich Dunin (eds), *Dance Structures: Perspectives on the Analysis of Human Movement* (Budapest: Akadémiai Kiadó, 2007), 53–102.

'Me'a lalanga and the Category *Koloa*: Intertwining Value and History in Tonga', in Atholl Anderson, Kaye Green and Foss Leach (eds), *Vastly Ingenious: The Archaeology of Pacific Material Culture: In Honour of Janet M. Davidson* (Dunedin: Otago University Press, 2007), 145–54.

'*Heliaki*, Metaphor, and Allusion: The Art and Aesthetics of *Ko e 'Otua mo Tonga ko hoku Tofia*', in Elizabeth Wood-Ellem (ed.), *Tonga and the Tongans: Heritage and Identity* (Alphington: Tonga Research Association, 2007), 65–74.

With Jo Anne Van Tilburg, Marshall Weisler, Claudio Cristino and Angela Spitzer. 'Petrographic Analysis of Thin-Sections of Samples from Two Monolithic Statues (*Moai*), Rapa Nui (Easter Island)'. *The Journal of the Polynesian Society* 117(3) (2008): 297–300.

The Pacific Arts of Polynesia & Micronesia. Oxford: Oxford University Press, 2008.

'One Plus One Equals Three [or More]: Dance Diversity as Intercultural Dialogues in the Pacific Islands', in Urmimala Sarkar Munsi (ed.), *Dance: Transcending Borders* (New Delhi: Tulika Books, 2008), 101–15.

'Dance', in Wolfgang Donsbach (ed.), *The International Encyclopedia of Communication, Vol. 3* (Malden: Wiley-Blackwell, 2008), 1165–66.

'Exchange Patterns in Goods and Spouses: Fiji, Tonga and Samoa', in Paul D'Arcy (ed.), *Peoples of the Pacific: The History of Oceania to 1870* (Aldershot: Ashgate, 2008), 253–59. [Reprinted from *Mankind* 11(3) (1978): 246–52.]

Edited with Markus Schindlbeck and Gisela E. Speidel. *Old Hawai'i: An Ethnography of Hawai'i in the 1880s Based on the Research and Collections of Eduard Arning in the Ethnologisches Museum, Berlin*. Berlin: Ethnologisches Museum Berlin, 2008.

'Preface', in Adrienne L. Kaeppler, Markus Schindlbeck and Gisela E. Speidel (eds), *Old Hawai'i: An Ethnography of Hawai'i in the 1880s Based on the Research and Collections of Eduard Arning in the Ethnologisches Museum, Berlin* (Berlin: Ethnologisches Museum Berlin, 2008), 9–11.

'Hawaiian Ethnography and the Study of Hawaiian Collections', in Adrienne L. Kaeppler, Markus Schindlbeck and Gisela E. Speidel (eds), *Old Hawai'i: An Ethnography of Hawai'i in the 1880s Based on the Research and Collections of Eduard Arning in the Ethnologisches Museum, Berlin* (Berlin: Ethnologisches Museum Berlin, 2008), 33–42.

'El arte Rapa Nui en el contexto de Polinesia y Oceanía [Rapa Nui Art in the Context of Polynesia and Oceania]', *Kuhane Rapa Nui, en las Islas del Pacífico* (Exhibition Catalogue) (Santiago: Fundación Centro Cultural Palacio La Moneda, 2009), 14–19.

'Two Unusual Wooden Figures from the Marquesas Islands', in Elfriede Hermann, Karin Klenke and Michael Dickhardt (eds), *Form, Macht, Differenz: Motive und Felder ethnologischen Forschens* [Form, Power, Difference: Motives and Fields of Ethnographic Research] (Göttingen: Universitätsverlag Göttingen, 2009), 141–48.

'Lakalaka and Mak'yong: A Story of Two Masterpieces (Keynote Address)', in Mohd Anis Md Nor, Elsie Ivancich Dunin and Anne von Bibra Wharton (eds), *Transmitting Dance as Cultural Heritage & Dance and Religion: Proceedings of the 25th Symposium of the International Council for Traditional Music (ICTM) Study Group on Ethnochoreology* (Kuala Lumpur: Cultural Centre, University of Malaya and Ministry of Information, Communication and Culture of Malaysia, 2009), 1–7.

(Head Curator) *James Cook and the Exploration of the Pacific* (Exhibition Catalogue). London: Thames & Hudson, 2009.

'Preface', in Adrienne L. Kaeppler (ed.), *James Cook and the Exploration of the Pacific* (Exhibition Catalogue) (London: Thames & Hudson, 2009), 8.

'Captain Cook's Three Voyages of Enlightenment', in Adrienne L. Kaeppler (ed.), *James Cook and the Exploration of the Pacific* (Exhibition Catalogue) (London: Thames & Hudson, 2009), 18–23.

'Enlightened Ethnographic Collections', in Adrienne L. Kaeppler (ed.), *James Cook and the Exploration of the Pacific* (Exhibition Catalogue) (London: Thames & Hudson, 2009, 55–60).

'Enlightened Encounters in the Unknown Pacific', in Adrienne L. Kaeppler (ed.), *James Cook and the Exploration of the Pacific* (Exhibition Catalogue) (London: Thames & Hudson, 2009), 88–92.

'"To Attempt Some New Discoveries in that Vast Unknown Tract": Rediscovering the Forster Collections from Cook's Second Pacific Voyage', in Michelle Hetherington and Howard Morphy (eds), *Discovering Cook's Collections* (Canberra: National Museum of Australia Press, 2009), 49–65.

(Text and Catalogue Writer) *Hawaiian Featherwork: Catalogue Raisonné of pre-1900 Feathered-God Images, Cloaks, Capes, Helmets* (Exhibition Catalogue), edited by Willem de Rooij and Benjamin Meyer-Krahmer. Düsseldorf: Feymedia Verlagsgesellschaft mbH, 2010.

Polynesia: The Mark and Carolyn Blackburn Collection of Polynesian Art. Honolulu: University of Hawai'i Press, 2010.

'Interpreting Ritual as Performance and Theory (Association for Social Anthropology in Oceania 2010 Distinguished Lecture)'. *Oceania* 80(3) (2010): 263–71.

'Introduction to the Dress of the Pacific Islands', in Margaret Maynard (ed.), *Berg Encyclopedia of World Dress and Fashion, Vol. 7: Australia, New Zealand, and the Pacific Islands* (Oxford: Berg, 2010), 367–74.

'The Beholder's Share: Viewing Music and Dance in a Globalized World (Charles Seeger Lecture Presented at the 51st Annual Meeting of the Society for Ethnomusicology, 2006, Honolulu)'. *Ethnomusicology* 54(2) (2010): 185–201.

Holophusicon: The Leverian Museum: An Eighteenth-Century English Institution of Science, Curiosity, and Art. Altenstadt: ZKF Publishers, 2011.

'Tau'a'alo: Paddling Songs as Cultural Metaphor', in Birgit Abels (ed.), *Austronesian Soundscapes: Performing Arts in Oceania and Southeast Asia* (Amsterdam: Amsterdam University Press, 2011), 223–40.

'Contributions of Tupou II to Tongan Art and Society', in Tangikina Moimoi Steen and Nancy L. Drescher (eds), *Tonga – Land, Sea and People* (Nuku'alofa: Tonga Research Association, 2011), 68–77.

Edited with Barbara Sparti, Judy Van Zile, Elsie Ivancich Dunin and Nancy G. Heller. *Imaging Dance: Visual Representations of Dancers and Dancing.* Hildesheim: Georg Olms Verlag, 2011.

'The Hands and Arms Tell the Story: Movement through Time in Eighteenth-Century Dance Depictions from Polynesia', in Barbara Sparti, Judy Van Zile, Elsie Ivancich Dunin, Nancy G. Heller and Adrienne L. Kaeppler (eds), *Imaging Dance: Visual Representations of Dancers and Dancing* (Hildesheim: Georg Olms Verlag, 2011), 87–102.

Lakalaka: A Tongan Masterpiece of Performing Arts. Nuku'alofa: Vava'u Press, 2012.

'Playing with Fire: Contemporizing *Pele*, the Volcano Goddess', in Elsie Ivancich Dunin, Daniela Stavělová and Dorota Gremlicová (eds), *Dance, Gender, and Meanings: Contemporizing Traditional Dance: Proceedings of the 26th Symposium of the International Council for Traditional Music (ICTM) Study Group on Ethnochoreology 2010: Třešť, Czech Republic* (Prague: Academy of Performing

Arts in Prague and Institute of Ethnology of the Academy of Sciences, 2012), 132–38.

'Dynamic Dialogues: Writing Dance as Tradition, Contemporanity, and Fusion', in Mohd Anis Md Nor (ed.), *Dancing Mosaic: Issues on Dance Hybridity* (Kuala Lumpur: Cultural Centre, University of Malaya and National Department for Culture and Arts, Ministry of Information, Communication and Culture of Malaysia, 2012), 17–26.

'Ritual, Theatre, and Spectacle: Exploring the Rituals of Saint George's Day', in Elsie Ivancich Dunin, Anca Giurchescu and Csilla Könczei (eds), *From Field to Text & Dance and Space: Proceedings for the 24th Symposium of the International Council for Traditional Music (ICTM) Study Group on Ethnochoreology* (Cluj-Napoca: The Romanian Institute for Research on National Minorities, 2012), 139–42.

'Una introducción a la estética de la danza', in Silvia Citro and Patricia Aschieri (eds), *Cuerpos En Movimiento: Antropología de y desde las danzas* [Moving Bodies: Anthropology of and from Dances] (Buenos Aires: Editorial Biblos, 2012), 65–73. [Spanish translation of 'An Introduction to Dance Aesthetics'. *Yearbook for Traditional Music* 35 (2003): 153–62.]

'New Observations on Nukuoro Wood Sculptures: Lost, Found, Dormant and Dubious', in Christian Kaufmann and Oliver Wick (eds), *Nukuoro: Sculptures from Micronesia* (Riehen: Fondation Beyeler; Munich: Hirmer, 2013), 152–65.

'Music and Dance as Export and Import: A Case Study of Japan in Europe, and Hawai'i in Japan'. *Yearbook for Traditional Music* 45 (2013): 214–30.

'Chanting Grief, Dancing Memories: Objectifying Hawaiian Laments'. *Humanities Research* 19(3) (2013): 71–81.

'Power, Prayer and Plumage'. *Hali: The International Magazine of Antique Carpet and Textile Art* 175 (2013): 90–99.

'Eduard Arning: Hawai'is ethnografischer Fotograf/Eduard Arning: Ethnographic Photographer of Hawai'i', in Wulf Köpke and Bernd Schmelz (eds), *Blick ins Paradies: Historische Fotografien aus Polynesien* [A Glimpse into Paradise: Historical Photographs of Polynesia] (Hamburg: Museum für Völkerkunde Hamburg, 2014), 87–103.

'Hawaiian Stone Pestles', 'Hawaiian Octopus Lures', 'Hawaiian Fishhook', 'Maori Canoe Prow' and 'Marshall Islands Stick Navigation Chart', in Cara McCarty and Matilda McQuaid (eds), *Tools: Extending Our Reach* (Exhibition Catalogue) (New York: Cooper Hewitt, 2014), 26–28, 48, 52–53, 110, 150–51.

'Recycling Tradition in the Arts of Polynesia', in Anne E. Allen with Deborah B. Waite (eds), *Repositioning Pacific Arts: Artists, Objects, Histories: Proceedings of the VII International Symposium of the Pacific Arts Association, Christchurch, New Zealand* (Canon Pyon: Sean Kingston, 2014), 5–16.

'The Edinburgh Hawaiian Feathered Cloak and Museum Guessalogs'. *The Hawaiian Journal of History* 48 (2014): 171–74.

'Sister Malia Tuʻifua, Descendant of Chiefs, Daughter of God'. *The Journal of the Polynesian Society* 123(2) (2014): 169–83.

With Michele Austin-Dennehy. 'Smithsonian Collections', in Jan Salick, Katie Konchar and Mark Nesbitt (eds), *Curating Biocultural Collections: A Handbook* (Surrey: Royal Botanic Gardens, Kew, 2014), 22–25.

'From Hawaiian Temples and Chiefly Courts to Festival Stages in Japan', in Elsie Ivancich Dunin and Catherine E. Foley (eds), *Dance, Place, Festival: 27th Symposium of the International Council for Traditional Music (ICTM) Study Group on Ethnochoreology 2012* (Limerick: The Irish World Academy of Music and Dance, University of Limerick, 2014), 90–93.

'Two Hawaiian Dancers and their Daughters'. *The Journal of the Polynesian Society* 124(2) (2015): 189–207.

'Lost Objects, Questionable Localities, and Other Cook Voyage Enigmas'. *Pacific Arts* NS 14(1–2) (2015): 78–84.

'From the South Seas to the World (via London)', in Jeremy Coote (ed.), *Cook-Voyage Collections of 'Artificial Curiosities' in Britain and Ireland, 1771–2015* (Museum Ethnographers Group Occasional Paper, No. 5) (Oxford: Museum Ethnographers Group, 2015), 256–98.

'Gifting, Trading, Selling, Buying: Following Northwest Coast Treasures Acquired on Cook's Third Voyage to Collections Around the World', in James K. Barnett and David L. Nicandri (eds), *Arctic Ambitions: Captain Cook and the Northwest Passage* (Seattle: University of Washington Press, 2015), 171–89.

With Queen Nanasipauʻu and Mary Lyn Fonua. *Tonga's Royal Family: Photographs from Royal Collections*. Nukuʻalofa: Vavaʻu Press, 2015.

Edited with Leah Caldeira, Christina Hellmich, Betty Lou Kam and Roger G. Rose. *Royal Hawaiian Featherwork, Nā Hulu Aliʻi* (Exhibition Catalogue). Honolulu: University of Hawaiʻi Press, 2015.

'*ʻAhu ʻula* in the Shape of a Trapezoid', in Leah Caldeira, Christina Hellmich, Adrienne L. Kaeppler, Betty Lou Kam and Roger G. Rose (eds), *Royal Hawaiian Featherwork, Nā Hulu Aliʻi* (Exhibition Catalogue) (Honolulu: University of Hawaiʻi Press, 2015), 38–39.

'Hawaiian Featherwork in the Age of Exploration', in Leah Caldeira, Christina Hellmich, Adrienne L. Kaeppler, Betty Lou Kam and Roger G. Rose (eds), *Royal Hawaiian Featherwork, Nā Hulu Aliʻi* (Exhibition Catalogue) (Honolulu: University of Hawaiʻi Press, 2015), 40–57.

'Ethnographic Treasures in The Hunterian from Cook's Voyages', in E. Geoffrey Hancock, Nick Pearce and Mungo Campbell (eds), *William Hunter's World: The Art and Science of Eighteenth-Century Collecting* (Surrey: Ashgate, 2015), 247–62.

'Culture, Conservation and Creativity: Two Centuries of Polynesian Barkcloth', in Peter Mesenhöller and Annemarie Stauffer (eds), *Made in Oceania: Proceedings of the International Symposium on Social and Cultural Meanings and*

Presentation of Oceanic Tapa, Cologne, 16–17 January 2014 (Newcastle upon Tyne: Cambridge Scholars, 2015), 2–14.

'Rapa Nui Rising', in Karen Stevenson and Katerina Teaiwa (eds), *The Festival of Pacific Arts: Celebrating over Forty Years of Cultural Heritage* (Suva: University of the South Pacific, 2016), 165–81.

'Objectifying Pele as Performance, Material Culture, and Cultural Landscape', in Mary Jo Arnoldi (ed.), *Engaging Smithsonian Objects through Science, History, and the Arts* (Washington, D.C.: Smithsonian Institution Scholarly Press, 2016), 91–103.

'Tongan Dance: Concepts, Genres, and Movements', in Terry E. Miller and Andrew Shahriari (eds), *World Music: A Global Journey (4th Edition)* (New York: Routledge, 2017), 71–73.

'Tongan Dance: Poetry in Motion', *Asia Pacific Dance Festival: Beyond Borders* (Honolulu: University of Hawai'i, East West Centre, 2017), 21–25.

'Capturing Music and Dance in an Archive: A Meditation on Imprisonment', in Kirsty Gillespie, Sally Treloyn and Don Niles (eds), *A Distinctive Voice in the Antipodes: Essays in Honour of Stephen A. Wild* (Acton: Australian National University Press, 2017), 429–42.

'Tangible Objects, Intangible Knowledge: Barkcloth as Cultural Expression in Oceania', in Michel Charleux (ed.), *Tapa: de l'écorce à l'étoffe, art millénaire d'Océanie: de l'Asie du Sud-Est à la Polynésie orientale* [Tapa: From Tree Bark to Cloth: An Ancient Art of Oceania: From Southeast Asia to Eastern Polynesia] (Paris: Somogy Art Publishers; Tahiti: Tapa Association, 2017), 16–20.

'Introduction to the Smithsonian Barkcloth Project; and Tangible and Intangible Knowledge Embedded in Tahitian '*Ahu* and Hawaiian *Kapa*', in Michel Charleux (ed.), *Tapa: de l'écorce à l'étoffe, art millénaire d'Océanie: de l'Asie du Sud-Est à la Polynésie orientale* [Tapa: From Tree Bark to Cloth: An Ancient Art of Oceania: From Southeast Asia to Eastern Polynesia] (Paris: Somogy Art Publishers; Tahiti: Tapa Association, 2017), 414–21.

'Two Tongan Dance Forms in Modern Contexts', in Kendra Stepputat (ed.), *Dance, Senses, Urban Contexts: 29th Symposium of the International Council for Traditional Music (ICTM) Study Group on Ethnochoreology* (Graz: Institute of Ethnomusicology, University of Music and Performing Arts Graz, 2017), 165–72.

'John Lafarge, A Contemporary Artist in Samoa, 1890–1891'. *Pacific Arts* NS 16(2) (2017): 20–30.

'Fijian Art From the US Exploring Expedition'. *Journal of Museum Ethnography* 31 (2018): 169–86.

With Jo Anne Van Tilburg. *The Iconic Tattooed Man of Easter Island.* Warren, CT: Floating World Editions, 2019.

'Notation, Texts, Translations and Interpretations', in Elizabeth Wood-Ellem (ed.), *Songs and Poems of Queen Sālote* [updated reprint] (Nuku`alofa, Tonga: Vava`u Press, 2019), 342–397.

'Queen Sālote's Poetry as Works of Art, History, Politics, and Culture', in Elizabeth Wood-Ellem (ed.), *Songs and Poems of Queen Sālote* [updated reprint] (Nuku`alofa, Tonga: Vava`u Press, 2019), 26–65.

'A Kato Mosi Kaka and other Treasures from Tonga from the US Exploring Expedition', in Jane Milosch and Nick Pearce (eds), *Collecting and Provenance: A Multi-Disciplinary Approach* (Lanham: Rowman & Littlefield, 2019), 257–268.

'Tongan Brass Bands: An Expanding Tradition'. *The World of Music (New Series)* 8(2) (2019): 39–56.

Jess Marinaccio is a Technical Support Officer for the Ministry of Justice, Communication and Foreign Affairs in Tuvalu. She received her PhD in Pacific Studies at Victoria University of Wellington, New Zealand. Previous to this, she was awarded a Master's in Chinese literature from National Taiwan University and, later, worked as a Mandarin-English interpreter for the Tuvalu Embassy in Taiwan. Jess's research focuses on Tuvalu-Taiwan cultural diplomacy, as well as understandings of diplomacy and indigeneity in Taiwan and its Pacific allies. She has published relevant articles in *Issues & Studies*, *Asia Pacific Viewpoint*, *ANU In Brief*, *International Journal of Taiwan Studies*, *International Journal of Cultural Policy* and *The Contemporary Pacific*.

Index

Aboriginal flag, 247–48
aesthetics, 9
   North Malaitan, 256, 258–59, 271
   of *kaufe*, 258–59
   Indigenous terms for, 289
   Polynesian, 112–13
   Sama-Bajau, 146, 151–53
   of *tango argentino*, 47–48
   visual a. of the dancing body in early twentieth-century Chuuk, 191
ainimae narrative dance, 270
airport art-art, 206
akalo or *agalo*, 261–62, 266, 273nn11–12
Alebua, Dominic, 257–58, 272n4
allokine, 46, 72
Alver, Brynjulf, 67–68
American anthropology, 68
American Board of Commissioners of Foreign Missions (ABCFM), 182–83, 186, 193n2, 193n4
American Protestants, 184, 188
Americanization, 218
analysis
   cultural, 181
   dance, 67, 109, 138, 141
   of dance culture, 129
   of dance style, 205
   data, 51, 53–56, 60, 64n26
   emic, 139, 142
   ethnoscientific, 143, 153
   etymological, 219
   of *igal tarirai*, 147
   linguistic, 144, 154n1, 288
   of listeners' imaginings, 21
   of Malaysian dance, 143–47

   movement, 50, 61, 85, 90, 94, 103n1
   of movement structure, 70, 139
   of *ocho atrás* (see *ocho atrás*)
   of realizations, 77
   structural, 71–72, 77, 83, 141–42, 144, 152, 197
   of structured movement systems, 61, 138, 198
   of transcriptions, 80
   visual, 2, 51–53
   of visual culture, 3–4
Anger Dance, 83, *84*
ANTENNA, 201
antivisual approach, 5
Apogevmatini tis Kyriakis, 205
'Are'are, 265
Arizona State University, 237
art
   North Malaitan concept of, 255–58
   spirituality as, 255
   visual, 6, 11, 110, 146, 217, 222
'Arutahi, Ma'iari'i, 122
asgama, 249
Atkinson, Henry, 247
aurality, 109, 111, 119, 130

Bacon, Pat, 93–94, 101–102
Bagandan music and dance, 132n11
Bakale, Lucy, 260–61
Bando, Mikayoshi, 280
barasili, 256, 259–71
   body ornaments, 267–69
   contemporary, 262–63
   dance ornaments, 270
   definitions for, 261

female dancer's costume, 267–70
Indigenous Instrumentation, 263–66 (see also *falake*; *kisi kisi*; *o'o*)
natural plant ornamentation, 270
songs, 262–63
barkcloth, 121, 124, 229–30, 241, 241n1, 281 (see also *tapa*)
Beamer, Mahi, 23
Belfast, 8, 198, 286
Bennigsen, Rudolf von, 187
Berger, Harris M., 3, 22, 37n17, 117–18, 128
Berlin, 245, 247–50
Berlin Society for Anthropology, Ethnology and Prehistory, 247
Berndt, Ronald, 167, 171n9, 171n12
Bevacqua, M., 216, 218
Bharatanatyam, 132n8
Bishop Museum, 8, 10, 67, 70, 90, 131n7, 279, 291n1
  Archives, 33
Blacking, John, 198–99, 286
Blom, Jan-Petter, 68
Boas, Franz, 138
Bollig, Laurentius, 179, 186, 189–90
Buenos Aires, 45, 47–48
body, 29, 71
  ballet, 112
  Christian, 187
  Chuukese, 183, 188, 192
  cultured, 42
  dancing, 4, 6, 111–13, 140–42, 152, 182, 191–92, 229, 233
  hula dancer's, 27–28, 30
  Indigenous, 180, 182, 191–92
  inscriptive, 38n28
  listener's, 30
  as object of visuality in the hula world, 22
  perceiving with, 27–32
  phenomenal, 118–20
  as research tool, 42
  sartorially objectified, 26
  as sound, 113–15
  tourist, 27
Boonjie goldfields, 246

Cairns, 246
capoeira, 37n16, 127

capturing technology, 43. See also motion capture
Catholic Church
  Jubilee of, 179, *180*
Celebes, 144
Cem, Ismail, 205–6
Center for Russian and East European Studies, 232
Cepeda, Jeremy, 220, 222
Chamoru culture, 218
chant
  dance, 190
  as means of cultural repair, 219
  as method of teaching and learning, 220
  in Oceania, 217
  Pacific Island, 215
  protection, 191
  revitalization, 217–218, 220
  revitalizing *fino' håya* through, 219
  rituals, 218
  sociocultural and biophysical effects of, 216
  sociopolitical and physiological effect of, 218
  as somatic depository, 222
  as somatic transformation, 216–19
  See also *lalåi*, *mele*
Chenoweth, Vida, 168–69
choreme, 144, 147–151, 153
choreomusicology, 5, 111, 120, 132n13
Christensen, Dieter, 158, 287, 292n16
Christian churches, 274n22
Christian music, 289
Christianity, 179, 186, 188, 191, 257 261–62, 268, 280
Chuuk, 11, 125, 179–92, 193n1, 193–94nn5–8
Chuukese dance, 180–81, 187–89, 192. See also *pwérúk*
Čilipi village dance events, 234–35
Čilipi village dance group, 234
Clarke, Barry. *See* Ng:tja, King
Clarke, George, 246
collaborative ethnography, 37n23
collaborative research, 10, 90–92, 95, 97–98, 100–102, 103nn3–4
colonialism, 4, 180–82, 216, 218, 220, 222
  American, 24, 30, 215

in Chuuk, 192
Spanish and American, 215
visual, 4
colonization, 181
American, 219
of the senses, 221
communication theory, 70
communicative competence, 143–44, 153
Concert Glee Club, 27, 30, 36n15
conventional rich images (CRI), 22, 24–27, 36n10
Cook, James (Captain), 10, 159, 198
Cook Islands, 113, 115, 122
Corbin, Alain, 29. *See also* landscape: auditory
corporeality
 imperial, 181, 183, 189, 191–92
 of colonial discourse, 181–82
corroboree, 249
courting, 11, 159–70
Cowell, Henry, 83
Cross-Cultural Dance Resources (CCDR) Collections, 237
cultural intimacy, 203

dance
 analysis (*see* analysis: dance)
 anthropology, 10, 104n11, 198–200, 217
 as aural experience, 111–13
 codification of, 47
 concept, 72–74
 cosmopolitan, 45
 description, 71, 74–76, 78–80
 ethnology, 8, 10, 104n11, 139–40, 242n8, 288
 as expression of colonial solidarity, 188
 performance model, 120–21, 126–27
 as play-performance, 142–43
 realization, 72–74, 76–79, 85
 representation (*see* transcription)
 as resistance to imperialism, 180
 as Satanic practice, 184
 sonic power of, 114
 as sounded art, 110
 as structured movement (systems), 10–11, 140–42, 159, 201
 traditional, 67–69
 twentieth-century, 68

dance-music relationship, 82–83
dancer
 dancer's voice, 110–111, 116, 118–19, 129–30
 as singer, 114
 as sound producer, 113
 See also body
dancing defiance, 181, 184
dancing politicians, 202, 205–6, 209, 210n4
decolonization, 216, 219
 somatic, 11, 219, 222
desiccation process, 246
diaspora
 Chamoru, 216–217
dissociation, 50–53, 56–57, 61
 angle, 53–56, 64n27
Dubrovnik weddings, 234–35

embodiment, 20, 120, 142
 dancer as e. of musical sound, 110
 gesture and, 132n13
 kinaesthetic, 97
 of subjectivities, 142, 215
 sensory, 216
 somatic, 221–22
embodied sovereignty, 218
embrace
 close (*cerrado*), 49
 flexible semi-open, 49
 open (*abierto*), 49
emic movement perspective, 95–98
emic analysis of movement systems. *See* analysis: emic
emic perspective, 97–98, 154n1
Enoch, Leeanne, 250
Ethnographic Museum, Zagreb, 229–30, 239
ethnography
 autoethnography, 92, 103n4
 collaborative, 37n23
 Hua, 165
 Internet, 37n23
ethnoscientific concept, 139, 141
ethnoscientific analysis. *See* analysis: ethnoscientific
experience
 bodily, 34
 constitution of, 21

embodied, 34, 51, 215, 222
emotive, 125
interpretive, 34
intersensorial listening, 32
kinaesthetic, 28
lived, 21–23, 27–29, 35, 112, 119, 121, 129–30
musical, 22, 27, 34
listeners' e. of ghost gesturing, 29
of 'Puamana', 30
shared, 110, 119, 128–30, 259, 271
structures of, 119
experiential writing. *See* listening-writing exercise
explication interview technique, 82

faʻatūʻati, 127
falake, 263–66, 268, 270–71
rhythms, 63–64
Farden family, 23, 25
Farden ʻĀluli, Irmgard, 22
Farden, Charles Kekua, 22
faʻataupati, 113, 130n5
fataʻabu (high priests), 262, 266
Fern (German dance teacher couple), 79, 87n15
Festival of Pacific Arts, 1, 2, 215, 219, 221, 260, 273n9
film, 3–4, 41, 43, 74–75, 79–80, 86, 204, 231, 236–37
documentary, 180, 231, 235, 238–39, 241
ethnographic, 188, 232, 235
Sa o Roma, 239
Völkerkundliche Filmdokumente aus der Südsee aus den Jahren 1908–1910, 189–93, 193–94nn5–6
fino' håya (Chamoru language), 216, 219–22
First Methodist Church Tongan congregation, 284
flower
motif, 122, 126–28
pua, 122
tiare tahiti, 110, 122–28
folklore, 68–69, 288
folk dance
collecting, 68
collector, 87n11

European folk dance research, 68–70
movement, 72
revival, 68–69
folk festival, 235
Fortune, Reo, 168
fōtea, 115
Fowler Museum, 233, 236
French traditional dance, 69

gagaku, 280, 286
gaze
colonial, 139, 189, 191
dancer's, 7
imperial, 182, 192
tourist, 26–27
Gee, James Paul, 34
gender of the researcher, 285–86
German colonial government, 187
ghost gestures, 22, 27–31
Gillison, Gillian, 165–66, 170n4
Giurchescu, Anca, 63n18, 71
Greco-Turkish rapprochement, 205
Greek dance, 210n1
rebetiko dance, 204–5, 207 (see also *rebetis*)
tsifteteli, 203
zeibekiko, 197, 202–9, 211n9
Greek politicians, 11, 197. *See also* Papandreou: Andreas; Papandreou: Yiorgos; Tsochatzopoulos, Akis
Greekness, 204
Guåhan (Guam), 1, 11, 214, 216–19, 221–22, 223n1
Barrigada, 217
Hågatna, 216
Guilcher, Jean Michel, 69

Hamburg South Seas Expedition, 188–89, 193n5
Hanna, Judith Lynne, 70, 140
Hanna, Thomas, 216
Hawaiʻi, 8, 20, 22, 24, 30, 35n1, 36n4, 70, 103n2, 114, 122, 124, 181, 199, 201, 280–81, 290
Honolulu, 8, 10, 20, 33, 67, 158, 170n1, 279, 283, 291n7
Waikīkī, 24, 279
Hawaiian communication, 33

Hawaiian cultural revival, 27
Hawaiian genre theory, 37n24
Hawaiian literacy (*see* literacy)
Hawaiian music, 22, 24
Hawaiian Renaissance, 20, 35n2
Hawaiianness, 30
Hays, Terence, 168, 170n4, 171nn15–16
historical music and dance in the northwest Pacific, 182
Holt, Hokulani, 110, 113
Hopoʻate, Vaisima, 282
Hotahota, Coco, 115
Huahine, 122
hula, 6, 9–10, 19–20, 22, 24–25, 27–31, 35n2, 90, 98, 103n2, 103–4n6, 104n14
   ancient (*hula kahiko*), 36n11, 91, 103–4n6
   costume *or* dress, 26, 36n12
   dancer, 25, 31, 131n6
   gestures, 26, 28
   hapa haole, 91
   kumu (teacher *or* master), 27, 91–97, 100–102, 103–4n6, 110, 113–14 (*see also* Bacon, Pat; McKinzie, Edith; Zuttermeister, Noenoelani)
   lineages, 93
   modern (*hula ʻauana*), 22, 28, 36n11, 103–4n6
   movements, 19, 22, 94–95
   motifs, 90–92, 94–98
   pahu (drum dance), 19, 49, 94, 103n1, 181
   Pahu (book), 90, 93, 98, 101, 103n1
   schools, 27, 37n25
   songs, (see *hula kuʻi* song)
hula kuʻi songs, 21–23, 28, 30, 32
   Hiʻilawe, 26, 30, 32, 37n18
   Puamana, 22–28, 30, 32, 36n12, 37nn18–19
hupahupa dance, 115
Huukena, Teiki, 125

I Fanlalaiʼan, 214–22
   chant compositions, 219
   performance of, 221
imagination, 20–22, 24, 26–27
imagining-how, 21, 23, 26

imperialism, 180–81, 191
improvisation, 69, 146, 149, 208–9
Indigenous agency, 181
Indigenous dance, 143, 180, 182, 189, 192
   studies, 139–40
Indigenous epistemologies of dance, 110, 120
Indigenous Repatriation Program, 245–48
Indigenous sensory activism, 215–16, 222
intangible cultural heritage, 73, 142, 239, 242n3 (*see also* UNESCO: Convention for the Safeguarding of Intangible Cultural Heritage)
intangible culture, 11, 231
International Council for Traditional Music (ICTM), 8, 140, 159, 229, 244, 279, 287–89, 292nn15–16
   dance, 287, 292n15
   Study Group for Folk Dance terminology, 71, 86n7
   Study Group on Ethnochoreology, 6, 8, 67, 71–72, 140, 229, 231, 287, 290, 292n23
   Study Group on Music and Dance of Oceania, 8–9, 244, 279, 290, 292n22
International Folk Music Council, 170n1
International Musicological Society, 158
intersensorial representation, 34–35
Iraklio (Crete), 206
Iriarte, Leonard, 214–21
Iriarte, Lynn, 219
Iriarte Sgambelluri, Juanita, 219
Ivančan, Ivan, 233, 236
Ivens, Walter George, 263, 266, 270

James Cook University, 249
Japanese dance (*nihon buyo*), 280
Jawaiian songs, 31, 37n20
   Unity, 31–32, 34, 37n22
Jirrbal group, 249

Kaeppler, Adrienne, 1–2, 6–7, 8, 67, 72, 118, 130, 170, 192, 206, 209, 222, 229, 241
   on aesthetics, 258, 271
   awards granted to, 9
   contribution to Southeast Asian ethnochoreology, 138–39

on dance as visual manifestations of social structure, 192, 201
on dance research, 70–71
on film as research method, 41, 211n7
on *hula pahu*, 19–20, 181
influence on Dance Anthropology in Greece, 197–201
international affiliations of, 8–9
interview with, 11, 279–91
definitions of dance and music, 7, 159
definition of arts, 256–57, 271
ethonscientific approach, 140–44, 154n1
hula pahu project, 90, 94, 96–98, 100, 102
on music as visual art, 109–10, 214–15, 217, 222
on notating traditional dance, 73
on Polynesian dance performance, 120–21, 128, 132n8, 132n12, 153
publications by, 293–316
on repatriation, 244–45, 250
on safeguarding lakalaka, 73–74, 231
on Tongan dance, 71, 181, 230, 263
on style, 46
work of, 7–11, 158–59
Kalākaua, King, 19, 35n2
Kamehameha (Schools), 20–21, 27, 32, 36n15, 37n26
students, 20, 27–28, 33–35, 36n8, 36–37n15, 38n27
kåna, 216, 218, 220–22
Kānaka Maoli, 20, 35n1
kaufe, 258–59, 271, 273nn6–7
Karamanlis, Konstantinos, 202
kastom, 257–58, 261–63, 265, 270
dress, 263, 267–68
drums (see *o'o*)
songs (see *barasili*)
story, 262
tabu, 262
kinaesthetic consciousness, 29
kinemes, 144, 147, 288
kinetic songscapes, 27–32, 35
kisi kisi, 263–66, 271
Klaatsch, Hermann, 246, 252n5, 252n7
Kodak Hula Show, 24
Koloamatangi, Lasinga, 284–85
Konavle, 234

Korčula Island, 229, 231, 241n2
Korčula Town Museum, 231
Korean dance, 280
Korean music. See *kugak*
Kubary, Jan, 190
kulintangan, 145, 147
Krämer, Augustin, 188–89
Kuala Lumpur, 231
kugak, 7

Labanotation, 50–51, 57–61, 63–64nn22–23, 64n31, 72, 77, 86n1, 90–98, 101–102, 103n1, 104n7, 104n14, 281
scores, *58*, 75, 77, 90–93, *96–97, 99–100*, 235
Ladas, Cristina, *44*, 49, 52, 56–57, 59, 64n28
Ladas, Homer, *44*, 49, 52, 56–57, 59, 63n19
Laguåña, Carlos, 220
Lahaina, Maui, 22–23, 25
lalåi, 214, 216–19, 221–22
landscape
auditory, 29
interlocutory, 32
visual, 29
Lange, Roderyk, 68–69, 86n1
Lassiter, Luke, 37n23, 100–102, 103nn3–5, 104n12
Lau-Mbaelelea, 255, 257–60, 264
art, 256–257
dance costuming (see *kastom*: dress)
homes, 259
societies, 257
learning to perform, 42, 62n2
Levi, 185–86
listening-writing exercise, 21, 32–35, 38n27
literacy, 32–33, 37n25
Logan, Robert, 183–85
love magic, 160–61, 167

Malaitan philosophy, 257
Malanda, 245, 251
Malaysian dance, 141, 143, 153
igal, 11, 143–54
titik tarirai, 147–149
Mana'o Company, 31, 37n21

Manahiki, 115, 132n9
Māori music, 214
Māori *haka*, 218
marching dance (*maas*), 189, 194n7
Marquesas Islands, 113–16, 122, 124
   Hiva Oa, 132n10
Masiala, Modesta, 260
mask dance, 189, 191 (see also *pwérúk, tapwaanú*)
Mataʻele, Kalo, 281
McKenney, Luana, 23
McKinzie, Edith, 93
McManus, Aʻima, 23
media artefacts, 202
media-related transformations in Greece, 202
   deregulation of Greek television, 202, 210n3
MEGA, 201
mele
   books, 33, 37n24
   oli, 19
   hula, 19
   hula kuʻi, 19
   hula ʻōlapa, 19
Merleau-Ponty, M. 3, 29
   on perception, 119–20
Micronesia, Federated States of (FSM), 11, 158, 179, 181–183, 191–92, 193n1, 193n3
   Chuuk (*see* Chuuk)
   colonial period, 179, 191–92
   historical accounts of, 181
   Mortlock Islands (*see* Mortlock Islands)
Miljević, Marko, 49, 52, 56–59
militarization, 218, 222
minen móót (sitting dance), 189–91
minen wúútá (standing dance), 189–90
mission
   American, 187–88
   Anapau, 183–85
   Protestant, 183, 188–89
missionaries, 180, 184, 186, 189, 191–92, 291n11
   ABCFM (*see* American Board of Commissioners for Foreign Missions)
   Catholic, 268
   Christian, 179

Protestant, 179, 183, 193n3
   See also Bollig, Laurentius; Logan, Robert; Price, Francis; Moulton, James; Snelling, Alfred; Stimson, Martin
moai kavakava, 229–30
modernity, 4, 19, 182, 188, 204
Molitau, Kaponoʻai, 113
Montevideo, 45
morphokines, 144, 147–151, *152*, 288
Morris, Mark, 83–85, 87n16
Mortlock Islands, 187–89, 191, 193–194n5
Mortlockese dance, 189 (see *pwérúk, tapwaanú*; *pwérúk, tukuyá*)
motif (dance), 72, 74, 90, 144–153, 205, 283. *See also* hula: motifs; *ocho atrás*; round dance: motives
motion capture (mocap), 10, 43, 45, 50–51, 53, 56–57, 59–62, 63nn6–7, 64n24, 64n26, 64n28, 64n30
Moulton, James, 291n11
Museum of Macedonia, Skopje, 236–38
Museum of Tropical Queensland, Townsville, 245
music as visual art, 110, 217, 222
musicking, 145, 147

Nanasipauʻu, Queen of Tonga, 283–84
National and Kapodistrian University of Athens (EKPA), 200
Nea Dimokratia, 202
New Zealand, 122, 124, 181, 199, 217, 286, 289
Ng:tja, King, 245–51, 252n5, 252n7, 252n9
   breastplate of, 245–47, 252n6
Ngadjon-Jii, 245, 252n4
noh, 280
North Malaitan dance music, 263
Northern Thracian dance, 198
Norwegian couple dances, 71
Norwegian folk dance movement, 67
Norwegian Centre for Traditional Music and Dance, 67
notation, 6, 45, 60, 73–77, 86, 140
   dance, 42, 62n5, 64n29, 104n13
   movement (*see* Labanotation)
   See also Tongan notation
Nukuʻalofa, 9, 291n10

Oceanic artefacts, 229–31
ocho atrás, 43, 53–57, 60–61, 63n18, 64n24, 64n28
　as style determinant, 49–59
　technique, 50–52, 56
oʻo, 263, 265–66, 274n18
oral tradition, 73, 222, 261, 274n21
Oslo, 68

Pacific Arts Association, 9
Pacific dance, 1, 11, 128, 158
Pahinui, Gabby, 26, 37n18
Palaʼu Bajau, 144
Pan-Pacific and Southeast Asian Women's Association, 281
Panhellenic Socialist Movement (PASOK), 197, 202, 208–9
Papandreou
　Andreas, 197, 202–3, 206, 208, 211nn5–6
　Andrikos, 205
　Margarita, 208
　Nikos, 205
　Yiorgos, 203, 205–9, 211nn5–6
Papua New Guinea, 11, 158–60, 244, 255, 291n12
　Awa, 169
　Benabena, 166–67
　Eastern Highlands Province, 161, 169
　Chimbu, 161, 163–66, 169–70, 171n7
　courting (*see* courting)
　Fore, 168–69, 171n12
　Gahuku, 166
　Highlands provinces, 161
　Inoke-Yate, 167
　Jiwaka, 161, 164, 170
　languages of Eastern Highlands Province, *162*
　Madang, 164
　music and dance, 158
　North Tairora, 169
　South Tairora, 169
　Usarufa, 167–69
participant observation, 71, 201
perception, 1, 3, 20–22, 26–27, 34, 42, 51, 117, 119–20, 128–30, 132n13, 216, 220

Petrović, Maja, 49, 52, 56–59, 63n20
Petrovski, Daniel, 238–39, 241
phenomenological method. *See* listening-writing exercise
phenomenological perspective, 21–22, 28
phenomenology, 3, 10, 21, 110, 119–20, 200
　Merleau-Ponty's, 29
Píliu, Neri, 49, 52, 56–60
poetic texts, 22, 111, 129, 142, 153. *See also mele*
poetry, 109, 112, 120, 129, 142, 283
　Hawaiian, 22, 33 (see also *mele*)
　in motion, 1, 115, 153
　sung, 6, 110, 115, 190, 217, 229
politicians as media stars, 203
politics, 2, 197–99, 203, 210, 237
　of chant revitalization work, 216
　dance, 180–81, 187
　Greek, 202, 205
　dance, 187, 191
　dance and p. in Greek society, 201
　dance as tool for, 198
　dance as expression of, 209–10
　of imperial confrontations in music and dance, 182
　lineage, 183
　music and, 11
　national identity politics in Greece, 205
　of performance (dancing), 180–81, 189, 191–192
　of representation, 35
Polynesian Cultural Center, 285
Polynesian dance, 36n12, 109–111, 114–15, 120, 128–30, 132n8, 138, 142, 153, 158, 285
postcolonial dance recovery, 218
postmodernism, 200
Price, Francis, 179, 183–88
pseudo-events, 201
Pukapuka, 122
pwérúk, 184, 188–90
　contexts of, 184
　éwúwénú (sitting dance), 184, 189–90, 194n8
　pisimóót (sitting dance), 184, 190
　tapwaanú (mask dance), 189
　tukuyá (stick dance), 184, 189

Queen's University Belfast, 8, 198–99
Quiñones, Yanina, 49, 52, 56–60

Rapa Nui, 8, 198, 229–230, 279, 290, 292n21
rebetis, 209, 211n10
reconciliation, 245, 248
   Action Plan, 250
redintegration, 24, 36n7
Regional Nordic Ethnology, 68
reinvigoration of tradition, 245
repatriation, 11, 244–51, 252n1
   ceremonies, 245, 247–50, 252n8, 252n8, 252n11
   of King Ng:tja, 244–51
representation, 4–5, 6, 22, 37n23, 122, 126, 180, 203–4
   dance, 42–43
   of dancers' bodies, 53, 152
   intersensorial, 34
   lyric, 30
   politics of (*see* politics: of representation)
   of text, 115
representative government, 198
resistance, 11, 180, 182
   colonial, 219
   spiritual, 218
Richardson Young Women's Christian Association (YWCA), 281, 291n7
Ringlenner. *See* round dance Ringlenner
Romani holiday. *See* Romani St. George's Day
Romani community, 237–39, 241
Romani costume, 236
Romano Ilo – Skopje Association, 237–39
Romani St. George's Day, 231, 235–37, 241, 242n3
   museum exhibition, 236–41
round dance
   motives, 78–80, 82–83
   paradigm, 78
   Reinlender, 79, 82
   Ringlenner, 78–80 (*see also* transcription of Ringlenner)
Røros, 78–79, 82

Sabah, 144, 153–154
   Semporna, 144, 147, 151–52

safeguarding, 73–74, 87n9
   Indigenous Chamoru knowledge, 218
Sakellariou, Rita, 206
Sālote, Queen of Tonga, 281–84
Sama-Bajau, 11, 144, 146, 151–54
   aesthetics (*see* aesthetics: Sama-Bajau)
Sāmoa, 113
Sāmoan, 288–89
   clothes, 286
Schoetensack, Otto, 246
Seeger, Charles, 34
   Lecture for the Society for Ethnomusicology, 9
self-monitoring writing technique, 34
shamisen, 280
Shamoto, Masatoshi, 280, 291n5
shouts
   as cues, 117
   as emotive reactions, 118
sinulog, 6–7
Skopje, 231, 235–41, 242n11
Šuto Orizari, 237, 239
Smith, Barbara, 70, 158, 280
Smithsonian Institute, 8–10, 67, 70, 198
Smithsonian Folklife Festival, 114
smoking ceremony, 249–50 (*see also* repatriation ceremonies)
Snelling, Alfred, 186, 193n4
social identities, 22
social media, 4, 61, 238
socialism, 198
Society for Ethnomusicology, 120
Solomon Islands, 11, 221, 255–58, 260, 268–69, 272n1, 272nn3–4, 273n13
   art forms, 255, 257–58, 272 (see also *barasili*)
   Auki, Malaita, 260, 273n9
   flag, 269
   identities, 257
somatic resonance, 217
somatic transformation, 217–19
somatics, 216
sound writing, 38n28
soundingness, 109, 111–112, 117–20, *126*, 129
South Slavic immigrant communities, 232, 235

Souza, Mihana, 23
Spider Henry, 249–50
spirit medium, 145, 151, 183–84, 186, 188, 192
spirit possession celebrations, 189–90
spiritual energy. See *kāna*
spirituality, 214–15, 222, 255, 257
Stevenson, Robert Louis, 6
Stimson, Martin, 188
Stolpe, Knut Hjalmar, 290
structural functionalism, 201
structuralism, 9, 138
structured movement systems, 61, 139–44, 152–54, 181, 198–199, 201 (*see also* analysis: of structured movement systems)
style
  among Greek refugees from Northern Thrace, 198
  barasili performance, 261
  barasili traditional dress, 267, 270
  hula, 31–32, 36n11, 90–91, 103–4n6
  igal, 144, 146
  of news, 201
  'ōte'a, 116
  pre-Christian movement, 19
  of structured movement systems, 143–44, 152
  zeibekiko, 206, 208
  See also analysis: of dance style; courting: styles in the Eastern Highlands; *ocho atrás*: as style determinant; tango argentino
sword dance, 231, 241n2
Sydney, 247
Szeged, 229–30

tagunggu', 145–47, 151
Tahitian dance, 109–111, 115, 118–19, *126*, 127, 132n9
  heiva, 112, 130n6
  'ōte'a, 115–17
  soundscape of, 117–18
  tapriata, 115, *116*, 132n10
Tahitian rituals, 127–28
Takwa Barasili Dance Group, 260, *267*, 270, 273n9

tangible items, 229–30, 241, 258
tango, 68, 208
tango argentino
  community, 46, 48–49, 51, 59, 61
  as coupled social dance, 46
  motif (see *ocho atrás*)
  movement (see *ocho atràs*)
  styles, 43, 45–49, 61, 63n13 (*see also* tango variants)
  translocal, 45–47, 61
tango variants
  canyengue, 48
  fantasia, 48
  for export, 48
  liso, 48
  milonguero, 47–50, 61, 63n17, 63n20
  new tango (*tango nuevo*), 47–49, 61
  organic tango, 49–50, 61, 63n19
  orillero, 48
  salón, 47–50, 60–61
tapa, 110, 121, 124, 198, 282
tattoo
  Tahitian, 110, 121–26, 131n5
  Marquesan, 124–25
  Polynesian, 125
taualuga, 113, 131n5
temporality, 6, 192
territorialism, 220, 222
theatrical performance, 77, 204
thick description, 199
tiare tahiti. *See* flower: *tiare tahiti*
Tongan dance, 1–2, 6, 9, 70–74, 103n1, 104n10, 138, 141, 181, 230, 263, 281, 283, 286
  lakalaka, 73–74, 181, 199, 229–31, 283, 285
  me'etu'upaki, 285
Tongan items, 229–30
Tongan funerals, 282–83
Tongan notation, 284
Torres Strait Island Expedition, 4
tourism, 24
Townsville, 245, 247–50, 252n9
traditional societies, 201
transcription, 42, 71–75, 87n10
  of Anger Dance, *84*
  dance movement, 10, 76–79

descriptive, 75
    of Ringlenner, 81
    of *titik tarirai*, 148
    process of, 79–80
    theatrical dance, 83–85
Tsitsanis, Vasilis, 206
Tsochatzopoulos, Akis, 203, 211n5
Tupou I, King, 282, 284
Tupou II, King, 284
Tupou III, Queen, 284 (*see also* Sālote, Queen of Tonga)
Tupou IV, King, 282, 284
    coronation of, 9, 283
Tupou V, King, 284
Tupou VI, King, 284

Ukrainian dance, 7
Ulster Museum, 198
UNESCO, 70, 239, 287, 292n15
    Convention for the Safeguarding of Intangible Cultural Heritage, 69–70, 73–74, 230–1
University of Bergen, 68
University of California at Los Angeles (UCLA), 231–32
    Museum of Cultural History, 231–33, 235–36
    Yugoslav Exchange Program, 232, 235, 242n4, 242n6
University of Guam, 220–21
University of Hawaiʻi, 8, 70, 91, 103n1 279–80, 291n4, 292n20
University of Maryland, 8
University of Otago, 217
University of Wisconsin, 279

verbal movement description, 97–98, 102
vision, 1, 3, 21, 29, 139, 183, 191, 214, 220
    colonial (*see* gaze colonial)
    imperial (*see* gaze imperial)
visual anthropology, 3

visual capture, 117
visual culture, 2–6, 199
    analysis of (*see* analysis: of visual culture)
visual documentation, 231, 237–38
visuality, 3, 22, 191–92, 218, 256, 259–60, 271
    in repatriation ceremonies, 245, 247–49
    of *kugak* (see *kugak*)
visualization, 5–6, 21, 24, 27, 51, 53
    of dance, 10, 189
    data, 45, 55, 60, 63n8
    of emigrant locations, 232
    of female body, 124
    of music and dance, 4
    of sound, 110, 115–18
vocal literature, 222

Waikīkī. *See* Hawaiʻi: Waikīkī
Washington D.C., 8, 67, 70, 198
ways of sensing, 260
Wesleyan Methodist Centenary Church, 291n10
Wilhelm II, Kaiser, 188
worldview, 11, 216, 218
    Chamoru, 214–17, 219, 221–22
    somatic, 214

Yugoslav dance zones, 232–36
Yugoslav museum exhibit, 233–35, 238
Yugoslavia, 231–232, 238
    costumes from, 231–36
    dance from, 11, 231
    Kingdom of, 232
    Socialist Federal Republic of, 232, 242n12

Zagreb, 229–30, 232, 235, 239, 241
    museum (*see* Ethnographic Museum, Zagreb)
zouk, 37n23
Zuttermeister, Noenoelani, 93–94, 101–102, 114

www.ingramcontent.com/pod-product-compliance
Lightning Source LLC
Chambersburg PA
CBHW071332080526
44587CB00017B/2814